# VAMPIRES · DRAGONS · AND EGYPTIAN KINGS

# VAMPIRES · DRAGONS · AND EGYPTIAN KINGS

## YOUTH GANGS IN POSTWAR NEW YORK

*Eric C. Schneider*

PRINCETON UNIVERSITY PRESS · PRINCETON, NEW JERSEY

Library of Congress Cataloging-in-Publication Data

Schneider, Eric C., 1951–

Vampires, dragons, and Egyptian kings : youth gangs in
postwar New York / Eric C. Schneider.

p.    cm.

Includes bibliographical references and index.

ISBN 0-691-00141-3 (cloth : alk. paper)

1. Gangs—New York (N.Y.)—History—20th century. I. Title.

HV6439.U7N467 1999

364.1'066'09747109045—dc21      98–33530 CIP

This book has been composed in Dante

The paper used in this publication meets the minimum
requirements of ANSI/NISO Z39.48-1992 (R 1997)
(*Permanence of Paper*)

http: // pup.princeton.edu

Printed in the United States of America

10   9   8   7   6   5   4   3   2   1

For Joani Unger (1951–1998) and Gary Stoller

# CONTENTS

# ILLUSTRATIONS

# ACKNOWLEDGMENTS

ONE OF THE PLEASURES of finishing a book is acknowledging those who have assisted you along the way—and one of the terrors is forgetting someone essential. I have benefited from close readings of several chapters by the Chester Avenue seminar: Len Braitman, George Dowdall, Howard Gillette, Sally Griffith, Ed Johanningsmeier, Emma Lapsansky, Adele Lindenmeyer, Cindy Little, Margaret Marsh, Randall Miller, Marion Roydhouse, and Sarah Tracy. Josh Freeman, Brian Gratton, Ruth Horowitz, Lynn Lees, Amanda Seligman, Rob Snyder, and Marc Stein have commented on different chapters of the book. Michael Katz has always been enormously supportive of my work. Elaine Simon, my co-teacher of the senior seminar in urban studies, invited me to present my research to the undergraduate department colloquia, which I did on several occasions. Ron Huff kindly supplied me with a work in progress. My editor, Brigitta van Rheinberg, has been a delight to work with and has enthusiastically supported this project from the moment she heard about it. Tom Pederson of the cartography lab in the Graduate School of Fine Arts at the University of Pennsylvania produced the maps for the book.

My work was dependent on the assistance of local informants. The Reverend Norman Eddy welcomed me to East Harlem and provided my initial contacts with several former gang members. Both Claude Brown and Piri Thomas took time from busy schedules to speak with me, Gilbert Diaz explained the streets of the 1950s, while Dan Murrow gave me an entry into the Fordham Baldies, with whom he had been a street worker. Ramon Diaz told me about "The Conservatives," a group of ex-gang members that he helped go "social"; Nestor Llamas explained the operations of the New York City Youth Board; Willie Connena talked about growing up in East Harlem and running a storefront for the Youth Board in the Bronx; the Honorable John Carro told me about East Harlem and the Youth Board; Manny Diaz discussed social work in East Harlem; Pete Pascale provided a history of Italian settlement there; Joseph Monserrat provided an informal history of Puerto Rican migration; Nicky Cruz went far beyond his autobiography in explaining gangs; Seymour Ostrow discussed law practice in East Harlem; Ken Garrett provided insight into gangs in Brooklyn; Michael Reisch informed me about Washington Heights; and John Nolan filled me in on the later history of the Youth Board and the resurgence of gangs in the South Bronx. Jose Castro and Joseph Gonzalez discussed growing up on the Lower East Side and their work with gangs, while Sonny Arguinzoni did the same for Brooklyn. I have benefited from the generosity of Kurt Sonnenfeld, who shared documents and insights from his position as the informal historian of the Youth Board. Gail Peck told me of her life with Salvador Agron and helped make him real to me. My greatest debt is to the former gang members who agreed to be interviewed for this project. To preserve their privacy, I have cited their interviews using only their initials, and I hope they accept this anonymous acknowledgment as heartfelt thanks.

No historian would be able to work without the dedication of librarians and archivists. I would like to thank Lee Pugh of the Interlibrary Loan office at the University of Pennsylvania, who unflaggingly searched for obscure items for me. The staffs at the New York City Municipal Archives, especially Kenneth Cobb, the Union Theological Seminary Archives, Special Collections at Columbia University Library, Special Collections at the City College of New York, the Social Welfare History Archives at the University of Minnesota, the Balch Institute for Ethnic Studies, the Schomburg Center for Research in Black Culture, the New York Public Library, Special Collections at the Brooklyn Public Library, and the American Friends Service Committee Archives all have provided crucial access to manuscript collections. William Power, director of technical services for the New York County District Attorney's Office, provided me with court records and the use of his office.

I have enjoyed the help of several research assistants: Eric Palladino, Lexie Adorno, Sacha Adorno, Tracy Feld, and especially Jeremy Feinstein, who spent part of his summer digging through the collections at the Social Welfare Archives.

Research in New York City would have been impossible without the hospitality and friendship of Joan Zoref and Roy Israel, Ellen Garvey and Janet Gallagher, Tom Tuthill and Nancy Stiefel, and Suzanne Strickland.

My greatest debt is to my family. Janet Golden is both my best and most severe critic and I cannot conceive of doing intellectual work without the benefit of her wisdom. She and our children, Alex and Ben Schneider, also remind me that there is more to life than intellectual work.

Finally, this book is dedicated to my friends Joani Unger and Gary Stoller, who have always inspired me with their dedication to social justice and their belief in the possibility of change. Joani fought colon cancer with her usual optimism, good humor, and courage, and Gary kept hope for us all.

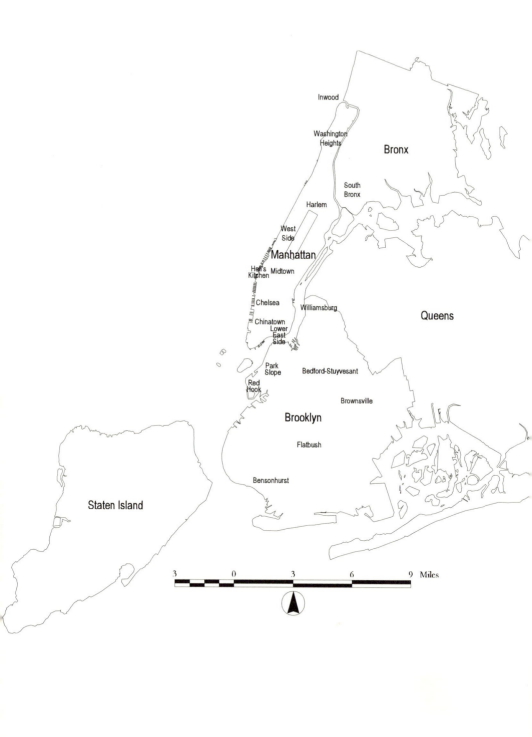

Inwood

Washington
Heights

**Bronx**

South
Bronx

Harlem

West
Side

**Manhattan**

Hell's
Kitchen Midtown

Chelsea

Williamsburg

**Queens**

Chinatown
Lower
East
Side

Park
Slope

Bedford-Stuyvesant

Red
Hook

Brownsville

**Brooklyn**

Flatbush

Bensonhurst

**Staten Island**

3          0          3          6          9   Miles

# Crossing 96th Street

I STILL RETAIN a New York City adolescent's sense of boundaries. Taking the First Avenue bus uptown to interview former gang members in East Harlem, I found myself watching the cross streets carefully after we got to 96th Street. I had ventured into alien territory, something I never would have done as a teenager. Well beyond the turf in which I and my friends felt comfortable, 96th Street divided Spanish Harlem from the rest of the Upper East Side of Manhattan, and in my youth I took such boundaries seriously.

I remember one winter's afternoon, standing near the corner of "our" block, 88th Street between Second and Third Avenues, when my friends and I came face to face with a group of Puerto Rican kids. They had probably come from East Harlem, and their turn from Third Avenue onto our street was a blatant challenge, for boys did not wander accidentally into strange neighborhoods in groups. I recall that we eyed each other for what felt like an eternity, and then our group stepped aside and let them pass. I can no longer recollect what words were spoken, although there were some, nor do I remember discussing what happened with my friends. I do recall my rage and humiliation, watching them glide down the block, knowing that their superiority, their presence, had been affirmed, just as ours had been negated.

My friends and I formed a street-corner group, common enough in working- and lower-middle-class New York. We inherited the block from an older group that had been broken up by the draft, work, steady girl-

*Opposite page:* P.1. New York neighborhoods.

friends, and, for one or two, college. They had been the Bad Ones and so we became the Little Bad Ones, at least for a summer, after which I don't think we were called anything at all. Building superintendents routinely chased us from their "stoops" (stairs leading from the street up to the door); young women walked a gauntlet between two lines of hard, staring eyes and endured occasional catcalls; the deli owner guarded his beer case when we came in; and our late-night rowdiness sometimes resulted in a phone call to the local precinct house. But in the tradition of street-corner groups, we kept our block safe from outsiders, and crime, aside from our own petty delinquencies, was largely nonexistent. When we left the block as a group, it was to play ball against the walls of a massive brewery on a nearby street that separated us from the far tougher Irish kids to our immediate north. To the west and south stretched Silk Stocking Manhattan, where boys did not hang out on street corners, carried tennis rackets rather than stickball bats, and swam at the boys' club instead of the East River. It is a measure of New York's parochialism that all of my friends, except one, were Catholic; of German, Irish, Italian, or Polish descent; and the children of postal workers, cooks, domestics, and small shopkeepers. To us, Jews, Protestants, African Americans, Asians, and Latinos all belonged to exotic other species and lived in New Yorks distant from our own, even if only a few city blocks away. To a passing sociologist, we might have looked like a gang defending the insularity of our world. But we were not: we lacked a key element in defining a gang, which is engaging in a pattern of conflict. Unlike a gang, we allowed others to walk down our block.

In writing this book about street gangs and masculinity in postwar New York, I have often thought of the meaning of that winter afternoon's meeting and the confrontation that never materialized. What I did not understand at the time now seems abundantly clear: we backed down from a fight because we could afford to. While none of us was wealthy, or even modestly middle-class, our parents paid parochial school tuitions and imbued us with aspirations of going to college. Even those of us from single-parent or female-headed households had models of masculinity available who were rooted in a world of work, family sacrifice, and obligation. At the same time, we enjoyed the freedom of the city. We did not live in an area teeming with other youths organized into warring age-graded groups. Our immediate universe felt restricted, but we could travel through other neighborhoods without the badge of color immediately drawing attention from other adolescents. Our collective self-worth was not defined by our turf, nor was any individual's identity wrapped up with a street reputation for toughness. Our masculinities were created in a variety of ways, and street brawling did not have to be one of them, although I believe we would have defended ourselves if attacked. On that afternoon, we backed down for a hundred reasons, including fear, but most important, we did so because our manhood was not at stake in the defense of a city block.

Many of the individuals encountered in this book did not have the luxury of retreat. Gang members fought and treated each other brutally for a number of reasons—to defend ethnic pride, to protect turf, to avenge the honor of a girlfriend, to enjoy the spectacle of another's suffering, or to break up the monotony of daily life. The most significant reason was that masculine identities were created through confronting and besting enemies, by testing and probing for weaknesses even among friends, and in posturing and negotiating on the street before the critical eyes of one's peers. Image, honor, and masculinity were all intertwined in a public presentation of self that required a public defense. A blow to any one of these elements threatened to unravel a precariously woven identity.

The stakes wagered in public confrontation were so high because, in many sections of New York, other supports for masculinity were so few. The hustler, pimp, gambler, numbers runner, and petty criminal—the streets themselves—were unambiguously male and defied the female dominions of home, church, and school, as well as the class subordination demanded by the workplace. Rebellious adolescents saw family and work as hopeless encumbrances, while "street culture," the art of getting by and putting on, promised freedom and encouraged adolescents in poor neighborhoods to apprentice themselves to the most dominant males in sight.

At the same time, the legitimate alterego of street culture—a male "shop floor culture"—was less attainable in postwar New York. Shop floor culture combined resistance to work discipline with a celebration of male sexual privilege, drinking, and fighting. Shop floor culture facilitated adolescent males' transition from school and family to the workplace by incorporating, and to some degree, taming elements of street culture. But shop floor culture rested on the availability of physical labor in industry, on the docks, or in the construction trades. In the 1950s, these jobs, although declining, were still relatively plentiful; they were not, however, always available to African Americans and Puerto Ricans. Street culture, constructed around public assertions of dominance and confrontation, was the most accessible way for those adolescents excluded from masculinized labor to form masculine identities for themselves.

While both my group and our Puerto Rican opponents shared in street culture to some degree, there was not much ecological support for it in my neighborhood. There were no knots of unemployed men standing on the corners, the local prostitute lived with her lesbian lover, we never saw a pimp on the street, and drug use and sales, if they occurred in the neighborhood, were not visible to us and thus remained absent from our consciousness. Alcohol abuse and wife-battering were known to all of us, and consumption of alcohol and dominance over women seemed to be part of the natural history of becoming a man, just like racism and anti-Semitism were an unquestioned part of our being "white" and Catholic in the 1960s.

We shared enough with our opponents to understand them, but we were not similar enough to be forced into confronting them physically. For us, class and "race" intersected to produce a measure of privilege just large enough to allow us to avoid a fight and still maintain our masculine identities. Our opponents were able to assert their dominance by simply walking down the street, so that they did not feel it necessary to push hostility into attack. Other boys on other occasions, galvanized by fear and pride, did not back down in their confrontations, and their battles sometimes left city streets littered with mangled bodies for police, reporters, and historians to discover and use to trace the meaning of their conflicts.

I started this book with a search for information about one of those conflicts. While completing work on a previous book, I read and saved an obituary about Salvador Agron, the Capeman, published in the *New York Times* in 1986. The *Times* reported that Agron had led the Vampires in an attack on a group of boys in a midtown Manhattan playground in 1959, killed two of them, and became the youngest defendant ever sentenced to death in New York State. Prominent liberals rallied to save him from the electric chair, and while in prison, Agron became literate, acquired his GED, took college courses, and wrote poetry and political tracts. The case and his trial raised questions about Puerto Rican and African-American migration to New York, ethnic relations between the migrants and the dominant Euro-American communities, and the meaning of youth violence in postwar New York. I found the district attorney's files about the case, but Agron's confession and the first volume of trial minutes were missing, having been borrowed by an earlier researcher and never returned. As a result, my project on Agron evolved into one on street gangs in New York, and my focus shifted from the 1950s to the entire postwar period. I became interested in answering a series of questions: Why did the period from the mid-1940s to the mid-1960s witness an explosion of gangs? How did gangs mediate between adolescence and adulthood? How did poor adolescents react to competition for space and resources? Why did some adolescents choose to shape their masculine identities through gang membership?

In order to present my argument about masculinity and the formation of gangs in postwar New York, I have used both a chronological and a thematic organization for this book. In the first chapter, I present the structural context needed to understand street gangs. I examine economic change, the effects of migration, and the impact of urban renewal and slum clearance in pitting African-American, Puerto Rican, and Euro-American youth against each other. Chapter 2 is chronological and analyzes the increase in gang violence after World War II as "racial" boundaries were transgressed. In chapter 3, the focus shifts to case studies of two neighborhoods, Washington Heights in the 1950s and East Harlem from the 1930s to the 1950s. I show that gangs were organized territorially and were able to integrate different ethnic identities into gang membership. The next four chapters are thematic in format. Chapter 4 makes an argument for the centrality of masculinity in understanding gangs, especially as rebellious youth rejected the authority of school, family, and workplace and established their own criteria for determining worth. Chapter 5 examines language, clothing, style, music, place—the elements of a "gang culture" that transcended ethnicity and united gang members even as they fought each other. In the sixth chapter, I look at the process of leaving gangs and at the different paths into adulthood available to gang members, while chapter 7 examines the impact of gang intervention programs. Chapter 8 is chronological and analyzes the decline of gangs in the mid-1960s, especially the role of heroin in the process, and the reasons for gangs' reemergence less than a decade later. In my conclusion, I compare the gangs of the postwar period with those in modern New York and argue that gangs have shifted from social to economic organizations.

Throughout this work I have tried to balance agency and structure—to see gang members as actors and to understand the world as much as possible from their point of view, while recognizing that gangs existed within a larger context of power and inequality. These interests drove me to search through the archival collections of settlement houses, to study gang member autobiographies, to examine mayoral papers, to read volumes of newspapers, to interview former street club workers for the New York City Youth Board as well as former members of the gangs with whom they worked, and to walk around and observe many New York neighborhoods. Gradually I found myself drawn across 96th Street.

# VAMPIRES · DRAGONS · AND EGYPTIAN KINGS

## The Capeman and the Vampires

THE MURDERS of Robert Young and Anthony Krzesinski, like most gang homicides, were not premeditated. The boys had stopped off at a playground on the way home from a movie, and they lingered to talk to some of their friends before facing the stifling August heat of their apartments. The playground, basically a concrete slab between 45th and 46th Streets, was surrounded by five-story tenements and hidden from the traffic on Manhattan's Ninth and Tenth Avenues. The unlit park was not the sort of place one stumbled on by accident, and local youths went there to smoke marijuana, drink beer, and have sex. Two sixteen-year-old prostitutes brought their customers there to be rolled by local toughs, and it was rumored that male homosexuals cruising Times Square were also lured there and beaten. On a corner nearby stood the White House Bar, headquarters of the last remnants of the West Side's Irish organized crime groups. Although the neighborhood—known as Hell's Kitchen—had been infiltrated by Puerto Rican migrants, "Spanish" boys knew the park was "white" and, except for a couple of local youths, they rarely ventured there and they never went in groups.[1]

Thus it was surprising when, shortly before midnight on August 29, 1959, five Puerto Rican boys, including a mysterious caped figure, strutted defiantly into the park. Seeking to avenge a beating suffered by one of their friends, and perhaps expecting to encounter a rival gang, the Nordics, the boys scouted the park carefully before approaching the group of "Americans" chatting on the park benches. They asked if anyone

*Opposite page:* I.1. The playground between 45th and 46th Streets in Hell's Kitchen.

had seen Frenchy, their friend who was supposed to finger the boy who had beaten him, but no one knew where he was. After retreating into the darkness, the Spanish boys returned a few minutes later, having rendezvoused with the rest of their raiding party, a coalition of Vampires, Young Lords, and Heart Kings. Now twelve or thirteen strong, they filtered back into the park and blocked the exits. One walked over to the Americans and flicked on a cigarette lighter to illuminate their faces while asking if any of them had beaten up a Spanish fellow or belonged to any "clicks." Replying "no" to both questions and growing anxious at the strange encounter, a group of five boys and a girl started to leave, but a Spanish boy blocked their way, declaring, "No gringos leave the park." Another boy, Rogelio Soto, asked if they were liars and hit one of the Americans; suddenly fists were flying, broom handles, garrison belts, and bottles were swinging, a sharpened umbrella was jabbed into a boy's stomach, and the boy with the cape flashed a silver-handled knife that he plunged six inches into Robert Young's back. Two boys grabbed Anthony Krzesinski and held him down while Salvador Agron, the Capeman, stabbed him in the chest, piercing his heart and his lung. While Young and Krzesinski managed to run out of the park despite their wounds, Ewald Reimer was cornered by four boys, who punched him until Agron stepped in and stabbed him in the stomach. Reimer broke free, but was tripped and stomped until someone said, "He has had enough." Meanwhile Young, with the help of his friend Tony Woznikaitis, struggled up the stairs to Woznikaitis's apartment. Woznikaitis recalled, "I pushed open the door and Bobby staggered in. He fell flat on his face on the living room floor. I got some water for him, but he didn't move." Krzesinski ran in the building next door and pounded on doors, crying for help. Sixteen-year-old Edna Zorovich opened her door: "The kid was lying there moaning. He put his hands up and grabbed my wrist. He held on very tight. It hurt. Then he must have died." In a matter of a few minutes, two boys were dead and one was seriously injured, all because of mistaken identity, ethnic tension, and rumors of a rumble.[2]

The next morning New York awoke to an uproar. Neither Robert Young nor Anthony Krzesinski had been gang members—they were not tough enough according to local youths. Moreover, they were the summer's ninth and tenth gang-related homicides and the third and fourth in a week.[3] While there were other innocent victims of gang violence that summer, this case, far more so than any of the others, captured public attention. Because of the publicity and the volume of documents produced, the case opens a unique window onto the gang world of the 1950s and the issues of ethnic and class marginalization and the problems in defining masculinity that led adolescent males to confront each other on city streets.

## NARRATIVES OF VIOLENCE

Six narratives of gang violence emerge in the Capeman case. The first appeared in the tabloids in the initial days after the incident and supplied stereotypical images of Puerto Rican gang members. A second narrative, apparent on the streets, is about ethnic conflict. The third narrative, created by public officials, liberals, and the minority communities, was designed to diffuse ethnic conflict by focusing on the violence of individual psychopaths. Prosecutors and police spoke of councils of war and premeditated murder and created a fourth narrative. The fifth narrative belongs to Salvador Agron, who provided his own view of his case and the causes of gang violence. Finally, using a variety of sources, I will reconstruct the gang members' viewpoint of the causes and meaning of gang violence.[4]

### The Media's Narrative

New York's tabloids immediately sensationalized the Capeman case and provided the public with enduring images of it.[5] The *New York Journal American*, the *Daily News*, the *New York Mirror*, and the *New York Herald Tribune* provided front-page headlines and published lurid photographs of mangled bodies, glaring delinquents, grieving family members, and innocent victims. Pictures of Young and Krzesinski that emphasized their youthful innocence were juxtaposed with shots of their bloodied corpses. Photos of the other attack victims showed bandaged white youths looking stunned at what had befallen them. Then photographs of the raiders appeared as police made arrests and brought in witnesses for interrogation. The newspapers showed them dressed in brightly flowered shirts that emphasized their island origins, and reporters encouraged them to

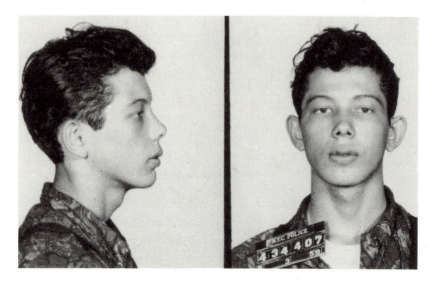

I.2. Salvador Agron, the Capeman.

provide outlandish or sinister nicknames that stressed their "otherness."
Photographers captured the Capeman, Salvador Agron, giggling with his
friends and shrugging off the accusation of murder; Tony Hernandez,
dubbed the "umbrella man," staring impassively at the camera or seeming
to glance admiringly at Agron; Hector Bouillerce, soon to be redeemed
as a prosecution witness, sneering defiance; Nestor Hernandez (no rela-
tion to Tony), Francisco "Baboo Charlie" Cruz, and José "Frenchy" Cordero all peering with heavily lidded eyes at the viewer as if they were
nodding out on heroin. The cameramen egged the boys on and then
displayed the "evidence" of their callous disregard for human life. These
photographs, the posturing of the suspects, and the names of the gangs—
Vampires, Young Lords, Heart Kings—constructed an image of the
Puerto Rican as an alien and a predatory gang member.[6]

The press demonized Salvador Agron in particular. The media called
Agron the leader of the Vampires and said that he enjoyed masquerading
in his cape and leaping out of the shadows to terrify passersby. Reporters
wrote that he was known as "Dracula," "Zorro," and "Machine Gun Sal"
and had been a member of the Mau Maus, a fearsome Puerto Rican gang
in Brooklyn responsible for a number of murders. The *Mirror* went the
furthest, calling Agron a "creature of the night" like the vampire he imi-

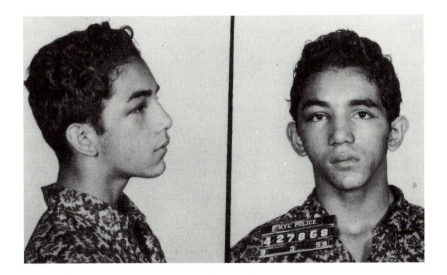

I.3. Tony Hernandez, the "umbrella man."

tated, and reported that Agron's family "saw him only in his torpid daylight hours." Agron contributed to the creation of his image by seizing the opportunity offered by the press and enacting the tough guy role. Following his arrest, Agron rejected the Bible offered by his mother, declaring, "I don't care if I burn; my mother can watch." After his interrogation by police, Agron faced reporters who asked him how he felt about the killings. Answering with a nonchalant shrug, Agron parried most of the questions until someone asked if he felt like a "big man" appearing before the microphones. Finally losing his temper, Agron snapped, "I feel like killing you," a remark headlined in the papers with the comment that Agron was "still feeling homicidal."[7]

The report that Agron's gang was made up of individuals who were actively or passively homosexual added to the notoriety surrounding the case. Tony Hernandez said that he hung around the Vampires for a "goof" because its social circle included "lesbians and fairies," but, a friend assured reporters, Hernandez really liked girls. It was Agron who was "queer," who apparently enjoyed having sex with other men, and several stories referred to him as the "effeminate hoodlum." Violence, a sexual identity perceived as deviant, and the report that he, like a majority of the defendants, had come from Puerto Rico only to be supported on

welfare in New York made Agron the quintessential outsider, an inhabi-
tant of a subterranean world who had surfaced to wreak terror on the
innocent, hard-working, and law-abiding majority.[8]

The image of the Puerto Rican as gang member was not created by
the media in the immediate aftermath of the Capeman case; rather the
press drew on symbols already familiar to most New Yorkers. *West Side
Story*, produced on Broadway in 1957, explored the ethnic hatreds that
rippled through New York neighborhoods as Puerto Rican and African-
American migrants moved into areas that had traditionally been Euro-
American. Bernardo and his Puerto Rican gang, the Sharks, had staked a
claim to the turf of Riff and the Jets, who declared, "We fought hard for
this territory and it's ours." The play had a humane vision, it portrayed
the aspirations of Puerto Rican migrants sympathetically, it explored the
similarities between the Puerto Rican and Euro-American gang members, and it pointed out the futility of violence. But *West Side Story* also
trafficked in the symbols of gang culture: switchblades, colors, midnight
rumbles, boys in pompadours and leather jackets. The play, which drew
power from the newspaper stories of ethnically based gang conflict that
were posted at rehearsals, created a language and a reservoir of symbols
that the public detached from the context of the play and used to interpret
gangs. None of these symbols was more potent than that of the knife-
wielding Puerto Rican gang killer.[9]

Yet the response to the Capeman case was not merely a construction
of the media or of popular writers. It would be a mistake to interpret the
reaction to the case simply as testimony to the vivid imaginations of
headline writers and the ability of the press to tap and enlarge ethnic
stereotypes. Although the press certainly helped arouse the Euro-American population, the images wielded by the media were so resonant because they captured emotions expressed on the streets, and most of those
emotions had to do with what people called "race."

## The Narrative of the Streets

The killings stirred the "racial" resentments that lurked beneath the
surface of daily life. "Race" is not an essential or unchanging biological
category, but a social one used by groups to distinguish among themselves in the competition for goods and resources. As a social construct,

"race" is a fluid term with different meanings in different points in time. In mid-twentieth-century New York, the city's predominant groups— Jews, Germans, Italians, and Irish—were still referred to as "races," and conflict among them had shaped politics, access to relief, and the organization of the economy. After World War II, the massive expansion of African-American and Puerto Rican communities redefined these conflicts, created unity among Euro-American groups around their "whiteness," and focused resentment on the newcomers.[10] Adult competition for housing, jobs, and the perquisites of political life fueled the confrontations among adolescent groups, while efforts by African Americans to integrate New York's schools in the 1950s led to boycotts and threats of violence by Euro-American parents.[11] In such a context, incidents such as the Capeman killings easily reignited the smoldering embers of "racial" conflict.

The sharpest reaction, understandably, came from local residents who knew the victims of the gang attack. Monsignor Joseph McCaffrey, the parish priest who said the requiem mass for Anthony Krzesinski, used naturalist metaphors in his sermon, comparing the Puerto Rican gang members to beasts who needed to be caged. McCaffrey whipped up already tense feelings, declaring, "Let us meet force with force in this war against juvenile criminals." Similar sentiments echoed in the streets near the precinct house. As the number of individuals arrested and interrogated grew, hundreds of spectators gathered outside calling for a lynching and chanting, "Kill the spics, kill the spics."[12]

Letters to the newspapers and to New York Governor Nelson Rockefeller repeated expressions of ethnic hatred. Correspondents recommended vigilante patrols, greater discretion for police use of force, proposals to limit access to welfare, and pleas to stop coddling criminals. In the first eighteen days of September, an average of fifty-eight letters or telegrams arrived per day at the governor's office expressing concern about delinquency and gang violence. Although the number declined by half over the next several weeks, the outpouring was sufficiently notable to merit a special memorandum to the governor's staff. About a quarter of the correspondents were from out of state, others were not city residents, and about a fifth offered constructive advice or pleaded with the governor not to succumb to prejudice. But many of the letters from city residents dripped vitriol. For example, one Park Avenue resident proposed that young criminals "be whipped publicly at a whipping post," while another writer insisted that the gang murders were the result of "letting loose so many persons of an inferior racial, mental and cultural development." Racial integration, he continued, was "against Natural [*sic*] law." The governor was told that "all criminals of the stinking and substandard mob of Puerto Ricans" ought to be deported, and another correspondent claimed that "the worst scum of P.R. and the south" came to New York because of the ease in obtaining welfare.[13] The letters reflected all the stereotypes of Puerto Ricans and African Americans and linked crime, welfare, and social change to the arrival of the migrants. The reaction was that of a people challenged in their dominance, forced to accommodate newcomers who rejected New York's color line and who pushed their way into new neighborhoods and the city's public spaces. In the discourse of the streets, African Americans and Puerto Ricans were nearly always the aggressors.[14]

It is easy, but too facile, to dismiss these reactions to the Capeman case simply as racism. To be sure, racism tinged the responses to the case. The fact that Young and Krzesinski were white meant that the case received much more attention than if they had been African American or Puerto Rican. Usually when the objects of African-American or Puerto Rican gang attacks were Euro-American, the press played up the attack and accentuated the innocence of the victims. For example, when a Puerto Rican gang called the Navajos murdered Billy Blankenship in the Bronx in 1955, he was described as a model boy whose father was active in the fight against delinquency. His participation in an earlier street fight between the Navajos and the predominantly Italian Golden Guineas was overlooked until discovered by a zealous defense attorney. By then Blankenship had already been covered by the mantle of innocent victimhood.[15] But to focus only on racism elides the anguish and righteous anger felt by family and friends of the victims of a brutal crime. And, in the case of Young and Krzesinski, further investigation sustained the presumptions of innocence.

Neither Young nor Krzesinski had been arrested or had a reputation for being troublesome. Anthony Krzesinski, sixteen, was one of four children of Mrs. Frances Krzesinski, who was separated from her husband and who supported her family as a hat-checker at the Waldorf Astoria. Tony had quit school and worked as a messenger for a downtown publishing house. Robert Young, sixteen, the foster child of Ed and Florence

Fontine, still attended school at least occasionally and worked as a delivery boy for a grocery store to supplement his foster father's wages as a truck driver. His older brother, also raised by the Fontines after the mother died eleven years earlier, was in the Air Force.[16]

The murders of Young and Krzesinski crystallized the fears of white working-class New York. The Fontines and Krzesinskis represented the people left behind by the fabled prosperity of the 1950s. They had sacrificed and worked hard but owned very little, except for the communities they had created in New York's hardscrabble neighborhoods, which they could not or would not abandon. Now, they believed, these communities were being threatened by a rising tide of crime that corresponded with the arrival of the newcomers. Evidence came in the form of innocent youths struck down by outsiders in the heart of their own turf.

In the first days after the killings, public officials scrambled to respond to the outcry over the case. The magistrate who arraigned Agron and the other defendants promised "drastic action," meaning "quick hearings, [and] a quick trial," while the district attorney prepared to charge the defendants with first-degree murder. The police department added 1,400 patrolmen to the streets and a U.S. Senate subcommittee quickly convened a hearing on juvenile violence in New York. Local politicians held emergency summits on crime, demanded a citywide curfew for children and adolescents, called for "nightstick justice" and the expansion of rural "work camps," and proposed a moratorium on Puerto Rican migration to New York. In sum, there was a "moral panic" as the majority community mobilized to condemn the Puerto Rican delinquents who symbolized all that was wrong with New York.[17]

New York's Puerto Rican and African-American communities commented less on the Capeman case per se than on the "racial" outcry it provoked. Puerto Rican leaders and the Spanish-language media organized a publicity campaign to defend their community. They emphasized the law-abiding nature of the vast majority of Puerto Ricans and pledged to supply volunteers to work with young people in boys' clubs and community centers. While indicating their support for any effort to combat delinquency, they emphasized its social and economic roots and applauded the restraint shown by Police Commissioner Stephen Kennedy. African-American leaders and the leading African-American newspaper, the *Amsterdam News*, condemned calls for vigilante justice and restrictions on the migratory rights of American citizens but endorsed proposals to increase the number of police. They also reminded New Yorkers that long-term proposals for fighting delinquency included better schools, better housing, and improved job opportunities. With the support of the minority communities and the more liberal elements in the city, a third discourse about the Capeman case began to emerge.[18]

### The Narrative of Liberalism

New York officials in their comments on the case denied the existence of any ethnic hostility—despite the evidence on the streets, in their mail, and in the subtexts of their own public declarations. Instead, they supplied an alternative reading of events based on the work of academic researchers and investigative reporters. This narrative, while acknowledging that social and economic conditions helped produce delinquency, held that gangs were unstructured, informal groups that demanded and received little loyalty from their members, and that gang violence was senseless, random, unorganized, and committed by psychopaths. By focusing on problematic individuals, public officials reassured New Yorkers of the fundamental health of the social system and dismissed the possibility that gang conflict had any larger meaning.[19]

Public officials moved quickly to air their view. In briefing the press on the progress of the Capeman case, Deputy Police Inspector Frederick Lussen declared that "no racial tensions were involved at all." Mayor Robert Wagner, Jr., in a televised address to the public, bluntly declared:

> Eight days ago, a group of hoodlums, dedicated to murder and mayhem, invaded a playground on our West Side, and proceeded to commit both those crimes. It shocked you and it shocked me. Possibly my shock was even the greater, because . . . I had the full knowledge that this was a playground we had built . . . for the decent children of a neighborhood.
>
> It was a neighborhood in which the playground approach to the juvenile problem seemed to be working. Then a gang came in from the outside, beat up the occupants, and committed murder.

One might argue that the juxtaposition of "decent children of a neighborhood" with the murderous "outside" hoodlums implied a code for "race" that viewers, surfeited with images of Puerto Rican gang members, could interpret for themselves. But the mayor went on to reject explicitly any "racial" interpretation of the incident: "What fomented this? Tense race relations? The police tell me no." Governor Nelson Rockefeller, who called for a summit on juvenile violence in the aftermath of the Capeman case, also rejected the idea that race played a role in the incident. The governor listed the causes of juvenile delinquency, and what he left off is as notable as what he included: delinquency, the governor avowed, was the product of "neglect by parents, broken homes, poor living conditions, unhealthy background, economic deprivation, mental disturbance and lack of religious training." Rockefeller and Wagner believed that social conditions bore some causal relationship to crime, but thought they could be ameliorated painlessly by an expanding economy and traditional liberal programs. In addition, neither wanted to confront the politically explosive issue of ethnic relations. Instead, they created a narrative based on the violence of aberrant individuals.[20]

This shift in the public discourse about the Capeman case was also in the interest of the minority communities. Though they might have preferred more acknowledgment of the effects of discrimination, economic marginality, and social injustice, minority spokesmen were interested primarily in defending the respectability of their communities. Nothing was to be gained by linking violence too closely to poverty and suggesting that the poor might commit murderous assaults. In an era of liberal consensus and civil rights optimism, minority leaders could easily overlook the frustration of adolescent gang members. It made more sense to agree that Agron and his co-defendants were not representative of Puerto Rican youth and that their crimes were deviant acts.

Several New York newspapers also stepped back from the initial emphasis on ethnic confrontation and joined the new consensus about the case. The *Times* reminded readers to distinguish between the law-abiding majority and the few lawless Puerto Ricans. The *Post*, warning of a "racial civil war," called on the mayor "to speak out bluntly and plainly against the ugly racist talk now being heard in too many places in the city. It is time he challenged with all the moral authority of his office the use of 'Spic' as a dirty word." Such forthrightness was rare. The *Daily News*, the *Mirror*, and the *Herald Tribune*, after stirring the cauldron of ethnic hostility, now remained silent about ethnic relations, while the *Journal American* (part of the conservative Hearst chain) cheered on those readers wishing to form vigilante patrols to protect their neighborhoods. The *Journal*, in its editorial cartoons, portrayed juvenile delinquents as untamed savages with blood-drenched hands, but without any discernible ethnic characteristics. While African Americans, Puerto Ricans, white liberals, and elements of the press stressed the social conditions that produced delinquency, they could agree with conservatives that gang members were deranged and murderous thugs in need of restraint.[21]

Certainly there was much in the Capeman case to support the view that gang members were social misfits who engaged in violence for "kicks." According to the district attorney's records, the group of boys who went to the playground on 45th Street expected to meet five or six hundred Italian or Irish boys. Apparently some of them did not know each other's names, and only a couple were friends with Frenchy, whose honor they were supposedly upholding.

The participating gangs had little apparent reason to protect Frenchy or defend his access to the park. They represented different neighborhoods: the Heart Kings came from Second Avenue between 117th and 119th Streets on the edge of Italian East Harlem, while the Young Lords (80th Street between Amsterdam and Columbus Avenues), and the Vampires (72nd Street and Broadway) were from the West Side of Manhattan, but many blocks from the Hell's Kitchen area. The playground at 45th Street was not adjacent to anyone's turf, it did not hold a resource (such as a swimming pool) that might attract youngsters from around the city, and there was little reason to contest anyone's ownership of it. Even within the logic of the gang world, the raid made little sense.[22]

The foray seemed to be the product of little planning, again suggesting its seemingly random nature. According to the police, the boys did agree to meet around midnight on August 29 at the playground and to bring knives, "gasoline bombs," and a shotgun. But some boys thought their enemies were Irish, while others claimed they were Italian, or just "Americans." A couple of boys agreed to go along at the last minute. No one seemed to know how many boys might be waiting for them or the exact strength of their raiding party. Their initial purpose, while not exactly innocent, was to walk the street: to challenge the enemy by swaggering as a group through the heart of his turf, which, of course, meant going armed. Failing to find any challenge on the street, the boys returned to the playground. Young, Krzesinski, Reimer, and the other victims of the attack just happened to be in the wrong place at the wrong time. Frenchy, who instigated the raid and who was supposed to bring the Molotov cocktails, never showed up. It was easy to interpret the incident as the product of an aimless search for excitement—typical of gang activity, according to most adults.[23]

The raiders also seemed to fulfill the expectation of politicians, investigative reporters, and social scientists that only the maladjusted participated in gang violence. Several of the youths had arrest records and had spent time in reformatories. Each youth's life seemed to be a variation on a similar theme: a migrant from Puerto Rico, often alienated from family, out of work or only occasionally employed, unskilled, a school dropout. Rogelio Soto quit school at age sixteen to work as a Western Union messenger before taking a job in a factory making the ribs for umbrellas. At the time of the incident, he had been unemployed for several months. His mother had divorced her husband back in Puerto Rico and had moved to New York in the late 1940s with her two children. Raphael Colon, twenty-seven, homeless, had arrived from Puerto Rico four years earlier and worked as a dishwasher. Colon slept in the homes of other gang members or in the halls or on the roofs of apartment buildings. Francisco Cruz, seventeen, president of the Heart Kings, worked as a painter's helper and contributed $15 a week to supplement the incomes of his stepfather, a truck driver, and his mother, who worked in a Hoboken, New Jersey, candy factory. Cruz had migrated from Puerto Rico in 1957, and, unhappy in New York, he had discussed returning to the island. José Rivera, twenty, vice president of the Vampires, worked in a candle factory in Brooklyn and he was married with a four-month-old daughter. Tony Hernandez, seventeen (the "umbrella man"), came from Puerto Rico in 1949 and lived with his father, who worked in the linen room of the Hotel Victoria, his stepmother, who was a garment worker, and three siblings. Hernandez had quit school after the seventh grade and tried to get a job but was unsuccessful. He had spent twenty months in reform school, where he won trophies for weight lifting. Despite his strength, Hernandez was small and apparently ran away from home after being threatened by a gang and moved into an apartment on 77th Street, where he joined the Vampires. He had a reputation as a sharp dresser and it was implied that he earned his money as a prostitute. Nestor Hernandez, seventeen, vice president of the Heart Kings, had come from Puerto Rico three years earlier to live with his mother and stepfather. He had gone to school for seven years in Puerto Rico and for nearly two years in New York, but he had a limited command of English. He also worked in a factory. Frenchy Cordero, eighteen, held as a material witness in the case, had come from Puerto Rico three years earlier and worked in a delicatessen. He had recently lost his job and had served some time in a reformatory for rolling drunks and for attacking a teacher. Hector Bouillerce, seventeen, who became a witness for the prosecution, had lived in New York since he was eleven. He had recently quit his job as a photo printer to join the Marines. Only shared ethnic and class marginality linked these youths together.[24]

It is clear in retrospect that the raiders were the sons of New York's Puerto Rican working class—and very similar in situation to Robert Young and Anthony Krzesinski. Several came from homes broken by desertion or divorce and had spent some time supported by welfare, but it is more notable that their parents, like most Puerto Ricans and African Americans, were participants in the low-wage and unskilled service sector of New York's economy. Most of the youths seemed fairly responsible, holding jobs as messengers or delivery boys to help support their families. After their arrests, however, the press directed attention to the raiders' lack of full-time employment, to their truancy from school, to their records as delinquents, and to their idling on street corners waiting for trouble to happen. These factors fit the stereotype of the violent gang member.

Of all the members of the raiding party, Salvador Agron appeared to be the most severely disturbed. Agron had spent most of his early childhood living in a Catholic poorhouse in Mayaguez, Puerto Rico. His mother, Esmeralda Rodriguez, eloped at thirteen with a thirty-two-year-old street cleaner, Gumersindo Agron. Esmeralda bore two children, including Salvador, born in 1943, before fleeing from her husband's beatings and taking refuge in the poorhouse. Except for about a year with his father, Agron lived in the institution for the next eight years. There the children were kept in the nursery, which was segregated by sex, and Salvador was allowed to see his mother only on Sundays or on those occasions when he was able to steal his way into her quarters. Agron ran away frequently, claimed that he heard voices telling him to do bad things, and upon several occasions slashed his body with razor blades. By the time Salvador left Puerto Rico at age nine, he had spent virtually his entire life separated from his family, had showed symptoms of psychosis, and was unable to read or write.

Esmeralda Rodriguez divorced and remarried. Her new husband, Carlos Gonzalez, a self-proclaimed Pentecostal minister, brought her and her daughter to New York in 1951. Salvador remained behind in the asylum until his parents sent for him the following year. The family lived in a three-room cold-water flat on the Lower East Side until moving to another Puerto Rican community in the Navy Yard section of Brooklyn. Salvador's mother worked in a belt factory and his stepfather in a blueprint factory, and they left the children to their own devices during the day. Agron's stepfather proved to be an unsympathetic parent. Neither Salvador nor his sister, Aurea, were allowed to dance, sing, play the radio, or hang nonreligious pictures in the home. To keep the children from eating too much, the parents padlocked the refrigerator. Aurea found her salvation in school, but the other students disliked Salvador and called him "crazy." He constantly skipped school and spent most of his time on the streets avoiding his stepfather's beatings. Eventually, Salvador's parents took what for a Latino family must have been an especially difficult step. They admitted familial failure and Salvador's stepfather entered a delinquent child complaint in Children's Court in July 1953. Salvador was again institutionalized at age eleven, first in the Youth House for observation and then in the Wiltwyck School for Boys.

The Wiltwyck School, despite its progressive reputation, did little for Salvador besides providing him with some instruction in English. He was released in 1956, having reached the age limit of thirteen, and returned to his parents' home in Brooklyn. Again he rarely attended school and, instead of being a tough gang member, he was a victim of gang beatings. His mother returned him to Puerto Rico, where he lived with his aunt for a short time before she passed him on to his father. The senior Agron, disabled by a stroke, was no better equipped to handle Salvador than were his mother and stepfather, and Salvador ran the streets until he was committed to a reformatory for assaulting another boy. Salvador's behavior declined even more rapidly in the reformatory. He banged his head against the walls and claimed he saw demons in his room and heard voices. Salvador was handsome and he engaged in sexual relations with other boys at the reformatory despite the efforts of the directors to prevent it. He ran away several times but was always recaptured, until his mother arranged for him to visit his father and then helped him flee to New York. He returned in November 1958, but again was unable to get along with his stepfather. Salvador alternated between staying with his sister, who had married at age fifteen to escape the family, and sleeping in abandoned buildings. Finally, he found refuge in a street club, the Vampires, whose president lived with a thirty-year-old male lover and where Agron's sexual identity was not an issue.[25]

The Salvador Agron revealed in court records possessed all of the traits of the socially marginal. He was a member of a minority group, a school dropout, a delinquent, a welfare recipient, he engaged in same-sex relations, and he exhibited symptoms of psychosis. He served as prima facie evidence that gangs attracted severely disturbed individuals who might explode into violence at any moment. With case histories such as these as evidence, commentators created a convincing narrative that gangs were loose collections of the aberrant.

### A Narrative of Crime and Punishment

None of the elements of the first three narratives was apparent in the fourth narrative—the one the district attorney prepared for the jury. Where the tabloids wanted to boost sales and give expression to white outrage, and liberal officials and minority group leaders wanted to tamp down ethnic hostility, the district attorney only wanted to gain a conviction. In order to prosecute Salvador Agron and his co-defendants for first degree murder, the district attorney had to make a case for premeditation, not random violence. Agron had to be seen as a calculating gang leader plotting the raid that led to Young and Krzesinski's deaths, not an out-of-control psychopath. The prosecution had to emphasize the immediate sources of conflict, not some larger explanation of the social forces impinging on gang members. Therefore, the prosecutor's narrative is framed most narrowly, focused only on who did what to whom.

The police discovered that the immediate cause of the playground attack was a dispute over drugs. José "Frenchy" Cordero had apparently offered to sell some "reefers" to the mother of John Diaz, a Puerto Rican boy who lived in the Hell's Kitchen neighborhood and who was an accepted visitor in the playground. When Diaz heard about the attempted sale, he was outraged and threatened Frenchy with a beating. To gain revenge, Frenchy made up the tale that he and other Puerto Ricans had been beaten up by American boys in the playground. The incident, according to police, had nothing to do with "race" and was the product of a warped imagination.[26]

The district attorney was faced with explaining why the Vampires, Heart Kings, and Young Lords rushed to Frenchy's defense when many of them did not know who he was. To do this, the prosecutor described a meeting of gang members on a street corner before the attack as a council of war among several "organizations" and argued that the three gangs had discussed forming an alliance. He maintained that Frenchy's tale provided the gangs with an opportunity to prove their courage and cement their ties.[27]

The district attorney also had to supply Salvador Agron with a motive for killing two boys whom he had never met. The prosecution portrayed Agron as a vicious gang leader who wanted to become president of the gang and who used the attack in the park as the occasion to solidify his position. The press, caught up in its own creation of the Capeman, never questioned the accuracy of this image. Though the district attorney's narrative made for a good story and rationalized his choices for prosecution, it was the weakest point in the state's case against Salvador Agron.

Agron possessed none of the characteristics of gang leaders. At sixteen, he was the youngest of the Vampires—which included men in their twenties—and he was physically not as strong as most adolescents his age. He had been rebuffed continuously by gangs and had been attacked on several occasions, none of which was conducive to high status as a gang member. Social workers described him as passive aggressive, always provoking conflict but unable to handle its consequences.[28] Far from being a leader, Agron was eager for acceptance. He may have wielded the knife in the rumble to prove he had heart, or he may simply have felt it necessary to be armed given his lack of physical prowess. Whichever was the case, it seems clear that Agron found in the Vampires the sense of belonging and acceptance that was missing in his home and elsewhere in his life. He was willing to do anything to preserve this sense of security— even kill. But it is very unlikely that he led the Vampires into action.

It is also doubtful that Agron acted with the premeditation demanded by the first-degree murder charge brought against him. The court testimony shows that the knife used in the killings belonged to Johnnie Rojas, the president of the Vampires and that it was acquired by José "Pepe" Rivera, the vice president, for use in the rumble. Pepe supplied the knife to Agron, who carried it to the playground. Witnesses related that Agron had declared he was going to stab someone, but he had made similar claims before. Agron himself maintained that though he wanted to hurt someone with the knife "he didn't think that it might kill him." Agron made his statement to the assistant district attorney after having spent four days without food hiding in a tenement in the Bronx and after being subjected to eleven hours of questioning by police, who also failed to provide either food or water or to inform Agron that he had a right to counsel. Police routinely abused prisoners, and several of Agron's co-defendants testified to receiving the "third degree" at the hands of police and showed evidence of bruises. Yet even in this state, Agron only admitted to wielding the knife and the police could not elicit a statement of intent to commit murder.[29]

Questions can also be raised about Agron's ability to distinguish between right and wrong. Several social workers and probation officers had noted his "schizoid traits," and his history of delusions and bizarre behavior was available to the court at the trial. A psychiatric evaluation performed in 1965 concluded that he was not psychotic: "Psychiatric examination at this time reveals a cooperative male who makes excellent contact with the examiners. His speech is relevant and coherent. His sensorium is clear. No delusions nor hallucinations were elicited. His affect is appropriate."[30] An examination performed six years later is not evidence of his state of mind in 1959, but it is notable that his attorneys did not attempt an insanity defense. It is likely that Agron met the legal standard of sanity despite the evidence of his occasional delusions. Ultimately, the issue of Agron's sanity is less important than that of his image.

The Agron presented to the jury by the prosecution was a ruthless gang leader who participated in an elaborate council of war and who swore to stab anyone who got in his way. Agron made the district attorney's narrative much more convincing by his behavior. He seized the limelight offered him, for this was his moment of triumph, his only recognition as a man worthy of note. His public statements and his swaggering before the press fit the image of the Puerto Rican gang killer so much in the public consciousness and helped to convict him.

The jury that convicted Agron was primed to do so. New York had an English language literacy test for voters, and, as a result, about half of New York's Puerto Ricans were excluded from the polls. Since jury lists were drawn from the pool of eligible voters, Puerto Ricans were severely underrepresented on jury panels. For example, only three individuals of Puerto Rican birth appeared on a grand jury panel of two thousand persons in 1959. In New York, one also had to believe in the death penalty in order to be a juror for a capital case. As a result, the jury that convicted Agron was an all-male, all-white jury that was unrepresentative of the city's population and probably disposed to view the exploits of Puerto Rican gang members harshly. They found Salvador Agron guilty of first-degree murder and made no recommendation for mercy. Both Agron and Tony Hernandez, the youngest of the defendants, received the death penalty; the other five defendants were found guilty of or had pled guilty to manslaughter charges and received lesser sentences. Although Hernandez's conviction was overturned on appeal, giving him the opportunity to plead guilty to manslaughter, and Agron's death penalty was eventually commuted, their convictions represented white New York's revenge.[31]

### The Narratives of Salvador Agron

Salvador Agron offered his own—conflicting—narratives of gang violence, although they appeared years after the fact. In a letter to the *New York Times* in 1975, Agron argued that during the wave of teenage gang violence in the 1950s, "One either fought or one either [*sic*] became the punching bag of rival gangs." He blamed New York's social agencies for not redirecting the energies of young people and he noted in his own case the absence of parental guidance and the influence of a pervasive "Bohemianism" that undermined traditional moral values. (Bohemianism may have been a veiled reference to his engaging in sex with other males.) He explained that "in becoming a victim of my social conditions it made me act in a way as to make victims of others." Agron maintained that he had been redeemed while in prison: when "facing the shadows of death, it occurred to me that one must do his best to take evil and turn it into good. It is due to this acknowledgment of life and reality that I have been able to maintain the little humanity that was left within me."

Agron was hoping to be paroled at the time, and he went on to make a case for his rehabilitation. "I have learned how to write poetry, received my high school equivalency, put legal petitions together in block letters. . . . I have also received my regents diploma, and at the present time . . . I have received college credits." He argued that everyone imprisoned for gang violence in the '50s was back on the streets. He asked, "How much is enough? How long does it take to correct or rehabilitate a first time offender?"[32]

Not until another four years had passed did the state of New York agree that he was rehabilitated. In 1979, on the verge of his release from prison, Salvador Agron gave an interview to the *New York Times*. By this time his tone had changed. Now he claimed to have been a "gang leader" who at sixteen had been "proud of his exploits in crime with the Mau Maus in Brooklyn and the Vampires of the West Side of Manhattan." He said that he had been a founding member of the Vampires, who had gone to the park to confront the Nordics. However, he maintained that he could not remember "actually plunging the knife" into anyone, and he claimed that his confession to the killings was false. "Somebody in that park did it and it wasn't me. I just took the blame. I had a nasty attitude . . . [and] I said here are the cameras, it was my chance to sort of jump back at society and I started insulting people back. I was exaggerating." According to the rules of the Vampires, the youngest member took the blame in a crime, and Agron was the youngest. "My cape had no blood. My knife had no blood. The other knife with the blood of the victim was suppressed by the prosecution. It was forgotten. But I can't feel the guilt." He argued that there no longer was any point in lying: "I've done the time for it. But the truth is the truth."[33]

What was the truth? Agron's first account was in many ways self-serving. He wrote it to arouse sympathy, to place the murders in a larger context, and to make a case for his rehabilitation and parole. Agron did not mention his exploits as a gang member, and he made no attempt to avoid responsibility for the murders. By the time of the second account, his release had already been agreed to and one might argue that with everything decided Agron could afford to be more honest. Instead, he postured for the press. Agron invented himself as a member of the Mau Maus and a founder and leader of the Vampires, even as he denied responsibility for the one act that gave credence to his account. Apparently

Agron still yearned for recognition, for respect, for manhood, even as he shrank from the deed that in the gang world bestowed these attributes upon him.

### Masculinity and the Gang

There are few hints in the district attorney's records, the court transcripts, or the newspapers about the defendants' worldview, their understanding of violence, or their justification for it. This—the gang members' narrative—must be pieced together from a variety of other sources, and it anticipates some of the arguments made in the remainder of the book. According to gang members, they fought purposefully, according to established norms, and did so for ethnic honor, personal reputation, and to defend their masculinity.

Gangs battled over resources, and these struggles took on a meaning much larger than access to a specific site, becoming especially intense when the opponents were of a different "race." Schoolyards, parks, and playgrounds usually belonged to a specific gang and had to be defended against outsiders or wrested away from the dominant group. Gangs seeking to gain "rep," or a reputation for being tough, were relentlessly expansionist, defeating and incorporating elements of other gangs into their group and staking claim to a widening sphere of influence until they met an equally powerful foe. Settlement houses, schools, or boys' clubs, which were supposedly neutral sites, usually sat square in someone's turf, and while the institution might ban gang paraphernalia and try to settle disputes through mediation, the streets outside were the scenes of a violent gauntlet as gangs fought to control admission. Truly rare commodities like swimming pools engendered the greatest conflict; members of the out group traveled there only in numbers large enough to fend off an attack, which in itself was provocative.[34] Control over facilities conveyed power and prestige, usually in excess of their use value, and battles over access became a contest over the relative ability and worth of the competing groups. From this perspective, a fight over access to a playground, even a barren slab of concrete, was anything but a senseless conflict.[35]

Since a raiding party entered enemy turf and expected to be attacked, it went armed. But gang members rarely went on a raid with the expectation of killing or being killed. Rumbles and raids were designed to terrorize an opponent, to enhance one's reputation, to drive another group from an advantaged position or from possession of a resource, and to test the manhood of a foe or of a newly initiated member. In the process, both gang members and bystanders were hurt and sometimes died. Gang weapons became deadlier over time as shotguns, Molotov cocktails, and handguns replaced homemade zip guns, car aerials, switchblades, bicycle chains, and lead pipes, and this had an obvious effect on fatalities. But death was a by-product of violent confrontation and not its chief object; rumbles were like combat in war—a few moments of intense, exhilarating, terrifying, and random action. Killing was something that gang members were aware of and accepted fatalistically, but it was rarely premeditated.[36] When the Vampires, Young Lords, and Heart Kings descended on the playground, they were prepared for mayhem, not murder.

Contrary to the impressions of adults, gang victims were not chosen randomly. Gangs rarely targeted adults, young children, or female adolescents, and gang members largely avoided attacking "coolies"—young males who were known not to be gang members. Violence was applied "rationally": reputations were made only by confronting equals, who by their style, walk, and language indicated that they were "down boppers." Gangs looked for signs of gang membership—capes, berets, narrow-brimmed alpine hats, canes, and other gang paraphernalia—when planning an attack. However, in the absence of telltale signs, other markers were used. Gender, ethnicity, and age were convenient substitutes, and adolescent males in enemy turf were presumed to be members of enemy gangs. Of course this meant that coolies in other neighborhoods—boys such as Robert Young and Anthony Krzesinski—were sometimes the mistaken victims of gang assaults.[37]

Ethnic hostility almost certainly had a part in the case. The assembled Vampires, Heart Kings, and Young Lords believed Frenchy's tale about being beaten up by American boys because it fit their experience. Euro-American gangs, with at least the tacit support of adults, enforced neighborhood boundary lines by violently assaulting minority group members, particularly adolescents, who crossed them. Retaliatory raids occurred not only to gain revenge but to defy attempted intimidation, to assert that a group had a place in society and the right to use public streets and public facilities regardless of what others thought. Asserting control over the playground at 45th Street was an attack on white domination and an assertion of Puerto Rican honor, and gang members understood it as such. (For example, some African-American gang members in Harlem showed their understanding of the case by treating the defendants as heroes and carrying newspaper clippings about the incident in their wallets.)[38]

Honor and masculinity, as sociologist Ruth Horowitz has found, were the most important components of the gang members' worldview because they were at the core of their identities.[39] Masculinity is socially constructed and opportunities to define it are dependent on social context. In working-class New York, this meant masculinity was created on the streets by showing dominance over other males, fearlessness in confrontations, and adeptness in the performances of street life. Puerto Rican adolescents, already marginalized by class, language, and ethnicity, found few legitimate means for establishing a masculine identity. Like other boys from working-class neighborhoods, they joined gangs because they failed at school, had miserable home lives, were excluded from the job market, or knew that they qualified for only the most menial positions. Gangs provided a means of transcending these circumstances, of allowing adolescents to establish themselves as part of a "street elite," and to define a masculine identity in spite of the humiliations of everyday life. In gangs, adolescent males proved themselves, acquired respect and honor, and demonstrated their masculinity by humbling a foe. Violence arose out of the need to meet these intangible goals.[40]

Cross-cultural analysis of masculinity suggests that it is frequently defined through aggressive, risk-taking behavior, and those who fail the public tests of masculinity are derided as being feminine or childlike.[41] In the gang world, this polarity was defined through "heart" and "punk." To have heart meant to be daring and courageous, to be a reliable fighter, to be manly; being called a punk was the worst insult imaginable, one that implied cowardice, weakness, and effeminacy. (In fact, the term "punk" was used along with "fuckboy" to define the passive or "female" role in the prison homosexual hierarchy and indicated someone who was weak and could be dominated or raped.) Having heart meant a willingness to fight, regardless of the odds, and to withstand death or a beating instead of backing down. Even enemies could respect each other for having heart; no one respected a punk.[42]

Honor and masculinity for those marginalized by the larger society were difficult to attain, readily threatened, and vigorously defended. The case histories of the young men in the Capeman incident suggest that they faced uncertain job prospects, were alienated from school, and desired recognition and prestige. The readiest way for them to obtain recognition was in the public arena provided by gang conflict. A reputation that inspired fear in others—that of being a down bopper or a cold killer— was a gang boy's most valued and most vulnerable possession, one that simultaneously ensured safety and challenge on the street. A reputation brought the pleasure of recognition, but required constant defense against the slurs, imagined and real, of others.[43] The rumored beatings of Puerto Rican boys by the Euro-American youths who frequented the 45th Street playground could not go unchallenged, for too much was at stake. Within the gang world, attacking members of what was seen as a rival group—even if unarmed—was both honorable and necessary.

For Agron and the Vampires, the challenge to masculinity may have been more pointed. As individuals who engaged in same-sex relations, they probably felt an extra spur to prove that they were not effeminate punks who could be pushed around, as Agron and Hernandez both had been upon other occasions. Since male homosexuals were the rumored victims of attacks in the playground, revenge for some earlier encounter could also have played a role in mobilizing their forces. The resort to violence was not the result of boredom or a random search for kicks but an ultimate test of masculinity and character, proof that they possessed heart and deserved to be counted among the warriors of the street. In a working-class world dislocated by economic change, reshaped by migration, and reorganized by public policy, the only thing an adolescent male could count on was heart.

## Remaking New York

NEW YORK is the most dynamic of cities and remakes itself every generation. Swathes of the city are torn down and recreated, new inhabitants colonize old neighborhoods, and tendrils of a new economy sprout and spread, choking off older growth, while promising to make the city flourish anew. It is this dynamism that sustains New York's place as a world-class city. However, Manhattan's glitter hides the social costs of uneven development. While the benefits of innovation and reinvention concentrate in the hands of a relatively small number of developers, traders, and investors, whose decisions are enshrined in Manhattan's skyline, the costs are borne disproportionately by the poor and the dispossessed, who are hidden in the "inner" city or the "outer" boroughs. Their neighborhoods disappear or are invaded by newcomers; their jobs migrate to other locations; their schools, hospitals, and public services are overwhelmed and underfunded; and their children create their own divergent cultural and organizational forms, including street gangs.

Four factors reshaped the postwar city and supply the context for understanding New York's street gangs. The first and most obvious was the transformation of New York's economy between the 1940s and the 1960s. Adolescents observed their parents and friends closely to see how they fared in the labor market. Decisions to remain in school or to drop out, to learn a trade or to take a factory job, to put up with a boss's demands or to quit and return to the street corner were based on adolescents' understanding of the marketplace. Migration, especially in the 1940s and 1950s, was the second factor affecting gangs. Immigration restriction laws had cut off the largest flow of Euro-Americans into the city, but African

Americans and Puerto Ricans continued to see in New York a beacon to a better life. Migration picked up speed in the postwar years, and the arrival of the migrants set up a bitter contest for residential space, jobs, and resources. Urban renewal, the third factor, was largely a product of the 1950s and early 1960s and worsened the competition for space among poor New Yorkers. Projects to make civic improvements, to construct highways through the city, and to build public housing wiped out older areas and contributed directly to conflict. Finally, suburbanization, which soared in the 1950s, fostered the illusion that social problems would disappear with prosperity and mobility.

Adolescents in the postwar period were not even aware of the reordering of the urban system going on around them—even if they were intimate participants in the process. They experienced the frustration of looking for work as low-skilled jobs left the city; they saw the effect of migration as Euro-Americans, African Americans, and Puerto Ricans vied for resources; they witnessed the bulldozing of tenement districts; and they watched their more affluent neighbors fleeing to the suburbs. These experiences affected the daily lives of all New Yorkers, and they generated tremendous tension in the city, especially among the young.

## THE NEW YORK ECONOMY

New York became the first postindustrial city, beginning its shift from a city of goods to a city of services as early as the 1920s. New York's economy, unlike that of Chicago or Detroit, was never dominated by a few heavy industries. Rather, the city's working class found jobs in thousands of small manufacturing establishments producing garments or machine tools, in printing, in construction, or on the docks. However, occupational categories in manufacturing and mechanical industries suffered the greatest losses in jobs between 1910 and 1930, and during the Depression unskilled laborers and semiskilled factory operatives had the highest levels of unemployment.[1]

These signals of the impending shift in the economy were easily missed. World War II acted like the fever that restores temporarily the flush of life to a dying patient. During the war, New York's harbor proved to be the engine for job creation: the Todd Shipyards in Brooklyn operated on around-the-clock shifts readying ships for the Allies; employment in the Brooklyn Navy Yard rose from 17,000 to 71,000; and the Brooklyn Army Terminal processed thousands of soldiers ready to ship out to Europe.

Major war production, however, was located outside of the city. Centered in adjacent Nassau County on Long Island, airplane construction added 100,000 workers in this field during the war. Other war production bypassed the New York metropolitan region altogether. By the end of 1942 only seven companies in New York City had won bids (totaling just in excess of two million dollars), as the city's typically small firms had difficulty acquiring major contracts. Some New Yorkers followed the example of other Americans and left their homes in search of employment, while state officials encouraged war contractors upstate to hire the city's unemployed. Still, the number of unemployed in New York City remained higher in 1942 than it had been in 1939.[2]

Eventually, war's prosperity trickled down to New York, and it had a profound impact on the young. As a result of Mayor Fiorello La Guardia's lobbying, Franklin Roosevelt ordered federal officials to push contracts toward New York City firms, and finally, in 1943, the city achieved full employment. The nation as a whole also responded to the demand for wartime labor. Eighty-four percent of the male population in the United States aged fourteen and over was either working or in the armed services in 1942. The selective service started drafting eighteen- and nineteen-year-olds in 1943, and employers began hiring women and even younger workers in order to keep up production. The Children's Bureau discovered that the number of minors employed illegally throughout the nation nearly tripled between 1942–43 and 1944–45. Not surprisingly, high school enrollments in the city and in the nation plummeted as youngsters seized the opportunity to earn money and assert their independence. In New York City high schools, the dropout rate averaged 55 percent during the war years.[3]

Irving Shulman captured the experience of the wartime boom in his masterful novel about Jewish street gangs, *The Amboy Dukes*. Shulman's protagonist, Frank Goldfarb, is tempted to drop out of school by the easy money to be earned in Brooklyn's war industries. His friend Moishe asks him why he is wasting time in school: "'Why don't you get working papers and make ... [yourself] some real dough before the Army gets you?'"[4] It was a thought that clearly occurred to many adolescents during the war.

Despite the boom created by the war, the long-term prospects for youths without a high school education were not good. The sluggish recovery of New York's economy in the early 1940s pointed to past weaknesses and presaged future problems. The revival of manufacturing during World War II was only temporary. Youths, like the fictional Goldfarb, dropping out of school and expecting to follow their parents' paths into the manufacturing sector would face stiffening competition for fewer jobs in the postwar era.

The loss of blue-collar jobs was the most significant aspect of New York's economic transformation for working-class adolescents. The advantages that had once held manufacturers in the city—proximity to transportation terminals, access to energy sources, an adequate labor supply, paved streets, sewers, and the other amenities of urban infrastructure—were offset by mounting "diseconomies." Narrow, congested streets slowed truck movement and added to the costs of handling freight; high land costs prohibited expansion while assembly-line production required the horizontal, rather than vertical, organization of space. At the same time, highway construction freed manufacturers and wholesalers from reliance on locations near the city center, and employers saw in relocation the opportunity to substitute unorganized and cheaper labor for unionized shops. As a result, in the two decades after World War II (1948–1967), the city lost 45,000 manufacturing and an additional 39,000 wholesaling jobs. Retailing showed the greatest losses—115,000 jobs—as stores followed their middle-class clientele to the suburbs. Although New York retained some declining low-wage industries (such as garment-making) and some light manufacturing, emerging high-wage industries showed a marked preference for locating in suburban counties.[5]

The federal government played an important role in the shift of New York City's economy. Defense expenditures grew to meet the demands of the cold war, but the revenue did not flow into the city. Some defense industries continued to expand in Nassau County, creating a demand for labor and spurring suburbanization. The county population grew from

660,000 in 1950 to 1.3 million in 1960 as five aerospace/defense contractors dominated the county's economy and became the largest employers in the metropolitan region.[6] However, defense spending did not significantly benefit the New York metropolitan area. More tax dollars leached out of New York's economy than federal programs returned to it, and taxes paid by New Yorkers helped fuel the aerospace/defense boom in the West and South. Military bases in the Sun Belt expanded while those in New York City curtailed operations and eventually closed, thus adding to the erosion of blue-collar jobs.[7]

Despite these losses, New York's postwar history was not one of stagnation and decline but of transformation. The reinvention of New York as a provider of services preserved the city's financial health, as the service sector gained 122,000 jobs between 1948 and 1967 and emerged as the city's leading employer.[8] New York solidified its position in financial and legal services, insurance, and government, and in so doing, added clerks, secretaries, and information processors—pink- and white-collar workers—along with brokers and bankers.[9] Overall employment in the city remained high, but gradually the nature of available work changed as New York led the way into the postindustrial economy.

Not all groups were affected equally by the emergence of a service-based economy. New York's economy was racialized, with African Americans systematically excluded from some sectors (such as manufacturing and construction), and with Euro-American groups established in economic niches that "belonged" to them and that improved their group's chances in the new economy. The Irish (in government and civil service) and the Jews (in garment manufacturing and retail) had bases from which to launch succeeding generations into the service-sector economy. Italians were overrepresented in construction and as a result they had made little economic progress by the middle of the twentieth century. In contrast, African Americans actually lost ground as other groups took over services (such as catering) that they traditionally had provided. Puerto Ricans had not succeeded in acquiring a secure foothold in the urban economy and were in the worst position of all in the postwar city. Italians, African Americans, and Puerto Ricans thus occupied the bottom of New York's occupational categories and endowed their children with few advantages to assist them in an economy gradually orienting itself to the production and distribution of services.[10] These were blue-collar children competing in an increasingly white-collar city.


MIGRATION, A NEW DEMOGRAPHY,

AND THE "TIPPING POINT"


Migration was a second force in the remaking of New York. Migrants from the southern Black Belt, Puerto Rico, and the rest of the Caribbean responded to the lure of the city and of course could not anticipate the changes in the urban economy. They pursued the promise of work, the hope of equal citizenship, and the potential for forming their own communities. During the war, industrial cities like Chicago, Detroit, Pittsburgh, Milwaukee, and Buffalo offered more immediate access to jobs. But Harlem and El Barrio had been prewar centers of African-American and Puerto Rican cultural and political life, and as New York's economy picked up, so did migration.[11] If the North was the promised land, New York was its Jerusalem.

New York's African-American and Puerto Rican populations increased rapidly after the war, while its Euro-American population grew slowly and then declined. European immigration had already slowed because of immigration restriction and subsequent Depression and war. As a result, the white population in the city peaked at 7.1 million in 1950 before beginning its steady decline. Meanwhile the number of African Americans and Puerto Ricans climbed steadily. The 300,000 African Americans who lived in New York City in 1930 increased to about 460,000 in 1940, and after another decade, to nearly 750,000. The Puerto Rican population (most of which was counted as "white") grew from approximately 45,000 in 1930 to just under 250,000 in 1950. By 1960, the Euro-American population had fallen to 6.6 million, while the number of African Americans grew to 1.1 million and the Puerto Ricans to about 612,000.[12]

The youthfulness and geographic concentration of New York's Puerto Rican and African-American populations were important factors in the emergence of gangs. Both groups of migrants contained disproportionately large numbers of adolescents who were of prime gang-formation age. The New York Department of Planning estimated in 1956 that 37 percent of the city's Puerto Rican population (both first and second generation) was under the age of twenty.[13] In 1960, youths nineteen and under comprised 37 percent of the city's African-American population, while the comparable figure for Euro-Americans was 29 percent, reflecting differences in birth rates and the outmigration of white families with children. Although white youths still outnumbered African-American and Puerto Rican youths citywide, those residing near expanding African-American and Puerto Rican communities undoubtedly felt beleaguered.[14]

Location was key in the emergence of gang conflict in the postwar period. The clustering of so many African-American and Puerto Rican youths in segregated neighborhoods gave ecological support for the creation of gangs. African-American and Puerto Rican youths crowded into schools, entered the labor market, and resisted being segregated in the oldest and most overcrowded districts, and they formed adolescent peer groups that competed for recreational space. Conflict occurred primarily in New York's borderlands, where neighborhoods touched (as will be seen in chapter 2), and Euro-American gangs defended their turf while African-American and Puerto Rican gangs formed to contest their control.

What happened in these areas was that gangs passed the "tipping point." The tipping point is an epidemiological term that explains how diseases must reach a certain threshold level, or a critical mass, in order to spread epidemically. Before reaching that point they can be managed, but once the threshold is achieved, they become very difficult to contain. Recent medical studies of violence have applied epidemiological theory to analyze the distribution and extent of behaviors—such as homicide—that act like infectious diseases.[15]

With gangs, this model works well. It suggests that the concentration of a large number of adolescents, especially from hostile ethnic groups, in a limited geographic area would spark the organization of gangs as adolescents decided they needed to protect themselves from the hostile intentions of others. The existence of gangs in turn would increase the likelihood of hostile encounters, which would set off an escalating cycle of violence. This is precisely what happened in New York's borderland communities.

## African-American New York

African-American migrants entered a Harlem that was dense, poor, and hemmed in by hostile white neighbors. The sociologist Irving Louis Horowitz, in his memoir of growing up in Harlem around 1940, recalled that "turf wars [among youths] were bitter in Harlem because the area proved to be so inelastic. Unlike the usual neighborhoods of New York, there was little spillover and scarcely any movement at the boundaries." African-American expansion out of central Harlem was blocked by Central Park to its south, and by white neighborhoods on all of its sides. Italian and "Spanish" Harlem to its east, Washington Heights to its north, and Manhattanville to its west became interracial battlegrounds in the postwar period as residents violently resisted "invasion" by African Americans trying to push out the borders of their community.[16]

Because Harlem's boundaries were so inelastic and expansion was resisted so actively, African Americans leapfrogged into other areas of settlement. Bedford-Stuyvesant and Brownsville in Brooklyn became predominantly black, as did the St. Albans-Jamaica section of Queens and a portion of the South Bronx, and these areas also witnessed gang activity as black adolescents encountered harassment. Even with African-American expansion into these other areas, Harlem remained extraordinarily congested.[17]

African-American Harlemites acted to establish control over their neighborhood by expelling lingering Euro-Americans. Adolescents participated in general troublemaking, harassment, and muggings of white residents and storeowners, which can be interpreted as part of a drive to claim central Harlem's turf for African Americans.[18] Irving Horowitz remembered the persecutions of being one of two white children in his school and one of a handful remaining in the neighborhood. "We never walked through the side streets of Harlem. We ran. Only along the main thoroughfares . . . did we dare pause to walk." Interracial fights were nearly a daily after-school occurrence until his parents finally decided to move to Brooklyn. Horowitz's father's dreams literally turned to ashes in the 1943

*Opposite page:* 1.1. Central Harlem. Central Harlem in the 1940s was surrounded by white neighborhoods that resisted its expansion.

Harlem riot, when looters destroyed his shop. From another perspective, the Black Panther Kwando Kinshasa recalled harassing the white students at Resurrection School whenever he and his friends lost lunch money to the tough older boys—"as we used to say, 'Resurrection pays!' " Encountering hostility and discrimination in the streets and in school, African-American adolescents took revenge where they could. By 1960, Harlem was 94 percent African American and 4 percent Puerto Rican.[19]

While gangs attempted to enforce residential boundary lines, more systematic exclusion occurred in the labor market. Private employers, unions, and state agencies all practiced discrimination in employment. Both union- and management-run training programs routinely excluded African-American applicants, which prevented them from entering manufacturing and construction employment. The public utilities, which accounted for a rather large 5 percent of New York City's employment, had a workforce that was approximately 1 percent African American. State employment agencies cooperated in excluding African Americans from better employment by listing only menial jobs in their Harlem offices. African Americans finally began to enter service-sector jobs in the 1940s, but only as whites left them for higher-paying positions in war-related industries. African Americans then found work as dishwashers, busboys, and launderers in the same restaurants and hotels that denied them service as customers. African Americans ran into the color line wherever they turned.[20]

The concentration of African Americans in low-level service jobs helped keep them poor. In 1949 an African-American family in New York earned 70 percent of what a white family earned, and the ratio remained unchanged over the next decade. Notably, while African-American women's median income in 1960 was nearly the same as (more than 90 percent of) that of white women, the comparable figure for males was 68 percent. To a large degree, the well-being of the African-American community rested on the domestic labor of its women. Naturally, this was a recipe for poverty.[21]

Residential segregation and discrimination in employment reinforced each other. Poverty limited African Americans to the poorest neighborhoods, and job discrimination kept them poor. While adults moved from one employer to another in search of better working conditions or a slightly higher wage, and families moved from one apartment to another seeking lower rents or better facilities, within a closed system such movement did not produce improvement. While the inner city of the 1940s and 1950s nurtured a small African-American middle class and a larger working class that provided leadership to the community, their example was countered by the unemployed men idling on corners whose existence questioned the viability of the work ethic. The drinking, gambling, carousing, and fighting of male street life spoke to young males of an alternative to hard work in a discriminatory labor market.

The experience of the older generation created a dilemma for the young. On the one hand, African-American youths sought jobs desperately because of the relative poverty of their families. More Harlem teenagers searched for jobs than others in their age group nationally; the most pressing issue was finding an employer willing to hire them.[22] Work was extremely important to young African-American men, even if its reward was unclear. Yet at the same time, youths feared taking the same dead-end jobs that their parents had. Not surprisingly, some African-American youths resisted being pressed into the labor market and they dismissed the usual unskilled, low-paying jobs held by their parents and peers as "slaves"—a bitter commentary on the dashed hopes of migration. For them, manhood was created in the streets rather than in the labor market.[23]

African-American migrants did not come to New York City because they were mired in hopeless dependency, unwilling to work, submerged in a culture of poverty and criminality, or hopeful of collecting welfare checks. They came to make better lives for themselves and their children, and they endured the failure of their dreams. But, as the author Claude Brown noted, "The children of these disillusioned colored pioneers inherited the total lot of their parents—the disappointments, the anger. To add to their misery, they had little hope of deliverance. For where does one run to when he's already in the promised land?"[24] Youths like Brown created an alternative to the white-dominated world that so dispirited their parents. Through their gangs they established their own rituals, norms, and standards for defining themselves as men.

### Puerto Rican New York

Puerto Rican migrants also came to New York to escape poverty and unemployment. A crisis in the agricultural economy of the island pushed the migrants into motion, and they chose to come to New York

City. Puerto Rico's population doubled between 1900 and 1950, but economic opportunities did not keep pace. Large sugar plantations had virtually wiped out subsistence farming, and though sugar production required a large workforce, much of the work was seasonal. Farmers who had lost their land became part of a migratory agricultural workforce that followed harvests from Puerto Rico to the mainland. Puerto Rican activist Iris Morales reported that her father, a sugarcane cutter, arrived in New York in 1947. "He was the oldest son of about nine children, so when things got rough, he came over here to make some money . . . to send back to the family." Displaced farmers also migrated to Puerto Rican cities and swelled urban shantytowns such as San Juan's El Fanguito and La Perla. However, the lack of employment opportunities in Puerto Rican cities (despite the government-sponsored industrialization of Operation Bootstrap) and the segregation and economic exploitation encountered by agricultural workers in the South made New York the destination of choice. Nearly 90 percent of migrants interviewed in 1948 reported that they never considered going anywhere else. For Puerto Ricans too, New York was the promised land.[25]

Migration to New York ceased temporarily during World War II, only to increase dramatically immediately thereafter. Some thirteen thousand Puerto Ricans entered New York in 1945, and that number nearly tripled the next year. The establishment of air links to New York City immediately after the war replaced a four-day sea journey with a six-hour flight and reduced the cost of a ticket from $85 to $35, making the Puerto Ricans notable as the first airborne migrants.[26]

New York's Puerto Rican migrants seemed poised for success in the city. A 1948 sample of Puerto Ricans living in East Harlem and Morrisania in the Bronx revealed that migrants came in their most productive years (half were between twenty and forty-nine years of age), 90 percent had lived in one of Puerto Rico's urban centers before coming to the mainland (only 28 percent of the islanders were urbanized), and over one-third had had white-collar and skilled jobs in Puerto Rico. These were not unskilled, agricultural workers, like Iris Morales's father: while 39 percent of the island population engaged in agricultural work, only 5 percent of the migrants had done so. Despite these advantages, many migrants experienced downward mobility in New York, with nearly half of them employed in unskilled jobs. The migrants were more educated than their

1.2. Puerto Rican migrants arriving in New York.

island counterparts, had experience in urban settings, and possessed valuable job skills, yet they landed in declining, low-wage jobs.[27] Why were they not more successful?

Puerto Rican migrants, like immigrants from the Caribbean and African Americans coming from the South, entered the world's most advanced economy. They competed with groups long established in the city who had well-defended economic niches, and they were able to find jobs only in those sectors of the economy abandoned by the more advantaged. Moreover, the migrants' educational advantages were relative. While the migrants were educated when compared to the islanders, they fared poorly when compared to both "white" (non–Puerto Rican) and "nonwhite" New Yorkers. In 1960, 40 percent of white New Yorkers and 31 percent of the city's nonwhites had completed high school, but only 13 percent of the city's Puerto Ricans had done so. One might expect that New York–born Puerto Ricans would do significantly better, but they did not. Because of New York's high levels of residential segregation,

Puerto Rican and African-American youngsters attended overcrowded, often ancient neighborhood schools, which left them unprepared for the city's elite academic high schools. Instead they attended vocational schools, which were not geared to prepare their students for the emerging service-sector economy. Seventy percent of Puerto Ricans worked in the three lowest-paying job sectors in 1950 (garment making, service establishments, and light manufacturing), and a decade later that figure had not changed.[28] The city's educational system simply did not function as a pathway into higher-paying, more skilled jobs. A combination of discrimination, segregation, poor education, and the transformation of New York's economy left Puerto Rican migrants trapped in ethnic niches that would not allow them or their children to advance.

Puerto Ricans encountered the same color line that African Americans did. Puerto Ricans had many communities in New York, which might at first suggest their relative integration into the city, but in fact this is misleading. The center of Puerto Rican life was in East Harlem, and by the 1950s the barrio ranged between 100th and 120th Streets and from Third to Fifth Avenues. The barrio expanded slowly and could not absorb all the new migrants because its boundaries were as inelastic as those of Harlem. Edwin Torres, who grew up in East Harlem and eventually became a judge, noted in his novel, *Carlito's Way,* that the barrio's Puerto Ricans were "boxed in": "Irish on the south, Italians to the east, Blacks to the north and west." As a result, Puerto Rican settlements continued to be dispersed in Brooklyn, lower Manhattan, the upper and lower West Side, and in the South Bronx. By the early 1950s, there were eleven Puerto Rican communities in New York City.[29]

Despite this dispersion, Puerto Rican areas of settlement were not distributed randomly throughout the city but were linked closely to those of African Americans. Puerto Rican settlements existed on the edges of African-American ghettos—on the east and west sides of Harlem, in the South Bronx, in St. Albans-Jamaica in Queens, and on three sides of Bedford-Stuyvesant in Brooklyn. Puerto Rican and African-American communities remained linked in space and were subject to similar forms of discrimination, which undoubtedly heightened Puerto Rican sensitivity to color.[30]

Racial discrimination was an insult new to Puerto Ricans in New York. Although distinctions based on color existed in Puerto Rico, they allowed more gradations than did those on the mainland. Puerto Ricans, particularly those of intermediate color, found the rigid discrimination practiced in New York's biracial society a novel and painful experience. Maria, a young migrant, expressed her preference for Puerto Rico over New York, saying, "In Puerto Rico you've got no problems with colors." Observers believed that the migrants clung to Spanish at least in part as a way of distinguishing themselves from lower-status African Americans, even if this meant more problems in adjusting to mainland society.[31] As a result, Puerto Rican migrants sometimes were unwilling to venture beyond the familiarity of a Spanish-speaking neighborhood. As one youngster put it, "Like the only thing we knew was that block. You never went out of that block." The block was invested with social and cultural meaning as the literal center of the universe that had to be defended against all challengers.[32]

Puerto Rican youths incorporated New York's racial distinctions into their family and social lives. Puerto Ricans called themselves "Spanish" and denied any identification with African Americans. In East Harlem, dark-skinned Puerto Ricans organized the Viceroys, while their light-skinned rivals formed the Dragons. While both groups fought with the white (largely Italian) gangs to the east and with African-American gangs to their west, the most bitter conflicts were with each other. Even within families darker-skinned siblings felt the sting of their lighter brothers' and sisters' prejudice. Mario recalled, "I was always denounced for being black by my family because I was the blackest person in it." The trauma of American racism was expressed not only through self-hatred but also in acts of violence against those of other colors.[33]

Young Puerto Ricans, like young African Americans, viewed New York through the lens of their parents' disappointments. They entered the labor market reluctantly, having seen the discrimination faced by their parents and knowing that they were condemned to futures busing tables or pushing carts in the garment district. They saw the promises of advancement through schooling as unreachable or as cynical attempts to get them to surrender their Puerto Rican identities.[34] Thus, some Puerto

Rican youths created their own world on the streets where masculinity was defined through gang membership, where worthiness could be proven, and where the insults of others could be avenged.

## THE REORGANIZATION OF URBAN SPACE

The third major force that remade New York was its physical reconstruction after the war. Urban renewal, highway construction, and the building of public housing literally reshaped the city but at great cost to the poor. New York began the postwar period with a terrible shortage of low-cost housing. Urban renewal, which frequently took the form of clearing older residential sections to make way for institutional, business, or upper-income residential development, worsened the problem. Highway construction had the same effect, as building expressways meant tearing down residential districts in their paths and sending low-income residents searching for housing. Public housing construction could not keep up with the displacement problem and never began to address the already existing need for low-cost housing in the city. The combination of these programs disrupted the social ecology of working-class New York.

The reconstruction of New York's urban landscape was a visible process, but its effect on street gangs was not obvious. By reshaping urban neighborhoods and upsetting traditional boundaries, these programs forced the poor into competition for residential space. Neighborhood transition for each group, always fraught with difficulty, became even more tense as residents worried about finding safe, affordable housing. At the same time, renewal projects helped drive low-skilled jobs out of the city, thus intensifying competition in the labor market, while public housing projects reinforced segregation by concentrating the poorest families into high-rise facilities that were not integrated into the local community.

Competition for space resulted from the city's extraordinarily tight housing market. In 1950, the city had an unheard-of 1 percent vacancy rate, with an even lower rate for low-cost housing. Tenements that had been condemned and boarded up in the late 1930s during Mayor Fiorella La Guardia's reform administration were reopened a decade later as landlords exploited the need for housing among the poor. Both Puerto Ricans and African Americans paid high rents for little space, often doubling up with other families or finding spots as lodgers. Reports circulated of "hot beds," where lodgers slept in shifts, and of single-family houses carved up illegally into multifamily units. A survey of Puerto Rican tenants in the mid-1950s showed that approximately one-third shared bathing and toilet facilities with at least one other family and that, because of their reliance on furnished rooms, Puerto Ricans paid more in monthly rents ($49 on average) than nonwhites ($43) and whites ($37).[35] To solve the crisis in housing, New York City took advantage of federal legislation and began massive urban renewal and public housing projects. The results, however, were not entirely what planners had intended.

The federal government funded slum clearance and housing construction as part of a larger effort to revive the economy during the Great Depression. The Public Works Administration cleared slums and constructed approximately 25,000 dwelling units nationally over a five-year period. However, in 1937 alone, New York City demolished 25,000 substandard apartment units. Under Mayor La Guardia's administration, the city tore down a total of 8,840 buildings and made no provisions for the estimated quarter of a million displaced residents. In response to an impending crisis, New York Senator Robert Wagner sponsored the United States Housing Act of 1937, which created a federal housing authority and supplied funds for public housing construction. However, the bill provided only nominal relief to New York City: 115,000 families applied for the 11,000 units opened by 1940. By the end of the war the city's housing situation had grown desperate.[36]

The second attempt to address the housing crisis occurred with the Housing Act of 1949. A hybrid political coalition that was more interested in urban renewal than in public housing shaped the legislation.[37] Public housing advocates were the least powerful members of this coalition, as the results of the legislation showed. The bill authorized the construction of 810,000 units of public housing over six years, a number that was never reached. While both Democratic and Republican administrations reneged on the promise to build public housing, they did fully fund Title One, the 1.5 billion dollar urban renewal provision of the housing act that supported the clearance and redevelopment of older residential districts near the downtown.[38]

Urban renewal had a significant impact in the spatial reordering of New York. Title One required that projects be predominantly residential, but it did not require the construction of low-cost housing, even for those who lost their homes to urban renewal. As a result, low-income residents were evicted while public funds subsidized the construction of luxury housing and quasi-public institutional developments. Robert Moses, New York's legendary impresario of construction, headed the Mayor's Committee on Slum Clearance and refashioned the appearance of the city.[39] Important projects included Lincoln Center (the midtown home of the performing arts), the New York Coliseum, the Manhattan campus of Fordham University, the New York University–Bellevue medical center, and a refurbished downtown Brooklyn that included space for Long Island University and Brooklyn Hospital. Urban renewal created the cultural, medical, and intellectual infrastructure of the modern city, but at the cost of housing for the poor.

Public investment in the city sparked private investment as well. Between the end of the war and the middle 1950s, New York added about two million square feet of office space per year, and building soared again in the latter half of the 1950s.[40] Midtown Manhattan, especially Park Avenue, became the locus for glass- and metal-sheathed corporate headquarters in the early 1950s, while Chase Manhattan Bank constructed the first major postwar high-rise in lower Manhattan in 1960 and began the renewal of the Wall Street area.[41] The publicly subsidized reconstruction of New York for the benefit of medical, cultural, and educational institutions secured the way for corporate reinvestment in the city, and New York's shimmering glass towers symbolized the emergence of the new service-based economy. But redevelopment meant the loss of industrial jobs and small businesses—between eighteen and fifty thousand jobs were lost through urban renewal, according to one estimate—and most of these were the types of jobs that had provided entry into the labor market for the city's blue-collar children.[42]

The massive postwar reconstruction of New York's highway system was another part of the city's physical remaking and added to the dislocation problems caused by urban renewal. Robert Moses planned on adding over one hundred miles of new expressways to link the suburban outposts of New York's metropolitan region, and many of these miles cut through the heart of city neighborhoods. Although three planned cross-Manhattan expressways were defeated, the Cross-Bronx, the Bruckner, the Van Wick, and the Brooklyn Queens Expressways, among others, became part of the postwar highway system that blasted through urban neighborhoods as if they were so much bedrock. At least five thousand persons were displaced by the Cross-Bronx Expressway alone, which had the added effect of blighting a once thriving neighborhood. As Marshall Berman, the literary critic, recalled, "When the construction was done, the real ruin of the Bronx had just begun." Like urban renewal and the construction of public housing, the public works projects unloosed streams of displaced tenants searching through older neighborhoods for low-cost housing.[43]

Studies of the displaced revealed the dimensions of the relocation problem. In its own study, the City Planning Commission found that less than 30 percent of the 170,000 dislocated tenants found their way into public housing, and it admitted that it did not have the faintest idea of what happened to the rest.[44] That admission was not surprising since the city left tenants displaced by building projects to their own devices, despite legal requirements that they be rehoused. For example, refugees from Moses's Cross-Bronx Expressway moved from one building to the next "like gypsies," complained one tenant, always one step ahead of the wrecker's ball. The city's Tenant Relocation Bureau not only failed to find them permanent homes, but it also threatened to cut their relocation allowances if they resisted moving.[45] City officials promised tenants on Title One sites that those who could not afford apartments on the open market would be placed into public housing; critics discovered that public housing was fully occupied and that planned construction would absorb only a fraction of those dislocated by city projects. Instead the displaced crowded into whatever accommodations they could afford. Despite the construction of public housing projects, the same number of substandard units existed at the end of the 1950s as had at the beginning. So many low-cost dwellings had been torn down and so few replacements had been built that the poor simply expanded the slums by moving into other older districts.[46]

A disproportionate share of the displaced were African Americans and Puerto Ricans, and tensions increased as they moved into peripheral white working-class neighborhoods. While only about 13 percent of the city's population in 1950 was Puerto Rican or African American, these groups comprised 37 percent of the displaced. African-American residents expelled by "Manhattantown," a Title One project on the Upper West Side, expressed their anguish at leaving an inexpensive integrated neighborhood and their anger at being forced back into Harlem, while in the East Bronx, Jewish residents complained that muggings and crime had been brought by new black and Hispanic migrants. Samuel Lubell, a political scientist who interviewed residents in the East Bronx in 1948, concluded, "Those who could fled the area. Their flight, in turn, quickened the influx, trapping those who could not flee." All over New York ethnic villages were being squeezed as people were set in motion.[47]

The public housing that was constructed in the city reinforced residential segregation. Robert Moses had referred to certain developments as "colored projects," and he followed the traditional practice of segregated housing development. The city had designated Williamsburg Houses in Brooklyn for whites and the Harlem River Houses for African Americans, while private developers, most notably the Metropolitan Life Insurance Company, followed similar practices. Other public projects were built in borderline areas—such as East Harlem, Brownsville in Brooklyn, and the South and East Bronx—that seemed destined to become incorporated into a larger area of African-American or Puerto Rican tenancy. The results of this building were disconcerting. Large swathes of the Lower East Side were cleared to form a phalanx of public housing projects that marched up the East River; East Harlem had the largest number of projects in the city; and ninety-six project buildings were constructed in the South Bronx alone. These sites were part of the new vertical ghetto that towered over the communities in which they were built.[48]

Public housing policy, as conceived in Washington and implemented in New York, was deeply flawed. The object of providing safe, decent, and affordable housing lost out to the interests of slumlords, real estate moguls, and downtown developers. Public housing construction occurred not on vacant or peripheral land, but on expensive, congested slum property.[49] As a result, high-rise buildings with few frills became the most feasible form of construction, and massive developments were shoehorned into small-scale neighborhoods, which were overwhelmed.[50] Planners viewed public housing as temporary assistance that supplemented the private market rather than as an investment in permanent

1.3. The James Weldon Johnson Houses, shown here under construction in 1947, covered from 112th Street to 115th Street in East Harlem.

communities. As a result, residents were not integrated into the fabric of the neighborhood.[51] Public housing remained a stepchild to urban renewal and never contributed to resolving the tensions among ethnic communities, which a dramatic expansion of high-quality, low-cost housing might have accomplished. Private interest hijacked public good.

Urban renewal, the building of a modern highway system, and the construction of public housing reshaped the city, revitalized its commercial core, and preserved a sector of the city for the middle class. However, the spatial reordering of the city also destroyed working-class neighborhoods, eliminated working-class jobs, worsened ethnic competition for low-cost housing, and reinforced residential segregation. Because public housing remained a poorly funded, poorly designed afterthought, urban public policy contributed to the problems caused by economic dislocation and migration and heightened the insecurity of working-class New Yorkers.

SUBURBS AND SEGREGATION

The effects of housing shortages and public policy decisions might have been worse had not nearly one million white New Yorkers (about 14 percent of the white population) abandoned the city between 1950 and 1960.[52] Suburbanization—the fourth major transformation of post-war New York—had been occurring since the middle of the nineteenth century, but its pace accelerated in the postwar years with federally subsidized mortgages that used tax dollars to sponsor segregated suburbs for middle-class and upwardly mobile working-class whites. Suburbanization and the federal policies that sponsored it contributed to the deterioration of older areas in the city as public policy abandoned those who were left behind.

Federal policy spurred the growth of a segregated urban system. Federal housing programs aimed to revive and extend home ownership, but they created national standards for evaluating property that discriminated against older city neighborhoods and actively discouraged loans to racially mixed areas. Such areas were considered hazardous and coded red (thus the term "red-lining"), and they withered without the availability of mortgage money. (Private lenders adopted the same principles and also declined to make loans in these areas.) At the same time, federal standards favored new construction of single-family homes in areas that were "harmonious" racially and defended by deed restrictions that limited sales to other whites. Even though such restrictive convenants were declared unconstitutional in 1948, the Federal Housing Administration allowed their use until 1950, and after that the agency continued to funnel money to areas that were socially and racially stable. Federal policy fueled the flight from the city and abetted the creation of all-white suburbs.[53]

A second piece of federal legislation that refashioned the urban landscape was the 1956 Interstate Highway Act. The act provided fifty billion dollars over ten years to build 41,000 miles of highway. By paying for 90 percent of construction costs, the federal government made participation in the interstate highway system irresistibly attractive. Robert Moses, an ardent fan of the automobile and a consultant in the drafting of the highway act, wooed interstate highway officials for funds to complete the system of parkways, urban expressways, tunnels, and bridges that circum-

navigated New York. Between 1955 and 1965, Moses built over four hundred miles of federally sponsored roadway in the New York metropolitan
area, which aided the dispersal of economic activity and residents
throughout the region.[54]

Federally sponsored programs gave wings to white flight, and the postwar movement out of the city was unprecedented. In the 1950s the city
as a whole experienced a loss of 990,000 whites, who left areas such as
East Harlem, the South Bronx, and Brownsville. Euro-American families,
especially those with children, fled these neighborhoods for the outer
reaches of the Bronx or Queens, or they left the city entirely. As one
former Brownsville resident remembered, " 'I saw friends, whose fathers
were doing well . . . and one by one they began to move out of the
neighborhood, some to Sheepshead Bay and Flatbush, more to Queens,
some to Long Island, some to Jersey. They had upward mobility. . . . And
with the blacks moving in there came a great fear.'" The push of ethnic
succession combined with the pull of inexpensive, accessible, and segregated suburban housing to draw many financially able white families out
of the city.[55]

Other federal policies worked indirectly to bring prosperity and suburban homeownership within the grasp of many more Americans. Government management of the economy smoothed out the business cycle and
kept recessions fairly short, while the cold war and the government-sponsored revival of foreign markets helped keep American industry busy.
Unionized labor won generous contracts in this era of economic growth,
and real wages rose by 50 percent, which enabled Americans to increase
their consumption of goods and services. Forty-four percent of Americans
owned their homes in 1934; by 1972, nearly two-thirds did so. Reaching
these homes required access to a car, and in the four years following the
war, Americans purchased over 21 million automobiles. Refrigerators,
televisions, and other appliances filled these new homes—and created
jobs for those manufacturing them—and the ethos of consumerism
helped foster a myth of classlessness that permeated American society.
Anyone who worked hard could afford the purchase price of the American Dream, or so it seemed.[56] One effect of this was to render the poor
invisible.

In an era of prosperity, it was natural to assume that poverty and its
associated problems would wither away. Scholars proclaimed that the

United States was a classless society, and studies showed that the number of the poor, however measured, was declining. African-American and Puerto Rican migrants who were isolated in urban neighborhoods and members of the white working class who were unable to afford a suburban retreat or were unwilling to abandon an ethnic neighborhood were ignored in the policy debates of the 1950s. To the degree that social scientists paid attention to the poor, they described them, in the social work jargon of the day, as "multiple problem families" who were part of the "hard to reach." The sources of poverty, they claimed, lay in the culture of the poor or in their character deficiencies rather than in the structure of society.[57]

While policy debates and popular concern ignored the poor, adolescence, delinquency, and the emergence of a youth culture became a national obsession.[58] Experts analyzed gang violence in the same terms as poverty—defining it as the product of a separate lower-class culture, claiming gang members were pathological misfits and labeling delinquents as suffering from the inability to defer gratification or to make the transition to adulthood.[59] While social scientists investigated gangs, it was youth culture that took center stage as middle-class America pondered its young. Parents, lawmakers, and shapers of public opinion investigated rock 'n' roll, analyzed the content of comic books, and worried about middle-class adolescents copying James Dean's scowl, gyrating like Elvis, or wearing Marlon Brando–like leather jackets. Concerns about youth culture merged with fear of delinquency and gangs. Even such an astute reporter as *New York Times* journalist Harrison Salisbury mistook the gang problem he found in poor neighborhoods as a symptom of a generational disease that threatened to infect suburban America.[60]

Observers did not understand that gangs were not the product of youth culture but were rooted in a working-class world turning upside down. A declining job base; the influx of African-American and Puerto Rican youths into a hostile environment; public policies that wiped out neighborhoods, ignored the displaced, and reinforced segregation; and the gradual abandonment of the city by better-off whites all fueled an urban crisis that adolescents felt and acted on in their gangs. As New Yorkers discovered in the aftermath of World War II, there was violence back in the old neighborhoods, and much of it stemmed from racial conflict carried on by street gangs.

# Discovering Gangs:
# The Role of Race in the 1940s

I N SEPTEMBER 1945, Mrs. Thelma Neston, fed up with the adolescents in her Brooklyn neighborhood, sent a letter to Fiorella La Guardia, the mayor of New York. She wrote, "I am a respectable American Negro citizen, mother of eight children. . . . In the community where I live . . . conditions are becoming so that our children's lives are in constant jeopardy, day and night." She pleaded with the mayor, "Will you advise us what we, the decent Negro mothers of Brooklyn, can do to get protection necessary to shield our children?"[1] Like countless other ordinary New Yorkers in the immediate postwar period, Mrs. Neston was in the process of discovering gangs, while the police, press, and public officials ignored the problem.

According to many theorists, social problems are not discovered by ordinary people. In a now classic work in sociology, Howard Becker attributed the discovery of social problems to "moral entrepreneurs."[2] Anthropologist Walter Miller has described youth gangs as originating in an unchanging lower-class culture. Since this culture has endured over time, Miller attributes apparent changes in gang activity to shifts in media attention.[3] Here his views dovetail with a more recent work in cultural studies by Stanley Cohen, who also emphasizes the role of media in defining social problems through the creation of "moral panics."[4]

These theoretical positions abstract youth gangs from their social and economic context and deny their historicity. They also rob working-class adolescents of their one token of agency: their ability to cause trouble.

Street gangs were not discovered by moral entrepreneurs, media moguls, or municipal officials looking for issues to stir the electorate. Gangs forced themselves into the consciousness of reluctant public officials in the aftermath of World War II through interracial clashes that can be documented through a variety of sources. The effects of gang violence are seen in a rising juvenile homicide rate and in the increasing arrests of juveniles for murder and manslaughter. Though a moral panic about youth culture occurred during the war and the public was primed to discover unruly adolescents, neither the public nor officials were prepared for ethnic conflict carried on by youth gangs. Street gangs in the postwar period confounded both public and scholarly understandings of what gangs were and how they behaved.

## Boys' Gangs

Memoirs and novels set in the early twentieth century on the Lower East Side of Manhattan, in Brownsville in Brooklyn, or in East Harlem casually mention gang membership as part of growing up. The musician Samuel Chotzinoff recalled that "every street [in lower Manhattan] had its gang," and wars with other "streeters" were common. The real challenge, he remembered, came from the Irish Catholics on Cherry Street, who asked not only what street a strange boy came from, but whether or not he was a "sheeny." Jewish gangs defended elderly immigrants from having their beards tugged, protected rabbis from showers of stones and debris, and defended shopkeepers from having their windows broken.[5] A Jewish teacher who had grown up in East Harlem and returned to teach at Benjamin Franklin High School remembered similar ethnic conflicts from his youth at the turn of the century:

> When I was a youngster . . . a common sight was a street battle between the Jewish and Irish boys, living on either side of the New York Central Railroad on Park Avenue. I remember taking part in several of these brawls. One day the Irish boys would raid "our" territory, turning over pushcarts, breaking store windows and beating up every Jew in sight. Another day saw "our" side retaliating on Irish home grounds. . . . Those were the good old days![6]

The gangs this teacher later observed in the East Harlem of the 1930s and 1940s did much the same thing as had the gangs of his youth. Only their ethnicity had changed. Italian gangs now fought Puerto Rican ones over the use of the "public" educational and recreational facilities in the neighborhood. One Puerto Rican youngster wrote his music teacher at Benjamin Franklin High School, "In the 3rd Ave, about six or eight Italians runs to beat us, as soon as I seen them, I escaped running but my friend can't and they beated him and one of the Italian fellows took his violin. Now I hasn't any violin to practice the lessons. As there are so many trouble I don't now how to go to school as it is located in the Italian Zone."[7] Youth gangs were hardly innocent, but their conflicts were generally nonlethal and so commonplace as to arouse little concern. As these accounts suggest, adolescent gangs did not exist independently of a neighborhood social structure, and they frequently enjoyed adult tolerance—if not support—for their rituals of ethnic purification. Only as gang conflict became racially charged and more violent did the gang emerge as a social problem that required a response by authorities and a new interpretation by scholars.

Initial studies of gangs emphasized their unproblematic nature. These studies used the term "gang" very loosely to describe children's play groups, bands of criminals, and street-corner groups. The first students of gangs—child-guidance experts—described them as originating in boys' play groups, and they emphasized that the "gang instinct" was perfectly natural. "Probably everyone," one author assured parents, "has been in a gang of some sort." Even discussions of gang-inspired delinquency and gang fights stressed their normalcy, placing their activities well within the range of boyish pranks. Belligerence and boisterousness were signs of a healthy male adolescent according to these boys' experts, who saw such traits as biologically determined characteristics. Authors argued that parents had much more to worry about with boys who did not defend themselves: such boys would fail the tests of masculinity and grow up to be effeminate and weak. Gang membership was far preferable; it signaled entry into a normal stage of adolescent or preadolescent male development.[8]

Other writers tended to subsume youth gangs into a discussion of adult criminal gangs. The modern study of gangs began with Frederic Thrasher's publication of an exhaustive survey of Chicago gangs in 1927.

For Thrasher, the absence of recreational activities and the problems faced by the children of immigrants, not some sort of biological instinct, generated the gang experience. Thrasher linked youthful play groups and adult criminal gangs, arguing that both emerged out of the social disorganization of the slum. He believed that the juvenile gang member could easily mature into the adult gangster unless the line of progression were interrupted. Although Thrasher took the activities of gangs—including boys' gangs—seriously, he did not apply a consistent definition of gangs and used neither age nor activity to distinguish youth gangs from older criminal gangs. Thrasher viewed bootleggers using tommy guns to fight over their markets and adolescent boys using rocks and fists to decide control over a vacant lot as part of the same phenomenon.[9] Similarly, Herbert Asbury, a journalist who published the first account of gangs in New York, did not distinguish between adolescent gangs and adult ones. Asbury's entertaining history of New York's underworld ranged from the antebellum Dead Rabbits to the Jewish gangsters in the turn-of-the-century Lower East Side, and though some members of both groups were adolescents, they were clearly part of adult criminal organizations.[10]

The first study to focus specifically on adolescents was William Whyte's well-known ethnography of a street-corner group in Boston's largely Italian North End, published in 1943. Whyte explored the group's recreational and associational activities, but he did not write about gang fights. While "Doc," Whyte's chief informant, told him about "rallies" against other Italian groups, these apparently were not serious or frequent enough to warrant extensive examination. Whyte's boys merited attention as an autonomous group, but they still fit into the framework of the larger, adult-dominated "street-corner society."[11] Before World War II, little in adolescent group behavior warranted specific consideration. The very fact that the term "gang" could be applied so indiscriminately to so many different groups suggests how unproblematic collections of adolescents were to public officials, urban residents, and scholars alike.[12]

## THE IMPACT OF WORLD WAR II

World War II marked a turning point in the discovery of the youth gang, although this occurred gradually and in three phases. First, public authorities discovered the problem of youth. Adolescents flaunted their independence from adult authority and participated in nightlife and commercial pleasures, as a superheated wartime economy absorbed their labor and supplied them with disposable income. Police rushed to reassert control over wayward youth, and rapidly increasing adolescent arrest rates made juvenile delinquency a topic of national debate during the war. Second, the race riots of 1943 linked the issues of ethnicity, youth, and violence. In Los Angeles, Detroit, New York, and other cities across the nation, African Americans, Latinos, and Euro-Americans battled over the color line. Usually young men were in the forefront in these disorders, which fueled concerns about out-of-control youth. A debate over race, youth, and crime initially ignored gangs, but finally, clashes in New York neighborhoods undergoing ethnic succession made gangs impossible to overlook any longer. First residents and then municipal authorities came to recognize their existence as a major social problem.

### War and Wild Youth

Commentators blamed increasing youth problems on "wartime conditions." With family life disrupted as older men joined the military and women moved into the workforce, stories abounded of "latchkey children" left on their own or with adolescents who handled adult responsibilities with varying degrees of effectiveness. Migration separated some families as men searched for defense employment, or it threatened to overwhelm boomtown communities and established neighborhoods as migrant families poured in. Even more problematic than rootless adults were the scores of rootless youths, able to free themselves of institutional and familial restraints.[13]

Concern about adolescent behavior initially focused on girls. In the past, female delinquency had been defined largely in terms of sexual activity, and little had changed by World War II.[14] Newspaper headlines warned of fourteen- or fifteen-year-old "Victory Girls" who exhibited their patriotism by picking up soldiers in dance halls, train stations, or on the streets. Girls, rather than their male partners, were blamed for the rising venereal disease rate, which sapped soldiers' health and delayed their military deployment. Prevention focused on controlling female delinquents, and their delinquency remained an issue of paramount importance throughout the war.[15]

Adolescent males who exercised adult prerogatives and threatened to overturn the hierarchy of age and class were another concern. Working-class males, including Euro-Americans, African Americans, Puerto Ricans, and, in the West, Mexican Americans, had money and entered the public spaces of downtown entertainment districts. These young men enjoyed a peculiar freedom that contrasted strikingly with the constraints placed on a wartime society. They had entered a liminal stage, not yet adults but no longer children, newly freed from the tyranny of school but not yet fully incorporated into the discipline of work, awaiting word of draft status, newly affluent with their wartime paychecks, and able to participate in the culture of poolrooms, juke joints, dance halls, and all-night movie houses.[16] A report on truancy for the New York Department of Education explained the adolescent's search for immediate gratification: "The boy's reasoning seems to be along this line, 'I'm going into the service soon, don't know what is going to happen, might as well enjoy myself while I can; what's the use of an education now?' " The mixture of relative affluence, uncertainty, and independence led to adult anxiety.[17]

The zoot suit became the most famous emblem of independent working-class youth. Latino, African-American, and Euro-American males employed the hip jive talk of the jazz world, plunged into the pleasures of the nighttime entertainment districts, jitterbugged, and wore zoot suits—outrageously flamboyant badges of youthful freedom. Zoot suits mocked somber military uniforms with their bright pastel colors and defied warnings of wartime shortages with their long coats, broadly padded shoulders, and voluminous pleats.[18] Irving Shulman, in his novel *The Amboy Dukes*, described the look of his working-class Jewish protagonists in Brooklyn's Brownsville neighborhood:

> The boys . . . wore pastel tan, blue, and gabardine suits: three-button jackets, ticket pocket, center vent, deep pleated trousers with dropped belt loops, pegged from twenty-four inches at the knees to sixteen inches at the cuffs. . . . Nonchalantly they swung long key chains that hung from a right or left belt loop, and the keys spun in continuous enlarging and contracting circles. The boys sported duck-tail haircuts: long, shaggy, and clipped to form a point at the backs of their heads.[19]

Most important, the zoot suit, while remembered as a form of dress favored by African-American and Latino youth, transcended ethnicity. At a time when African-American and Latino migrants poured into still-segregated cities, the zoot suit represented racial transgression for whites. Its wearing did not symbolize tolerance, however, as zoot-suited gangs still organized along ethnic lines. Rather, Euro-American adolescents appropriated African-American and Latino cultural forms—including bebop and the zoot suit—as the most provocative way of expressing both the joy of consumption after the long dry years of the Depression and their rebellion against parents, school, employers, and their impending incorporation into the war effort. Young African Americans employed the zoot suit to celebrate a bebop-based culture, reject the color line, and express opposition to the war. (The forms and meaning of gang culture are discussed more extensively in chapter 5.) African Americans wielded these symbols of resistance quite consciously: when Malcolm X reported for induction in 1943, he wore a zoot suit, talked jive, and threatened to organize black soldiers to fight segregation, which earned him the rejection he hoped for. This sort of overt rebelliousness, symbolized in the styles of adolescent dress, aroused a response on the part of authorities and the public at large.[20]

To gain control over adolescent behavior, police began arresting larger and larger numbers of youths. The Federal Bureau of Investigation reported that arrests of girls under twenty-one had increased by 55 percent between 1941 and 1942, in response to the hysteria over adolescent girls cruising for soldiers. Boys also had their activities checked, with juvenile courts reporting as much as a one-third increase in their caseloads of delinquent boys between 1942 and 1943. That many offenses were comparatively minor did not seem to matter. FBI director J. Edgar Hoover maintained that the surging juvenile crime rate threatened the stability of the nation. In New York City, the press began a sensationalized campaign about African-American crime following the murder of a fifteen-year-old white youth by three black adolescents in the fall of 1941. Story after story focused on the "Harlem crime wave," in which many of the perpetrators were young males, and these accounts merged into the coverage of increasing wartime delinquency.[21] Of all wartime phenomena, juvenile behavior was the most susceptible to control, and as a result, juvenile arrest rates soared. The wartime juvenile crime wave was produced as much by the effort to curb youthful behavior as by the growth of misbehavior itself.

Gangs formed a comparatively minor part of this overall picture. The Office of War Information (OWI) reported that adolescents, envious of the adventures of their older brothers and male relatives, had formed "commando gangs" that imitated military tactics, stole weapons, and initiated raids into enemy territory. The OWI also alleged that gangs were responsible for acts of theft, arson, and vandalism, but, surprisingly, its report still did not take gangs very seriously. The influence of the prewar gang boy studies is readily apparent. Federal officials continued to see gangs simply as boys' play groups that had gotten a bit out of hand.[22]

### Race and Riots

Interethnic clashes, beginning with the Los Angeles zoot suit riots of June 1943, were the second step in the process of discovering gangs. The zoot suit riots—actually attacks by Euro-Americans on Mexican-American youth—followed several months of tension between white servicemen and Mexican-American "pachucos." A number of servicemen had been mugged after leaving bars or while looking for sexual liaisons with Mexican-American women, and in the zoot suit riots they gained revenge. Soldiers, painfully aware of their impending shipment overseas, no doubt resented the freedom enjoyed by their rivals. Aided by civilians, they attacked Mexican-American youths, stripping them of their zoot suits, beating them up, and ritualistically cutting off their ducktails. The turmoil lasted for ten days until the military finally declared downtown Los Angeles off-limits to servicemen.[23]

Even though zoot-suited adolescents were the victims, not the perpetrators of violence, the riots reinforced an image of minority youth as criminal. Even the way they were discussed, as "zoot suit riots," erased the role of Euro-American servicemen in the conflict and focused only on the disorder of minority youth. The Los Angeles City Council considered a resolution making wearing a zoot suit a misdemeanor but finally decided that existing legislation on disorderly conduct sufficed to control Mexican-American youth. Newspapers, such as the *New York Times*, followed the lead of Los Angeles authorities and began to comment on the style of youthful troublemakers. The paper referred to "zoot-suit gangs" that engaged in thievery, fighting, and knifings and noted in local news stories when criminals wore zoot suits. The *Times* stories associated a certain style and young males—especially African Americans and Puerto Ricans—with crime and rebelliousness.[24]

These issues were brought home for New Yorkers later that same summer with the Harlem riot of 1943. The immediate cause of the Harlem riot was the rumored shooting by a white police officer of an African-American serviceman protecting his mother. Although the facts of the case were somewhat different, the rumor seemed credible because of accounts of police brutality and a series of shootings in Harlem, in which plainclothes police officers acted as decoys and then shot their would-be muggers.[25] Harlemites' anger at police abuse, at discrimination, at their higher rents for shoddier apartments, and at the color line in general exploded in attacks on white-owned stores and on police.

Young African-American males were leading participants in the looting and destruction that accompanied the riot. Author Claude Brown, who at the time was the child "mascot" of a gang called the Buccaneers, recalled the turmoil that accompanied the riot. When he went outside the morning after the riot, he did not recognize his neighborhood. Glass from shattered store windows littered the street, stores had been broken into, and a virtual army of police occupied Harlem. Despite the police presence, Brown and his friends took the opportunity to raid local stores for food on what was perhaps one of the few occasions when any Harlemite could have a full larder.[26] Another youthful participant in the riot, "R" (clad, the interviewer noted, in a zoot suit), described more serious violence that occurred farther uptown, where Harlem met a Euro-American community in Washington Heights, and where young men could attack whites directly:

> A trolley car comes along packed with 'fay people [white people] and a few colored people grabbing the trolley and the conductor to keep him from drivin' the trolley, while other people throw rocks and stones into the window causing serious accidents. Half-juiced . . . the rest of the people grabs the trolley and begins lifting it into the air while the other people that was in the trolley climbs the window. . . . [T]he cops run over to the scene of the crime and start whippin' asses like hell, beats one colored man dam [sic] near to death before he let go the trolley.[27]

Unlike race riots in the nineteenth or early twentieth centuries, in which whites were the aggressors, the 1943 riot (like the Harlem riot of

1935) involved African-American attacks on white-owned property and occasionally on white commuters. It followed a year of clashes nationally, as African Americans and Euro-Americans fought nearly everywhere the color line was crossed, especially on military bases and near defense plants where African Americans were taking traditionally "white" jobs.[28] In the Harlem riot, young African-American males, like Claude Brown and R, reveled in the carnivalesque reversal of the usual structures of power and order and gave voice to a new rebellious spirit to which white New Yorkers responded with predictable panic. R's warning, "I leave this thought with thee, Do not attempt to fuck with me," could be taken as an epigraph for a new era.[29]

### Race and Crime

One might expect that the disorders of 1943 would lead to a discovery of gangs, but they did not. There was no evidence of organized gang participation in the riots, and when public officials encountered reports of gang activity, they dismissed them as not serious. They were caught up in what they viewed as a more important public debate about increasing crime, which many white New Yorkers blamed on African Americans. In the public furor over race and crime, hints of the existence of street gangs were ignored.

The public debate over race and crime, initiated with reports of a Harlem crime wave and continued after the Harlem riot, was now refueled by the Brooklyn grand jury report of August 1943. Instead of beginning a discussion of the problems of migration, displacement, and poverty, the report sparked an attack on African-American migrants. Public authorities in turn, led by the liberal mayor, Fiorella La Guardia, defended the African-American community against charges of criminality. This highly charged atmosphere contributed to officials downplaying reports of gang activity.

The Brooklyn grand jury complained that Bedford-Stuyvesant's "Little Harlem" existed in a state of lawlessness. They found that "many school children have been beaten, robbed and otherwise mistreated on dozens of occasions." Walking the streets after dark had become perilous, and "many fine churches have closed completely because their parishioners do not dare attend evening services." Citizens traveling on subways and buses had been assaulted, and groups of young boys, armed with knives and other weapons, "roam the streets at will and threaten and assault passersby and commit muggings and holdups with increasing frequency." Youths under twenty-one years of age were responsible for most crimes. "These children form into little groups, run into stores, steal merchandise and run away. They break windows; they snatch pocketbooks; they commit muggings, holdups, and assaults." Law-abiding citizens armed themselves in self-defense, thus reinforcing a cycle of violence. The grand jury blamed young, male, African-American migrants for the upsurge in crime. Moreover, as evidenced by the frequent references to problems with "groups," the Brooklyn grand jury was in the process of discovering gangs.[30]

The grand jury report was inflammatory and fed the long-standing racism of many Brooklynites. White homeowners in Bedford-Stuyvesant had been concerned about the increasing presence of African-American families since the 1920s. They formed block associations to prevent sales to African-American families, and local institutions, such as churches, sought to limit contact between African Americans and Euro-Americans by encouraging the formation of segregated congregations. Community groups proposed building low-income housing in peripheral areas to isolate the minority population, while others suggested shipping welfare recipients back to their hometowns. Monsignor John Belford, pastor of the Nativity parish, in the path of black settlement, had written Mayor La Guardia to urge him to teach the black man "to live and act like a human, not an animal." When the grand jury convened in the summer of 1943, it became a new vehicle for white resentment and fear.[31]

Although the grand jury identified the activities of "groups" of African-American adolescents in particular, their report became a focus for racist reaction and a means of labeling an entire community as criminal. In the town meeting held after the grand jury's presentment became public, white Brooklynites, including Monsignor Belford, called for Mayor La Guardia's removal by the governor, hooted down African-American speakers, and cheered those linking African Americans ("sunburned" citizens according to a police officer who addressed the crowd) to the increase in crime and muggings.[32] The issue of gangs was lost.

Public officials and civil rights organizations defended the African-American community against charges of criminality. Mayor La Guardia sent hundreds of police officers to Bedford-Stuyvesant not, as critics noted pointedly, to protect the citizenry, but to conduct a house-to-house survey of residents to gather evidence to counter the grand jury's presentment. The Brooklyn branch of the National Association for the Advancement of Colored People called the charges exaggerated and expressed its bitterness over the racist terms of the debate, while the left-leaning American Labor Party denounced the grand jury as a political tool of the mayor's enemies. Over the next several weeks, various commissioners defended their administration against charges of lax enforcement of welfare provisions, the absence of recreational opportunities, and violence in the schools.[33]

Perhaps the most careful analysis of the grand jury presentment came from the police. Police Commissioner Valentine's investigation found that while some of the grand jury's charges were factual, the rate of increase in crime and juvenile delinquency in Bedford-Stuyvesant lagged behind that found elsewhere in Brooklyn. Moreover, because the migrant African-American population was younger than the resident Euro-American one, the number of adolescents susceptible to arrest had increased. Although the number of arrests was up, the arrest rate had not increased as dramatically, and less than 1 percent of the adolescent and young male population had been charged with a crime.[34]

When public authorities encountered complaints from Brooklyn citizens, such as Mrs. Neston, about street gangs, they responded defensively. In the highly charged political atmosphere of 1943, municipal officials were not ready to give any credence to reports about gang activity, whatever their source. Police investigated citizens' complaints, but they did so with the intent of discrediting them. As a result, it was another four years before the city began to mount a credible response to the gang problem.

### Ignoring Gangs

Brooklyn citizens echoed the grand jury's charges about gangs. Louis Schachter, an attorney, wrote the mayor about gangs whose accomplishments included "beating of women, aged persons and children. Purse snatching and petty theft is a common occurrence. These boys . . . are known as The Saints, Falcons, The Bishops, The Beavers, and The 627 Stompers, among other names." Schachter concluded, "From my speaking to these people [residents], it appears to me that they are in mortal fear of the gangs in the area." Edwards Cleaveland, the chair of a committee for interracial relations, wrote, "We are much concerned over the activities of gangs of young boys and particularly so since the recent murder on Jefferson Ave. . . . The published accounts of this murder mention such gangs as the 'Robins' and the 'Bishops' whose members organize gang fights with knives and home made firearms." These were the fears not of rabid racists but of citizens—black and white, young and old—who saw themselves as potential victims of gang violence. Cleaveland wrote, "We have known of the existence of these gangs and of the terror which they inspire in young Negro boys who do not belong to them."[35] Their voices were stilled, however, by the clamor over race and crime.

Public officials reacted skeptically to citizens' complaints about gangs. They rejected evidence of gangs, either by disparaging the credibility of witnesses or using the turn-of-the-century gang studies to reinterpret the meaning of what people were reporting. The police commissioner was among those who refused to acknowledge the existence of gangs in Bedford-Stuyvesant. Whatever offenses adolescents committed, they were, he argued, the acts of individuals and not of an "organized juvenile crime syndicate." The commissioner admitted that there were "groups of youths who associate together in this neighborhood, but such association is fundamentally no more expression of evil than the association of the members of a parish ball club." It was an expression of "natural instinct," a product of the "gang age." Commissioner Valentine borrowed the language and concepts of the early gang boy studies to dismiss residents' fear of gangs. Gangs were either the result of normal play activity or they belonged to the adult criminal world. No category existed in the gang boy studies for adolescent gangs whose playthings included firearms but who were not linked to organized crime. The Bishops and the Robins, according to Valentine, simply could not be.[36]

The police who investigated the complaints of the citizens who wrote to the mayor were equally dismissive. In response to Louis Schachter's letter, police officials visited the local boys' club, where the gangs were alleged to congregate. The director told the police that "there are no gangs of boys known as the 'Saints, Falcons, Bishops, Beavers or the 627 Stompers.'" Police investigating Edwards Cleaveland's letter reported that accounts of the Bishops and Robins had been "greatly exaggerated. . . . They are not true gangs in that the organization is not tight and controlled, and leadership is not the task of any one member. Often these groups form because of athletic contests, assume bizarre names and titles, and then when the athletic season is over they will remain together chiefly because they are from the same locality or street." There was no evidence of anyone being terrorized; police only found the "overexuberance of misguided youth." As for Mrs. Neston, she could not supply the police with any specific information, "only her personal opinion due to mischievous acts of the young people of the neighborhood and rumors from her friends."[37] Officials continued to apply the concepts of the prewar gang studies to discredit citizens' reports of adolescent gang activity. Public officials could not see the gangs in front of them.[38]

## GANGS AND NEIGHBORHOOD CONFLICT

At the same time that public officials rejected reports about street gangs, evidence of their activity began to mount. As gang conflicts began to rage across ethnic lines, it became difficult to ignore them. Although police and political leaders denied the existence of gangs, New York citizens were discovering them. In neighborhoods where ethnic succession was occurring, existing Euro-American gangs took on the task of defending turf against the in-migration of Puerto Ricans and African Americans. Bradford Chambers, a journalist trained in sociology, was one of the first commetators to note the proliferation of gangs and the increasingly intense nature of gang conflict as different ethnic communities came into contact. Chambers argued that while gangs had a long history in New York, the inspiration for contemporary gang conflict lay in ethnic and religious hostility. Gangs were to be found in many city neighborhoods, but their activities were most charged in borderline districts, where "fear, suspicion and antagonism" predominated. "The gangs in these communities have primarily one purpose—protective security." Here gangs were passing the "tipping point," as fear sparked gang formation and conflict followed.[39]

Chambers investigated an area on the Upper West Side of Manhattan near City College that he called "Mousetown." African Americans and

Puerto Ricans had breached the dividing line in west Harlem by crossing Amsterdam Avenue and moving west toward the Hudson, and the area's white youths were resisting. "When the traditional colored districts began to expand . . . the white boys' clubs, led by the Hancocks, the Rainbows, and the Irish Dukes, turned to conflict. In adjacent Harlem, the Negro Sabres, the Socialistics, and the Chancellors joined the battle." The key words here are "turned to conflict," as clubs or street-corner groups chose to become gangs and fight against African-American adolescents. This was a classic "defended neighborhood," in which corner groups patrolled the borders and watched passersby and, when faced with the "invasion" of another group, decided to resist.[40] Some white adults, worried about the changing composition of the area, encouraged gangs to attack African Americans. Chambers quoted one resident:

> "This here neighborhood used to be a darn nice place. But now the jigs and the spiks are moving in. They all stink like hell, and every last one of them carries knives and razors. It's not safe to live here now. These jigs are willing to work for less, so pretty soon we whites won't find no jobs and they'll take over the whole damn city. You know, I'm against these white kid clubs around here fighting each other, but if they can get to-gether and help keep out the colored, well . . ."[41]

Gangs responded enthusiastically to adult support by throwing rocks through the apartment windows where African Americans lived, painting swastikas on the buildings, and hurling trash, debris, and paint-filled bot-tles into the lobbies of apartment buildings. Needless to say, wandering adolescents, both black and white, were subject to attack by different gangs solely on the basis of skin color. The *New York Times* reported that Frederick Teichmann, Jr., a fifteen-year-old pastor's son, was escorting two girls home from services in the Mousetown area, when he was set upon and stabbed by an African-American gang that mistook him for a gang member. (Following what was reported as the "gang code," no at-tempt was made to rob Teichmann or to harm his companions.) Under such circumstances, many residents, particularly those with children, saw their only choice as to flee. Boys from families unable or unwilling to leave joined gangs because " 'it's just smarter for your health to belong, that's all.' "[42]

Skirmishes of the variety found by Chambers were common in neighborhoods undergoing ethnic transition. All over New York, Euro-American adolescents forgot earlier rivalries and organized to defend neighborhood boundaries. For example, in the Tompkins Park neighborhood in Brooklyn, African Americans were moving into an area that had been largely Jewish, Italian, and Irish. White gangs had taken over an abandoned brewery, which was both a clubhouse and a fortress to which they retreated when threatened by others. A Brooklyn community organization became alarmed enough to hire a street worker to investigate the situation. He found that "there were a number of clicks [*sic*] that went to war, with the brewery and the street as battlegrounds. One fight was seldom enough. They fought for weeks at a stretch. When the police arrived the fighters had disappeared."[43] The white gangs included the Brewery Rats, the Pulaski Street boys, the Clover Street boys, and the Red Skin Rhumbas, all of whom were bitter rivals. However, "whiteness" provided a common denominator around which the rivals could rally. When threatened by outsiders, the white gangs formed an uneasy alliance that lasted until the immediate threat disappeared. "During quieter intervals the larger group called together to engage in gang warfare splits up into several smaller groups [that] go by different names than does the whole group." This seemed to be a reflection of their essentially defensive posture. The street worker argued that they were "afraid of the colored groups immediately to the south and seem to exist in most part as a means of common defense against these gangs." White youths remained somewhat disorganized because they did not yet feel as pressured as did gangs in the Bronx and Harlem. Tompkins Park had still managed to avoid "real gang warfare."[44]

"Real" gang warfare went beyond rumbles featuring chains, bats, car aerials, and rocks. Morrisania, in the South Bronx, was one of the neighborhoods where clashes were getting out of hand. Like other South Bronx neighborhoods, Morrisania had served as a refuge for Irish, Italian, and Jewish families fleeing the tenements of the Lower East Side or East Harlem. Now they felt under siege as Puerto Rican and African-American families followed in their footsteps. Father Banome, a Catholic priest at Saint Jerome's Church, reported, " 'I was just amazed at the struggle between them [Irish and Puerto Ricans], the absolute hatred and disregard. It manifested itself mainly in gang fights.' "[45] One such fight in the spring of 1945 between the Jackson Knights, a white gang, and the Slick-sters, an African-American one, resulted in the death of thirteen-year-old Jesse Richardson. Members of the Slicksters had stolen a pair of eyeglasses from a member of the Knights, who plotted revenge. When a group of Slicksters approached the corner candy store that the Knights used as their headquarters, the Knights opened fire on them and killed Richard-son. Police later confiscated two Springfield rifles, one Savage rifle, a bayonet, and two hundred rounds of ammunition.[46]

Most conflicts did not produce such a sensational outcome, even in neighborhoods where ethnic tension was high, and therefore were not reported in the press. Usually boys fought in school hallways or on the playground, or they beat up a rival caught without backup on the street, which were events that might lay the ground for a more explosive conflict later on. Ambushes or planned rumbles were infrequent, few gangs had access to real weapons, and when clashes occurred, nervous adolescents and single-shot weapons kept casualties low. Therefore, most gang con-flict remained below the line of sight of public officials and even the press.

Schools, which brought together youths from different neighborhoods, became sites of these more mundane forms of conflict. While most of New York's public schools remained highly segregated throughout this period, East Harlem's Benjamin Franklin High School attracted Italian, African-American, and Puerto Rican youths. The principal, Leonard Co-vello, developed an imaginative curriculum that involved his students in doing community research and that tried to foster ethnic tolerance. De-spite these efforts, essays written for an English class—for a publication on multiracial education—are full of references to interethnic clashes and indicate the on-going tension in the neighborhood.

Students at Benjamin Franklin encountered gangs and interethnic con-flict as part of the normal experience of living in East Harlem. One boy wrote of a shoe-shopping expedition that turned into something else. As he and a friend were walking, they spied a group of boys they knew carrying bats, sticks, rocks, and several knives. Rumors of a small boy being beaten set the group off on a hunt for African Americans to retaliate against. "About 106th Street we met a colored man about 35 years old. The biggest boy went over and hit him in the face. The man started to run away, but about 10 boys ran after him and caught him. Then they started to beat him up, hitting him with everything they could find. Meanwhile two city patrol men came over and . . . said, 'if you boys want to beat up niggers go down a little farther and fight, but stay away from our section. Get a couple for us too.' " This account was unusual only in that the attack involved an adult—and that it received explicit adult (and official) approval. Thomas Foudy described more common incidents: "Around our neighborhood we have had many gang fights between colored and white. In many instances boys have been seriously injured, and private property damaged." An Italian-American youth reported that he and his friends were standing around their block with their club jackets on when an African-American gang appeared and threatened to shoot them unless they surrendered the jackets. "When they got in the hall one fellow had a gun, another a pipe made of rubber. They made them take off their jackets. One fellow started a fight. He was beaten by the fellow with the rubber pipe. My friend could not do anything because if he did, he would get a bullet in his stomach. From this day, we are always having a fight with the Negroes."[47]

The ordinary conflicts among gangs, such as the ones Benjamin Franklin students wrote about, occurred beyond the realm of media or official attention. They were not the sorts of events that prompted mayoral investigations or caused social welfare agencies to send social workers into an area, and they rarely bubbled up into the consciousness of municipal officials.

However, a report of a riot at Benjamin Franklin High School sparked an official investigation of the school by the district attorney and prompted acknowledgment of the gang problem. The press reports of the incident were wildly exaggerated—the "riot" was actually just a fistfight among two groups of youngsters. But according to the New York Times, "Twice during the day street fighting broke out in which knives flashed, stones and bottles were flung from roof-tops and 500 white and Negro students and their elders battled eighty uniformed and plainclothes policemen." The Daily News was even more imaginative and upped the total to two thousand high school students battling in the street outside the school, with African-American students outnumbered four to one. The Daily News claimed that police escorted about a hundred students toward the subway, but "the march almost turned into a rout, as nearly 1,500 white students trailed the group, frequently breaking through the police phalanx to pummel the Negroes."[48] A minor incident, involving a handful of students, was blown up by the press into a full-scale riot.

Leonard Covello indignantly defended the reputation of his school against the "lies" of the press. He recounted that several white boys had attacked several African-American youngsters waiting for the bus, but the fight lasted no more than ten minutes and the white youths fled as soon as the police arrived. Covello foiled an attempt at retaliation the next day when he spotted a group of African-American youths carrying sticks and confronted them. No one had gathered on rooftops, no one had displayed any knives, and no pitched battles occurred in the street.

Leonard Covello, dedicated to creating a multiracial environment in his school and defensive about East Harlem's reputation, confronted evidence of ethnic conflict reluctantly. He apparently chose to ignore the ugly realities revealed in student essays, and his comments about the incident reflect his optimism that ethnic harmony could be achieved through education: "We had gotten the feeling that a racial clash between groups could not occur, particularly in the light of the good will and friendly relations which have existed between the different racial and nationality groups in the school over this eleven year period." Covello may have overestimated his influence on his students, but there is no reason to doubt his sincerity. He admitted ruefully that teenagers and young men in the neighborhood "do not like colored people and will take the occasion if a fight should occur, to attempt to beat up colored boys indiscriminately." Covello took comfort in the relatively minor nature of the incident that had occurred, but the district attorney's investigation revealed a school more troubled than Covello cared to admit.[49]

The district attorney's investigation corroborated Covello's account of the so-called riot, but it also revealed disturbing information about the school. Interviews with students indicated that a small group of youths bullied both teachers and other students: "All of the [fifty] boys interviewed, both colored and white, admitted that a large number of the boys at the school carry knives, razors and other dangerous weapons and that some of them exhibit them in front of the teachers and their fellow students for the purpose of intimidating them." A number of youngsters claimed that a group of older African-American boys controlled the bathrooms and demanded cigarettes or money as payment for entry, and they mentioned that these students were the ones carrying weapons.

Interviews with African-American students confirmed that they were armed, but the boys attributed it to the need for self-protection against the gangs in the neighborhood. The implication of the report was clear— even if the accounts in the newspapers were false, the school could not remain aloof from the conflicts occurring in the streets, which already were seeping onto school grounds.[50] Rather than being an interracial mecca, Benjamin Franklin High School brought together hostile groups. It was located in territory controlled by Italian gangs, and however welcoming the principal and staff, African-American students believed they attended at their peril. These students responded by attempting to create a space for themselves in the school through acts of intimidation. Like their zoot-suited peer "R," they, too, warned white New Yorkers: "Do not attempt to fuck with me."

All over the city, but especially in neighborhoods undergoing ethnic succession, gangs were organizing, street-corner groups were transforming themselves into gangs, and adolescents were arming themselves and engaging in bitter skirmishes. Disparate pieces of evidence—a district attorney's investigation, essays written by high school students, letters from besieged citizens, a racist grand jury presentment, the reports of social workers and journalists, and even fabricated news reports—can be assembled to peer into a world of ethnic conflict largely carried on by street gangs. The gangs that public authorities could ignore in 1943 had become a major social problem they had to confront. It was clear by the end of the war that gangs were carving up neighborhoods into spheres of influence as readily as Roosevelt, Churchill, and Stalin had divided the world at Yalta. A war abroad had been replaced by a war at home, and public officials and the press were finally forced to acknowledge it.

While ethnic conflict was the most important reason for the discovery of gangs, gang behavior—specifically the intensification of violence after World War II—contributed to it. It was no longer adequate to beat rivals up; instead they were "stomped," as gang members held a boy down while the others took turns kicking and jumping on his face and body. The greater availability of weapons meant that more youths were seriously hurt or even killed than in the past. Gang fighting had always been brutal, but observers claimed that it had become more so.[51] Here the influence of World War II seems most apparent.

## Gangs and War

War has frequently led to a postwar increase in violence in domestic society. An analysis of the effects of war on domestic homicide has shown that most nations have suffered a substantial postwar increase in their homicide rates. This relationship has held regardless of whether the nation won or lost the war, suffered major or lighter casualties, or encountered postwar prosperity or depression.[52] Sociologists Dane Archer and Rosemary Gartner argue that war legitimizes violence: acts that in peacetime would be considered horrific are described as heroic because they are sanctioned by the state and committed against an enemy. This violence appears to have a residual effect, not necessarily on combatants, but on noncombatants who have indulged in violence only vicariously during wartime.[53] This hypothesis is difficult to evaluate as it is not entirely clear how one measures the legitimation of violence in individuals. But there are two very concrete ways in which World War II affected adolescent street gangs.

After World War II, gangs acquired more sophisticated weapons and used more elaborate tactics. Thousands of young men—many in the prime age for committing acts of violence—were suddenly released back into civilian society. Veterans, returning to their old street corners and finding their use contested, supplied souvenir weapons, tutored their younger gang brothers in military maneuvers, and sometimes engaged in violent clashes themselves. Bradford Chambers observed that "for sticks, stones and bottles, they have substituted ice picks, knives and ingenious, home-made revolvers and rifles." Older gang members, comparing gang fighting before and after the war, agreed that the use of weapons became more common later. German Lugers—war trophies—appeared on the streets, and one former gang member explained that he borrowed his father's pistol when he went out on gang raids. From army surplus stores boys purchased garrison belts, which had heavy metal buckles that they sharpened and swung at opponents in close combat. Comic books advertised pistols that could easily be converted to fire .22-caliber bullets, which could be pocketed at any penny arcade shooting gallery. Occasionally rifles, bayonets, and even hand grenades made their appearance in gang arsenals.[54]

2.1. Boys' arsenal at the Bathgate Avenue Police Station, the Bronx, March 3, 1949.

Gang members acquired weapons eagerly because they brought their owners status, and they tipped the balance of power with other gangs. Gangs usually possessed only a couple of highly treasured weapons, and the privilege of using them was carefully guarded. "Carl Joyeaux," a leader of a "midget" division of the Bishops (the gang the police commissioner did not believe in), recalled finding a box of .38-caliber revolvers that had been hijacked from the Brooklyn Navy Yard and hidden: "The sudden haul made a spectacular difference in our division's chances. With our new artillery we might rise to be top club in the city. . . . I got ideas of becoming the Hitler of all the Little People [junior gang members]." Even the seniors in the Bishops were jealous of Joyeaux's arsenal, the possession of which allowed him to challenge the leadership of the older boys. Getting ready for a fight, Joyeaux and his followers readied their weapons: "As we loaded up, you could feel the tension. None of us had yet fired a real gun with live ammo at anybody. Just to wrap our fingers around the grip of a businesslike, blue-black .38 gave us a charge down to our toes." Real weapons supplemented the "homemades" boys usually used, and only nervousness and poor marksmanship kept casualties low.[55]

Street gangs employed the tactics of warfare in their conflicts. Gang fighting took place in the form of feints and sorties, war parties engaged in pincer movements to trap their enemies, gangs used decoys to lure rivals into deadly ambushes, and groups of boys "japped" lone members of rival gangs and beat them to a pulp. One gang ambush witnessed by Bradford Chambers involved a group of four young boys, junior members of a white gang called the Robbins, who snatched a baseball bat from a group of Buccaneers, an African-American gang. The Buccaneers gave chase, only to find halfway down the block that the Robbin seniors had blocked both ends of the street. Other Robbins, hidden on the roofs, began to hurl bricks and trash cans down on the trapped Buccaneers. Only the timely arrival of the police prevented serious injury.

On other occasions, the mixture of weapons and tactics proved lethal. A white gang armed themselves prior to setting an ambush for the Bear Cats, an African-American gang. After initiating a raid into rival territory, which they knew would require a response, the gang shot out streetlights on their block:

> "Then we see 'em coming in a car. Well, the lights in our block is out. so we sneaks up to the car and shoots bullets into the tires. It was real stuff. As the car slows up, down from the rooftops, where others in our club were hid, comes ash cans and garbage and bricks and every other goddam thing on top of the car. How the Bear Cats ever got away that time I'll never know, but they did, and that ended the fight for them. But another time, that same way, we killed a couple of jigs."[56]

Adolescent street gangs had become embroiled in ethnic conflict, employed new tactics, utilized new weapons, and had essentially taken on a new form.

It is difficult to estimate the death toll associated with this new form of gang conflict. Immediately after the war there was an increase in the juvenile homicide rate (the death rate per 100,000 adolescents aged ten to nineteen, with homicide listed as the cause of death) as well as in the number of adolescents (under twenty years of age) charged by the police with murder or manslaughter. The increases in the juvenile homicide rate and the murder/manslaughter arrests are difficult to interpret and will be discussed below, but first they must be placed in the context of what had over time become a more peaceful city.

New Yorkers, like other urban residents, had enjoyed over a decade of comparative safety—homicides had hit historic lows during the Depression and early war years—and they were unused to violence on the homefront. In most urban areas, the homicide rate had declined since the middle of the nineteenth century, with the exception of a post–Civil War surge, and historian Roger Lane has maintained that the discipline of factory work and the structuring of life by bureaucratic institutions pacified violent preindustrial populations.[57] More recently, historian David Courtwright has argued that the existence of a bachelor society promoted violence on the western frontier, while eastern cities, characterized by an excess female population and higher rates of family formation, became more peaceable over time. While offering different models of causation, both of these historians conclude that violence became less normative in urban areas. An apparent increase in homicide in the early twentieth century that peaked around 1930 is explained by prosecutions for "vehicular homicide," a category that then disappeared. Thereafter the rates in most areas declined sharply again until just after World War II. As a result, urban residents were unprepared for any increase in violence.[58]

New York City fits this general pattern. The homicide rate remained fairly stable until starting a steady increase during the late 1920s. The homicide rate peaked in 1930 and then fell precipitously during the Depression and the early war years. A homicide rate of nearly 5 per 100,000 in the late 1940s was 50 percent higher than the rate during the war years (see fig. 2.2).[59] New Yorkers undoubtedly reacted to their immediate historical experience, which was of a period of comparatively few homicides and little violence, and saw the postwar increase in homicides with alarm.

To be sure, criminal statistics must be used with caution. Arrest figures and the numbers of reported crimes are manipulated by police departments seeking funding, are distorted by sudden shifts in policy, and are susceptible to discrimination by class and ethnicity. Moreover many crimes—in some instances a majority—go unreported. However, the more serious the crime, the more likely it is to be reported. Crimes such

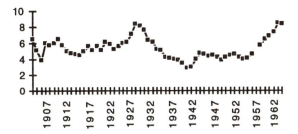

2.2. Twentieth-century homicide rate (deaths per 100,000) in New York City.

as homicide and manslaughter are less likely to be ignored or affected by a change in policy.[60] Since a homicide produces an artifact—a body—that must be photographed, dissected, weighed, analyzed, and somehow accounted for, one reasonable and widely accepted way to measure changing levels of violence is to analyze the homicide rate. By this measure, New York City was becoming a more violent place after the war.

The statistics for juvenile homicide and for adolescent arrests for murder/manslaughter must be interpreted carefully. A surge in either the homicide rate or in the number of youths arrested for murder and manslaughter would not necessarily prove that gang behavior had changed—not all juvenile homicides occurred at the hands of other juveniles and not only street gang members committed homicide. More important, the homicide rate for juveniles declined and then remained fairly stable in the 1950s, when gangs were very active, and increased dramatically in the 1960s, when gangs were less active. Therefore the juvenile homicide rate cannot be taken as a proxy for gang activity. However, increasing gang conflict would inevitably find expression in the homicide rate and in the number of youths arrested for murder and manslaughter. Both of these measures took a sudden jump in the mid-1940s.

The homicide rate for adolescents in New York City largely mirrors the pattern for adults in the years after 1940. In 1945 and 1946, the homicide rate for adolescents was more than double what it had been in the early 1940s (see fig. 2.3), as the introduction of weapons and military tactics took their toll. The homicide rate rose from 1.28 deaths per 100,000 in 1940 to 3.11 in 1945 and 3.45 in 1946 before beginning a modest decline. Although the homicide rate had its ups and downs thereafter, the rate never again fell to its prewar low.

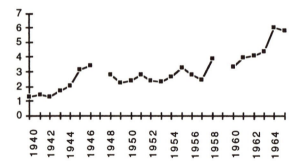

2.3. Adolescent homicide rate (deaths per 100,000) in New York City.

The number of adolescents arrested for murder and manslaughter also increased alarmingly in the postwar period (see fig. 2.4). As with the homicide rate, the number of juveniles arrested for these crimes more than doubled between 1940 and 1946, increasing from 34 to 88. In the same time period, adolescents accounted for an increasing proportion of the total arrests for murder and manslaughter. In 1940, only 12 percent of those arrested for murder and manslaughter in New York City were under age twenty; by 1946, they accounted for 25 percent of the total arrests. While both the number of juvenile arrests and their proportion of the total declined thereafter, it was clear to anyone who looked that adolescents were both the victims and the perpetrators of the most heinous crimes. Fear of violence and concerns about gangs reflected what was happening in the streets.

Adolescent street gangs forced themselves upon the public consciousness by the end of World War II. Accounts of rising juvenile delinquency rates, the Los Angeles zoot suit riot, increasing youthful independence, and ethnic conflict involving adolescents may have primed New Yorkers to discover street gangs. But if their perceptions were colored by news reports and their own anxiety about the war's effect on adolescents, it is also clear that they reacted to the experience of crime and disorder in their midst. New Yorkers, at least in certain neighborhoods, saw the evidence in the streets—in the knots of angry youths on the corner, in the wild rumbles in city parks, in the increasing number of adolescents accused of homicide, and in the mangled bodies in the emergency rooms and the morgue—that adolescent gangs had become more than play

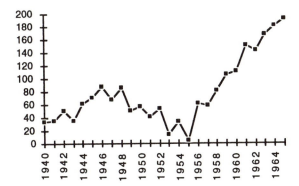

2.4. Number of adolescents arrested for murder/manslaughter in New York City.

groups, that their violence had little to do with profit and organized crime, and that their organization was due to something more sinister than a boyish "gang instinct." Increasing conflict among African-American, Puerto Rican, and Euro-American gangs, and the intensifying violence associated with it, led New Yorkers to discover the gang problem.

By the late 1940s, public authorities and private social welfare agencies caught up with Mrs. Neston and acknowledged what citizens had been saying for several years. Official recognition of the gang problem came with the formation of the New York City Youth Board in 1947, as public authorities scrambled to gain some control over gangs. The Youth Board funded projects initiated by private social welfare agencies that placed "street workers" with gangs in central Harlem and in Tompkins Park in Brooklyn. The Youth Board eventually took over and expanded street work into other neighborhoods, which were ethnic borderland communities similar to the ones discussed here. Street gang work was formalized by the establishment of the Council of Social and Athletic Clubs in 1950.[61]

Ethnic conflict explains why gangs were discovered in the 1940s, as communal warfare raged across racial boundary lines. But ethnic conflict does not explain either the organization of gangs or the basis of conflict once ethnic succession was completed. Gangs were organized territorially—they were rooted in place—and once ethnic boundaries were breached, they had the surprising capacity to integrate individuals of different ethnic backgrounds into membership.

## Defending Place:
## Ethnicity and Territory

N O ONE lived in New York. New Yorkers lived in neighborhoods—East Harlem, Hell's Kitchen, Red Hook, Washington Heights, and hundreds of others. These neighborhoods took on mythic meaning as residents stamped their image on the city and invented communities for themselves that promised stability amid the flux of urban life.[1] These communities were urban villages through which inhabitants organized their daily lives, and gangs were an integral part of the urban village's social ecology. Unlike some sociologists, I see gangs as an integral part of these organized communities.[2] Gangs established community boundaries, observed strangers, and, in some instances, guarded the area's ethnic purity.[3] In a city of ceaseless change, street gangs represented place.

Street gangs organized territorially; that is, they lay claim to a bounded geographic area, which became their turf, and drew their members from that area. As those geographic places changed with ethnic succession, gangs faced the choice of disbanding or of including members from other ethnic groups. Some sociological studies either presume that gangs were temporary phenomena that disappeared after new ethnic groups took over, or they link gangs with ethnicity without considering the possibility of change over time.[4] What I have found is that at least some gangs responded to ethnic succession by incorporating newcomers. What is most interesting about the gangs that became diverse is that they did not surrender their original ethnic gang identity; that is, they still used a language of ethnicity to describe their conflicts with other gangs. This chapter explores the seeming paradox of claims of ethnic exclusivity coexisting with ethnic heterogeneity.

In order to understand the relationship among place, ethnicity, and gangs, I have chosen to analyze two neighborhoods, Washington Heights and East Harlem.[5] These neighborhoods possessed different social ecologies: different levels of social organization, resources, ethnic populations, and rates of change. But both were "defended communities" in which street gangs supplemented adult institutions aimed at keeping outsiders at bay. Washington Heights is viewed in a moment of crisis in the 1950s, following a terrible murder as the defended community produced chaos, while East Harlem is seen undergoing a long process of change from the 1930s through the 1950s.

## A MURDER IN WASHINGTON HEIGHTS

Shortly before 10:00 P.M. on July 30, 1957, Michael Farmer and Roger McShane went for a walk and entered Highbridge Park in Washington Heights, perhaps intending to swim in the municipal pool. Local teens frequently sneaked in through a hole in the fence to swim in the evening after the pool had closed. The swimming pool was a treasured recreational resource; it attracted adolescents from all over northern Manhattan, but it was "owned" by a local gang, the Jesters. On several occasions Puerto Rican and African-American youngsters coming to swim had been called "Spicks" and "Niggers" and had been chased from the scene by members of the gang. One boy complained:

> "They kept on saying, 'You dirty Spick, get out of this block.' Every time I go in the pool, they said the same thing to me. I don't bother them, 'cause, you know I don't want to get into no trouble with them, but one day they beat me up. You know, there was about five of them, and they wouldn't leave me alone. They beat me up, and I had to take a chance and get the boys."

Only when youngsters from outside the neighborhood came in groups could they avoid being jumped by the Jesters, but then they ran the risk of provoking a full-scale rumble.

The evening that Michael Farmer and Roger McShane entered the park, the Egyptian Kings and an allied gang, the Dragons, decided to retaliate against this continuing ethnic intimidation. A call to a brother gang in the Bronx to supply cars and guns to help get "the Irish boys" had gone unanswered, and after hours of milling around outside their candy store headquarters, the Egyptian Kings and Dragons decided to raid the Jesters alone. Already a number of boys had drifted away, tired of the aimless waiting, or had headed home to meet parental curfews. The remaining Kings and Dragons filtered uptown in twos and threes, and seventeen of them completed the twenty-block walk to Jester territory, carrying knives, a machete, garrison belts, chains, and baseball bats. Either no one noticed them or no one bothered to call the police, and the raiding party arrived at their destination without incident. Scouts went ahead to reconnoiter, and when they reported that eighteen to twenty Jesters were loitering on a nearby street, the raiders headed into Highbridge Park, hoping to pick off stragglers.[6]

The Dragons, a largely Puerto Rican gang, seemed to have had the least at stake in any confrontation with the Jesters. Their turf was over forty blocks to the south, between 125th and 135th Streets, on the western edge of Harlem. Puerto Ricans began moving into this area in the late 1940s, and they were recruited for membership in both African-American and Euro-American gangs seeking to gain a numerical majority in the neighborhood. By the 1950s, the Euro-American population had fled or had been expelled, and Puerto Rican youngsters had become sufficiently numerous to form their own gangs.[7] Their natural enemies would have been nearby Puerto Rican or African-American gangs rather than the distant Jesters. The Dragons, only recently organized out of an amalgam of other gangs, had little cohesiveness and seemed to have little reason to venture so far uptown.[8]

One explanation for the Dragons' participation in the raid on Highbridge Park lies in their decision to call themselves "Dragons" in the first place. A group of youngsters began to organize a new gang after several existing ones had been broken up by arrest. Their choice of the name Dragons signified their affiliation with a powerful and well-established gang, the Dragons of East Harlem. This "parent" gang had affiliates throughout the city and aggressively sought to incorporate other groups and claim additional turf. It seems likely that local youngsters decided to become a division of the Dragons in order to share in their powerful aura and to feel that they were part of a citywide network of clubs that could be called upon for assistance. The raid into Highbridge Park provided them with an opportunity to prove that they were honorable and manly enough to bear the Dragon name.

The Egyptian Kings, identified as African American, lived much closer to Jester territory, and animosity between the two groups is more easily explained. The Kings controlled the area from 135th Street to 155th Street, between the Dragons and the Jesters on the northernmost edges of Harlem. With a neighborhood in flux, skirmishes between the Kings and the Jesters would have occurred naturally as groups of boys tested boundaries, visited friends or relatives, or attempted to use public facilities belonging to the other gang. The Jesters maintained that the Egyptian Kings repeatedly wandered northward, especially into Highbridge Park with its prized swimming pool. As one Jester informant put it, " 'We're mostly a defensive fighting team, you know, but they're offensive. . . . [I]f they don't come up, we don't fight. There's never been a time when we've invaded them when they haven't come up here first.' "[9] In the gang world, the fact that this was a municipal pool, available to anyone, had no meaning: the Jesters had the right to protect "their" pool from others, just as the Egyptian Kings knew that if they could wrest it away, honor and prestige would accrue to them. The Kings and the Jesters had a history of conflict, and the raid into Highbridge Park was only the latest installment.

The Egyptian Kings had another reason for going into Highbridge Park that night and for asking their allies, the Dragons, to accompany them. A number of the older Kings had been arrested and incarcerated, and the remaining Kings sought an alliance with the Dragons in order to regain their strength. The raid on the Jesters provided a perfect opportunity to put their newfound allies to the test. According to some accounts, the two gangs had merged their leadership shortly before the raid into Highbridge Park and referred to themselves as the Egyptian Dragons.[10] Whether the raiding party was an alliance of two separate gangs or a newly created single group, is less important than the fact that the group inherited the animosity between the Jesters and the Egyptian Kings and chose this moment to prove that they were worthy heirs.

As Michael Farmer and Roger McShane strolled through the park toward the swimming pool, they probably noticed a number of couples seated on the benches. Although several individuals had seen the collection of boys that had gathered in the darkness, no one thought to warn Farmer and McShane that trouble might lie ahead. McShane later recalled that as they approached the stairs in the park, he saw two young boys at the top with garrison belts wrapped around their fists. The two did not say anything, and McShane and Farmer ignored them and climbed the stairs.

Trouble began at the top of the stairs. McShane suddenly spotted the rest of the group lurking in the shadows: " 'I turned around fast, to see what Michael was going to do, and this kid came runnin' at me with the belts. Then I ran, myself, and told Michael to run.' " But Michael Farmer, who had had polio as a youngster, could not run as fast. He was quickly surrounded and asked if he was a Jester. The Kings and Dragons later claimed that Farmer replied that he was before they knocked him to the ground with a baseball bat and started to stomp him. One King recalled that he attacked Farmer while the boy was on the ground: " 'I kicked him in the stomach. That was the least I could do, was kick 'im.' " Another one of the raiders declared, " 'I was aimin' to hit him, but didn't get a chance to hit him. There were so many guys on him—I got scared when I saw the knife go into the guy, and I ran right there. After everybody ran, this guy stayed, and started hittin' him with a machete.' " McShane had run down a hill, but three gang members were waiting in ambush and grabbed him. The others, finished with Farmer, began to attack McShane. One boy remembered, " 'I just went like that, and I stabbed him with the bread knife. (Laughs.) He was screamin' like a dog. He was screamin' there. And then I took the knife out and I told the other guys to run.' " Another youngster later recounted that he wanted to know what it felt like pushing a knife through bone, and yet another recalled that McShane said "thank you" as the knife was withdrawn. McShane staggered to the street where he hailed a cab that took him to the hospital. Before blacking out, he told the driver that Farmer was still in the park. When the police arrived, they found Farmer still alive. According to the police notes, Farmer said, " 'The Niggers got me, the Egyptian Kings . . .' " before dying on the way to the hospital.[11]

The attack on Farmer and McShane and the feud between the Kings and the Jesters fits the model of a defended community, in which gangs mobilize for honor or to protect turf against outsiders. The way in which the two groups defined each other—the Jesters as "the Irish boys" and the Egyptian Kings as "the Niggers"—replicated the division between neighborhoods. By tradition, Washington Heights started where Harlem stopped.

## DIVIDED COMMUNITIES

As the African-American and Puerto Rican populations expanded, the line separating Washington Heights from Harlem retreated northward. The original dividing line between Harlem and Washington Heights was 135th Street, but in the 1920s, as African Americans migrated uptown and turned Harlem into a black neighborhood, first 145th Street and later 155th Street marked the retreating boundary. As one study found, "very often whole blocks of white residents fled at the first indication that a Negro would reside in the block." New barriers were breached as quickly as they were erected. One census tract north of 155th Street, within the "new" Washington Heights, was about 70 percent African American in 1940 and nearly completely black a decade later.[12] An African-American state assemblyman, whose family moved into the southern portion of Washington Heights, recalled the block busting used by real estate speculators to open the area to black settlement:

> "They had just begun to allow blacks to live west of Amsterdam Avenue, on 156th Street, and they did it . . . by emptying a building out first. . . . In those days they could afford to go through the building and say 'you better move because we're moving blacks in,' and they emptied the building out."[13]

Speculators profited from the panic as white families fled from southern Washington Heights toward Inwood, at the very tip of northern Manhattan, with their backs against the Harlem River. This repeated the trek that a number of the neighborhood's Irish families had made a decade or so earlier, when they fled from West Harlem (Bradford Chambers's "Mousetown" discussed in chapter 2) into Washington Heights. No doubt

this group brought with them the memory of the increasingly bitter gang conflicts of the 1940s, as white gangs had vainly resisted "invasion" by African Americans. Now there was no place left in Manhattan to which they could run.[14]

Irish Americans organized as defenders of Washington Heights. The Irish had created a dense network of kin and countrymen who clustered on specific streets, and even in particular apartment buildings, and supported Gaelic football clubs, stores, and bars that catered specifically to them. Historian Robert Snyder's oral histories of the community reflect the sense that the area was "all Irish" ("It took me a long time to figure out that there were other people in the world besides Irish people," one former resident told Snyder), and many inhabitants organized their social lives around the neighborhood's institutions—especially the parish church and school—seeing the rest of Manhattan as an alien country. Catholics were among the most rooted of urban dwellers, with their parishes forming the core of their urban villages. Everywhere they resisted change, especially integration, and Washington Heights was no exception.[15]

The irony is that the Irish were an insecure minority within the neighborhood well before the arrival of African Americans and Puerto Ricans. The Irish accounted for only about 12 percent of the population in Washington Heights in 1940, with higher densities within certain census tracts, while Jews made up about one-third of the population. Washington Heights was bisected by Broadway with the Irish living to the east of it and Jews to the west, especially in the apartment buildings near the heights overlooking the Hudson River (known as "the Jewish Alps"). But even in the areas of high Irish concentration, the Irish accounted for only one-fifth to one-quarter of the population. If Irish residents thought of Washington Heights as an Irish enclave, it was because their primary social interactions occurred within a dense ethnic network; it was not because of their numbers in the neighborhood.[16]

Ethnicity and religion thus provided sources of discord long before African Americans moved into Washington Heights. In the 1940s, Irish

*Opposite page:* 3.1. Washington Heights. The boundary between Washington Heights and Harlem moved steadily northward, while the community itself was divided by Broadway.

youths formed the Amsterdams and the Shamrocks who, egged on by the anti-Semitic Christian Front that held rallies in the area, attacked synagogues and Jewish-owned shops, and assaulted Jewish youths. Police, many of whom were Irish and lived in the area, exhibited little sympathy for complaints about anti-Semitism. A number of the Shamrocks were arrested in 1944 and the combined forces of political and church leaders managed to tamp down anti-Semitic attacks, but clearly this was an area shaped by ethnic conflict.[17] Conflict continued with the arrival of African Americans and Puerto Ricans.

Puerto Ricans moved into the area first. By identifying themselves as "Spanish" and by attending Catholic services, they succeeded in living in areas where African Americans could not. The increasing Puerto Rican presence probably raised concerns in and of itself, while also arousing fears that they were stalking horses for African Americans, who were continuously extending Harlem's northern boundary. By the early 1950s, the Irish community in Washington Heights felt that it was under siege.[18]

Washington Heights was organized to keep "others" out, and this was not just the response of adolescent gangs. Public schools, with the connivance of the school board, were informally segregated until the mid-1950s. Private institutions, including the churches, operated similarly. When Herman Farrell (who eventually was elected to represent the area in the state assembly) applied to the local parish school, he was told to go elsewhere even though he was Catholic. Farrell attended an all-black public school, which was located in an area of Washington Heights that had become African American. In order to get home, he had to dodge through the turfs of several white gangs.[19] Segregated institutions, closely knit ethnic networks, carefully patrolled borders, suspicious neighbors, and active gangs made Washington Heights a seething cauldron of ethnic hostility. The death of Michael Farmer was long in the making.

The most interesting aspect of the Farmer case is not the division within the neighborhood but the makeup of the gangs that fought over it. The relationship between ethnicity and place had always been problematic in Washington Heights, which had never been an "all-Irish" enclave. Now it was no longer "all-white" either. Despite the construction of the opposing groups as "Irish boys" and "Niggers," in fact both gangs were multiethnic. The "Irish boys," the Jesters, included African-American members, and five of the Dragons and Egyptian Kings, identified by Michael Farmer as "Niggers," were Euro-Americans. Diversity—not homogeneity—characterized both the neighborhood and its gangs.

In the rapidly changing environment of upper Manhattan, rigidly drawn lines demarcating one ethnic group's turf from another's simply could not be maintained. New populations moved in and eddies of older ones were left behind, and as a result, street gangs, which were organized territorially, came to include members of different ethnic groups. Despite this diversity in membership, gangs had corporate identities as "Irish boys" or "Niggers," which shaped their conflict with each other.

Ethnicity remained a defining category—and supplied the basis for fighting—but it could be negotiated on an individual level. Thus Euro-American members of the Kings and the Dragons were expected to uphold the gang's honor and identity, regardless of their own. The Egyptian Kings and Dragons, although seen by Michael Farmer as African American, were largely Puerto Rican with a few African-American and Euro-American members. Since the gangs came from Harlem (or southern Washington Heights, depending on one's perspective), an area that had been surrendered to African Americans, Puerto Ricans, and Dominicans, it was expected that they would represent these predominant ethnicities. However, Euro-American boys living in this area had no other gangs to join, and they felt some pressure to participate in gang activities. Some boys were able to stay unaffiliated, but not all could or chose to. Seeking membership in an uptown "white" gang was an impossibility; these boys were strangers in other neighborhoods, potentially spies for other gangs, and they would have found remaining in their own neighborhoods afterward a nightmare. The ambiguous "racial" status of Puerto Ricans—their racial liminality—probably made joining a gang with a large Puerto Rican membership a viable option for Euro-American boys. Since Puerto Ricans did not fit the black/white dichotomy usually imposed by race, they could more easily incorporate Euro-American members than an African-American gang, while also accommodating African Americans who wished to join.

The case of African Americans joining a predominantly white gang such as the Jesters has a similar explanation. As African-American families filtered into white areas, their sons confronted the same problems faced by lingering whites in a black community. Here, too, beatings might be followed by begrudging acceptance, especially if a declining adolescent population made it difficult to sustain a gang made up only of the favored group. A boy who proved he had heart earned respect in the gang world, regardless of ethnicity. Such a youngster would be asked to favor neighborhood honor and his identity as a gang member over his ethnicity, and if he were willing to do so, he could earn a spot in the gang.[20] The Farmer case shows how gangs integrated individual ethnic identities into a larger, corporate whole.

In the wake of Michael Farmer's slaying, public officials, commentators, and attorneys involved in the case adamantly rejected the idea that it concerned race. Police officials immediately issued disclaimers, portraying the incident in Highbridge Park as typical of the wanton violence of adolescent gangs and claiming that it stemmed from a bet over the outcome of a stickball game.[21] Sociologist Lewis Yablonsky, who used the Farmer case to analyze the "violent gang," dismissed gang members as sociopaths produced by disorganized slums.[22] Attorneys for the defendants did not introduce evidence of ethnically motivated attacks at the Highbridge Park pool into evidence, nor did the prosecution raise the issue of ethnic conflict. Moreover, the mixed composition of the raiding party seemed to be the logical counter to any such argument. The press followed the same line of reasoning. The *Amsterdam News*, the city's leading African-American paper, reported that "contrary to race baiting reports," there were no specific "racial overtones" to the Farmer incident. The paper supplied the ethnic composition of the raiding party as "nine Puerto Ricans, five Irish and three Negroes."[23] (Only seven of the seventeen assailants were fifteen or over, old enough to face trial for murder, and three of the whites, six of the Puerto Ricans, and one African American were charged as juvenile delinquents.) The Egyptian Kings and the Dragons looked like a multiethnic group of thugs.

Given the diversity of membership in these gangs, the references to ethnic honor seem puzzling. What was the meaning of an all-Irish Washington Heights to African-American Jesters, or of Puerto Rican or African-American honor to Euro-American Dragons and Egyptian Kings? Was ethnicity just so much window-dressing used to defend unspeakable acts of violence? I think the language of ethnicity is important to understanding gangs. It allowed them to appeal to honor and citizenship in asserting rights of access to parks or city streets, while defenders of place used ethnicity to express the values of stability and community. In other words, ethnicity can only make sense in the context of gang culture. As will be seen, honor was of paramount importance to the Egyptian Kings and Dragons, while place mattered most to the Jesters.

Defense of ethnic pride ennobled gang conflict. The Egyptian Kings and Dragons went to Highbridge Park to avenge ethnic insults and to defy the Jester warning that "Spicks" and "Niggers" would not be allowed to swim there. The Kings' and Dragons' wish to defend African-American and Puerto Rican access to Highbridge Park propelled them into action and allowed them to imagine themselves as street warriors and men of honor.[24] But it is likely that this was a more compelling motive to the African-American, Puerto Rican, and Dominican gang members than to the Euro-American ones. The seven defendants tried for murder had their case histories discussed extensively, and they provide some insight into the possible motivations of individual members.

Charles "Big Man" Horton went to Highbridge Park for reasons of honor. Born in Alabama, where he had started to work in the cotton fields at age seven, Horton had a reputation to uphold and he probably found racial epithets an unbearable insult to his dignity, a reminder of the Jim Crow segregation he thought he had left behind. Leroy "the Magician" Birch, also African American, had retired from active member-ship in the gang, but it was his misfortune to run into the raiding party on their way up to the park. "The Magician" agreed to go along for old times' sake, to defend the honor of the gang. (Birch confessed to participating in the killing when, according to another defendant, police detectives attached wires to an exposed electrical circuit and threatened to electrocute him, telling him if he was such a magician, he ought to be able to escape.) Lencio "Jello" De Leon, born in the Dominican Republic, claimed that Michael Farmer himself had led a group of Jesters in chasing him out of the neighborhood and had called him a "Spick" sometime before the fatal confrontation. For George Melendez and Louis Alvarez, president of the gang, who had scoured the neighborhood to round up boys to attack the Jesters, Puerto Rican honor was at stake. Alvarez had been told by the Jesters, " 'We don't want you Spicks up here no more.' " For these individuals, the renewal of hostilities with the Jesters provided an opportunity to assert their self-worth, to prove that they were men, and to lay claim to their civil rights by declaring that it was not acceptable to exclude them from a public pool on account of their ethnicity.

But Richard Hills, who was white, the son of an engineer and the only defendant in the case living with two parents, in all likelihood found ethnic honor a less urgent matter. Hills later claimed that he had been drafted by the Egyptian Kings, but this version of events seems to have been designed to provide him with a defense at his trial. Gangs rarely drafted members—they were too unreliable and posed too great a risk of cooperating with police if caught. Moreover, other evidence suggests Hills's willingness to join the gang. Hills kept "Big Man" Horton's machete hidden in his apartment, fought other gang members as his initiation into the Kings, and chose to go along to Highbridge Park when other boys who had gathered that night drifted home before the fateful march. Another white boy in the neighborhood, Hills's friend, had also been approached by the Egyptian Kings, but decided not to join, a choice that was reinforced by a parental decision to forbid him from going out by himself. While this was no doubt a difficult surrender of adolescent autonomy, it was a choice that Hills did not make. Hills, like co-defendant John McCarthy and the three white boys charged in the case as juvenile delinquents, became caught up in the group's larger purpose even if they did not fit the simple categories of "Nigger" and "Spick" imposed on the group by the Jesters. They were Egyptian Kings and Dragons, and if the gangs decided to avenge ethnic insults, then their honor—and consequently their manhood—was at stake as well. Michael Farmer saw the raiders as "Niggers," despite their overwhelming Puerto Rican membership, because most had darker skins and came from the portion of Washington Heights that was becoming Harlem. Even Hills and McCarthy looked like "Niggers" because they were Egyptian Kings.[25]

For their part, the Jesters wanted to defend a community overwhelmed by change. They held a conception of community inherited from their parents and reiterated in the institutional organization of the neighborhood, which could not help but define change as bad. Communal memory included the inexorable expansion of Harlem westward into the formerly white enclave of west Harlem and northward into Washington Heights. The Jesters' defense of place was fed by conversations about the deteriorating neighborhood, the rising crime rate, and the nature of the "others" that were moving in. The Jesters wanted to hold on to "their" pool, "their" park, "their" neighborhood, and "their" place in the city, but the futility of the quest was underscored by reports that despite their attempts at intimidation, already two-thirds of the pool users were African American and Puerto Rican—and by the ethnic composition of their own gang.

Over time the correlation among gang, ethnicity, and place diverged in many New York neighborhoods. Despite this divergence, gang members continued to talk about ethnicity when describing their conflicts. It was the language of their parents and it gave voice to their battles over place. The defense of ethnic community provided gang members access to a field of honor on which to wage their battles. Those battles, for both old-timers and newcomers, were about asserting that one had a place in the city.

## East Harlem

The character of East Harlem in the 1950s is suggested by an interview with Manny Diaz, a retired social worker. The interview provides evidence of the division in the neighborhood between the Italians and the Puerto Ricans, and it suggests the relatively privileged status of Italian gangs, which were protected by organized crime, as well as the level of organization and the political influence of East Harlem's Italians. Here was a powerful defended community that was seemingly impervious to change.

Diaz was familiar with East Harlem when he arrived there as a social worker in 1953. He had grown up in East Harlem and had been a member of the East Harlem Dukes when gangs fought more with fists than with firearms. Diaz became the first Puerto Rican social worker hired by the Union Settlement House. By the 1950s, the block on which the settlement house was located had become nearly two-thirds Puerto Rican, although nearly 90 percent of the patrons of the Union Settlement were Italian. Diaz believes that he was hired to make the settlement more inviting to Puerto Rican residents, who naturally saw it as the property of the Italians. As head of the teenage division, he ran a basketball program and a game room, and he took youths camping and on outings. His work had not yet had a chance to attract a new clientele when he had a run-in with the Red Wings, East Harlem's largest and most powerful Italian street gang: "I was at the settlement two weeks . . . when one night some of the Red Wings came in, four of them had guns, and they announced that by Christmas they were going to get rid of the Spicks and the Niggers at the settlement house."

Diaz confronted them and told them that no guns were allowed in the settlement, that they had to show respect for all members, and that they were suspended for two weeks because of their behavior. "They laughed in my face," Diaz remembered, but they left without incident. Worried about the confrontation he was sure would come, Diaz went to the local precinct and requested a police presence at the settlement. Diaz recalled:

> We opened up about seven o'clock in the evening. I expected trouble and sure enough, the second day, I'm in my office . . . and the door man, the membership secretary, says, "The Red Wings are here."
>
> So I went down and there were like twenty-two Red Wings, sixteen-seventeen-year-old kids, but they had one guy who was over twenty . . . dressed like a dream. . . . And he walks in—and he was their mouthpiece obviously—he walks in and says, "I hear you won't let my boys in."
>
> "I'll let your boys in in two weeks provided no weapons, they respect the other membership, [and they] abide by the rules of the house."
>
> Then he says to me, "Don't you live at 1062 Colgate Avenue in the Bronx? Don't you have a wife named Alice? Don't you have a two-year-old named Lisa?"
>
> Now, Eric, staff people didn't know this, I think my boss didn't know this, the settlement didn't know this, and this guy has a dossier on me.
>
> So I said to him, "Are you trying to intimidate me in front of this officer?" Because the officer was standing right next to us.
>
> This guy says, "Oh, Joe. He's one of the boys, he's from 106th Street." At this point, this officer kind of melts away, a wimp.
>
> I turned on him and I said, "You motherfucker . . . you had better pray that my wife doesn't get run over by a cab, that my daughter doesn't fall down some stairs, because I know how you work . . . so you better pray because if anything happens to my wife or my daughter, I'm going after your throat, just me and you."

The guy says, "Oh, Manny, be a good guy." That's the first time he called me Manny, and I knew I had him when he said Manny. "Yeh, I'll be a good guy. When these guys come back in two weeks . . . they can come back into the settlement."

He turned around and he says to them, "Okay, guys, come back in two weeks."[26]

In the confrontation between Manny Diaz and the Red Wings, the gang members undoubtedly felt emboldened by their "connections" to organized crime and believed they could challenge adult authority. The young Mafiosi negotiator—perhaps himself a graduate of the Red Wings—wanted to stick up for "his boys," but at the same time, he had to restrain the gang. While organized crime protected Italian gangs, it also curbed their behavior: rumbles brought police and interfered with business, and the Italian gangs were admonished to act defensively only. The Red Wings were forced to give ground when the attempt to intimidate Diaz failed. Mobster supporters of the Red Wings were happy to negotiate for them, to suggest a threat, to demonstrate their control over the police force, and to show their access to confidential information, but they had little at stake in who used a settlement house in a portion of East Harlem already taken over by the Puerto Ricans. Standing up for Italian honor, maintaining ownership of a recreational resource, and defending the community against "Spicks" and "Niggers" had meaning only for the adolescent Red Wings. Racketeers wanted an amicable settlement, for men of business were reasonable as long as face-saving accommodations could be reached. The Red Wings proved that they had power, and they were allowed to return to the settlement—after serving their two-week suspension.

Just as the Italians surrendered control of the settlement house, they also surrendered control of East Harlem. Here resistance was stiffer and the process took several decades to complete. Italian East Harlem, in the middle decades of the twentieth century, seemed to defy change. Depression and poverty, then war and the tight housing market, held Italian East Harlem in place and served the illusion of permanence. After World War II, however, the pace of change quickened, as did the friction between East Harlem's predominant ethnic communities—the Puerto Ricans and the Italians. Puerto Rican and Italian gangs defended ethnic communities and they both underwent a similar process of change: they incorporated other youths into their membership while the language of ethnicity continued to supply the justification for violence. Eventually even the Red Wings included Puerto Ricans.

## ITALIAN EAST HARLEM

In the early twentieth century, East Harlem exemplified the diversity and rapid social change that characterized New York neighborhoods. Bounded by 96th Street on the south and 125th Street on the north, the East River on the east, and Fifth Avenue on the west, East Harlem housed a variety of ethnic groups, including Irish, Jews, Germans, Finns, and Italians, and it later added Puerto Ricans and African Americans. In the 1920s, approximately 45 percent of East Harlem's population was Jewish, but the Jews vanished almost overnight: the 1923 population of slightly more than 100,000 Jews was reduced in 1930 to 2,900, or 3 percent of its total just seven years earlier. The Puerto Ricans pushed out the Jews, settling first in the southwest corner of the neighborhood, and then moving north and westward, until they merged into the expanding African-American sections of central Harlem. Movement east of Lexington Avenue was resisted by Italian East Harlem, first settled in the 1890s. The area of Italian settlement contracted over time and eventually was absorbed into the barrio. But in 1930, East Harlem housed the largest Italian-American community in the United States.[27]

Italian East Harlem, even in its heyday, was never exclusively Italian, although it had a much higher concentration of Italians than Washington Heights had of Irish. Three census tracts in the center of Italian East Harlem had between 79 and 85 percent Italian population (foreign stock) in 1930, which fostered a sense of power and permanence.[28] But

*Opposite page:* 3.2. East Harlem. The barrio began around 99th Street and Madison Avenue and ran northward. Expansion to the west was halted by Central Harlem at Fifth Avenue, while expansion to the east was resisted by Italian Harlem. Note the presence of public housing projects that covered entire square blocks.

East Harlem's physical ecology helped determine its fate. It was a solid working-class neighborhood, spotted with industrial sites, and with both single-family brownstones and a large stock of old tenements. The tenements made East Harlem ripe for urban renewal, and their demolition for the construction of public housing in later decades completed the transformation of the neighborhood from Italian to Puerto Rican.

The Italians of East Harlem, despite their number, were not secure in their majority. Their community was hemmed in by hostile neighbors, and Italian gangs were the active defenders of the community from these "others." "Tony," a founding member of the Red Wings, explained, " 'The Red Wings were all Italian—no Spanish, no Irish, no nothin'—just Italians. We wanted to keep the people we didn't like in line—other races, religions, gangs.' "[29]

This spirit of defensiveness characterized the social organization of the community. Italian Harlem was intensely provincial, anchored by a local moral order, and organized through age- and sex-graded peer groups into what sociologist Gerald Suttles calls a "segmentary system." This social system, by categorizing residents into groups, allowed them to negotiate their way safely through the neighborhood by distinguishing between those who were known and those who were potentially dangerous strangers.[30]

The public world of Italian Harlem was male and hierarchical. One analyst observed a strict rank ordering in the local park; a group of boys playing handball stopped playing when the local gang's "tots" division indicated that they wanted the court. The juniors, who were slightly older, in turn displaced the tots, only to have the seniors come along and demand playing time.[31] In the evenings, older men gathered to gossip on the stoops or to play cards and drink, while younger ones congregated on the street corner or in the pool hall. Virtually no block was without its candy store—investigators counted over five hundred in East Harlem in the 1930s—which was usually the hangout for the local gang and often where residents played the numbers.[32]

Social and athletic clubs were the most potent symbols of this organized community. Located in storefronts, sparsely furnished, and decidedly male, the approximately fifty clubs found in East Harlem in the 1930s linked the world of street gangs, racketeers, and politicians. They

3.3. Private social and athletic clubs linked the legitimate and illegitimate male worlds of Italian East Harlem.

provided political workers and organized voters in return for favors, immunity from prosecution, and access to graft and power. (Today, in what remains of Italian Harlem, one can still find an occasional storefront occupied by old men playing cards, cars double-parked outside, immune from tickets, as a mute witness to faded but still present power.) Members of street gangs expected to graduate into the adult social and athletic clubs, which included upstanding citizens and businessmen as well as former street fighters. An unsympathetic journalist described—with much hyperbole—a boy's advancement from one group to the next in the neighborhood:

> So soon as [a boy] puts on long trousers, slicks his hair down and takes to
> clipping instead of biting his nails, he frequents the back rooms of candy
> stores, the poolrooms and restaurants that blaze a wide trail through the
> section and the social clubs on Second Avenue that consist of a room with
> a pool table and some chairs and a state charter. Here they plan hold-

ups and recite . . . their adventures in love and banditry. They graduate
from knives to pistols to Thompson sub-machine guns; from petty larce-
nies and neighborhood sweethearts to organized rackets and imported
"molls."[33]

Certainly not all social and athletic clubs were made up of racketeers,
nor were their activities principally illegal. But, as Manny Diaz's interview
showed, organized crime had a visible presence in the neighborhood and
provided a career path for those youths who were rebellious and talented.
Not only could they find upward mobility through a career in the rackets,
but the local crime family could be counted on to intervene with authorities when necessary. (The Youth Board also recognized the special circumstances of Italian East Harlem. It refrained from placing a worker with
the Red Wings and instead called the local dons when a problem arose.[34])
One individual, who because of his abilities as a boxer was able to reject
recruitment efforts by gangs, recalled, " 'You could do two things when
we were kids—you either became a thief and eventually go into the rackets or you could go to school.' "[35] Social and athletic clubs, street gangs,
and the rackets defined East Harlem's public space as a masculine, defended, segmented, and bounded domain. Not every individual had to
belong to such groups, but everyone owed them deference.[36]

Italian Americans succeeded in inventing a community that seemed to
defy the flux of urban life. With its heavily concentrated Italian-stock
population, it supported major political figures, such as Mayor Fiorella
La Guardia and Congressman Vito Marcantonio, and served as the base
for one of New York's major crime families. Religious processions conse-
crated the streets and conveyed the impression of an eternal, divinely
ordained order. Italians in East Harlem had greater social capital and a
more cohesive community that they sustained longer than did the Irish
in Washington Heights. Street gangs such as the Red Wings utilized violence to preserve their community, but their activities were embedded in
a larger public order dominated by adults. But even here change came,
and with surprising rapidity. Gangs could not prevent the influx of Puerto
Rican families, the gradual movement of Italians out of East Harlem, or
the effects of public policy decisions to construct vast public housing
projects in the neighborhood. And when the neighborhood changed, so
did the gangs that defended it.

## "Spanish Harlem"

Spanish Harlem, the "barrio" that served as the heart of Puerto Rican settlement in New York, was organized in a pattern similar to that of Italian Harlem. It, too, was a segmented neighborhood that mirrored Italian Harlem's organization of public space. Bodegas (small grocery stores), storefront Pentecostal churches, "township clubs," carefully tended gardens in vacant lots, intensive interaction among Spanish-speaking peers on the street corner, and active gangs defined the barrio and established it as a defended community.[37]

Family networks formed the basis of the Puerto Rican community. Boarders, either relatives or townsfolk from Puerto Rico, lived in nearly one-fifth of the Puerto Rican residences surveyed in 1948.[38] Boarding provided the family with added income and assured at least minimal supervision of young migrants to New York. Migrants with families sometimes left one or more of their children behind with relatives, sending for them when they could, or they returned children to the island for schooling or when they got into trouble in New York. Illness brought visits from kin to help tide the family over during a difficult period, and migrants returned home to their relatives during times of unemployment. To earn a living, women took in sewing and flocked to the garment industry, but families remained patriarchal in name if not always in practice. As in Italian families, Puerto Ricans guarded their daughters' honor, while adolescent boys enjoyed more freedom to participate in street life.[39]

Age-based peer groups in the barrio created a hierarchical structuring of public space. Play groups, street-corner groups, gangs, and social and athletic clubs shared the streets. In both clubs and gangs, the age range extended from boys of ten or twelve to men in their twenties, organized into tots, juniors, and seniors. The different age groupings were independent of one another but younger boys, the tots and the juniors, were aware that the seniors would bail them out if necessary. " 'You see, usually the Juniors, if they can't finish a fight . . . [or if] some older fellows from the other club jump in . . . [will] come back and get the Seniors.' " Occasionally, even older adults became involved in the disputes, and fights among the juniors could evolve into neighborhood brawls. Street-gang members graduated into the adult social and athletic clubs, but in the barrio, these organizations had more difficulty controlling youthful behavior. They lacked the institutional clout of their Italian equivalents since they did not have the same political and racketeering ties and because male authority itself existed on an unstable foundation.[40]

The marketplace did not offer Puerto Rican men a secure basis for patriarchal authority, and this, in turn, reinforced the use of the streets to define manhood. A sample of households in Puerto Rican–dominated census tracts found that males held jobs as unskilled workers in the service sector (22 percent), as factory operatives (29 percent), or were unemployed (10 percent).[41] Puerto Ricans also lacked access to the more organized sectors of the illegal economy, which the Italians of East Harlem continued to dominate. Subject to layoffs and frequent job changes, male household heads had to rely on income from wives and other family members. The strain that this caused in the family is suggested by the author Piri Thomas, who recalled a period in his youth when his mother worked and his father stayed home and helped with the housekeeping. Exploding in frustration one day, his father started punching the apartment walls, and when warned by his wife that he would hurt his hands, he replied, " 'What good are they if I can't use them to do a man's work?' "[42]

If male authority within the family was problematical, it still could be asserted in the street. The street served as a public arena for the display and definition of masculinity, and, as a result, the significance of minor slights was magnified. Not only were other sources of honor few, but also the audiences for dramas of confrontation were large. Both individuals and groups strove to enhance their reputations, which encouraged Puerto Rican gangs to act aggressively. Where Italian gangs fought defensively to preserve their community, Puerto Rican gangs were primed to prove that they had a place in East Harlem.[43]

## ETHNIC SUCCESSION

Puerto Rican and Italian rivalry on the streets of East Harlem first became apparent in the late 1930s, as the Puerto Rican population began to swell. In the fall of 1938 a series of clashes occurred around Lexington Avenue between 104th and 110th Streets. Over a period of several days, small groups of youths crossed into the other's territory and engaged in hit-and-run attacks, beating up youngsters unfortunate enough to be caught alone or engaging other groups in fights before retreating. Apparently the confrontations came to a head in mid-October when a group of about fifty Puerto Rican youths crossed into the Italian section. News of the invasion spread, and an equally large group of Italian youths gathered to meet them. "A general scrimmage and hand to hand fighting occurred after the first exchange of bottles, stones and other missiles. Confusion was added by the hurling from roofs, of bricks torn from chimneys by Italians. . . . The police fired several shots into the air when they arrived on the scene and the combatants from both sides took to their heels." In response to the situation, the city stationed a policeman every three blocks and patrol cars circled the area for several days. Border skirmishes continued, especially with the population shifts of the postwar period, and youths growing up in East Harlem described lives that were carefully circumscribed in order to avoid confrontation.[44]

Borders in East Harlem were well known and crossings were rarely accidental. As a result, youths—and not just Italians and Puerto Ricans—organized their lives around a few blocks and were painfully aware of the dangers that lay beyond them. Walter Sheppard, a student in English 7 at Benjamin Franklin High School, was one of a small number of African Americans who lived in East Harlem. Sheppard argued that he "felt submerged in the white majority" and "isolated from his own race living in West Harlem." He went on to say that "practically all public playgrounds, clubrooms, dancehalls, etc are not open. . . . Very few blocks are available in which to play, and the public parks are dangerous unless Negro youth goes in a large enough crowd to protect itself." Puerto Rican students felt similarly, noting that while there was room at the Boys' Club on First Avenue a few blocks to the east, "Puerto Rican boys near Madison Avenue cannot find a place to play. They are unwilling to go a few blocks because it means crossing Lexington Avenue [into Italian East Harlem]."[45] Programs by the Good Neighbor Federation to promote harmony between Puerto Ricans and African Americans failed because the Puerto Ricans, "who predominate in that area, eventually drive the Negroes away." When the 23rd Police Precinct organized social and athletic events, "it was found that Negro boys would invade the dances in groups and break them up." One former member of a Puerto Rican gang recalled that

Italian boys in the Jefferson Park pool "held me under water and almost drowned me," and that on another occasion, following a basketball game sponsored at the park, the team was chased "all the way from Pleasant Avenue to Lexington." Italians, too, expressed their fear of crossing borders. One social worker found that many children had never been to Central Park because their parents were too afraid of what might happen to them. Even groups taken on outings by adults went blocks out of their way to avoid crossing certain streets.[46] East Harlem, like Washington Heights, was divided into ethnic villages, and gangs attempted to enforce this order on the streets.

What is remarkable about this portrait is how quickly it changed. Italian East Harlem, densely populated, politically powerful, and highly organized, reached its ascendancy in the 1930s, but two decades later it seemed but a shadow of its former self. Already in the 1930s, sociologist Frederic Thrasher's research team noticed that birthrates were much lower in Italian Harlem than in the sections populated by Puerto Ricans and African Americans. Thrasher concluded that younger families, especially those that were more middle class, had begun to move out of the neighborhood.[47] This process of change slowed during the Depression and World War II. Most residents were too poor to move during the Depression. As late as 1939, the unemployment rate in Italian East Harlem was nearly 30 percent, and 10 percent of those who were working found employment on temporary public works projects. War finally brought full employment but little housing construction, and only with the end of the war could residents think about the possibility of moving to the outer reaches of the Bronx, Queens, or even the suburbs. The lure of affordable, modern, single-family housing drew younger residents away from the old neighborhood. The approximately 80,000 Italians who lived in East Harlem in 1930 declined to less than 50,000 by 1950, while over the same time period the Puerto Rican population grew from roughly 13,000 to over 63,000.[48]

Public policy also contributed to Italian Harlem's demise. Urban renewal—in the form of public housing—finished off the process the Italians themselves had started. With their political clout, it might seem surprising that East Harlem's Italians were unable to fend off public housing. In fact, East Harlem's political leaders welcomed its construction but could not predict its effects.

Some form of reconstruction of East Harlem was probably inevitable. A survey of housing done during the Depression revealed that 90 percent of the structures in East Harlem had been built before 1901; in Italian East Harlem, nearly 85 percent of the tenements lacked central heating, two-thirds lacked a tub or a shower, and over half did not have private toilets. Housing in the Puerto Rican sections was in much better shape, with a higher percentage of apartments having central heat and bathing facilities than in the city's housing as a whole. Thus it was logical for city planners, community leaders, and reformers to focus on the Italian sections as the sites most needing renewal. Italian ascendancy in politics and Mayor Fiorella La Guardia's ties to Franklin Roosevelt ensured that funds would be made available for the reconstruction of East Harlem, but few Italians would ever live in the housing that was built.

East Harlem became the home of nine public housing projects—the largest concentration of public housing in the city—which changed the social ecology of the neighborhood completely. Massive high-rises that covered whole city blocks (see the map of East Harlem) replaced small-scale tenements and brownstones and displaced many of the original residents of the area. Public housing had garnered political and public support in Italian Harlem, but by the time most of the projects were finished in the 1950s, Italian families, some with several earners, no longer met the income requirements for admission. The effect of public housing construction on Italian East Harlem can be seen by looking at the sites where housing was built: whites made up 34 percent of the site residents where the Washington Houses were built, but only 8 percent of the tenants; they were 81 percent of the site residents at the Wagner Houses, and 21 percent of the tenants; and they were 64 percent of the inhabitants at the Jefferson Houses site, and 28 percent of the tenants. While it would be an exaggeration to say that building public housing drove Italians out of East Harlem—they had been departing for over a decade—that was the perception of the inhabitants. Pete Pascale, a long-time resident of East Harlem, his voice quivering with still-felt anger, recalled that "they were making East Harlem a ghetto." As people said at the time, the bulldozers move in, the Italians move out.[49]

The decline of Italian Harlem did not mean the end of gang confrontations. Red Wings, Viceroys, Dragons, and Enchanters, among others, continued to battle, but the retreat of Italian Harlem and the declining number of Italian adolescents brought an increasing diversity in gang membership. As in Washington Heights, gangs organized within territorial limits and included members of different backgrounds as the population shifted. One youth told a reporter that " 'a lot of the clubs have kids of all nationalities, so long as they live on the block.' " Lingering Italians were included in Puerto Rican gangs and adopted their corporate identity, while the Red Wings could no longer be "just Italians" and began to recruit from Puerto Ricans living in their area. As one Puerto Rican gang member put it, "The gangs used to be strictly according to whether you were a Puerto Rican or an Italian or something like that. Now, you hear all this talk about Italian gangs and Puerto Rican gangs, but it's not all one way or the other. The Italian gang that's left up north has maybe twenty guys who are Puerto Ricans." The Enchanters, initially made up of African Americans and dark-skinned Puerto Ricans, were among the first to be organized on an interethnic basis and incorporated Italian members. Other gangs soon followed their lead.[50] The "Italian" Red Wings defended Jefferson Park, just like the "Puerto Rican" Enchanters asserted the right of Puerto Rican access to it. Like the Jesters and the Egyptian Kings, these gangs battled as corporate entities defending ethnic communities in spite of the individual makeup of their membership.

Italian East Harlem best exemplifies Gerald Suttles's model of the defended community. It was an ethnic neighborhood, seemingly anchored by churches and schools, identified by clubs and stores, defended by gangs, represented by politicians, and blessed by priests. But it melted away through suburbanization, ethnic succession, and the unanticipated results of public policy, and the Italian hold on East Harlem proved to be no more permanent than the Irish hold on Washington Heights.

Because of the centrality of change in New York's neighborhoods, many gangs could not remain ethnically homogeneous. Gangs were spatial entities, organized by neighborhood, and as those neighborhoods changed, gangs assumed a more heterogeneous ethnic membership. Despite this diversity, gang members clung to a language of ethnic exclusivity in their defense of place, but not because they were oblivious to the population shifts in their communities or ignorant of the backgrounds of fellow gang members. Diversity could be tolerated as long as individuals submerged their individual ethnic identities to the identity of the gang. Ethnicity remained of symbolic importance because it ennobled gang conflict and it elevated the status of gang members by turning them into defenders of community. Whether asserting rights of access or of citizenship, like the Dragons and the Egyptian Kings, or protecting a beleaguered community, like the Jesters and the Red Wings, adolescents were transformed into men of honor. Adolescents felt the unseen hands that remade their neighborhoods, and they lashed out at each other with ethnic honor as their rallying cry.

But ethnicity could not always be called upon as a justification for conflict. When the African-American Bishops battled the African-American Chaplains, territory—not ethnicity—explained their rivalry. As Harrison Salisbury declared, "propinquity" was a major source of conflict regardless of the ethnic makeup of the rivals.[51] The obvious question to ask is why territory was invested with so much meaning that adolescents were willing to kill, maul, or die to assert control over it. The answer lies in the fundamental difficulty of imagining oneself a man in poor or working-class neighborhoods.

*Becoming Men:*

*The Use of the Streets in*

*Defining Masculinity*

CLAUDE BROWN, in his autobiography, *Manchild in the Promised Land*, remembered the lessons of his youth: " 'Don't mess with a man's money, his woman, or his manhood.' This was the thing when I was about twelve or thirteen. This is what the gang fights were all about."[1] Some might be surprised that a thirteen-year-old had money, women, and manhood enough to defend. But "manhood" and "masculinity," the creation of a male identity, are defined culturally, and their purchase prices change over time and vary according to ethnicity and by class—in other words, by temporal, cultural, and structural factors.[2] Ethnic conflict in the 1940s brought gangs to public attention, and gangs organized themselves around the defense of place, but neither ethnicity nor place explains why adolescents joined gangs. The roots of gang membership are found in the difficult transition to manhood and in the vulnerable masculinities of working-class Euro-American, Puerto Rican, and African-American adolescents.

Evidence about gangs and masculinity can be drawn from autobiographies, oral histories, conversations recorded in gang workers' field notes, comments by gang members in studies by social workers, journalists, and academics, and my own interviews with former gang members. These sources were created for different audiences and contain only partial truths: former gang members recalled "war stories" to entertain a visitor;

radicalized activists put their gang experiences in political perspective; reporters or gang workers wanted to convey what it was like on the streets; and writers were interested in narrating a powerful story. Nonetheless, common themes emerge from these different sources about the ways in which adolescents struggled to create masculine identities. Youths encountered problems with school, the labor market, and family, and each of these will be examined in turn. Young men who rejected the demands of these principal sites of adolescent socialization found in street gangs the opportunity to win power, prestige, female adulation, and a masculine identity. The elements for this masculinity were assembled through shows of force against others and through domination over adolescent girls.

## Schools

Schools were the first mainstream institutions encountered by working-class youth, and they patterned the nature of gang members' rebellion as well as its outcome. In the first place, schools made the assertion of masculinity difficult. Attendance required submission not only to adult authority, but also to those who were different because of gender, class, and ethnic origins. The first choice facing youngsters was between cooperation and resistance, and for some youths, school provided a target for rebellion. But overt defiance of teachers or fights with other students resulted in suspension or intervention by police or social workers. Some adolescents learned to negotiate their way through school, while others skipped school without triggering some punitive action until they reached the age of sixteen, when they could drop out. The choices of truanting and dropping out materially affected an adolescent's future status. Youths who entered the labor market without having met the educational and behavioral standards conveyed by high school graduation were assured of being fit only for the low-wage, low-skill, "casual" labor that they so dreaded.[3]

Problems with school are a consistent theme in gang members' narratives, especially those of African-American and Puerto Rican youths. Differences of class between teachers and students were compounded by ethnic differences, low expectations, and, frequently, racism. Teachers rewarded behavior that gang members considered demeaning or that seemed to denigrate ethnic identity. A Puerto Rican youth recalled, "Even at that point we knew that to the extent that we became white—we would advance in school. To the extent that we spoke properly—we would get Satisfactory or Excellent on our report cards. To the extent that we conformed—we were accepted."[4] New York City schools did not offer regular bilingual instruction until 1958; prior to that, Spanish-speaking students were placed in classes below their intellectual ability or even with the mentally retarded.[5] For many average students, school meant tedium: "The subjects were so boring and teachers seemed to be more wooden than the desk you had to sit behind."[6] Some gang members found the curriculum unchallenging. For example, Carl Joyeaux, who eventually attended medical school, claimed that teachers underestimated his intellectual abilities because he was black, and his boredom with the standard curriculum led directly to his truancy and involvement in gangs.[7] Some teachers humiliated their students, especially in the face of ethnic differences: "When you go to school, like, the teacher used to tell you, 'Oh, man, you dumb—like, you nothing but a little boy,' and shit like that. So all the young brothers used to have that complex of the teacher calling them a boy, and they wanted to prove it to themselves they were a man."[8] From the gang member's perspective, the curriculum was irrelevant, the teachers prejudiced, and attendance meant submersion of a masculine self to meet (usually) female demands for obedience, silence, and order. Not only could masculinity not be won in school, it was actively subverted by school's organization and demands.

Adolescents who attended school regularly were derided as "school boys," and the term captures the contempt in which they were held. Even though gang members created elaborate gradations of status among themselves and engaged in bitter rivalries, the ultimate distinction existed between gang members—men—and school *boys*. Gang members emphasized the unmanly dependence of school boys. Claude Brown, for example, referred to them as "kids," in contrast to his friends, who were daring, tough, always in trouble, and familiar with the streets. "I felt that since I knew more about life than they [school boys] did, I had the right to regard them as kids."[9] Felipe Luciano, a former member of a Puerto Rican gang, admitted, "I was vicious when it came to fighting, simply because I didn't want to be considered a schoolboy, you know."[10] School boys sometimes had to pay protection money in order to go back and forth to school or to a job, and a school boy was always liable to be "sounded" for his "cowardice."[11] In the streets, school boys were less than equal. (Although it may have been possible to do well in school and keep the respect of more streetwise peers, it did not appear as a possibility in these sources.)

This unequal status brought some measure of safety in the neighborhood. School boys were off-limits during gang wars—contests of honor could only be fought between equals, and as one interviewee pointed out, "You could not prove you were tough by beating up someone who would not fight back."[12] On those occasions when an invading gang mistakenly attacked a school boy, gang members became incensed at the violation of the code.[13] School boys could not be legitimate targets because they belonged to the world of the subordinated.

Although they tried hard, not even gang members could fully escape this subordinated world. As long as they were under sixteen years of age, they remained subject to truancy regulations as well as parental enforcement of school attendance. Until they could legally drop out, gang members avoided school as much as possible. Claude Brown played hooky, arguing that when he went to school he only got into trouble. Usually it started with a fight with the teacher, who would send him to the principal's office. After arguing with the principal, Brown would be suspended until he came back with one of his parents. To avoid all the problems, Brown simply skipped school.[14] Piri Thomas found that it was fairly easy to duck out of school. Once attendance had been taken, he simply slipped out of his seat and snaked along the floor until he got out the door. Most of the time the other students in the class cooperated and pretended not to notice anything. Another alternative was to ask permission to go to the bathroom and then disappear.[15] Absence did not necessarily affect passing. As JT put it, "If you were tough enough, they passed you because if you went up, you wouldn't come back."[16] Joseph Fernandez, former New York City superintendent of schools, and as an adolescent, a member of a gang called the Riffs, noted in his memoirs that "school wasn't something you gave a lot of thought to, just somewhere you had to go. And I *didn't* go, very often, once I was old enough to sample the alternatives."[17] Fernandez's experience was not unusual. The New York City Youth Board found that gang members tended to quit school at the earliest possible moment and prior to that attended infrequently.[18]

When gang members attended school, they brought with them the rivalries that originated in their neighborhoods. Instead of islands of safety or neutral zones, schools, according to Kwando Kinshasa, were "for all practical purposes an extension of the street." Kinshasa's grade school was located down the block from Stitt Junior High School, one of the toughest in Harlem. "Every day at lunch time, these older bloods from Stitt would come on down to the grade school to get some lunch money." Boys had to fight, or run and be labeled a punk.[19] Schools (or, more accurately, hallways, school yards and bathrooms) either "belonged" to a particular gang to which everyone paid tribute or drew members from a number of gangs, setting the stage for conflict among them.[20] Another former gang member went to Junior High School 40, which members of the largely Puerto Rican Sportsmen and the largely African-American Crowns attended: "It was very dangerous just going to school because I wasn't a Crown or a Sportsman at the time and therefore it was open season on me for anybody."[21] As this memoir indicates, some boys joined gangs to gain protection in school. JC, in an interview, recalled being shaken down on his first day at Patrick Henry Junior High School in East Harlem. An African-American youth told him to pay two cents for the free school lunch. Refusing to pay or to be intimidated, JC agreed to fight the boy after school. That afternoon JC and several of his friends went to meet his assailant, who had brought along members of his gang. The boy then backed down, telling JC, "I didn't know you were one of the guys [i.e., a gang member]."[22]

Schools were contested territory, only the contest was not just between teachers and students, but among gangs. All gang members recognized the danger inherent in a setting that mixed boys from different neighborhoods and with different gang affiliations. Gang members who attended a school in which their gang was a minority faced continual threats. Shorty, a member of a Bedford-Stuyvesant gang, the Pythons, told his Youth Board worker that he dropped out of Boys' High in Brooklyn as soon as he turned sixteen: "See, I used to go down there and get in gang fights with the Robins [another African-American gang] . . . and get beat up by them all the time, so I decided to quit."[23] Even if gang members had found teachers welcoming, the curriculum relevant, and learning important, they still would have had to overcome their fear. (Recall the investigation of Benjamin Franklin High School, discussed in chapter 2.) It was easier not to go.

Of all the reasons for nonattendance, the most interesting is some gang members' rejection of the association between schooling and success. Despite hearing from teachers, parents, Youth Board workers, and no doubt others that completing school meant access to good jobs, some boys reacted cynically to promises of opportunity.[24] Evidence for this is fragmentary, but it is apparent that some adolescents recognized the class and ethnic barriers they would have had to surmount to complete school and obtain decent employment. They took the experiences of their parents and older friends as evidence of the futility of making the effort.

Kenneth Marshall, an African-American Youth Board worker in Brooklyn, recorded in his field notes a conversation with one boy who at least partially understood the systemic barriers to opportunity. This adolescent had quit high school just one year prior to graduation, and Marshall urged him to go back and finish his education so that he would qualify for better jobs. " 'Look at Langston,' " the youth replied. " 'He graduated from high school with the cabinet maker trade. What kind of job did he get? In a factory, that's what.' "[25] This young man probably interpreted Langston's difficult job search as resulting from racism. Although prejudiced employers may well have played a part in Langston's problems, the economy did also. In New York's declining blue-collar sectors, training for skilled occupations such as cabinetry no longer meant much. (Ironically, the factory jobs that this youth scoffed at would soon disappear as well.) The irrelevance of the school's vocational programs, the structure of the local economy, and encounters with prejudice all shaped the job possibilities and decision making of adolescents.

Among themselves, youths were even more bitter. Marshall reported a conversation in which several boys assailed "Chester," a school boy from the neighborhood. " 'Tell me something, high school boy,' " sneered one, " 'what are you studying so much for? What you think it's going to get you?' Ronny chimed in, 'Hey Chester, I hear they got you up for a Western Union job.' The other boys snickered. Bones, feigning incredulity, said, 'What you say, man? You mean Mr. High School Graduate is gonna be nothin' but a Western Union boy?' "[26] These adolescents believed that they would be shunted into low-skilled, low-paying service sector work no matter what their educational attainments—or their age.

Messenger "boys" were not always adolescents, and the job exemplified the world of dead-end work. These youngsters combined the historical significance of the term "boy" to African Americans with its school boy associations and its more obvious meaning ("Western Union boy") in the service sector to attack both Chester's decision making and his masculinity. Chester had accepted subservience in school and now was going to be a step-and-fetch-it at work. While they were already men, Chester was doomed to remain a "boy."

Experience ingrained this logic into youths. What could one say to the young man who noted that his mother had a high school diploma and, after working eighteen years as a nurse's aide, made $1.25 an hour? He commented, "I quit school to help my mother with the bills. I began making cheap jewelry at $1 an hour. And here is where I dug that the piece of paper—that diploma—didn't mean much as far as employment was concerned. My mother was just making 25 [cents] an hour more than I, and she had that piece of paper plus an eighteen-year head start."[27] Hard work meant as much in the promised land as it had in southern cotton fields or on Puerto Rican sugar plantations, and school did not seem like the way to avoid that bitter fate.

Gang members believed that the school's promise of opportunity was hollow, but this perception did not necessarily lead to a challenge to school authority. Since it was possible to drop out of school, gang members' rebellion was channeled away from school and into the streets. Resistance was expressed individually, through dropping out, and gang members never created an oppositional culture—one that actively and collectively confronted the shortcomings of the school system. Instead, the youths created an alternative culture—one that shielded them from the humiliation of school failure and the pain of discrimination and provided them with a different standard for self-evaluation. The gang offered them a stage on which their masculinity and self-worth could be proven, but it did not lead to a demand for a serviceable education. In the gang, adolescents created a refuge, where they could create their own standards of masculine achievement, try on street identities, and at least postpone a rendezvous with the labor market.[28]

Of course, not only gang members dropped out of school. A New York State Department of Labor study done in 1957 revealed that only 36 percent of males in New York City between the ages of twenty and twenty-four had completed four years of high school. The statistics, when broken down by ethnicity, revealed that 38 percent of Euro-Americans, 21 percent of Puerto Ricans, and 25 percent of non-whites and non–Puerto Ricans (i.e., African Americans and a small number of Asians) had finished four years of high school.[29] Graduation from high school had not yet become the norm for working-class New York males, and most of them did not become gang members. Nonetheless, high school was becoming an increasingly central institution in adolescent life in the 1950s—63 percent of seventeen-year-olds graduated from high school nationally in 1960—and part of a growing credentials market that regulated entry into the labor force.[30] African-American and Puerto Rican youths and those white dropouts without the family connections to get them into high-paying construction or manufacturing jobs faced a future of low-skilled, low-paying work in the service sector. Schooling, as practiced in most schools in poverty areas, certainly did not guarantee success for these youths, but rebellion against school almost certainly guaranteed failure. Gang members bore an additional burden: rebellion against school frequently meant rebellion elsewhere as well, and despite the shield offered by the juvenile court, many former gang members entered the labor market with a police record.[31]

## The Labor Market

The second major theme in gang members' narratives revolved around their encounters with the labor market. Their feelings about the marketplace were decidedly ambivalent. They desperately needed work, yet they would quit or get themselves fired after a short time on the job. While ridiculing peers who took low-paying jobs, they besieged street workers with requests to help find them factory jobs or work in a restaurant. While proclaiming their rebellious attitudes toward the boss, they humbly returned to the marketplace again and again. Gang members attempted to resolve this contradictory stance toward the marketplace by actively shaping the conditions of their employment. Frequently they worked until they had achieved some short-term objective, such as money for clothing, and then quit the job, or they used the opportunity to steal goods for their own use or for resale. By covertly resisting the authority of the employer, they could maintain an independent, manly stance, even if they thought of the work they performed as unmanly. Adolescents needed money and so the labor market, unlike the school, could not be avoided indefinitely. Rebellion was tempered by need.

The labor market was not well prepared to absorb those who left school. Young workers found that demands for experience or educational requirements limited their opportunity to gain entry-level jobs. In addition, class, gender, and ethnic factors restricted access to the labor market. The unemployment rate for New York City teenagers in 1960 was 9.6 percent, or nearly double the rate for adults, but racial and gender patterns are even more revealing: white fourteen- to nineteen-year-old males had an 11 percent unemployment rate (compared to 6 percent for females), while non-white males in the same age group had a 19 percent unemployment rate (compared to 16.5 percent for females). The labor market deflected these youths onto the streets, and in 1962 the New York City Youth Board estimated that 65,000 teenage males were out of school, out of work, and ready for trouble.[32]

Many gang members found themselves woefully unprepared for work because of their lack of attention to education. Vincent Riccio, a Youth Board worker in Gowanus, a white working-class section of Brooklyn, recorded a poignant conversation with Tommy, who confessed his terror at entering the workplace: " 'I'm fourteen and I can't read one fucking word. . . . There ain't no jobs where the boss don't say, 'Hey, kid, write down this,' or 'Add these numbers for me.' Add! Hell, I can't *write* those numbers.' " After arguing that he could still find a job, the boy told Riccio he was afraid to leave Brooklyn. Astounded that a boy who was fearless in a gang fight could become so timid, Riccio asked him what was so frightening about a subway trip to Manhattan. Tommy replied, " 'You don't have to read no street numbers to steal hubcaps. You don't have to know which subway to take to get to a rumble.' " Tommy found his way around Brooklyn only because he knew that the Coney Island subway was the "bull's eye subway," with two red circular lights indicating the route it was taking.[33] Although Tommy's case was extreme, many more boys were unfamiliar with the protocols of job hunting. Calling for appointments, dressing properly, writing letters, filling out application forms, and exhibiting appropriate behavior all posed major difficulties for them.[34]

Racism also accounted for problems in the job hunt. Street workers in the Central Harlem Street Clubs Project (a privately funded forerunner of the Youth Board's gang project) recorded one African-American gang member's hopeless plea, " 'Where does following the straight and narrow get you? Anyway, what's the use of looking for a job? Nobody wants a nigger.' "[35] Roy, of the Spanish Kings, told Steve Klein, his gang worker, that he feared rejection because of his Spanish accent, while Piri Thomas recounted how he and a light-skinned Puerto Rican friend interviewed for jobs as door-to-door salesmen. His friend was hired immediately while Thomas was told to wait for a call back when "new territory" opened up.[36] The Brooklyn office of the Youth Board was sufficiently concerned about racial discrimination to call up prospective employers who listed jobs with them to see if African-American boys would be hired. "About 50 percent have specified that they cannot take Negro boys because 'I'm not prejudiced myself, but my customers wouldn't like it.' "[37] These adolescents' fears of discrimination and their expectations of poor treatment were well founded.

Once they had jobs, adolescents found they were a disposable and a readily exploited commodity. Kenneth Marshall discovered that the gang members with whom he worked were frequently asked to work overtime and rarely given any extra pay, "nor did any of them really know how much they were being paid. When, with my help, they computed the hourly wage, they saw that it was far below the legal seventy-five cents minimum."[38] Adolescents "knew" they were exploited even if the conditions under which exploitation occurred remained mysterious.

Gang members also learned from observing their parents' encounters in the labor market as garment workers, launderers, cooks, and maids. Joseph Fernandez's parents were typical: "My dad did anything to make a buck. He ironed sheets and mended shirts at the Commodore Hotel on 42nd Street. He washed windows on skyscrapers, worked as a deliveryman for a handkerchief factory, drove cabs, drove trolleys, drove buses. My mother worked, too, when she could, as a seamstress . . . then for some time as a maid at Columbia University."[39] Gang members were not trapped in a culture of poverty nor did they lack a work ethic. Rather, they knew that their parents' jobs involved low pay, little security, high turnover, and no future, and that despite their hard work, the families remained desperately poor and still required occasional assistance from the welfare office. The message was clear: society did not respect or reward hard work and honest labor by the poor.

Gang members and their families had such a difficult time in the marketplace because they were limited to the secondary labor market. That is, they entered a labor market that was divided internally into segments—a primary labor market that was itself divided, and a secondary labor market. While positions in the primary sector paid reasonably well, with benefits, security, and opportunity for advancement, jobs in the secondary labor market were created by companies on the periphery of the core or primary economy. These companies had smaller profit margins and suffered from greater competition with other firms. They therefore had less liberal labor management policies and provided lower-paying jobs with few or no benefits and experienced high turnover among employees.[40]

African-American and Puerto Rican youth entering the secondary sector of the labor market were doomed to stay there. Though nearly all youths began with these sorts of jobs, as white workers aged and gained experience, they generally advanced into more secure and higher-paying positions. As seen in chapter 1, they had the advantage of ethnic niches that provided them with a means of entry into a job network. Minority group members consistently found themselves excluded and limited to the low-wage sector, regardless of their work history.[41] Based on the experience of his relatives and friends, a gang member could reasonably conclude that " 'even if they hire you, they'll only pay you beans and give you the dirtiest job in the place.' "[42] The only jobs open were the ones " 'where you could save your money for a thousand years and still wind up with nothing.' "[43] Asked about job opportunities in his youth, one former gang member scoffed, "Sure you could find jobs—if you wanted to be a busboy."[44] African-American youths found jobs in the garment district pushing clothing trucks along the street—"working for Mr. Goldberg"—and as messenger boys, but dismissed these sorts of jobs as "slaves" or "yokes."[45] The language is evocative: employment in the low-wage sector of the economy was the equivalent of chattel slavery. Young men were no better than draft animals "yoked" to a plow, fated to remain harnessed and driven.

There was very little in a job as a slave or a yoke to sustain a masculine identity. Periodic layoffs, low wages, few benefits, disrespect for the value

of one's labor, and little possibility for improvement emphasized marginality, lack of power, and subservience—not the qualities needed for the
creation of masculinity. Encounters with the labor market delivered body
blows to masculine self-respect, and gang members regarded the market
place warily.

Despite their experience with the labor market and their largely accurate assessments of what their future as unskilled labor would bring,
many gang members still hoped to become gainfully employed. They
continually discussed how to look for work, asked friends how they were
faring in their jobs, or requested information from their street workers
about the availability of jobs. Youth Board workers frequently used their
ability to connect boys to the labor market as their "in" with the gang.
Adults hanging around street corners trying to make contact with street
gang members were almost universally suspected as being police officers,
narcotics pushers, or homosexuals. But an introduction by a local priest
or minister as a "job man" invariably meant acceptance for the gang
worker.[46] Because of their poverty, gang members attempted to gain entry
into the legitimate world even as they created an alternative world in
the gang.

Gang members resolved their ambivalence about the job market by
trying to control the conditions of their labor. They resented the regular-
ity and discipline of the workplace and they responded by skipping work,
pilfering from the stock room, or fooling around on the job. (Of course,
participation in the hidden or underground economy through theft and
trading in stolen goods characterizes employee behavior in many settings
and certainly is not limited to the poor.)[47] Youths quit their jobs because
of real or perceived discrimination or because they realized they were
being crassly exploited. "Otto" reported to the Youth Board that he
worked a variety of jobs, but he never held them for very long. For example, "He had worked for two days as a dishwasher in a restaurant, but
the fact that he worked there brought so many of the fellows into the
restaurant, he had been let go."[48] Steve Klein found that Roy, a member
of the Spanish Kings, who had worked as a shipper, requested a raise
shortly after being hired. The boss explained that he was a good worker
but that he could not be paid more than the other workers who had been
there longer. Three weeks later Roy quit and "seemed bitter about the
experience."[49] Another one of the Spanish Kings told Klein that if he got

angry at the boss, " 'Fuck him—I just leave the job.' "[50] Manny Torres summed up the gang member's response to minimum wage jobs when he declared, "Society . . . needs niggers, and they'll take 'em where they can find 'em, regardless of color. But I'm not going to do it!"[51]

Despite high unemployment rates, discrimination, and lack of education, gang members' experience with the market was less of exclusion than of episodic involvement. They found jobs, quit them or were fired, spent time looking for other jobs, and then repeated the process. Because they were adolescents, most did not have significant financial obligations and could endure periods of unemployment and be somewhat cavalier about their lack of skill and periodic layoffs. They had more of an opportunity to be agents, even if factors of class, ethnicity, and power constricted their level of agency. Bringing friends into a restaurant and giving them food, stealing merchandise from employers, and working long enough to earn the price of some consumer good were means of resisting exploitation, of demonstrating defiance of the marketplace, of proving that one had some shred of masculine independence. Adolescents participated in the marketplace, but they did so according to their own terms as much as possible.[52]

Of course, these were short-term strategies. Just as gang members manifested their resistance to school by dropping out and then suffered the consequences of a poor education, they responded to the marketplace by quitting jobs or getting themselves fired, and then remained trapped in a secondary labor market. Their reaction to exploitation or discrimination was individual rebelliousness. They did not "oppose" the market or organize to challenge its authority; instead, the gang served as a source of support in their individual rebellions. But the gang could do nothing to change the conditions under which they labored, and sooner or later poverty forced them to confront the marketplace again. The labor market structured the gang member's experience of work and resistance, just as the school patterned his form of adolescent rebellion.

## FAMILY RELATIONS

Relationships with family members form the third theme found in gang members' narratives. Gang members sometimes referred to the gang as a family, which suggests its alternative role to their own families.

This did not mean that families were absent from gang members' lives. Gang members came from two- and single-parent families, from families where parents worked hard, from families enmeshed in street life, and from families disrupted by drugs or alcohol. One common theme found in discussions of family life was an adolescent's failure to discover an appropriate model of masculinity. Sometimes youths rejected a model based on honorable labor, and other times they lacked such a model; in both cases they found an alternative on the streets. Men on the corner, pimps, criminals, gamblers, and petty hustlers were a constant reminder that masculinity could be defined aggressively, independently, and arrogantly through street life. Gangs proved an apprenticeship for earning a street identity.

Claude Brown, Carl Joyeaux, Piri Thomas, Joseph Fernandez, and many of the gang members I interviewed came from two-parent families. Nearly all of them tried to hide their gang membership from their parents ("my mother would have had a fit" was one refrain). Since street-corner groups were ubiquitous in these neighborhoods, a boy's denial of membership in a gang or a defense that police arrested him just because he was hanging out on the corner seemed quite plausible. Gang membership could be hidden for some time, especially by those members on the periphery of the group. Core members, however, had too many brushes with police and too many bruises—or worse—from rival gangs to be able to deceive parents indefinitely. They suffered harsh discipline when detected as truants or arrested by police, and many endured parental beatings as the price of gang membership.

These adolescents went beyond ordinary adolescent rebellion; their gang membership threatened the continuation of normal familial relationships. Youths rejected their parents' way of life and responded to parental discipline by staying away from home, which was referred to as a "prison," and finding their freedom through the gang. These youths repudiated not their families so much as the conditions imposed on their families by the labor market and the welfare system. They were determined to live differently and dreaded the possibility that they would follow in their parents' footsteps.[53]

Because they feared becoming like their fathers, gang members rarely discussed them in admiring terms. One observer of East Harlem wrote of one boy, "Matthew grew up with a sense of defeat from the start because he saw only beaten men around him, men with no fight left in them, men like his father."[54] Though this smacks of melodrama, it captures the sense of foreboding adolescents must have felt when approaching adulthood and seeing the dead-end lives led by many adult males in the neighborhood. Dion DiMucci, the rock 'n' roll star and a member of the Fordham Baldies, wrote that his father never managed to hold a steady job and allowed his wife to support the family, which earned him the contempt of male family members: "It was hard to respect a man like that and, for me, respect was everything."[55] Claude Brown also recorded the devastating impact of seeing his father grovel before a judge: "And I used to think he was a real bad nigger. But not after that. I knew now that he was just a head nodder."[56] If the legitimate world stripped their fathers of the ability to maintain masculine identities, then the sons would turn to the illegitimate world for father figures. Gangs attracted the rebellious, those who were tough enough to try on a street identity, and who, like Claude Brown, dared to be "men" at age twelve or thirteen.[57]

When adolescents looked for ways to assemble masculine identities, they inevitably encountered the criminals, hustlers, and former gang members of the neighborhood. These men had money, women, cars, and expensive clothes and offered a tempting counterpoint to those who "yoked" and led lives that were drab and difficult. Henry Hill saw his hardworking father never able to afford a vacation or to move out of their cramped house, and he vowed not to follow in his path. As a youngster, he ran errands for Paulie Vario, a member of the Lucchese crime family, who provided a model of masculine power and authority: "To me being a wiseguy was better than being president of the United States. It meant power among people who had no power. It meant perks in a working-class neighborhood that had no privileges." By contrast, working men such as his father "were already dead."[58]

Youths grew up in neighborhoods where gangs were a fixture and provided an opportunity to try on a street identity. Bobby reported that "when I was a kid, the gangs were a very big thing. It was like hero worship. The heroes of the block were the Bad Motherfuckers and the Wizards. They were the thing we wanted to be."[59] Carl Joyeaux grew up on a block in Brooklyn controlled by the Bishops, and he recalled that all the small boys "imitated their insolent strut."[60] Street life beckoned to

youths from their earliest years in these neighborhoods as a way of defining masculinity.

Some adolescents carried on the tradition of male relatives or other
neighborhood males who had been gang members. They understood
that they inherited responsibility for maintaining the reputation of the
neighborhood and that the eyes of their elders were upon them, measuring them to see if they lived up to the masculine ideals created for them.
JT developed a fearsome reputation as president of East Harlem's Viceroys, but creating a street identity was made easier because he followed
in his two older brothers' footsteps.[61] RG explained that the Fordham
Dagger Juniors became the Fordham Baldie Juniors after receiving permission from both groups of seniors. The Baldies were a more well-
known and feared group and their reputation better fit the desires of the
Dagger Juniors. RG's was the third generation of Baldies in the Bronx's
Arthur Avenue area, with a lineage going back to the Depression.[62] Gang
members were chided if the older males in the neighborhood thought
they were letting down the reputation of the gang. When members of
the Robins came to visit a girl in the territory of the former Greene
Avenue Stompers, an older youth called the younger boys punks for letting strangers come into the area. " 'I mean, like if a guy didn't live in
the neighborhood, he wouldn't dare show his ass anywhere around here.
Man, this corner right here—two, three years ago—used to be the *baddest*
in the city. Even the cops used to be afraid to come through here.' " He
believed that the younger boys needed a pep talk to remind them of the
honor that was theirs to defend.[63]

While some youths rejected models of masculinity based on work,
others had no model to reject and fled to the gang from disrupted or
abusive families. Gang worker Vincent Riccio described the situation
among the Euro-American gang members with whom he worked in
Brooklyn, where alcoholism among the longshoremen was a common
problem and poverty haunted the households. Some women supported
their families through prostitution with the sailors and dockworkers
from the Brooklyn waterfront; one boy confided in Riccio that "he found
his mother in bed . . . five times with different guys" when he came home
unexpectedly.[64] Another youngster, whose father had deserted his family,
recalled waiting for the welfare check at the end of the month when food
was scarce: "My brother, sister, and myself used to fight each other for

scraps of food on the table."[65] Mario, whose father allegedly began drinking after his experiences as a medic in World War II, recalled that his father tried to do the right thing, "but the alcohol just wouldn't let him." His mother resisted his father's beatings and finally they separated; Mario reported that he saw his father every couple of years.[66] Narratives of beatings, alcoholism, occasionally drug abuse, and, of course, intense poverty framed decisions to stay away from home and to create an alternative world with one's peers in the gang. Gang members from disrupted families relied on each other for emotional support as much as for anything else.[67]

Perhaps the best evidence for the familial support provided by the gang comes from Vincent Riccio's oral history. Riccio maintained that the kids "actually like each other" and shared whatever they could. "They have sympathy towards one another. They're always sorry for the guy who has to sleep in the cars because he was kicked out of the house, and one always tells him to 'come to my house' if it's possible, if he can sneak him in, if his mother didn't mind."[68] Boys without money for a show or a meal were treated by the others, while those without clean clothes for a dance could expect someone to step forward and loan them some.[69] Members reported that the gang was sympathetic to the situation of those on parole. JS, who had been the war counselor for his gang, told Kenneth Marshall that the gang would support him in "cooling" his role. " 'Yes, sir . . . they even tell you to,' " knowing that JS would get in even more trouble if arrested again.[70]

Members sometimes described the gang in romantic terms, emphasizing the support it provided. Speaking of one member's effort to kick a drug habit, the president of the "Cherubs" said, " 'We told the guy he didn't kick the habit, he was out of the crew. We were *through* with him. So he kicked it. Cold turkey.' "[71] Even if this was not literally true, it expresses a metaphoric truth: members believed that the gang provided support and saw them through tough times, and this belief cemented the relationships within the gang. Reporter Robert Rice accompanied gang worker Nestor Llamas on his rounds with his gang, the "Avengers," and recorded a conversation in which "Louie" described his reliance on the gang to help him break his drug habit. " 'Now it's different because I'm with the guys [gang]. A couple of guys came the other day, man, they had just seen the connection and they're going to get a straight, and they say, 'Come on, Louie, come on, man. We got the coins.' I say, 'No good, man.' I felt no urge.' " Louie admitted that he sometimes still wanted to score a "nickel" but, he added, " 'the guys want me to be good.' "[72] When *New York Times* journalist Harrison Salisbury asked a member of the Cobras what the purpose of the club was, he replied that it was a social club made up of friends who were " 'all for one and one for all.' "[73] Again and again, gang members discussed the gang in terms of protection, security, and community identity.[74] The gang served as "family"; in fact, for a gang member such as Felipe Luciano, the gang constituted his whole social world. As Luciano maintained, " 'We had our gang, we had our identity, we had our own community.' "[75]

Romanticism aside, it is clear that the gang provided adolescents with a sense of belonging, solidarity, and community that was missing elsewhere in their lives. For some boys, the gang formed a replacement for an absent or dysfunctional family, one that helped them survive the harshness of street life. For others, the gang supported them in their rebellion against their families and the impoverished world in which they lived. Like schools and the labor market, families pushed the rebellious into the street.

## Masculinity

Gang members defined their masculinities in the streets through their relationships among themselves and with girls. Gang members organized their own norms, codes of behavior, and rituals and created a distinctive "subculture" as a refuge from the pressures of working-class life.[76] The gang culture they created provided standards for measuring the achievement of masculinity. However, gang culture was vulnerable, the gang world was heavily mediated, and the masculinities that gang members created were precariously defined.

Gang members' masculinities were insecure for two reasons. The first was external: the gang through its activities provoked intervention by the police, the Youth Board, and other agencies, which reinforced a sense of vulnerability. The second reason was internal to the gang world: a gang member's masculinity rested on a street reputation that invited challenge by other gang members.

Gangs inevitably encountered public agencies that had different no-
tions about who controlled the streets. Truant officers pursued those
under sixteen who did not attend school; police moved them off street
corners, subjected them to random searches, and watched for violations
of the law; judges sentenced those found guilty of crimes; probation officers pushed them into the labor market or into training programs; and
street workers entered their candy store hangouts and clubhouses. Already marginalized because of class and frequently ethnicity, gang members had their sense of marginality reinforced at every turn. Even the
gang was subject to pressure, reminding gang members how fragile their
creations were.

Pressures internal to the gang world also made masculinity difficult to
maintain. A gang member's proudest achievement—his reputation for
toughness, bravery, shrewdness, and "heart," in sum, his masculinity—
was never above challenge. It rested not on ascribed status, in the possession of a skill, or in material production, but on the quality of his public
performance as judged by his peers. Whether participating in a rumble,
engaging in verbal jousting by "sounding," "toasting," or "playing the
dozens," competing with a rival for the affection of a girl, or being especially vicious in attacking a foe, a gang member knew that his performance was being weighed. Masculinity was negotiated on the streets
before an audience attentive to the nuances of public insult, and though
minor slights from inferiors might be ignored, challenges from peers
went to the core of one's masculinity. Masculinity was defined and maintained in the complex interplay between younger males seeking to enhance their reputations by besting others through hustles or in fights and
older males defending the status they had earned. Masculinity depended
on meeting the next challenge, on continuously eliciting bravos from the
audience.[77]

Violence against others, including adolescent females, was the surest
way of assembling a masculine identity. The violent act negated the
shame of poverty and allowed an adolescent the opportunity to imagine
himself as a person who could exercise power, who could intimidate others through terror, and who would exact revenge for a perceived slight.
While the model of the street criminal was available to adolescents of all
ethnic backgrounds, it was particularly alluring for African Americans.
Historian Lawrence Levine has excavated the figure of the "badman"

from African-American folklore. The badman, a stock character in folk-tales, inspired fear in all, including whites, with his pure evil. He epito-mized racial rebelliousness, becoming a heroic figure even to those who did not follow his example. All African-American adolescents recognized the "badman," who frequently stood no farther away than the nearest street corner. For Puerto Ricans and Euro-Americans as well, the neigh-borhood was populated by toughs and wiseguys. While school, family, and the labor market demanded subservience and promised humiliation, the street—and the gang where adolescents could model a street per-sona—afforded status, power, and entry to manhood.[78]

Gang boys displayed their masculinity on a public stage in rituals of violence enacted before their peers. Elaborately negotiated "fair ones" (fistfights between the champions of their respective gangs), rumbles be-tween gangs, and raids into enemy turf involved displays of courage in defense of honor. These contests allowed participants to be rank ordered and determined the hierarchy of the gang. Gangs formed what might be termed a brutal brotherhood.

Membership in a gang provided a boy with pride and respect, which the legitimate world could not supply. Claude Brown recalled that he and his friends looked upon themselves as the "aristocracy" of the neighbor-hood, members of what sociologist Jack Katz referred to as the "street elite." Gang membership conveyed a sense of superiority to others in the community who, in Brown's words, "didn't know anything."[79] Bobby described the sense of self-worth he derived from the gang: "It was like you were trying to say to the world, 'This is *me*, man, I'm alive, you dig, and I got somethin', and I live in this community, and I'm somebody here. I'm a leader. . . .' Especially if you were a leader of a gang."[80] Walk-ing down the street and having adults make room for you on the sidewalk conveyed a sense of the power that came from being in a gang with a reputation for being tough.[81] "All you had was your turf," Bobby said, "there was nothing else. All you had was this pride in being an *hombre*, in being bad and taking care of your people."[82]

The elite had to fight to improve or maintain reputations. Gangs usu-ally organized themselves offensively or defensively. That is, like individ-ual members, they were "image promoters," seeking to build a fearsome reputation, or "image defenders," content to remain in their turf but aware of slights to honor and ready to take on any invaders.[83] Offensive gangs sought to spark conflict as a way of taking over new territory, luring new members, or simply of gaining a reputation as "bad." Offensive gangs were frequently "juniors" seeking to inherit the mantle of an older group or to establish their own reputation. The aggression of the group was related to the individual's drive for status. News of a successful raid spread rapidly and drew in new recruits anxious to share an aggressive group's reputation for toughness and eager to establish their own street presence. Image promoters anticipated the opportunity to best a rival and sought out situations in which rivals might be provoked.[84] Though defensive groups—frequently older, established gangs—did not seek out conflict, they did not avoid it either because that was dishonorable and might suggest that they were "turning punk" and in danger of losing masculinity as well as reputation. As one former gang member wrote, "Gangs were the only symbols of masculinity in the ghettos of America," and perceived threats to that masculinity could not be ignored.[85] Thus conflicts started easily, with rumors of insults or a simple walk down the block sufficient to spark a confrontation.

Gang members gained their reputations as masculine tough guys through individual acts of courage. These actions, performed before an audience, were discussed and evaluated, and if notable enough, were re-told and relived afterward. Such tales, often embellished, formed the lore of the gang, announced its place in gang cosmology, and informed initi-ates of the reputation they were expected to uphold. In one such story, ES, a warlord for the Dragons from East Harlem, together with one other Dragon chased members of the archrival Italian Red Wings deep into their turf—while carrying only an empty pistol. This established ES's reputation and proved that the Dragons had more heart—and were better men—than their foes.[86] A certain bravado, such as standing in the middle of the street and challenging members of a rival group to shoot, as Carl Joyeaux did, distinguished the leaders from the followers and justified the deference they were given. "Ronny," a leader of the junior division of Brooklyn's Greene Avenue Stompers, earned the respect of older gang members as well as the admiration of other gangs by refusing to run in gang fights and beating those members of his gang who did. When the Stompers' gang worker, Kenneth Marshall, visited the rival Nit Hill, one of the Nits asked about Ronny and commented: " 'That Ronny was a *down* little stud back in the days we was bopping strong.' "[87] By showing they had heart, gang members gained honor and status among friends and foes alike. Reputation was the currency of the streets, and the individual who amassed it stood atop his peers, the "baddest" and most manly of all.

Part of securing this identity involved the willingness to use violence, which was an integral part of the gang member's persona. Youngsters seeking to gain reputation searched for opportunities to prove to their peers that they could be more awful than anyone else. Manny Torres recalled that as a thirteen-year-old member of the Stars, he would walk around with his chest out, bumping into people and hoping they would object, so he could "pounce on them and beat 'em into the goddamn concrete."[88] This willingness to act violently with no show of mercy proved how hard and how manly he really was. Violence was curiously impersonal, part of an aura that was developed for its own sake. Adults, even those familiar with gangs, did not always understand this. A youngster who had walked into the middle of a gang fight between the Nits and the Gents described a vicious stabbing to Kenneth Marshall. Marshall assumed that the Nit had a personal grudge against the other boy, but he was told, " No. He didn't even know him. He was just one of the guys they caught, that's all.' "[89] If violence was masculine, mercy was equated with weakness, a sign of effeminacy. Acting with brutality, treating an enemy as if he were not even human, just an object to be stomped and torn, assured the gang member that he was really a man.

The need to be brutal could override any other considerations. Past ties meant little if youths were in rival gangs, even if, as sometimes happened, they had grown up together or shared previous gang membership. For example, Kenneth Marshall found out that a former El Quinto, who had defected to the Chaplains, "knifed several of his former buddies" in a gang fight.[90] What was important was not the object of violence, but violence itself. It was the willingness to "burn" a rival in a drive-by shooting, to stab another boy in a gang fight, or to stomp someone unlucky enough to be caught without his friends that proved that one had heart and deserved to be a member of the gang. Nicky Cruz, a member and later president of the Mau Maus, recalled the exhilaration he felt after his first rumble: "I felt good. I had seen blood run. I had shot someone, maybe killed him."[91] This was the gang member's baptism, his initiation into the elite. Through violence, he acquired a reputation and proved he was a man.

The process of creating and protecting a reputation began very early. Even young boys were encouraged to settle differences through fighting, a theme that Claude Brown returns to repeatedly in his autobiography. Fights between little boys drew an audience of both peers and adults, who urged them on to see which one was tougher. The winner was accorded respect and earned the right to strut through the neighborhood. The fights established a pecking order on the street, and lower-ranked boys deferred to those who could beat them. At the top, however, boys jostled for position and struggled to maintain the reputations that earned them respect on the street. As he got older, Brown was expected to take on bigger kids, which meant that he had to become more vicious in order to beat them. Brown gradually began to feel the weight of his reputation. Fists no longer were sufficient to sustain it, and Brown feared that soon he would be expected to kill someone to preserve his status: "[I]f I didn't, I would lose my respect in the neighborhood."[92] Adolescents constructed masculinity through the repeated performance of violence before an audience and came to feel that they had no choice but to heed the curtain call. Piri Thomas echoed the same theme. Through challenging and fighting the leader of the gang on his new block to a draw, Thomas felt that he had established himself. But he noted that he could not afford to relax: "In Harlem you always lived on the edge of losing rep. All it takes is a one-time loss of heart."[93]

Loss of heart brought shame and devastating rejection. A boy who ran or failed to show up for a rumble suffered physical chastisement, the disdain of his peers, and the mockery of local girls. A repeat offense meant a severe beating and expulsion from the gang, for a failure of heart was equated with the loss of manhood. Someone who was cowardly became a non-person without friends and self-respect. While a good fight, even if resulting in a loss, was usually enough to maintain status, this was not always the case. When one of his friends told Claude Brown that another friend, Bucky, had been voted out of the gang, Brown protested that Bucky was one of his oldest friends. But he agreed with the decision when he heard that Bucky had been beaten up by a white boy. "When I heard this, there was nothing I could do. . . . That kind of news spread fast, and who wanted to be in a clique with a stud who let a paddy beat him?"[94] When the stakes were so high, such hints of weakness had to be eliminated.

A reputation was a fragile commodity, always on parade and open to challenge. Public insult or humiliation had to be met, however difficult the circumstances, to appease the honor-based code. Gang members were marginal members of the labor force who had dropped out of school, most were poor, and the African Americans and Puerto Ricans had experienced racism and discrimination. They had no accumulated social capital to cushion them from a challenge, which went to the core of their masculine identities. As Bobby explained, " 'If you were a bad motherfucker you had a rep, and you'd die for your rep if somebody fucked with it because that's all you had.' " Masculinity that had no structural supports other than reputation was always vulnerable and trapped its bearer in escalating cycles of violence.[95]

## NEGOTIATING GENDER

Gender identities are not created in isolation from one another, and gang members negotiated masculinity through their relationships with girls. Gang members' attitudes about sexuality and gender were part of a widespread "working-class sex code."[96] Gang members frequently viewed girls in a purely instrumental fashion, and intimacy—with its demand for openness and vulnerability—seemed difficult or even beyond their reach. Relationships with girls simply provided another realm of competition among males in which gang members established precedence over one another, or they provided an opportunity for gang members to reaffirm their bonds. Gang boys earned respect by getting girls, either for themselves or for fellow gang members, for ritualized rape.

Single-sex peer groups—both gangs and street-corner groups—were nearly universal in working-class and poor neighborhoods. One aspect of social settings dominated by male peer groups is the tendency to define girls and women as part of a subordinated "other." As anthropologist Peggy Sanday has argued, socializing males within a segregated setting—

regardless of class—reifies male dominance and nurtures the seeds of violence against women. While some women in working-class neighborhoods were protected and gained power through their incorporation within the family, those outside of the family system were fair game for exploitation and rape. In addition, the family did not protect women against domestic violence. The behavior of gang members toward girls and young women should be understood in this context. Their activities existed along a continuum of "normal" male behavior, with only a short distance between domination and force. Gang members were at one end of that continuum, but their expressions of sexual violence were not far removed from those of other men, especially in single-sex settings.[97]

The categorization of girls within the gang world reflected the dichotomy between the protected and the unprotected and shows how easily these lines blurred. Gang members divided girls into three groups: "debs," "lays," and "nice girls." Debs were partners or gang "wives" to the members, and they acted as spies during times of intergang tension, went along on raids, and concealed weapons for the boys. They frequently were organized into their own groups, usually with names that were the female diminutives of the male gang name (i.e., the Rangers' debs would be the "Rangerettes"), but with their own leaders and forms of initiation. Debs played an important, quasi-independent role in the gang and were distinguished from "lays," who were used exclusively for sexual purposes. However, if a deb broke up with her boyfriend, she had the choice of dropping out of the group or taking up with another member. The latter choice involved some danger, since the new boyfriend would be teased mercilessly about taking a "cast-off" and might be induced to break up with her on that account. If she continued to hang around the group, her status might quickly descend to that of a lay. As Kenneth Marshall pointed out, "Once a girl had a reputation for promiscuity she was hard pressed to refuse any boy who made a pass at her since he might then force her to submit."[98] Carl Joyeaux recalled, "Bams were what we called our female auxiliary members, from the jingle, 'bam, ram, thank you ma'am,'" and he stated that "if a bam refused a guy, he would slap her in the puss."[99] Debs had status, derived from their relationships to male gang members and from the useful services they provided the gang, while lays were free for the taking and subject to the threat of rape. The line between the two was easy to cross and whether or not a girl did so depended on her skill in negotiating her relationships with male gang members.

"Nice girls," not debs, were gang members' serious girlfriends, and they were outside the world of the streets. Nice girls existed within the protected category, in the system of chaperonage, church groups, and school. A gang member might seek a serious girlfriend from outside the neighborhood, where his gang membership might be unknown and where a girl's sexual history would be unknown to the gang. As gang worker Vincent Riccio recalled, the gang member's attitude toward girls was that "everybody lays, everybody should lay . . . with the exception of the girl he's going with, who's a nice girl."[100] However, intimacy, when it was found, brought its own set of constraints. Choosing a steady girlfriend offered a gang member a way out of the street, if he wanted to use it. "Going steady" required a regular source of money and was cited by observers and gang members as a reason for leaving the gang.[101] For those who tired of the personal costs of street life, a serious relationship with a girl provided an acceptable escape (this is discussed further in chapter 6), but it also meant entering the world of casual labor. Dating a nice girl therefore posed a serious dilemma—did one seek love and intimacy and face being forced back into a labor market that undermined one's sense of manliness, or did one forgo them to remain in the shelter of the gang where masculinity could be maintained?

If boys felt ambivalent about their relationships with nice girls, the pervasive ethos of conquest offered an easy way out. One way for a gang member to acquire status, aside from fighting, was through the conquest or pretended conquest of girls. Piri Thomas noted that "getting yourself a chick was a rep builder. . . . It was part of becoming *hombre*." Bob Collier recalled that "one of the girls I was laying the love rap to was thought of as the finest sister downtown, and I knew if I could make it with her, it would raise my standing a lot." Boys bragged about "getting over" (persuading a girl to have sex because of a good rap), which earned special praise when the girl was not known to be promiscuous. Having sex proved a girl did not deserve the nice girl distinction, while bragging about it added to a boy's renown. Of course, sexual conquest was not at all unique to gang members, although it may have been accentuated by the competitive process of defining masculinity in the gang setting.[102]

Hostility and suspicion frequently characterized the individual relationships between boys and girls. Several sources mentioned that boys used
condoms only if a girl insisted and then, to get even, pricked a hole in
the bottom with a pin.[103] Pregnancy was the girl's problem. As Carl Joyeaux put it when his girlfriend told him that he was becoming a father,
" 'That's a smile. . . . The whole club and his brother have been banging
you.' " When she protested that she was sure he was the father, he replied, " 'Stop jivin'. Any how, what difference does it make?' "[104] Kenneth
Marshall observed members of the gang he worked with sitting on a
stoop when a group of girls, including the pregnant ex-girlfriend of one
of the boys, walked by. The boys began singing a popular song, "Because
of You." "At one point when they had reached the words 'Because of
You' D. O. [the former boyfriend] yelled out, 'You got your belly full!' "
which provoked peals of laughter. One of the other boys suggested they
throw something at the girls. "Somebody got the idea of filling up a bottle
of urine and throwing it. . . . The bottle was passed around until it was
filled. Several of the boys regretted that they had no contribution to offer.
[A.] took the bottle and gave it to D. O. saying, 'Here, man, now wait till
you get right up on them before you throw it.' "[105] Getting over, getting
a girl pregnant, making a fool of a girl, or publicly mistreating her proved
a gang member's independence and fed his male ego. These were tri-
umphs of masculinity that increased a boy's esteem in the eyes of his
peers.

Girls from outside the neighborhood were both objects of desire and
suspicion. Boys earned honors by taking girls from other neighborhoods
who were the "property" of other gangs, but at the same time they worried that the girls might be spies or agents sent to set up a gang member.
JP, in a conversation with Kenneth Marshall, told him he refused to walk
his girlfriend home because she lived in Assassins' territory and her
brother was a member of the gang. He feared his girl would lead him
into an ambush. When Marshall said it was unlikely that someone with
whom he was sexually intimate would do such a thing, JP asserted that
it was not at all unusual and that his gang set up rivals this way all the
time.[106] Deception undermined the apparent search for intimacy, and suspicion between the sexes reinforced the notion that only one's peers were
a source of genuine friendship and support.

"Line-ups" or gang rapes followed naturally from the fraternity of the gang. Rape occurred in a ritualized fashion that cemented ties among the gang members and celebrated their shared male dominance. Just like a stomping victim's blood provided a communal baptism, anointing the participants as members of an elite, the rape victim's body served as a sexual communion, joining the participants together, assuring them of their power, and providing an appropriately masculine alternative to heterosexual intimacy.

Gang members treated rape as an ordinary experience. The street workers from the Harlem Street Clubs project found that line-ups were the subject of amusing stories told in bull sessions among the boys. They found the boys laughing as one recounted, " 'When I came along Pluck had just finished and I went over to the girl. She said, 'Pluck said he was going to be the only one.' I said to her, 'What did you say?' I picked up my fist. She started to argue and I said, 'Come on move your leg over.' "[107] Considerable status accrued to the gang member who acquired a girl for a line-up. A particularly handsome or suave individual might take a girl out on a date and then "bring her to his neighborhood and not only score, he would also get her to be involved with two or three other of his friends." Vincent Riccio—from the perspective of the 1950s—claimed that the gang members he worked with "very seldom" used a threat of violence; on most occasions "the girls were willing to lay."[108] Jerry Della Famina recalled that one or two girls in his Brooklyn neighborhood submitted to group intercourse, which he did not consider rape "because they went along with it." But he also noted that the girls "always came from the lowest-level intelligence grading in the schools."[109] Alcohol or drugs were used to incapacitate a girl and therefore physical force probably was not necessary. Daniel Belknap, a Youth Board worker in Brooklyn, persuaded the members of the Pythons to intervene in a gang rape taking place in the park. One of the boys admitted that he felt bad because " 'that girl goes for me. She wanted me to fuck her and I don't think she cared when you [another gang member] came around, but now she's got all those guys in the park; she'll be there until morning.' " When the group went to get her, Belknap noted that she seemed very groggy and had difficulty walking, but he commented, "I felt that she was almost willing."[110]

The comments of gang members and gang workers alike indicate how unproblematic line-ups were. (Their openness is a striking contrast to the present. Anthropologist Philippe Bourgois called the subject of rape taboo for discussion and only after months of fieldwork did his informants speak to him about it. No one that I interviewed broached the topic.[111]) Rape was interpreted from within a working-class sex code shared by street worker and gang member alike in which girls "knew" what would happen if they continued to hang out on the streets and therefore bore responsibility for it. Rape, violence, and consent were not issues, and the ethos of conquest ensured that they would not be raised. Gang members recounted their exploits proudly and did not differentiate between voluntary and forced intercourse when counting coups. In the homosocial world of the gang, girls—debs, lays, and nice girls alike—possessed value only in their relationship to a gang member as a marker of status, an object of pleasure, or an opportunity for group bonding. Violence against them was a natural and unquestioned consequence.

Rape, like other gang activities, followed an established protocol. The line-up encapsulated the gang members' relationships with one another, with each individual's measure of prestige and masculinity precisely calibrated by his place in line. The individual who brought the girl to the group generally went first, followed by the other members in order of status. Riccio recalled that Mousie, the butt of gang humor and the lowest status member, always went last. Riccio also told of another occasion when Sonny, then one of the leaders, contracted gonorrhea in a line-up, but no one else did. Sonny declared, "'It must have been Noke-noke [who] had a dirty cock—he had her before me.'" The guys then all ranked Sonny because he was in line after Noke-noke, an individual with no status in the gang, "for Sonny changed things since those days."[112] The gang rape reinforced the hierarchy within the gang, but at the same time, it cemented the group's cohesiveness. Even the most subordinated male was included in the group, his masculinity confirmed by his place in line and his dominance over a prostrate female.[113]

Gang members also assaulted male homosexuals, and some gang members engaged in same-sex relations, usually with older males in exchange for cash or drugs. Some specialized as "fag rollers" and would pick up men and then rob and beat them, justifying their brutality as punishment of "fairies."[114] "'After this queer bastard blew us,'" a gang member told Lewis Yablonsky, " 'we beat the hell out of him—but good.' "[115] Other youths simply engaged in sex as an economic exchange. Poor and in need of material goods, gang boys approached same-sex relations with the same utilitarian attitude with which they regarded heterosexual relations. Vincent Riccio found that when the boys went to the movies "one or two of them would always pick up a queer, so they could go in the men's room and get a five dollar bill, or a dollar bill, or a blow job."[116] As long as they did not play the "female" role and be penetrated, or limited themselves to being fellated, same-sex relations did not threaten their masculinity. Older working-class cultural norms, which did not identify a male as gay as long as he was the dominant sex partner, continued to be prevalent among these youths, much to the bewilderment and consternation of middle-class observers. However, homoerotic tensions within the gang had to be confronted.[117]

One way of understanding violence against both women and gay men is as a way of purging homoeroticism. The gang was for these adolescents their major source of comfort and friendship, and the powerful feelings of intimacy that arose could only have been faced indirectly. In addition, accounts of gang rape stress their performance aspect, as youths gathered around to watch their peers engage in sex. Rape was a voyeuristic act of male bonding, as Philippe Bourgois has found, that also aroused homoerotic feelings.[118] These feelings of desire, when projected on others who were then punished, could be safely eliminated. Violence allowed masculinity and intimacy to co-reside in the gang.

Gang members' masculinity was perpetually tested, as was the gang itself. Whether attacking other gangs, fighting among themselves, beating up gay men, or dominating young women, gang members endlessly pursued group solidarity and engaged in a relentless search for reputation. The very structure—the gang—that they created to shield themselves from the adult world and used to define their masculine identities continuously invited attack by rivals and intervention by police, social workers, and other agents of middle-class society. The reputations gang members gained were sustained only by passing countless tests, which helps account for the levels of violence found in the gang world and in street life generally. Masculinity could be created outside of the legitimate world of school, work, and family, but it was not secure.

Schools, the labor market, and families deflected some adolescents into the streets. Unable to define themselves as men through these institutions, they created gangs that allowed them to resist the demands of the dominant society and to create alternative measures of masculinity. Adolescents also made a gang culture that served as a mediating space between gang members and the society in which they lived.[119] Through language, music, dress, and ritual, gang members created a social space for themselves that defined their world and invested it with meaning.

# Making a Gang Culture: Form, Style, and Ritual in the Gang World

$B$OPPERS knew each other. They recognized each other on the streets, even without knowing each other's names, or the neighborhoods they came from, or the gangs to which they belonged. Gang members shared a system of signs, a style, and a way of walking that other gang members knew how to read and interpret. Not all gangs shared in each of the forms of gang culture, but enough did so that gang members felt as if they lived in their own world and had created an alternative culture, one that distinguished elite boppers from mundane coolies. As Manny Torres recalled about walking around with his gang sweater on, "It was like a uniform, and you could go anywhere in the city and even if you ran into a rival gang, you could still identify with them. You would try and kill each other in a rumble, but an outsider was a mutual enemy."[1] Bop culture united gang members even as ethnicity and place divided them.[2]

Bop culture was the conscious creation of gang members. They formulated its rules, negotiated according to its tenets, and used it to organize their lives. Too often gangs have been seen as violent, short-lived, disorganized collections of misfits whose main purpose was thrill-seeking and immediate gratification.[3] To be sure, as the previous chapter shows, gangs should not be romanticized: they committed acts of terrible violence against other adolescents and residents of their communities. Yet gang members created a culture that was a rational attempt to establish order and meaning for themselves. This chapter analyzes the forms of bop culture: language, music, clothing, names, graffiti, the use of space, ritual, and social codes and roles.

Bop culture must be distinguished from "youth culture." Bop culture borrowed elements from both the dominant culture and subordinate ethnic and working-class cultures, but it recombined them in distinctive and unusual ways.[4] Youth culture, on the other hand, was created by adults in order to tap a teenage market.[5] It threatened the autonomy of bop culture since it appropriated and sanitized some of its forms for mass entertainment and consumption. By spreading elements of bop culture to middle-class youth, youth culture developed a cultural vocabulary that was shared across class and ethnic lines. (One reason middle-class parents found youth culture so threatening was because they thought their children were adopting both the form and the substance of working-class and ethnic alienation.) Bop culture evolved new forms as old ones became incorporated into youth culture and lost their ability to convey distinctive meanings for gang members.

## LANGUAGE

The place to begin analyzing bop culture is with its language. Gang members shared a language based on the jazz style—bebop—that gave them their name. In the 1940s, young, urban, African-American musicians rejected the sound of swing that had been adopted by white America. They formed small bands that allowed greater virtuosity and individual expression than the smoother, more popular big bands. Bebop had, in Imamu Baraka's words, a "harsh, *anti-assimilationist* sound" that challenged rather than lured listeners. Young musicians—called boppers— came from all over to Harlem's small after-hours jazz clubs, where they created their own social space and music. Like the zoot suits worn by black musicians, bop was adopted by young black males to express their rebellion and alienation, and it became literally a language as young men redefined its terms to express the values and meaning of gang culture. And, again like the zoot suit, the language and the music of bop spread far beyond the African Americans who initially gave it form.[6]

Gang members of all ethnic groups employed the hip language of the jazz scene for their own purposes. The language of jazz already signified a rejection of the dominant culture, and gang members rearticulated it and employed it as a code. A bopper played bebop, but in the gang world, a bopper was a gang member ready to fight. (Other variants were "diddleybopper," "bopster," and "jitterbug.") To bop meant to dance a new variation on the lindy hop, but it also described a gang member's style of walking that suggested someone listening and moving to bebop. Gang members referred to gang fighting as "bopping" or, in another reference to dance, as "jitterbugging." Musicians played a gig, which was also the gang name for a party, and they recorded music in a session, a gang name for a dance. "Cool" described a style of playing jazz, as well as an armistice between rival gangs, while "to cool it" required acting with patience and calmness. To be "down" meant to be with it and "down kiddies" were skilled street fighters, while "wild kiddies" fought with reckless abandon. To be "wasted" meant to be exhausted, sometimes because of drug use, but to "waste" a rival gang meant to annihilate them. "To swing" meant to be hip, which in the gang world meant being a gang member. The hip talked "jive," but in gang circles a "jive stud" was a liar. Gang members called their girlfriends "debs," which did not have an antecedent in music, but was clearly an inversion of debutante. Finally, "jazz" to a gang member meant worthless talk, which aptly captured their perception of the difference between the intellectualized rebellion of goatee-wearing, bereted musicians and the street fighter dressed down for battle. With their use of bop language, gang members constituted themselves as a cultural community.

Gang members' language changed slowly over time. The lexicon of gang terms included in journalist Harrison Salisbury's study of gangs, *The Shook-Up Generation*, published in 1958, is identical to that found a decade earlier. Gang members in the 1960s still used a term derived from World War II ("jap") to describe an ambush of rival gang members, and Geoffrey Canada, growing up in the South Bronx in the mid-1960s, still referred to the walk used by gang members as "bopping."[7] However, gang members were not frozen into a static culture created in the 1940s and then handed down to succeeding generations of boppers. Language and usage changed and reflected the incorporation of new styles, while some terms were given new meaning. By the late 1960s, gang members used the term "bop" to mean idle talk and a "bopper" or "bebopper" was someone who was inept or hopelessly out of step—as in listening to music that was no longer in vogue. A "diddeybopper" referred to someone who was upwardly mobile or pretentious, a "jitterbug" talked too much, and a "fish" was no longer a style of dancing but someone who could be fooled easily. Gang members reinvented and inverted the meaning of their own language in the effort to preserve themselves as a distinctive community. They negotiated among bop culture, the dominant culture, and an increasingly powerful commercialized youth culture.[8]

## MUSIC

Bop culture and youth culture intersected most clearly in music. Gang members, like other adolescents in the 1950s and early 1960s, listened to, played, and created rhythm and blues, doo-wop, and rock 'n' roll. Doo-wop, a form of rock 'n' roll that emphasized vocal harmonizing and that was related to both gospel and rhythm and blues, was the creation of both African-American and Euro-American (frequently Italian) artists. Street-corner acappella groups were part of the neighborhood social scene, and some gangs sponsored their own singing groups. Performers generally enjoyed a special status in the neighborhood and were accorded a unique freedom to move around gang turfs. When boppers and their debs "fished" or did the "grind," they did so to the sounds of the Jesters, the Bop Chords, the Big Bopper, and other artists whose names both derived from gang culture and were echoed in the names adolescents chose for their gangs.

Singing groups traded on their gang associations both for subject matter in creating music and to prove their authenticity. The link between gangs and popular music is shown by Dion DiMucci, who withdrew from the Fordham Baldies as his singing group Dion and the Belmonts (which retained the geographic reference to the Fordham Road–Belmont Avenue area of the Bronx) began to make it big. Anthony Gourdine, who attained fame as the lead singer in Little Anthony and the Imperials, had been a member of the Chaplains. Like Dion, Little Anthony was a peripheral member of the gang, participating in its activities, seeing it as a source of protection, but finding his music as an alternative source of identity and, ultimately, as a means of social mobility. Such stars were held in great regard by their former peers and admired as individuals who made it without capitulating to the world of yokes and slaves. But, like the music they created, Dion, Little Anthony, and other bopper-musicians left the gang world and became absorbed by youth culture.[9]

The development of rock 'n' roll illustrates the ability of the market-place to assimilate the forms of bop culture and tame challenges to the status quo. Rock 'n' roll, originally rhythm and blues repackaged for whites, had many crossover artists, and it attracted integrated audiences to its early concerts. This potential to bring together black and white teenagers in a shared experience, especially given the music's overtly sexual and rebellious messages, was simply too threatening to many Euro-Americans. White southerners are usually cited as responding most viscerally and angrily to rock 'n' roll, but this ignores the politics and culture of race in northern cities, where the sight of mixed—and frequently rowdy—audiences dancing together in downtown public spaces raised the hackles of public officials and parents alike.[10]

Rock 'n' roll initially challenged the tradition of a highly segregated urban popular culture that for most of the nineteenth and early twentieth centuries had defined itself consciously against African Americans. White audiences of different ethnicities and class backgrounds had been able to celebrate their "whiteness" (and, indeed, create a sense of whiteness) through the medium of popular culture that appropriated African-American forms while excluding African Americans. In the 1950s, traditional sites of popular entertainment, such as the downtown movie palaces, inner-city baseball stadiums, and amusement parks, became integrated. As they did so, they began to lose their white audiences. Only when these sites were removed to the safely segregated urban periphery did they again attract large numbers of whites. Supporters of rock 'n' roll had to confront the racialization of popular culture if the music was to be successful commercially. To reach a broader white audience, rock 'n' roll's promoters had to harness and institutionalize the music, strip it of its overt ethnicity, make it part of a commercialized youth culture, and have it performed in segregated venues. In the process, they robbed rock 'n' roll of its incipient challenge to racial protocol.[11]

Too much can be made of the latent challenge that rock 'n' roll posed to racial hatred. There is no evidence that gang members, who shared in the nasciently integrative music of rock 'n' roll, just as they did in an integrated gang culture, were thereby made more tolerant of ethnic differences. While they danced to music created by black and white musicians, spoke the language of bop, wore the common insignia of the gang world, and even participated in integrated gangs, they simultaneously spoke a language that referred to "Niggers" and "Paddies." Gang members inherited racialized views from their elders and the dominant society. African-American, Euro-American, and Puerto Rican gang members perceived themselves as defenders of ethnic communities, and sharing a bop culture did not change this. Simply put, a Euro-American gang could sing along with Little Anthony on the radio while planning a raid on an African-American foe and see no contradiction between the two.[12]

Boppers participated in youth culture and used its institutions for their own purposes. Because New York's many radio stations, their celebrity disc jockeys, and the independent record companies that supplied them with talent competed intensely to create audiences, their audiences had an opportunity to shape them. Most commonly, listeners affected the music recorded and played on the radio. Gang members sometimes used call-in requests to radio stations to signal fellow boppers, and stations were accused of fostering gang culture by referring to gangs and their exploits by name on the air or in dedicating certain songs to gang members. Gang members were part of the teenaged audience that helped create modern music, and, as noted above, they used the idioms of doo-wop and rock much as they had the earlier language of jazz. Over time "hip cats" created new terms that crept into the gang member's vocabulary. Rhythm and blues, doo-wop, and rock 'n' roll supplied a language and institutions that gradually replaced the earlier forms based on jazz.[13]

Music also created what might be called a choreography of the streets. Boppers carried themselves on the streets in a way that combined a musical fluidity with an aggressive masculinity. Walking "bop style" was both a challenge to other boppers and a warning that the individual was "wise" and not to be messed with lightly. Piri Thomas, a Puerto Rican living in an East Harlem block not yet claimed from the Italians, described walking like a bopper as he went to the market for his mother. Thomas adopted the style he "had copped from the colored cats I had seen, a swinging and stepping down hard at every step. Those cats were so down and cool that just walking made a way-out sound."[14] For Thomas, this was a way of asserting his right to walk down the street and declaring that he was unafraid. Other boys also employed the "diddleybop walk" aggressively. Carmen Sanchez recalled that boppers "would come through the neighborhood making a little jump every time they take a step, making their leg jump." This "walking tough" or "diddleybopping," together with loud and wise talking, served as a direct challenge to any bopper who claimed that street.[15] Israel Narvaez, a member of Brooklyn's Mau Maus, recalled that when they entered enemy turf, "We walked down the street like we owned it—doing the slow easy walk of the jitterbug, loosely swinging our shoulders, hips, and knees, bobbing and weaving to our own individual rhythm, tapping our bamboo canes [a trademark of the Mau Maus] in front of us."[16]

The flowing, nonchalant walk of the bopper, beating out time with his foot or with a cane, was the opposite of the hurried scurrying of the timid or the studied avoidance of streetwise adults. It announced the presence of the walker and it invited the gaze of passersby, who either had to confront a bopper or step aside. In the public theater of the streets, diddleybopping defined the walker as a man of power and assurance, as someone who had to be reckoned with and recognized. Like other elements of bop culture, it was intended to make the invisible visible and to defy assertions of order and decorum imposed by the dominant society.

## CLOTHING

Clothing also made boppers visible, as most gangs employed some insignia or wore an item of clothing that, like colors on a ship, declared the wearer's allegiance. Clothing would be worn in unusual combinations or colors that signaled the wearer's disaffection from the dominant culture. Gang styles changed as different items of gang clothing became adopted and commercialized through youth culture, which forced gangs to find new ways to present themselves.

According to the claims of popular culture, the item of gang clothing most associated with gangs was the leather or satin jacket. Norman Podhoretz recalled that his red satin Cherokees jacket was "my proudest possession, a badge of manly status." Some of the Brooklyn-based Mau Maus sported black leather jackets with a crimson double "M" stitched on the back, while others reversed the color scheme and wore red jackets with black armbands and a black double "M". Fully decked-out members wore alpine hats with wooden matches in the brim and carried bamboo canes to complete the ensemble.[17]

These are unusual examples, however. While some gangs wore club jackets, usually they were saved for special or ceremonial occasions and were not intended for public viewing. Other gangs avoided jackets because they literally could be read. Carl Joyeaux, a leader of the Bishops, dismissed another gang because they wore jackets with their club name written on them. "[Y]ou could tell they weren't bops because their club jackets bore the name, Barons, a dead giveaway to the cops." Jerry Della Famina declared bluntly that only "pseudo-tough guys" were jacket wearers, and gang workers maintained that obtaining jackets meant that a gang was ready to give up fighting and go "social." In these cases, instead of serving as a symbol of gang membership, the jacket became a way of indicating respectability—a sign of openness and peaceful intent. As club jackets became popular among teenagers across America, boppers invented different forms of attire to signal their allegiances.[18] (It is interesting to note that jackets made a comeback with the resurgence of gangs in the South Bronx in the 1970s. By then, youth culture had long abandoned jackets and therefore gang members could once again wear them.)

Jackets are a perfect example of how youth culture appropriated an element of bop culture and turned it into a commodity. Gang jackets were popularized among adolescents after Marlon Brando wore one as a motorcycle gang leader in the 1953 movie *The Wild One*. To many middle-class teenagers, jackets became the symbol of youthful rebelliousness, guaranteed to worry parents and teachers. Teenagers adopted styles that were associated with working-class gangbangers to indicate their own alienation from middle-class life—or simply because they liked the style. Middle-class adolescents expressed themselves through participation in youth culture and individual acts of defiance; they did not patrol the borders of their neighborhoods, organize age-graded divisions among the children in the area, or prepare Molotov cocktails to fight rival gangs and police. While the disaffection of middle-class youth was real, it was of a different magnitude than that of working-class adolescents, who suffered from severe economic and social dislocations in the postwar period. Parents, journalists, and public officials mistook the stylistic affectations of rebellion for its substance.[19] They saw the spread of leather jackets, Levi's, and rock 'n' roll as proof that juvenile delinquency was like a contagious disease spreading outward from the slums, rather than as the expression of clever marketing.[20]

As club jackets lost their semiotic power, gang members adopted similarly colored items, such as black chinos, or a combination of clothes that the cognoscenti knew signified gang membership. For example, the Robins, an African-American gang from Brooklyn, wore blue sweaters with a yellow "R" on the breast, and blue Esquire hats, with a lighter blue ribbon as a band. Manny Torres, a member of the Young Stars, described his usual gang attire as a "stingy brim [a hat known as a "stenjer"], a slick white shirt, and pressed brown khaki pants." Torres also carried a rolled-up umbrella, but the most important item was "the sweater with the stars." One Brooklyn gang, the Bishops, wore black jackets, strap boots, and black hats called "bleeckers" (because they were purchased on Bleecker Street in Greenwich Village). Hats were commonly used to display colors. The Beavers had black, fuzzy, felt hats, the Tiny Tims wore blue berets, and Brownsville's Black Hats based their name on their black chauffeurs' hats.[21] A group of boys walking bop style and wearing similar types of clothing needed no further announcement of their status.

Gang styles could be quite surprising, given the class origins of gang members. For example, for a period in the 1950s, African-American gangs in Central Harlem wore gray flannel suits or took to the streets in the "Ivy League look," with Harris tweed sports jackets, narrow dress slacks, dress shirts, and striped ties. Other gang members observed by Harrison Salisbury also paid careful attention to dress, appearing in gabardine half-coats, peg-top trousers, silk or dacron shirts, and black dress shoes. Since many of these young men walked around without the price of a meal in their pockets, an analysis of their elaborate self-representation and style reveals something of their core identities.[22]

In their styles, gang members defied both the dominant culture and that of their parents. The flamboyant zoot suits of the 1940s, discussed in chapter 2, were preeminently badges of minority youth that shocked observers. Although he was not a gang member, the young Malcolm Little (later Malcolm X) dressed in a wild zoot suit and he recalled the reaction he provoked: "I'd go through that Grand Central Station after-noon rush hour crowd, and many white people simply stopped in their tracks to watch me pass." The adoption of the zoot suit also marked Little's entry into the world of hustling and his eventual rebirth as "De-troit Red"; the cost of several zoot suits, accessories, and nightly trips to the dance halls could not be paid for by shining shoes or other forms of low-skill, low-wage, legitimate work. The zoot suit meant not only a symbolic rejection of the dominant culture, but also a literal rejection of a working-class work ethic that could not support the style. The parents of zoot-suited youths were no less startled than strangers at their chil-dren's transformation. African-American working-class parents, many of them southern migrants, stared across a cultural divide at their urbane, hip children. For white parents especially, the adoption of a zoot suit by a teenaged son symbolized an identification with (on the East Coast) a predominantly African-American style, even though as a gang member that youth might have acted to exclude African Americans from the neighborhood.[23]

While zoot suits shouted defiance of the dominant culture, flannel suits and tweed sports jackets subverted it. These clothes were more subtle in message, serving to confound the expectations of police, par-ents, and other onlookers. African-American gang members inverted the meaning of gray flannel suits—the foremost symbol of the dominant white culture—simply by having them adorn their black bodies. Instead of merging into what white critics saw as a faceless corporate culture, gang members used the suits to make themselves visible, both to their working-class parents and to the dominant culture they defied. Boys wore clothes associated with a status that neither they nor their parents could reach. While some parents, realizing that the goods their children dis-played were ill-gotten, no doubt punished their sons' defiance of respect-ability, others probably envied their sons' pluck and ability to acquire what they could not. The visibility provided by a good suit was also a form of protection from harassment. Claude Brown noted that he stole a new suit whenever he was planning to stay away from home ("cat out") for several days. The police were less likely to bother him if he looked "respectable," and even his parents were less likely to punish him, once the police brought him home, if he returned in proper dress.[24]

Other youths wore traditional work clothes as their gang attire. The adoption of work boots, jeans, and leather jackets by youths whose principal occupation was hanging around on street corners also signified a rejection of both parental and mainstream cultures. The key was the assembly of items of working-class clothing into a new ensemble: it was the combination of colors and types of clothing that indicated gang membership and implied a threat of violence to observers. Whether they chose suits, leather jackets, or work clothes, gang members took elements of working-class, ethnic, or the dominant cultures and reconstituted them in a particular bop style that was visible—if not always legible—to members of the non-bop world. Their style signaled their independence and at least temporary resistance to the marketplace and mainstream culture.[25]

Certain rules also applied to wearing gang clothing. Although gang members might wear special hats or other insignia to a fight, generally they saved suits and other expensive clothing for special occasions, such as visits to dance halls, dates, or trips downtown. Gang jackets, to the extent that they were worn, were saved for similar formal occasions and not worn when on the way to a rumble or to commit a burglary, where they might aid witnesses or police in identifying participants. Some gangs prohibited their members from wearing gang regalia unless they were otherwise neatly dressed, and some regulated members' behavior while acting as official representatives of the gang. The Cougars, for example, forbade members from getting drunk at dances while wearing club jackets. Even rival gang members were supposed to respect the parameters established by dress. When a member of the Clippers went walking with his girlfriend—who lived on a street claimed by the North Street boys—they encountered members of the rival gang. Taunted into action, the Clipper lunged at his rivals and wrestled one to the ground before realizing he had his "dating" clothes on. The boy leaped up and, appealing to the North Street boys' gang etiquette, challenged them to meet the Clippers in a rumble. After setting the time and place, the North Street boys allowed the Clipper to leave. This may have been an example of quick-wittedness on the part of a hopelessly outnumbered boy, but it is still notable that he thought of making an appeal to the gang code and that it worked. Gangs distinguished among everyday dress, clothing saved for special occasions, and the more rugged attire worn for gang fighting.[26]

Of course, gang fighting clothes had utilitarian as well as symbolic value. Many gang members wore heavily studded garrison belts, which made a useful weapon when the heavy brass buckle was filed down to a point and the belt was swung overhead in hand-to-hand combat. Heavy jackets offered a measure of protection against the thrusts of a switchblade or the swipe of a broken-off car aerial. A certain type of boot may have signaled gang membership, but it also served as a weapon when used to stomp a fallen opponent. Colored kerchiefs allowed opponents to distinguish between friend and foe, as did wearing a girlfriend's earring in the right ear.[27]

Clothing itself became a source of conflict. Because clothing had symbolic meaning, its loss threatened the honor of the group and its capture by a rival gang was a major victory. Manny Torres recalled the pride the Young Stars felt stripping club sweaters from fallen foes and bringing them back to hang on the clubhouse wall "like scalps." Kenneth Marshall, the gang worker, recalled seeing his gang waving something in the air as if it were a flag. When he approached the group he realized that they had stripped a rival gang member of his jacket and were parading around the street with it in a proud display of their prowess and their enemy's humiliation. Appropriating an enemy's clothing and "sporting" it brought the wearer status and recognition within the group and served as a constant jibe to the rival gang until it could gain revenge. Colors were a badge of honor that proclaimed the gang's identity; they had to be defended bravely and their wearers had to act in an appropriate fashion. Torres claimed that he would die for his sweater: "If you're going to take it off me, you've got to kill me first."[28]

## NAMES

The names of gangs and of gang members provided another way of becoming visible. Gang names suggested nobility, inspired fear, or implied that a group had transcended its local circumstances. In East Harlem, Puerto Rican gangs included the Viceroys, Enchanters, Young Lords, Latin Gents, and Cavaliers. It is notable how many gangs took names that had medieval or religious connotations, such as the Bishops, Chaplains, Crusaders, Dukes, Kings, and various forms of Knights, suggesting these gangs' identification with warriors and codes of honor. Gangs declared their predatory nature with names such as the Hawks, Scorpions, or Falcons, and they also announced their ethnic identities. The Bronx had the Golden Guineas and the Italian Berettas, while Brooklyn's Mau Maus, in a rare example of political consciousness, adopted their name from the Kenyan resistance fighters wreaking terror on British colonialists in the 1950s. Other groups wished to proclaim their local attachments rather than make some royal or historical allusion and adopted the identity of their corner into their names, such as the Greene Avenue Stompers. Some gangs took names (such as Beavers or Nits) that may have had some significance to them that is not immediately obvious. Of course it is possible to read too much into a name; Lewis Yablonsky, who did fieldwork on Manhattan's Upper West Side, recounted that his gang, the Balkans, invented their name in the police station after having been arrested for participating in a fight with another gang. Gangs were expected to have names, and the boys created an identity on the spot in order to meet police expectations.[29]

In the end, however, the names that gangs gave to themselves were significant. Through their names, adolescents signaled their transformation from street-corner loungers, truants, and refugees from difficult family situations into men with noble purpose. In their club names, youths reached for identities that transcended the limitations of their daily lives.

Gangs also changed their names, though not, as some would have it, as a result of disorganization.[30] Several gangs had dual identities, employing one for gang warfare and another in times of peace and when arranging social events. The Dumonts advertised the dances and parties they organized, but they became the Amsterdam Knights if preparing for conflict with another group.[31] Groups of boys might change names to signify adoption of a new role. For example, the Fordham Dagger Juniors reorganized as the Fordham Baldie Juniors because the name better fit their aspirations of becoming a feared gang, like generations of Baldies before them.[32] Other gangs reluctantly surrendered identities that had become too notorious. The "Cobras" emerged after a group of Royal Imperials had been tried and convicted of stabbing a subway motorman to death, and the "little people" or juniors felt that the name was too well known to the police.[33] Finally, finding a new name was imperative when a gang decided to go social. If the gang's claims to forswearing violence were to be taken seriously, it had to make a clear break with its past. A gang arrived at such a decision with great difficulty, as it represented a betrayal of previous generations of boppers and of their comrades who might have been imprisoned, and it allowed others to charge that they had turned "punk."[34] In these cases, the decision to change a name was not the result of boys' inability to organize or of the loose structure of their groups. Rather, it was the product of a careful, rational decision about the face a gang wished to present to both the adult and gang worlds.

The individual gang member presented his own face to the bop world through his street name. Virtually all gang members had nicknames—or street names—by which they were known to fellow gang members. Usually boys did not choose a nickname, but had one bestowed on them by their peers, which represented their acceptance into the gang. Nicknames sometimes referred to physical characteristics ("Shorty" or "Squinty"), to a boy's place of origin, or to a personality trait. Carl Joyeaux beamed at being christened "Frenchy" by the leader of the Bishops, and, while hiding the name from his parents, he wrote it boldly across the covers of his books at school. Some names were chosen in the hope of signifying terror: Manny Torres's brother Bobby, the designated "hitman" for the Young Stars, was known as the "Undertaker," while a number of individuals were called "Hitler" or "Goering" in the 1940s. Indian names, associated with bravery and defiance of authority, resonated with gang members, with "Geronimo," "Cy-Ox" (for Sioux), "Cheyenne," and "Cherokee" as particular favorites. Even friends might be unaware of a fellow member's given name and family name, knowing him only by his street name.

Some observers described the nickname as a "nom de guerre." It served to hide a gang member's identity from the police, especially after a crime or a gang fight had occurred, or from concerned family members. This may be true, especially since boys used a fairly limited range of names and a single neighborhood might have a number of boys with similar street names. Determining which "Shorty" did what to whom became a difficult task in the face of suspicious youths unwilling to talk to police. Nicknames also hid activities from other adults—teachers, welfare investigators, neighborhood gossips—who were unable to decode the language and symbols of the gang. But the nickname served a more important purpose than secrecy. The acquisition of a nickname marked a youth's baptism into the gang world. He had acquired a new identity, and he needed to build a reputation to give that identity substance. Instead of hiding who he was, a gang member wanted to proclaim this identity, to warn rivals and peers that he was someone to be reckoned with, and to brag about his feats, which adolescents did in foot-high letters in the public spaces of the neighborhood.[35]

## Graffiti

The nicknames of gang members and the names of their gangs graced the walls of abandoned buildings and subway underpasses, proudly proclaiming individual as well as corporate identities. Gang worker Vincent Riccio knew the names of members of his gang before even setting foot in their hangout: "All I had to do was walk the area and read of Buggsy, Dreamy Dick, Bo Bo, Joey Boy, Squatty, Squinty, Rocky, Hunk, Freddi, Shorty, and many others."[36] Graffiti served three functions: it defined turf; it provided the opportunity to issue a challenge or a warning; and it reported the neighborhood news. (The more recent phenomenon of "tagging" or "getting up," in which street names or initials were spray painted in highly stylized forms on subway cars, in tunnels, or seemingly inaccessible public sites, represents a new form of graffiti writing that is divorced from gang traditions.[37]) Graffiti supplemented the gossip networks in reporting who was seeing whom and which gang claimed current ascendancy. The journalist Harrison Salisbury learned to "read the news" on the subway stop walls in Brooklyn:

> The platform and stair walls of the Smith-Ninth station are covered with what first appears to be an embroidery of white chalk, red paint and black crayon. The tracery of lines is everywhere but it is not embroidery. It is a living newspaper of the streets. Here are the threats and taunts of rival gangs, the challenges and defiances. Here is word of neighborhood romance, old flames and new loves. Here bids are staked for leadership. Here bulletins are posted on the rumbles.[38]

Neutral spaces, such as the subway stop or a schoolyard, through which many individuals passed, were most appropriate for news writing and staking claims. No doubt only some local residents, present and former gang members, other knowledgeable teenagers, and a few outside initi-ates knew how to read the messages on the walls. To middle-class adults, they were another disquieting reminder of the existence of an otherwise inaccessible, but threatening, world.[39]

Gang members did not write graffiti at random throughout a neighborhood. They inscribed border regions most thickly, while leaving the central portion of their turf more free of wall writing. Graffiti that marked the edges of a gang's territory did not serve as a "newspaper," but as a warning to intruders that they had left whatever neutral zones might exist and were liable to being attacked. Border areas also attracted the attention of rival groups. Gangs trying to advance their claims to new territory might write over the "home" gang's markings and thus issue a challenge. Border areas offered ease of access, since rival wall writers did not have to venture deeply into enemy territory. In the core of a gang's turf, there was less reason to stake a claim and rivals were less likely to have the opportunity to write. Graffiti was the clearest announcement of a gang's presence, and through graffiti writing, gang members visibly claimed a part of the city as their own.[40]

In their language, music, way of walking, clothing, and writing, boppers inscribed themselves and their neighborhoods in a way that was visible both to other gang members and to adults. But gang members did not define themselves solely in terms of the outside world or in reaction to the dominant culture.[41] Gang members created their own standards of worth, established their own rules to govern their behavior, invented rituals to mark important transitions, and established their own social spaces within which they could practice their culture. Bop culture existed principally for boppers, not for working-class or middle-class adults, and this is most apparent in the aspects of bop culture that were less visible to outsiders.

## The Use of Space

Gang members supplemented their use of the streets, parks, school yards, or recreation centers by meeting in candy stores, abandoned buildings, apartments, clubhouses, and rooftops. These social spaces were generally private places, where gangs were unlikely to be observed by police, adults, or rivals. In the social geography of the gang world, the candy store was the most ubiquitous and commercial of these spaces.[42]

Candy stores dotted working-class areas, offering an opportunity for petty entrepreneurship that kept the proprietor rooted in the local neighborhood. Typically small storefronts, with a counter, a soda dispenser, magazine racks, and perhaps a jukebox and some stools or a small table, candy stores provided a place where gang members could meet, gossip, and, if space permitted, dance with their debs. A symbiotic relationship existed between the owner, whose slim profit margin depended on frequent small sales, and the gang members for whom the candy store provided a haven for hanging out. Owners relied on the gang's patronage and dispensed advice and small loans, and they occasionally aided gang members in avoiding the police. Carl Joyeaux claimed that his division of the Bishops stored their guns in a crate hidden in the basement of Lenny's, their candy store hangout. Lenny was unusually supportive, having been a gang member in his youth; few store owners risked angering the police. Most did not wish to know of the illegal activities of their gang patrons, but if they did discover something, they were expected to feign ignorance when questioned by police.[43]

As the most public of the private spaces used by gangs, candy stores were vulnerable to raids and adult intervention. Street workers, for example, knew to find gang members in their candy store headquarters and would come in, buy sodas, and spend money in the jukebox as a way of making contact with the gang. Police came by and rousted gang members for questioning about goings-on in the neighborhood. Rival gangs also knew which candy stores served as headquarters for gangs. RG recalled having a group of Young Lords, a Puerto Rican gang, come into the candy store that the Baldies used and threaten to shoot everyone; Manny Torres and the Young Stars threw garbage cans into the plate glass window of the headquarters of the rival Italian Hoods and opened fire with zip guns. When hostilities threatened, gangs would temporarily abandon their candy stores for more inaccessible or secure hangouts.[44]

Cellar clubs offered more privacy and less adult supervision than candy stores. Usually basement rooms located near the furnace or in some other area that was equally unrentable, cellar clubs were modestly furnished with a few mattresses, sofas, and chairs picked up out of the trash. Sometimes blankets hung on clotheslines to partition the space so that couples could enjoy a bit of privacy. A room in a tenement required some sort of accommodation with the superintendent of the building as well as a rent payment; to avoid this, gangs sometimes took over abandoned buildings. There, meetings, councils of war, and parties could be held with nearly complete freedom.[45] However, cellar clubs and buildings used by gangs presented the same problems that candy stores did. They might have been less visible, but they were no less known, and were subject to raids by rivals.

Apartments (usually the home of one of the members) were used to host "sessions" or parties. Supportive parents (or parents hoping to keep an eye on their children's activities and friends) sometimes outfitted a room in an apartment or in the basement of a house for recreational purposes or meetings. Working-class neighborhoods also had a tradition of apartment parties at which nominal admission was charged and the proceeds used for the rent or some other purpose.[46] Gangs employed the same policy, charging five or ten cents admission and selling refreshments by the glass. The living room, cleared of furniture, served as a dance floor, and a gang member served as disc jockey, spinning 45s on the record player. Since gang members rarely had much money, the success of a session relied on the gang's ability to attract adolescents from all over the neighborhood and even members of other gangs. Of course, news of a session was also an invitation to a rival group to crash the party (to "turn it out"), and sessions were the scenes of tense face-offs between rival gangs, especially when rivals danced with the hosts' debs.[47]

Gangs occasionally rented storefronts, but this usually indicated a gang's intention to "go social" (or "conservative"). Renting a storefront required an adult intermediary to help negotiate a lease, and since store-fronts were relatively costly, a gang had to be committed to raising money through charging members dues, selling raffle tickets, and hosting com-munity activities such as hiring a live band and sponsoring a dance. This in turn required negotiating with churches or community groups in order to rent a hall and even arranging for police supervision in order to fore-stall any possibility of conflict among guests. Storefronts were visible to police and passersby, and it was unlikely for a gang to acquire one unless it was changing its identity and orientation.[48]

Of all the gang hangouts, rooftops were the safest. Rooftops gave gang members a hidden and comparatively easy means of traveling around the neighborhood. Since apartment buildings were generally the same height and filled an entire square block, connected rooftops allowed youths to race from one street to another. Doors leading to the roofs were left open

5.1. The attached roofs of New York tenements provided recreational space and a means of escaping pursuers.

in strategic locations so that a gang member fleeing from police or a rival gang could sprint up the stairs onto the roof, leap over the airshafts, and disappear through another door in a building a half a block away. Stairwells led down into a maze of backyards and alleys that could be reached from the basement. Gangs left mattresses at the bottom of airshafts to cushion a fall, but members became adept at leaping from roof to roof even at night. The roof also provided a vantage point from which to observe the movements of potential enemies, and if a rival gang or the police could be lured onto a block, gang members hidden on the roofs

could rain ashcans, bottles, and bricks on the victims below. During times
of conflict the streets were particularly dangerous and might be abandoned altogether. JT claimed that on such occasions "you would see more
people on the roofs than on the streets." But the roof had more than just
strategic value. Gang members, like other city residents, would sleep on
the roof to escape the summer heat and would use the roof to fly pigeons,
drink, smoke marijuana, and have sex. The roof may not have been a
trouble-free paradise, as the Drifters put it in "Up on the Roof," but, as
anyone who has climbed a New York City roof at night will know, it was
a space in which adolescents could experience freedom and soar over the
city below.[49]

## Ritual

Like other social institutions, gangs screened applicants, established
codes of behavior, and supplied an informal list of rules and duties to
their members. Some analysts of gang behavior claim that standards were
kept low so that the social misfits who made up gangs could meet them,
but I have found that boys had to earn admission into the bop world and
then had to work to remain in good standing by demonstrating qualities
of toughness, loyalty, and heart.

Since each gang member bore responsibility for the collective honor
of the group, fellow gang members had to be sure that an applicant was
worthy of admission. Applicants, especially if they were unknown to
other boys in the group, underwent tests of character. These standards
could be relaxed under some circumstances. In highly structured gangs
that had age-graded divisions, a youngster might graduate from one
group to the next without undergoing a formal initiation. Simply by
hanging around long enough, a boy would become known and gain acceptance, and if he showed any particular talent, he might be actively
recruited for membership in the seniors. If an applicant were not known,
he had to pass a probationary period before gaining full admission to the
gang.[50]

Prospective members endured a variety of tests. In East Harlem's Red
Wings, a boy would be sent up to Third Avenue (where the police pa-

trolled since it served as a dividing line between Italian and Spanish Harlem) to "roll a spick" (mug a Puerto Rican) and bring back a watch or wallet to prove that he had done so. "Tony" argued that to be a Red Wing "you had to go a little farther, either stab a guy or do somethin' outstandin' that no other kids in the neighborhood would do."[51] Nicky Cruz was given a choice of initiations: he could be beaten up by five of the toughest guys in the Mau Maus, or he could stand against a wall waiting for a knife to be thrown at him. If he flinched or tried to run away, he would not be allowed to join the gang. (Or he could suffer a worse fate. Cruz described the brutal treatment of a boy who turned "chicken" in the initiation process. The gang leader declared he would "clip" the boy's wings and stabbed him in each of his armpits.)[52] Another gang leader reported that prospective members were shown a loaded gun, which was then secretly switched with an unloaded one. The boy would then be told to shoot one of the other members present, and he would be beaten up and kicked out of the gang if he refused. (He would also be beaten up if he pulled the trigger, but he would have gained admission.)[53]

Beatings, which could be quite severe, were the most common forms of initiation or promotion in the gang. Dion DiMucci had to take three punches in the stomach from each member, while Manny Torres fought five Young Stars in order to become the warlord. It was assumed that someone who could take a beating would be unlikely to run away in a fight with another gang or inform on his gang under the pressure of a police beating.[54] Surviving the initiation gained a boy the privileges of membership—such as use of the clubhouse, access to the debs, and the right to wear the gang's colors—but most important, it impressed upon the boy that he had left behind the world of coolies and school boys and had acquired a new status as an elite bopster.

Some gangs included a sexual liaison among their rituals. Writer Harlan Ellison, who joined a Brooklyn gang, the Barons, for a short time in the early 1950s, was admitted to membership after running a gauntlet of six boys with garrison belts. He was then expected to pick a girlfriend from among the debs to take into the next room. Ellison knew that this was in many ways a test of judgment. He had to avoid picking either a girl who was the "steady" of a fellow gang member or a girl who was

beneath his status—a "lay." "I had to pick a good-looking girl who was
not a bum, who was not strongly attached to any club member, who
wouldn't give me a hard time, but who would carry into her sexual meet
with me all the qualities of a 'good' girl, yet be hip enough to make me
a steady chick." The selection of a "gang wife" consummated his initiation into the gang.[55]

Sometimes this consummation ceremony was quite formal. When
William Gale reported on gangs in the South Bronx in the 1970s, he
observed that girls would be "married" to a gang member by the president of the gang. "Brides" wore white—or at least white towels wrapped
around their heads—and exchanged vows with the "groom," after which
the president cut their thumbs so that their blood could mingle and
poured a can of beer over their heads. The couple then retired for twenty-
four hours to a room from which everything had been removed except
for a single mattress, some food, beer, and a paint can that could be used
for relieving themselves.[56]

Other gang activities also had formal and ritualistic aspects to them.
Before a gang fight members passed around bottles of "Sneaky Pete,"
sweet wine sometimes mixed with other alcohol, in order to get ready
for action. Drinking served the practical purposes of dulling the con-
sciences and steeling the courage of gang members; as Dion DiMucci
claimed, "I felt my fear shrink when I was high."[57] But it was also a
communion rite that emphasized the shared risks of brotherhood and
bound the members together. Youths would affirm each other's courage
and reputation, retell stories of past exploits, and remind members of the
benchmarks of honor against which they would be measured. As members got drunker, louder, and wilder, individuals melded into the corporate entity of the gang and prepared to do its bidding.

After a fight, the returnees would gather and smoke marijuana as a
way of calming down and wait to hear back from members and assess
their losses. At quiet moments, when more reflection was warranted,
some gangs poured an offering of wine on the ground to memorialize
fallen or incarcerated comrades and to remind themselves that they belonged to a chain of warriors that reached back into the past and would
extend forward into the future. At such times, war stories would also be
retold, thus reaffirming old enmities, investing conflict with historical
meaning, confirming the status of the leaders, and assuring members

that, if hurt, killed, or incarcerated, they, too, would be remembered as individuals with heart.[58] The rituals of gang rape, discussed in the previous chapter, also served to unify the gang and reinforced the hierarchical rankings of the members. The world of the gang was encoded in ritual.

## SOCIAL CODES

Gangs created elaborate protocols for declaring war or establishing peace. "Warlords" represented the gang in negotiating the time and location of conflict and the types of weapons to be used. Sometimes, usually with the encouragement of gang workers, gangs elected champions who would square off in a "fair one" that involved only the two combatants in a fistfight that settled the dispute. On other occasions, warlords selected a schoolyard or a park in which the assembled gangs would fight. When the Young Stars arranged to fight the Hoods in Crotona Park in the Bronx, the two gangs agreed that combatants would meet at 10:00 P.M. and that clubs, chains, and knives—but no guns—were to be used. Both sides cheated. The Young Stars brought guns, and when they arrived at the park, they found that the Hoods had arrived early and arranged an ambush. Although the rules established for combat were frequently disregarded for lack of trust between combatants, gangs nonetheless at least attempted to regulate conflict. As Carl Joyeaux put it, "Although bopping clubs hardly fight fair, they rarely make war without declaring it first. Which is more chivalry than nations have shown since World War II."[59]

Gang conflict itself took on a ritualized form. Though gang fights could occur at any time, they happened most frequently in the summer, when school was out, large numbers of adolescents congregated on the streets at night to escape the heat, and time weighed most heavily on their hands. Summer began on Memorial Day, and gangs gathered in Prospect Park, at Coney Island in Brooklyn, or at Orchard Beach in the Bronx and initiated the summer gang-fighting season. The rumbles in Prospect Park were so well known that crowds gathered to watch both the official celebrations and the action in the park. Brooklyn resident Clarence Norman recalled, "We'd have a picnic on the Parade Ground and wait for it [the rumble] to start. We'd watch for a while, and then we'd all have to run." That gang fighting occurred according to a predictable cycle and took the form of a mass spectacle did not make it less terrible. It is evidence of planning, order, and ritual. Gangs organized fighting, like other aspects of gang life, according to established conventions.[60]

Peace negotiations were governed by rules that could be as elaborate as those of any international peace conference. Usually periods of fighting ended when leaders were incarcerated or the police presence was so extensive that no further operations were possible. At other times, boys who attended the same school or older advisors to the gangs might act to end the conflict. Mediators—community or religious figures or gang workers—arranged negotiating sessions in which rival gangs discussed the origins of the current dispute, agreed on a truce that would be renewed after a specified time, reestablished borders, and created safety corridors in which rival gang members could travel. (Mediation is analyzed more extensively in chapter 7.) The New York City Youth Board published recommendations to guide mediators through this difficult process. The time and place of the negotiating session were kept secret until the boys were in the car and on their way. Each gang's worker searched the boys for hidden weapons and the gangs arrived and left separately. Each group had a spokesman who outlined its grievances before an impartial mediator, who kept the two sides in order, summarized the meeting, worked out the terms of agreement, and provided each side with a copy of the terms. Because mediation was such a formal process it nearly always involved adults, but within carefully proscribed limits.[61]

Gangs established norms that guided the formal and informal behavior of their community. Most gangs avoided attacking coolies and adults both for reasons of status and to avoid police intervention. Gang fights generally took place between 5 and 9 P.M. so that boys had time to finish work and meet parental curfews. A wounded gang member might be aided into a cab, but he showed up at the hospital emergency room by himself so that his fellow gang members would not be held for questioning. Gangs sometimes agreed to establish neutral turf, such as the school or the community center, where rivals would be encountered unavoidably. They also allowed members to go to and from work unmolested, and they sometimes agreed to share a movie house by deciding on which side of the center aisle members of the respective gangs could sit. Special efforts were made to show respect for ministers, priests, and community elders. Some gangs did not allow members to steal, and one gang leader maintained that members were fined for cursing in the presence of a woman. While most gang members used alcohol and marijuana quite regularly, a number of gangs drew the line at heroin and threatened to expel anyone caught using it. Whether or not gangs usually abided by these rules (and frequently they did not) is less important than that the rules existed. Gangs did not inhabit an anarchic world but rather attempted to impose their own order and codes for behavior.[62]

## SOCIAL ROLES

In keeping with the existence of elaborate rituals and codes of behavior, gangs themselves were frequently highly organized. African-American and Puerto Rican gangs were larger than Euro-American gangs, with as many as seventy-five or a hundred members formed into age-graded divisions, and therefore had a hierarchical structure with well-defined leadership roles, including presidents, vice presidents, war counselors, and sometimes treasurers. Euro-American gangs were usually smaller—more similar to street-corner groups with only fifteen or twenty members—and had fewer, less-defined roles. Usually different activities—such as gang fighting, organizing social events, committing burglaries, and picking up girls—demanded different skills, and leaders existed in each of these areas.[63] Sometimes only the demand by the Youth Board that the "leaders" appear at a negotiating session with another gang forced a more deliberate delineation of power.[64] Despite the diffusion of power, Euro-American gangs were no more democratic than African-American or Puerto Rican ones. They, like most gangs, had charismatic leaders whose opinions were sought about everything. As Kilmer Myers, an Episcopal priest active in negotiating an end to lower Manhattan's gang wars, put it, the rank-and-file membership of a gang did not even go to the movies "unless the leadership approves."[65]

Roles within the gang were negotiated, as the leadership was subject to challenge and as members reaffirmed their status. "Ranking" (which literally reminded someone of his rank in the group), "sounding," or, among African-American youth, "toasting" or "playing the dozens" allowed members of the gang to challenge each other in a test of verbal

skill.[66] While leadership in a gang fight demanded a certain physical prowess and courage, overall gang leadership required a fair amount of intelligence, and the verbal agility involved in sounding tested the merits of
different aspirants to leadership. Generally, ranking reinforced the authority structure of the gang. Low-status gang members were the subject
of ranking sessions, although the activity included them in the rough
brotherhood of the gang even while reminding them of their place. A
conversation recorded by Kenneth Marshall suggests a fairly typical exchange. Freddy and Billy were making comments about each other's
clothing. Billy said, "Look at the outfit you have on now. I wouldn't give
my dog that stuff to wear!" Freddy replied, "O.K., man, you scored."
"Damn right I scored!" Billy chortled. "How could you come out on the
streets with stuff like that on?" Freddy replied that he was "not trying to
be sharp now," to which Billy retorted, "Damn right you're not trying to
be sharp."[67] Ranking also took the form of practical jokes. Vincent Riccio
recounted how the Gowanus Boys stripped one of their members, Mousie, in front of the girls and threw his clothes over the streetlight. Mousie
then had to climb the light pole naked to retrieve his clothing. Despite
the humiliation, Mousie kept coming back—he was one of the boys and
the ranking, however painful, was still a sign of his inclusion in the gang.[68]

Playing the dozens was characteristic of African-American gangs rather
than Euro-American or Puerto Rican ones. The dozens involved lewd
comments about family members, particularly mothers, and could expose severe hurts among boys who cruelly exploited their intimate
knowledge of each other's family situations. Claude Brown asserted control over his war counselor not only because he could stand up to him
in a fight, but because he knew he could taunt him about his absent
mother.[69] Kenneth Marshall observed that boys sometimes warned each
other off by declaring that they did not play the dozens, and persistence
after that point invited a fight.[70]

One might well ask what was the function of such potentially damag-
ing activity. The African-American community, in particular, highly prized
verbal skills, and boys learned the dozens and traditional "toasts" as important "manly" skills.[71] To hold one's own and survive on the streets
meant having a good "rap," and boys constantly practiced to develop their
ability. Verbal contests were also a form of entertainment and relieved the
tedium of hanging on the street corner for hours on end. Most important,

in the context of the gang, sounding defined the structure of relationships among members, serving to reinforce the leader's authority by virtue of his adeptness at the dozens.[72] The dozens reaffirmed bonds of masculine superiority over women, who were the usual vehicles for delivering insults, while they also confirmed the status of other males in the group. Insulting mothers may also have been a way of declaring independence from home and affirming identification with male street life.[73] The exchange of ritual insults elevated one player's masculinity over another's in a public forum, and only the ritualized nature of sounding and the cohesive structure of the gang prevented the tension from breaking out into violence.

Bop culture allowed gang members to negotiate with the outside world and with the gang world. Its symbols, codes, and rituals expressed both defiance of the dominant culture and the creation of meaning and order for gang members. It mediated between the worlds of working-class adolescence and working-class adulthood, and one can find in bop culture inversions of the dominant culture, working-class and ethnic cultures, and a commercial youth culture that frequently drew upon the bop world as a source of innovation. But as a subculture constructed by adolescents and young men, bop culture and the gang world it organized could not supply a permanent solution to the problems of working-class adolescents. Ultimately, gang members had to face leaving the gang and joining the adult world to which they were inevitably bound.

Bop culture allowed adolescents to defy school and the labor market, to mock the symbols of the dominant culture, and to defer the demands of working-class adulthood. Although the gang world provided only a temporary refuge from which participants removed themselves or were removed by adult authorities, the gang world itself proved resilient. When social workers, police, school authorities, and public officials attempted to invade it, they found how coherent a world gang members had constructed for themselves. Adolescents did leave the gang, but frequently it was on their own terms, and the choices they made were among street and organized crime, drug use, and the legitimate world of education and work.

# Leaving the Gang:
# Pathways into Adulthood

GANG membership did not last forever. Gangs were principally organizations of adolescents and young men, who, as they grew older, confronted the necessity of earning money, tired of the aimless hanging around on street corners, or became concerned that death, injury, or serious jail time awaited them. As "juniors" ascended to "senior" status, they watched what happened to the generation of gang members that preceded them and took stock of their situation. Youths considered the costs of gang membership—which escalated with age—and made choices about their futures. This chapter explores the different paths gang members took in leaving the gang. Some married and used the excuse of family to depart from the street scene; others decided that the costs of gang membership exceeded those of "yoking" and became reconciled to entering the labor market; and the armed forces beckoned to still others as a socially approved means for demonstrating manhood. However, only a minority fully escaped street life and drugs, and even fewer began the arduous climb up into the middle class. It was more common for former gang members to enter criminal careers that promised greater rewards than gang membership, or to use heroin, which replaced the gang as the center of their lives. For the unfortunate majority, the lack of education and social skills and an identity built around the aggressive defense of masculinity kept them in the streets after others in their cohort began to leave.

The process of leaving the gang is sometimes referred to as "maturing out," as if it were an inevitable life-stage phenomenon. I prefer to describe leaving the gang as the product of conscious decision making that was shaped by a variety of social and economic forces. Nor were these irrevocable decisions. Some young men left the gang but continued to be active in street life, while others drifted back and forth between work and hanging on the corner. In the postwar period, as in contemporary gangs, there were adults who associated with adolescent street gangs, and there was nothing "abnormal" about this. Because gang membership went to the heart of one's masculine identity and the economic and social environment remained unchanged, a decision to leave the gang community was a difficult one to make, especially for "core" members who had invested so much of themselves in the gang.[1]

The difficulties faced by youths trying to leave the gang should not be underestimated. Despite the efforts of street workers, the support of wives and family members, and the assistance of other adults, there was enormous pressure on young men to keep fighting. Rival gangs moved in to take over a power vacuum left by the disintegration of an established gang. Successive raids sometimes forced gangs to re-form, at least temporarily, to repulse attacks and protect their members, who reopened themselves to the risk of injury and arrest. Older, former gang members derided the loss of heart and masculinity by the younger ones trying to go social and goaded them into maintaining the honor of the gang.[2]

Sometimes gangs reinvented themselves and adopted a new identity to signify their intentions, but even this was not enough. The Conservatives, made up largely of former members of the Enchanters, opened a storefront clubhouse, painted the members' names on the walls for anyone to see, and sought help from the East Harlem Protestant Parish in organizing social activities. Members solemnly pledged to avoid violence, surrendered their guns, and agreed to get police protection. However, word that the Dragons were going down to 100th Street to attack them led a couple of the members to organize an ambush in self-defense. The police arrived at the same time the Dragons did, and it was the former Enchanters who were caught with guns firing at the Dragons, and two were arrested and incarcerated. Gang enmities ran deep and rival gangs would not let former enemies escape.[3]

The burden of a reputation that had taken years to develop was also difficult to shake. A gang member might decide to go by his family name, rather than his street name, in order to signify his retirement, but that did not mean others would respect his decision. When Nicky Cruz left the Mau Maus, he realized that he had to leave New York for his own safety, but most former gang members did not have that opportunity.

6.1. The Conservatives with Ramon Diaz in their storefront hangout.

Both police and community agencies eyed them with suspicion and discounted their claims of reform. The reputations that youths constructed dogged them for years as police picked up the known gang members whenever an incident occurred, and recreational centers and clubs barred them from membership. Forces from all sides conspired to keep a young man in the gang and on the streets, even as other less-prominent members of his gang cohort were able to leave.[4]

## CORE AND PERIPHERAL GANG MEMBERS

Sociologists (and gangs, too) distinguish between core and peripheral members, and this is a useful way of evaluating the relationship of the individual member to the gang. Usually gangs had a small number of core members and a much larger and frequently changing group of peripheral members. Youngsters were defined as peripheral members because they lived on the fringes of the gang, joining for some months or a year, but without finding the principal definition of themselves through their gang membership. Peripheral members may have affiliated with a gang for reasons of protection in tough neighborhoods or to try on a street identity. Both Dion DiMucci and "Little Anthony" Gourdine, mentioned in the previous chapter, found music more meaningful than bopping and saw themselves as peripheral gang members (" 'I was what you call a part-time Chaplain,' " maintained Gourdine), as did many other youngsters who did not become celebrities. Gang workers thought peripheral members were easier to peel away from the gang and involve in recreational activities or employment, while the core members required much more intensive work.[5]

Peripheral members of the gang might simply drift away. By failing to show up at the usual corner, by not participating in fights or rumbles, or by getting a job that interfered with hanging out, a youth could extricate himself from the gang. Such a decision involved some risks: taunts about turning punk were inevitable and getting beaten up by former comrades was possible. But peripheral members by definition had not invested all of themselves in the gang, they were usually not party to "official secrets," and their departure did not arouse deep feelings of betrayal. They had tried on a street identity and had decided to take it off, and it was rarely in the gang's best interest to try and hold them by force or to retaliate against them.[6]

Core members formed the heart of the gang. They had a larger investment in gang membership, interacted most intensively and regularly with each other, participated in gang rituals, and upheld the traditions of the gang. This group included, but was not limited to, the leadership of the gang. Although one had to be a core member in order to attain leadership positions, core membership did not translate automatically into high status. The core included individuals who were basically followers, the butts of practical jokes and the objects of sounding sessions, all of whom might have been lost without the gang. Social scientists have found that core members began delinquent activity at an earlier age, committed more serious crimes, continued to be subject to arrest and incarceration for a longer period of time, and engaged in criminal careers more frequently than did peripheral members.[7] When discussing the problems of leaving the gang, I am principally concerned with core members, for whom it was a more difficult process.

The possibilities and problems faced by core members leaving the gang depended on the circumstances of their departure. Those who began serious criminal careers, left the neighborhood either by enlisting or marrying and moving, or got lost in drug use chose acceptable means of loosening ties to the gang. However, a youth who withdrew from the core group without undertaking one of these more momentous changes could face a difficult time—including a serious beating.[8] Since core members knew the intimate details of gang activity, including criminal acts, their departure was both a betrayal and a security risk. There were rumors of gangs killing core members who tried to leave. When Nicky Cruz entered the Mau Maus, he was told, "Once a Mau Mau, always a Mau Mau," an explicit threat that he took quite seriously. It is possible that such killings took place, but I found no evidence of them. It is more likely that old enemies settled scores without paying attention to whether or not someone had left his gang. A core member leaving the gang for the legitimate world left his old friends behind but did not shed his enemies. That fact alone kept young men tied to their gangs.[9]

## Decision Making: Trauma and the Streets

Gang members' narratives frequently turn around a traumatic event. A crisis, such as incarceration, a serious injury, or the death of a friend, could jolt an adolescent into reassessing his life and reevaluating his gang membership. While this may be a literary device in gang-member autobiographies, other sources described similar "turning points" that led a gang member to reevaluate his membership.[10]

Perhaps the most prohibitive cost to remaining on the streets was the continually escalating price of maintaining one's reputation. Claude Brown knew that if he stayed in street life sooner or later he would be faced with having to kill someone in order to keep his position of respect. He also realized that once he turned sixteen, any serious criminal charge would bring an adult arrest record and increasingly long jail time. Ronny agonized over the revival of gang warfare in his Bedford-Stuyvesant neighborhood, afraid that he would be drawn in once again. These individuals had established reputations—no one could reasonably call them punks if they chose to walk away from further confrontations. Nonetheless, the agonies they went through—Claude Brown's constant headaches, Ronny's tortured, "I didn't want to be in it. I mean . . . I ain't punking out or anything like that, but I don't want to be messing around"—indicate the psychic cost of giving up gang membership and street life. Despite all this, some individuals found it the cheaper price to pay. Manny Torres admitted that it was "with some measure of relief" that he left his gangbanging days behind.[11]

A sentence to the reformatory provided a youth with a respite from the streets and sometimes caused him to have second thoughts about gang membership. JT was sent to reform school for four years on a weapons possession charge and recalled his incarceration as a blessing in disguise that "helped me wake up out of a bad dream." He realized that remaining in the gang world would inevitably lead to prison, and he returned to East Harlem determined to stay out of trouble. Israel Narvaez had a similar experience. After serving four and a half years for manslaughter following a gang killing, Narvaez was released on parole. "When I was released from prison, I had reached the breaking point. I knew that I couldn't take any more years—even months—behind bars."[12]

Sometimes acts of violence so startled a youth that they forced him to see his gang membership in a new light. For Nicky Cruz, the death of his close friend Mannie proved the catalyst. Trapped by a group of Bishops in their candy store hangout, Nicky and Mannie tried to duck out a side door into an alley. Nicky charged his enemies, who were momentarily startled and let him through, but Mannie, who had been knifed in an earlier confrontation with the Bishops, was unable to run fast enough to get away. When Nicky realized his friend was not with him, he returned in time to see Mannie stabbed:

> I saw the boy with the knife pull his arm back and with an underhand gesture jab the knife toward Mannie's ribs with great force. Mannie gasped and I saw him jerk upright. He remained erect against the wall for a short moment, and then started to collapse face first toward the concrete. As he fell, the boy with the knife viciously plunged it once more into his chest.

Nicky claimed that even as he watched the Bishops surround Mannie, he did not believe that they would kill him. Gangs were brutal—Nicky, Mannie, and the Mau Maus had kidnapped a Bishop, bound him hand and foot, and left him for several days in an abandoned building before re-

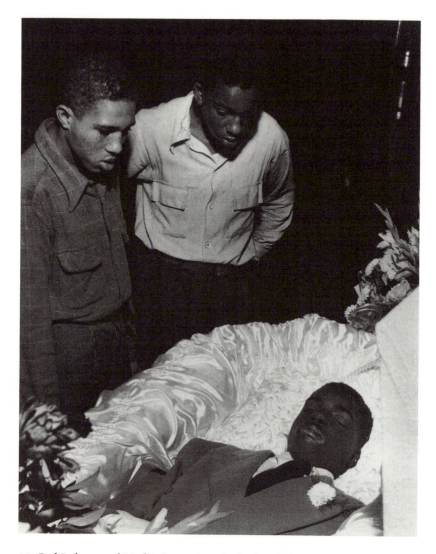

6.2. Red Jackson and Herbie Levy view the body of Clarence Gaines, killed by a rival gang.

turning to torture him by jabbing him around the face and neck with lighted cigarettes—but murder was not usually part of their repertoire. Mannie's death left Nicky stunned.[13]

Carl Joyeaux had already decided to leave the Deacons when he saw his friend Gent shotgunned on a Bedford-Stuyvesant street. As Joyeaux bundled Gent into a cab for the trip to the hospital, he pondered the senselessness of the shooting and his own responsibility for Gent's fate, since he had recruited him into the gang. As Joyeaux recalled it, he defied the calls for revenge by the other Deacons and, in a complete betrayal of the gang code, volunteered information to the police when they came to investigate the shooting.[14]

Even the death of a rival could spark a boy's conscience. Georgie, then a member of the Viceroys, recalled how several Dragons drove through 112th Street in East Harlem and started shooting at them. One of his friends was armed with a .38 and, when another boy managed to open the driver's side door, "Chico shot the Dragon in the head. He fell against the horn dead, and the car went out of control and went into that store on the corner of 112th and Madison." Georgie felt bad about the Dragon's death: "You know, you say, 'Ah, fuck it, yeah we killed a motherfucker, man.' But inside, you really say, 'Man, one of these days they probably come up to me and shoot me.' " Georgie thought of himself as lucky: "We stabbed a lot of guys, right, but never killed nobody, and we not doin' time."[15]

Crisis promoted introspection, but it did not help youths find their way out of the gang and out of the streets. Adolescents frequently needed the help of an adult to make the break from the gang, and a street worker, a local minister or priest, or even a reformatory official could provide crucial assistance.

## MENTORSHIP

Core members who found mentors to guide them out of the gang world were lucky. JC and JG formed close relationships with Nestor Llamas, their Youth Board worker, and eventually became gang workers themselves before entering New York's social service bureaucracy. For Carl Joyeaux and Claude Brown, it was Alfred Cohen, the director of the New York Training School for Boys, who took a special interest in them and encouraged them to develop their intellectual abilities. JT found help from Danny Murrow, who had been a gang worker with the New York City Youth Board before moving to JT's East Harlem neighborhood to direct the American Friends Service Committee's Friendship House. Kenneth Marshall, a Youth Board worker in Bedford-Stuyvesant, helped Ronny resist his gang's efforts to recruit him back into bopping. Although incidents in their lives led them to reconsider their commitment to the gang, the availability of adult sponsorship proved decisive in allowing these young men to leave the gang world.

For Nicky Cruz, it was a street-corner evangelist named David Wilkerson who provided key assistance. The stabbing death of his friend Mannie punctured Nicky's sense of invulnerability, left him with nightmares, and opened him to the possibility of a religious conversion. Wilkerson had come to New York from rural Pennsylvania to preach the Gospel to gangs after hearing about the Michael Farmer killing (discussed in chapter 3). Exhorting gang members to find Christ, Wilkerson challenged Nicky Cruz and other gang members to attend his services and eventually converted Cruz, who went on to attend divinity school and joined Wilkerson's Teen Challenge crusade. Although Mannie's death led Cruz to question his continued involvement in gang life, it was Wilkerson's presence that provided Cruz with the means of leaving the gang. Without the guidance of an adult, Cruz might have slipped back into gangbanging—as his friend Israel did—despite his disenchantment with it.[16]

Adult sponsorship frequently came in the form of a street worker. Both public and private agencies hired young men to make contact with gangs in their own milieu and to devise activities that might turn the gangs away from fighting. (Street work is discussed more extensively in the next chapter.) Street work depended on the worker's charismatic ability to reorient the gang, and social service agencies frequently found that ex-gang members were the best street workers. Former gang members were effective in communicating with gangs because of their shared experiences, and they were obvious role models for gang members. Street work projects served the important latent function of providing former gang members with employment and the opportunity to use their knowledge of street life constructively.

Street work became, in effect, an avenue of upward mobility. Five of the former New York City Youth Board street workers I interviewed had themselves been gang members, as had Vincent Riccio. All of my informants used their Youth Board experience to rise in the civil service/social welfare bureaucracy, and they attended college, frequently at night, in order to gain the credentials they needed to advance. (Street workers without college degrees remained frozen in street worker positions, and as the Youth Board became more bureaucratized and moved away from street work, at least a couple of the former gang workers were unable to adjust to finding other jobs.) Another form of street work—street-corner evangelism—served a similar function. Both Nicky Cruz and another former Brooklyn gang member, Sonny Arguinzoni, became ministers who worked with gangs. The existence of gang intervention projects, secular and nonsecular alike, provided at least a few former gang members with the opportunity to become educated and acquire middle-class status.[17]

## Return to the Labor Market

It was more common that adolescents made conscious choices to go "square"—to marry, take a legitimate job, or enlist in the military—without receiving any formal assistance. Gang members took the jobs they once had shunned and became reconciled to their place in the labor market. Marriage, especially to a young woman from outside the gang world, presented a perfect excuse to limit the time spent on the corner. In fact, according to criminologists Robert J. Sampson and John H. Laub, marriage and attachment to the labor market were the key variables determining an adolescent delinquent's cessation of criminal activity in adulthood.[18] These breaks with gang life when understood retrospectively appear inevitable as the results of a process of maturation. When seen prospectively, as gang members saw them, they appear to be choices made from a range of options. Gang members made conventional adjustments to adulthood because they decided the costs of unconventional choices were too high.

As adolescents saw harsher criminal penalties looming before them and had their fill of visits to the hospital emergency room or the funeral parlor, the terrors of the labor market began to pale. Construction work was a popular choice for young men because it retained a masculine ethic of rough work and independence, and it offered high pay.[19] Entry, however, was limited by ethnicity. African Americans and Puerto Ricans found that construction unions would not admit them into apprenticeship programs and then used their lack of appropriate training to refuse them permission to work. Piri Thomas replicated his Puerto Rican–born father's experience of repeated rejections from construction jobs. On the other hand, TS and RG, both Italian, left the Fordham Baldies to work construction once they were old enough to do so. TS commented that most of the guys in the neighborhood found jobs as construction workers: "We wanted money and we knew we had to earn it." Both of them found jobs because of family friends: "Every job I ever got was through somebody I knew," explained TS. RG came from a somewhat more advantaged background, and after his father's death, he took over the family's liquor store and eventually became a wine importer. For Euro-Americans, at least, connections through ethnic niches offered the opportunity to enter the labor market, acquire skills, and obtain well-paying and high-status work.[20]

For African-American or Puerto Rican youths, leaving the gang usually involved a return to arenas where they had failed in the past—such as school or the labor market. Subordination in these areas could not be justified in terms of masculinity; it was born of necessity and gang members tried to come to terms with unmanly obedience. Georgie, who returned to East Harlem from prison, reluctantly went to work in a garment factory. "Everytime I used to work and I used to see that foreman, he'd remind me of the prison guard. It always bothered me. . . . When I was working for my boss, like, it would remind me so much of a jail." AC took a job in a gas station after his parents returned to Puerto Rico. He was on his own and had to support himself; besides, he said, "You can't keep doing the same things." Others in his cohort became building superintendents or hospital orderlies. The choice to yoke was particularly difficult if a youth remained in the same neighborhood and faced the constant lure of the easy money and the seemingly successful life enjoyed by the hustlers. The decision to seek respectability anyway is a measure of the costs of remaining in the gang.[21]

## MARRIAGE AND FAMILY

Wives and serious girlfriends provided another key support for youths leaving the gang. Attention to one's spouse or to a "steady" was a socially acceptable reason to lessen the time spent on the corner and to loosen ties to the gang. Gang members sometimes linked the decision to look for legitimate work to the development of serious relationships with girls. RG, who married at age twenty-two, maintained that he would not have gotten a job if it had not been for his girlfriend and the need for a dependable source of income. He also admitted that he was tired of "being a target," and it seems likely that his relationship with his girlfriend provided an excuse to leave the gang, find work, and still maintain face in the neighborhood. TS married at age twenty and moved away from Baldie territory to another section of the Bronx, which made the break from the group easier.[22] Growing weary of street life, some gang members began to define gang fighting as "kid stuff" and used their relationships to distance themselves from the gang.

No one discussed male-female relationships in precisely these terms, although gang members were nearly universal in mentioning marriage as one reason why young men left the gang. In fact, the evidence suggests that some individuals made a deliberate choice to marry "nice girls" from outside the neighborhood as a way out of the gang. JC, for example, maintained that the debs were fine as girlfriends, but would not be appropriate choices for marriage. When he got married, he "picked a girl from a stable family" who had no relationship to the gang world.[23] As noted in chapter 4, gang members were ambivalent about their relationships with nice girls. Family life demanded a return to the labor market or, at least, to income-producing activity in the underground economy. Despite the fears of intimacy that plagued gang members' relationship with girls, a "nice girl" provided a youth with a lifeline out of the gang. Gang members did not have to make this choice and those that did, did so deliberately.

## Military Service

Enlistment in the military was in many ways the perfect solution for the gang member eager to escape the street but anxious to preserve his manly reputation. Military service took a youth away from the temptations of street life, it provided an acceptable reason for stopping gang fighting, and the military incorporated the symbols and language of masculinity so important to adolescents. Military service also offered a stage and an audience before which a youth could continue to demonstrate his masculinity.[24]

Gang members self-consciously used enlistment to escape the gang. One African-American gang member, turning seventeen, realized that his life was at a crossroads: " 'I had a lot of enemies in the Bronx, in Manhattan, and in other areas of the city because of my gang affiliation. And the illusions that I had of grandeur, of becoming an aerodynamics engineer, just didn't correspond with the objective conditions." In order to get out of the neighborhood and to gain time to figure out what to do with himself, Dharuba joined the army. It was the sort of decision that street workers encouraged young men to make.[25]

The Korean War broke up a number of the gangs active in the early 1950s. Several seniors of the Greene Avenue Stompers belonged to the same state guard unit, and when it was called up, the gang splintered, with the younger members unable to maintain the Stomper tradition and turf. Others enlisted for the sake of adventure. Carl Joyeaux analyzed the Korean War in gang terms. He wrote that after the outbreak of war "eight of our members turned it on the North Koreans and Chinese, who had raided the turf of the South Koreans, brother club of the Americans." NL enlisted in the Marines during the war to get away from the gang-banging in his South Bronx neighborhood ("the Marine Corps changed everything for me"), and he, like other returning veterans, took advantage of the GI bill to gain a college education.[26]

Vietnam had a similar, albeit more widespread, effect. MR noticed a decline in gang activity in the Inwood section in Manhattan in the mid-1960s, as young men were drawn off into the service. As the older Lords were drafted, the gang broke up and no one initiated the younger boys into the gang. SN also believed that the draft destroyed the continuity between gang generations in his neighborhood on the Lower East Side of Manhattan. Young men volunteered for the service or were drafted, which removed a critical mass of them from gangbanging.[27] (This is discussed more extensively in chapter 8.)

The military's appeal to young men is understandable. They found social approval for fighting, and the same spirit of heart and daring that marked them as men in the gang world distinguished them in the military. ES, a warlord in East Harlem's Dragons, enlisted in the army and stated proudly that his leadership qualities were recognized in the service.

He was the only Puerto Rican in his noncommissioned officers class.[28] Ability, rather than ethnicity or class, seemed to determine advancement.

Most important, unlike some of the other avenues to respectability, the military enshrined a cult of masculinity. The military services, especially the Marine Corps, employed masculinity to arouse and focus recruits' aggressiveness. In basic training, drill sergeants exposed any hint of weakness publicly and denounced it as unmanly, while referring to recruits as women or "faggots." The rituals and brutality of basic training were in some ways quite similar to those of the gang. They provided an initiation rite that separated true men from the weak, the despised, the effeminate, the world of women, homosexuals, and civilians. Only those who mastered the physical and psychological challenges of basic training, who submerged their individual identities to the will of the group, and who proved their ability to withstand pain and humiliation and to exact revenge on the enemy were admitted to full status as military men. Gang members could justify their unfamiliar obedience to orders in the masculinist terms of military authority, while the military used the adolescent obsession with proving one's manhood as a tool to establish discipline and exact obedience. And the Korean and Vietnam Wars, with their voracious appetites for manpower, provided poor adolescents with the opportunity to demonstrate their manliness in combat.[29]

In peacetime, however, the military was more particular about who joined. In 1959, youth worker Kenneth Marshall recorded notes of a meeting he attended with members of the Home Services Bureau. There he learned that individuals who had been committed to reform school for sex offenses, homicide, and armed assault were automatically eliminated from consideration as volunteers. Gang fighting and simple assault were not considered as serious. Since the nineteenth century, enlistment had been a choice given boys leaving reform school and it was used later by juvenile court justices as an alternative to commitment to a reformatory. The serious charges that sometimes faced adolescent gang members in the postwar period foreclosed that option, at least during the late 1950s when the cold war remained cold and the size of the military fell. (The army, the chief consumer of young men, declined in size by nearly 50 percent during the decade before beginning its dramatic Vietnam Era growth.)[30]

CRIMINAL CAREERS

Gang members lived in neighborhoods where crime was a viable and manly career. Such a "career move" was much admired and appeared to be a natural progression from gang membership, something sociologist Frederic Thrasher discovered in the 1920s.[31] Having spent several years on the streets, gang members were acquainted with local hustlers and might even have performed an occasional service for them. "Teddy," who eventually became a heroin dealer and user, was asked how he learned about criminal activity in the neighborhood. He replied that "by being a kid on the block, we knew everything." Teddy had been a gang member but soon became involved in organized crime. Teddy started out as a runner, making deliveries in the neighborhood, and he also worked as a lookout:

> I was working in this house that dealt in sex, alcohol, and drugs. There were girls there, and whiskey for sale, and narcotics. The police knew this was going on, but they didn't arrest anybody because they'd come buy [sic] and pick up their payoff. My position was more or less a hanger-oner or a flunkie. I used to put the liquor in the bottles. I'd add one shot of brown sugar that I cooked up on the stove to make it look just like whiskey. I would sit on the stoop, where I had a string with a bell. When somebody wanted some whiskey, they would come up in their car; I'd go up and get it, bring it out. I was a lookout man. If the cop came, I'd ring the bell and start running.[32]

Other gang members—not necessarily in their corporate capacity as gang members—had extensive experience in criminal activity, including burglary, car theft, and robbery. While most members might raid a delivery truck for food or steal from an outdoor vendor, only a smaller clique, who might share proceeds among themselves but not with other gang members, engaged in more specialized forms of criminal activity. These youths became acquainted with the neighborhood fences, gamblers, numbers runners, and narcotics dealers, and in effect, had apprenticed for criminal careers.[33]

There were three forms of criminal careers: membership in an Italian crime family, participation in non-Italian organized crime, and street crime. New York's Italian crime families sat at the apex of the underground economy and provided employment opportunities for illegal entrepreneurs. Members undertook professional burglaries, hijacked cargo from the docks and the airports, loan-sharked, ran numbers and other gambling operations, imported and dealt drugs, and engaged in labor racketeering, among other activities. They generally enjoyed political influence and therefore gained some protection from arrest and prosecution. Organized crime outside the Italian crime families involved similar types of illegal activities and relied on a network of associates, frequently individuals who had shared membership in the same street gangs. Finally, street crime and hustling included low-level drug dealing, pimping, stickups, muggings, and shoplifting. These activities required few or easily learned skills, yielded little return, brought low status, and involved greater exposure to arrest and incarceration.

Organized crime has traditionally served as a means of upward mobility for working-class youths with no other viable route to riches. Gambling, labor racketeering, after-hours clubs, and brothels had long provided opportunities for economic advancement. The lure of easy money proved overwhelming to some. One gang member, now serving time for murder, reportedly explained his leaving the gang for organized crime by saying, "Why kill someone for free when you can get paid to do it." In the postwar period, gang members wishing to enter organized crime found that the Italian crime families controlled access to the choicest enterprises.[34]

The Italian crime families, which rose to prominence during Prohibition, used their experience in the organization and distribution of bootleg liquor to organize the importation of narcotics. Although illegal entrepreneurship took many forms, narcotics dealing was among the most lucrative. Ralph Salerno, a New York City detective with the police intelligence unit, explained that until the 1960s, heroin importation depended on ties to a handful of Corsican dealers. Only Italian Americans and a few Jewish mobsters affiliated with them had the connections necessary to purchase heroin from the Corsicans, and as a result, the Italian crime families controlled sales and distribution in New York. As Salerno put it, "A big Italian dealer is going to sell it [heroin] in one-kilo, two-kilo, half-kilo lots to people that he knows and trusts well. You're not going to get others in the picture until you get down to what we used to call the 'ounce men.' "

The Italians had created an ethnic niche in organized crime, which (as in the legitimate economy) limited opportunity to members of the preferred group.[35]

Naturally some Italian-American gang members aspired to become members of the Italian crime families. RG mentioned that several of his younger brother's generation of Fordham Baldies joined the Mafia; TS said that he had several cousins who had done so; and a number of interviewees noted that talented youths in Italian Harlem's Red Wings were recruited for organized crime, which provided a clear ladder of opportunity for adolescent street gang members. (As seen in chapter 3, organized crime restrained street gangs because of their power and this promise of opportunity, but contrary to theorists Richard Cloward and Lloyd Ohlin, the presence of crime families did not prevent conflict gangs from organizing.)[36]

Not everyone possessed the talent to join the Mafia, however. Jerry Della Famina recalled that very few of his tougher acquaintances in Gravesend in Brooklyn made it. "The Mafia was not dumb; it didn't want most of the half-baked crazies who were posing over on West Tenth Street. Those who were too dumb for the Mafia never saw the light of day at home, on their twentieth birthday: they usually were in jail someplace, or on the run." And even those former gang members entering organized crime found fewer riches than they hoped for. "Tony" became involved with peddling narcotics in East Harlem before being murdered, while Vincent Riccio recalled that many of his gang cohort remained small-time bookies or numbers runners.[37]

Organized crime, like other parts of New York's social structure, had a color line. As New York's population changed, the Italian crime families employed African Americans and Puerto Ricans for street-level distribution and sales. However, African-American and Puerto Rican distributors remained lodged in the lowest echelons of organized crime, where they were most vulnerable to violent encounters with competitors, to arrest, and to incarceration. For example, Little Abner, who helped East Harlem's Dragons establish citywide alliances, had a less successful career in organized crime. Abner remained too undisciplined, reportedly crossed one of the "106th Street [East Harlem] Italians," and was found shot to death in the trunk of a car. "Luis Santos" first sold marijuana and then heroin but found that his connection refused to sell to him in quantity:

"The Italians controlled our area; they doled out the stuff in small portions so you could only get so much from them and you could never take over even a block." Santos dabbled too much in his own product line and partied instead of plowing the profits of his heroin sales back into his operation. He wound up imprisoned after a fight and believed he had been set up by rivals. In each of these cases, gang members had gone into organized crime, only to find themselves barely a notch or two above street crime. The color line that kept them from advancing also left them exposed. Usually professional criminals who were members of minority groups lacked the connections to public and police officials that shielded their higher-placed Euro-American colleagues.[38]

Over time, ethnic succession occurred within organized crime. African Americans and Puerto Ricans replaced Euro-Americans and constructed their own illegal organizations in the ghetto. (White mobsters led by Arthur "Dutch Schultz" Flegenheimer had originally taken over the numbers in Harlem from African Americans in the 1930s, so the development of African-American and Latino crime organizations in the 1960s was not entirely new.[39]) Where recruitment into the Italian organized crime families was based on kinship first and then ethnicity, African Americans drew on their youth gang friendships for partners in adult criminal activity, while Puerto Ricans relied on both kin and gang associations. "Harold Robinson," a former member of the War Dragons, an African-American gang from Bedford-Stuyvesant, recounted, "We haven't been a gang in twenty years. Man, we're in business pure and simple. . . . And we started moving in as the Italians lost muscle here." As youngsters, members of the War Dragons caught the eye of an African-American entrepreneur who advised them to give up rumbling and other "kid stuff" and come work for him. Five of the War Dragons began running numbers, protecting dice games, and working in an after-hours club and whorehouse, and the gang members gradually moved up from their entry-level jobs. As a professional criminal, Robinson still relied on his gang cohort: "Teddy, Tiny and Tim are still with me every day working numbers and we are into gambling at after-hours clubs. George now banks four of those spots and Teddy among other things picks up the cash every night." Through regular payoffs to the police in the local precinct, the former gang members rendered themselves less vulnerable to arrest and had succeeded in becoming major entrepreneurs.[40]

Illegal enterprise promised adolescents far greater returns than the unskilled jobs they otherwise would have competed for, even as it remained a risky and difficult route to success. DS, an African-American former gang member from East Harlem, became a numbers runner in Harlem, began a narcotics distribution ring, did some loan-sharking, and opened an illegal after-hours club. He relied on former members of his gang, the Comanches, to handle distribution problems, intimidate rivals, and help recycle the proceeds of his illegal enterprises. A group of seven met weekly at a local bar to discuss the problems that had arisen in their respective businesses and to agree on who should handle them. While DS was very successful, he eventually served an eight-year prison term on drug charges. Like other members of organized criminal groups, DS understood that doing time was an occupational risk. It still beat yoking.[41]

Street crime offered less money and greater risk for young men leaving the gang than did organized crime. The major difference between street crime and organized crime was in the level of skill involved. One informant explained to anthropologist Francis Ianni that street crime did not require any skill. You only needed a little moxie since "any jerk with a trigger finger can put a gun in somebody's face and get a few bucks." Claude Brown noted that several of his adolescent acquaintances became street hustlers, minor pimps, and low-level pushers, which meant constant exposure to the perils of the street. Their lives involved a nearly endless cycling in and out of jail. In the course of a criminal career, as ethnographer Mark Fleisher has argued, jail came to be seen as a relief from the streets, the only time a street criminal had access to housing, food, recreational opportunities, tutoring, and health care on a regular basis.[42]

Street crime was the career of the least skilled. Adult street criminals were too erratic to be allowed to join an illegal enterprise. Frequently they were drug addicts who could not be trusted, or they were men lacking the personality to organize their own operations or to catch the eye of a more successful criminal. In addition, their lack of education and social capital frustrated their attempts to rise in the underground economy. They remained street criminals because they were unwilling to face the unmanly subordination required in most unskilled work in the legitimate economy, and they were unable to do anything else.[43]

## Heroin

Heroin ("horse") offered yet another avenue out of the gang. Evidence differs on the amount of tolerance gangs had for heroin users: some threatened to expel those who used the drug, and, as seen in chapter 4, the threat of expulsion seemed to help some youngsters get off drugs. Other gangs allowed a certain amount of sniffing and skin-popping (in which heroin would be injected but not into a vein), especially as a way of coming down after a fight, and some members even injected the drug intravenously. In most gangs, however, regular heroin users formed only a small clique or used the drug individually and did not remain part of the core. Leaders who dabbled in horse generally lost status.[44]

Gangs mistrusted full-fledged heroin addicts, since their powdered dreams were more important than gang loyalty. Boppers were smart enough to understand that an addict going "cold turkey" in a cell would not stand up to police interrogation. Gang worker Vincent Riccio commented that while gang members would risk arrest to bring an addicted former member who had taken an overdose to the hospital, they would shun him on other occasions. "Charlie," whose social life had revolved around the gang, was no longer allowed to hang out with them after he had become a confirmed addict. He explained, " 'They told us, 'We don't want you junkies lousing us up.' . . . I don't blame them.' " Frequently gangs did not have to expel addicts. As Archie Hargraves, a minister with the East Harlem Protestant Parish, told a reporter, " 'The ones who get hooked drop out of the gang and drift off in little knots by themselves.' " The appearance of heroin use in a gang often foretold its disintegration, as addicts were consumed by "taking care of business"—hustling the resources necessary to support a habit, scoring, and nodding off into a narcotic bliss—and could not be counted on to support the gang.[45]

Users flirted with addiction, but addiction was not inevitable. Some adolescents limited their usage to weekends and never became addicted. Joseph Fernandez was a weekend user and claimed that his heroin use never interfered with other activities. Because he controlled his dosage, no one—parents, straight friends, school officials—ever knew that he used heroin. By all accounts, Fernandez was lucky; "Mannie" was more typical. Mannie claimed that first he used marijuana and then turned to heroin in his search to prove that he was the toughest and had the most heart of anyone in the gang. " 'From 'pot' you said you'd try a little 'sniffing' . . . to show that you were even 'badder' and then you went from 'sniffing' to 'skin-popping' . . . and then to 'mainlining.'. . . Then you were the 'baddest' in the whole club, and you didn't care what anybody thought, and you went off by yourself.' " In Mannie's case, heroin use led right out of the gang, as it did for most addicts.[46]

The presence of a large number of adolescent heroin users in a neighborhood led to a decline in gang fighting. (This is discussed in chapter 8 in the context of declining gang activity in the 1960s.) Narcotics sellers had no wish to attract the police attention that gang fighting drew, and heroin users wanted free access to supplies regardless of neighborhood boundaries. The constant search for a fix or for the money to purchase one took an addict far afield into different neighborhoods, which meant he could not afford to have a known affiliation with a particular gang. This virtually guaranteed that he could not be counted on for gang activities. Even ethnic differences faded in importance. Members of the largely Italian Fordham Baldies, who fought to keep African-American and Puerto Rican youngsters from crossing their turf to attend Theodore Roosevelt High School, later entered African-American and Puerto Rican areas in search of heroin. "You were scoring dope from Puerto Rican and black guys and in those neighborhoods, so you didn't want to fight them," RG maintained. As the seniors withdrew from the gang in larger numbers to become heroin users, they tried to discourage the juniors from reviving hostilities. One Youth Board worker wrote in his notes that the older members of his Bedford-Stuyvesant gang, who were then using narcotics, were afraid that if gang fighting recurred, they would be the ones picked up by police since they were the known gang members. Because arrest limited their access to illegal drugs, the seniors wanted to keep the peace.[47]

A few gang members maintained that heroin use replaced gang fighting as a test of masculinity. A powerful mystique surrounded the drug and dared adolescents to try it. By arguing that they had enough will to control their dosage, users defied the drug's power and proved their masculine prowess. Claude Brown recalled coming home from reform school and finding that his hip friends were all talking about horse and getting high. Suddenly, in his group, bopping was for kids and heroin was for men. Brown argued that even though heroin use pulled a youth out of gang fighting, no one accused him of cowardice. "They would just say that you were a junkie, and everybody knew that junkies didn't go around bebopping." Junkies retained their masculine pride by maintaining that they were too cool to fight.[48]

It is more likely that youths who were worn out by the tension of gang warfare or who found that the gang could no longer supply their emotional needs used heroin as an escape. Once a user became addicted, heroin became the center of the universe, transforming his consciousness of himself and his surroundings. One heroin-using former gang member told his street worker that after shooting up he looked at his slum world with great serenity. Fordham Baldie Dion DiMucci put it most evocatively:

> It was freedom like I'd never had. It was complete confidence: a magic potion that set the world right side up. Smack did for me what I couldn't do for myself. I wasn't afraid any longer. My doubts disappeared in a warm, embracing glow. That first time I did it, I remember walking down Crotona Avenue in the middle of the street, on the white lines, and looking up at the tenement buildings. I felt like it all belonged to me, like I owned the world and it was a beautiful place.[49]

Heroin users were at peace with their world, at least for a time. Rumors that someone was mainlining traveled fast in the neighborhoods, and the consequent loss of position in the gang provided a certain safety. They were recognized as retired from fighting and could travel beyond the confines of the old neighborhood without having constantly to check their backs. They had metamorphosed from diddleybops to heroin users, which had moved them out of the gang world. Heroin promised liberation and an opportunity, according to Manny Torres, to "walk on tiptoe with the gods." Heroin supplied a new meaning, a new set of rituals, new associates, and a whole new organization of life to replace that provided by the gang. Most users did not believe they would become addicts, and they did not see their futures written on the gaunt features of neighborhood junkies.[50]

# Intervening in Gangs:
# The Problems and Possibilities
# of Social Work

WORKING with gangs was a major facet of social policy in the postwar period. Settlement houses, churches, and public agencies tried to stop gang fighting and make it easier for individuals to leave the gang. Intervening in gangs took three forms: street work, institutionally based recreation/social programs, and community-wide intervention projects. Street workers ("detached workers") searched out street gangs, helped members find jobs, and provided counseling for gang members. Their most important role was serving as mentors and helping gang members make a conventional transition into adulthood. Institutions also developed programs to draw gangs off the streets, and they hosted recreation programs and mediated among warring gangs. Community organizing projects linked institutions together and developed a neighborhood strategy to create truces, to counsel gang members, and to work for community improvement. These distinctions blurred considerably in practice but they allow us to proceed from the individual, to the group, and then to the community level in analyzing gang intervention.

Virtually all intervention programs mediated gang conflict. Mediation involved face-to-face discussions between rival groups led by a negotiator with the aim of achieving a written agreement that resolved a conflict. Mediation may have prevented fights, but it also supplied gangs with the prestige and attention they craved and, as a by-product, with greater organizational coherence, resources, and sometimes new members. As a result, mediation was heavily criticized by those who saw gangs as a problem of policing, to be handled with nightsticks on the street and jail time after court. But, as gang worker Vincent Riccio put it, "If the Youth Board did nothing else, its idea of getting the kids together in a peace conference justifies its existence. An enormous number of young lives have been saved by these secret, macabre, powder-kegged gatherings of kids."[1] Mediation was only one form of gang intervention, but the differences of opinion about mediation reflected larger philosophical differences over approaches to gangs. Tension existed between social work and a policing approach, and in our own time, it has been resolved in favor of law and order. This chapter explores the successes, the failures, and the possibilities of social work.

## THE ORIGINS OF GANG INTERVENTION

In New York, gang intervention projects dated from the period immediately after World War II, when the adolescent gang problem was first identified. Private agencies initiated street work in Central Harlem, Tompkins Park in Brooklyn, and Morrisania in the South Bronx in response to the increase in gang violence and the resulting fatalities. But gang intervention was not devised in New York. These initial efforts were inspired by the Chicago Area Project (CAP), which also became the model for the New York City Youth Board and for other institutional and community-based gang intervention programs.

The Chicago Area Project opened in 1934 as the brainchild of University of Chicago sociologist Clifford Shaw. Shaw believed that organizing the indigenous community to solve its own problems was the best way to attack juvenile delinquency. A well-integrated community did not tolerate the illegal activities that lured adolescents into crime; it provided recreational opportunities, and it mediated between the institutions of the dominant society and local youth. Because of his democratic philosophy, Shaw did not impose a predetermined program on the community. Instead, CAP engaged local residents in reforming their own children according to their own means. Youth workers, both paid and volunteer staff from the neighborhood, participated in what became known as "curbstone counseling" because it took place outside of institutions. Curbstone counseling, the forerunner of street work, assisted youths in trouble with the law, provided advice on handling personal or family problems, encouraged adolescents to stay in school, and helped youths find work. CAP's philosophy also linked adults and adolescents in a joint effort at community improvement.

Most gang intervention projects in New York drew on CAP's example. However, few incorporated a similar respect for the community and for individual delinquents, and fewer still implemented its policy of community empowerment. Nonetheless, CAP is a useful benchmark against which to examine New York's gang intervention projects.[2]

New York's intervention programs focused on ending gang fighting, and they largely limited themselves to hiring detached workers. The Central Harlem project, for example, worked with four of the most aggressive gangs, which ranged in size from thirty-five to over one hundred members. Each gang had a street worker, who encouraged the members to plan social activities, including block parties, dances, and athletic events, that substituted for fighting. The social initiatives, project sponsors hoped, would demonstrate gang members' ability to do something constructive and improve both their self-image and their relationship with the community. At the end of the project, the directors concluded that it had been successful: none of the gangs had engaged in interclub warfare while under the guidance of their street workers.[3]

The end of gang fighting among the Central Harlem gangs, together with equally promising results from the South Bronx and Tompkins Park, led to a rapid expansion of street work. The New York City Youth Board, which opened in the Office of the Mayor in 1947, took over funding for the private intervention projects and eventually opened the Brooklyn Detached Worker Project in 1950. The Council of Social and Athletic Clubs replaced it, reflecting the expansion of street work to troubled neighborhoods throughout the city. By 1955, the Youth Board's Council of Social and Athletic Clubs had forty gang workers on the streets of New York.[4]

## STREET WORK

Like the private agencies, the Youth Board hired young street workers or detached workers to make contact with the gangs. Detached workers derived their name from their relationship to the sponsoring agency.

Unlike most social workers, who were psychotherapeutic in focus, agency based, and waited for the individual to come and request help, detached workers followed the curbstone counseling model and were rarely found in the office. They met gangs on the street corner, in the park, or in the candy store and at virtually any hour of the day or night.[5]

The first step for any detached worker was to locate and make contact with the gang. Locating the gang was the easy step. From graffiti on the walls, conversations with community leaders, store owners, and police, and by simple observation, street workers could identify the hangouts and core membership of the local gang. Gang worker Vincent Riccio "knew" the members of his gang before he ever met them simply by reading the inscription of names and the claims of gang dominance written on neighborhood walls. Sam Kolman, in his fictionalized account of working for the Youth Board, described his first identification of his gang:

> Then as I moved towards the far end of the luncheonette, I saw them. Four teen-agers, nattily dressed in expensive sports jackets and freshly pressed slacks, were beating out a soft tattoo at the back of the counter. . . . Something seemed to set them aside from the other teen-agers I had seen in the neighborhood. Each was wearing a fedora with an arched brim, the bebopper's hat.[6]

Gang workers learned the semiotics of the street and used their knowledge of gang culture to make contact with the gang.

The next step in establishing some sort of relationship with the gang could take months of work. "After literally consuming hundreds of cokes, gallons of coffee, playing the juke box, and just 'hanging around,' " noted one report, "this worker became a familiar figure and was invited to participate in conversations, to pitch pennies, and to play football with the boys."[7] Street workers were sometimes introduced to the gang by an intermediary, frequently an adult affiliated with a church or neighborhood settlement. Even then the process of winning acceptance took a long time. Richard Brotman, in his ethnographic study of the Amsterdam Knights, described the lengthy negotiations he undertook with the gang after being introduced by the director of a recreation center as a potential basketball coach. "Bobby," a Knight who occasionally attended the center, responded to the introduction by saying that he could arrange a meeting with the gang if Brotman could arrange for the sole use of the gym for basketball practice. The two danced around the issue before Bobby agreed to introduce Brotman to some of the other gang members, while Brotman remained noncommittal about the gym. After several encounters on the street corner, Brotman decided he could come around without "Bobby," and he began establishing relationships with some of the gang's leaders. After meeting challenges, such as climbing over fences to play ball in closed playgrounds, Brotman thought he was making progress with the group. He and the Knights returned to the issue of the gym and agreed that use of half of a court in the gym was a reasonable compromise. Still the Knights regarded him warily; he noted that he was called neither friend nor coach.[8]

Gang workers offered concrete services as a way of proving themselves to the gang. They set up athletic programs with cooperating recreational centers, visited gang members in jail, and found them jobs. After a worker assisted some twenty gang members in finding jobs, one youth said in admiration, " 'Man, you came around here and got us all working.' " With Brotman, the breakthrough came when the Knights asked him to attend a meeting where they would discuss the rules set by the recreational agency on use of the gym. For the first time, Brotman was invited to participate in a formal meeting of the gang.[9]

Once a relationship had been cemented, the gang worker began the real work of turning the gang away from fighting and criminal activities. Richard Brotman took pains to avoid passing judgment on gang activities or on gang members' opinions. Like other gang workers, he discussed the potential outcome if the gang were caught doing something illegal, rather than simply condemning it. When Brotman observed one of the boys stealing from the recreation center, for example, he pointed out to him that the group had signed for the equipment and that it would be foolish to jeopardize their use of the facilities with a theft. The youth agreed and returned the item. After accepting Brotman's judgment about an action, it became easier for individual members to ask him for advice on more personal issues, such as schooling, girlfriends, or joining the military. The youth worker tried to make gang members aware of the consequences of their actions, to think through decisions rather than acting impulsively, and to take responsibility for themselves.[10]

Of course, the purpose of gang intervention was to end gang fighting. Gang workers tried to identify the leaders of a gang, believing that if some of these individuals could be swayed, either the rest of the core and the peripheral members would follow, or the gang would splinter and become ineffectual. Kenneth Marshall, a Youth Board worker with Brooklyn's Greene Avenue Stompers, realized that the Stompers were made up of several subgroups, not all of which were equally interested in street fighting. Marshall chose one of these groups, which he identified as the "Angels," and concentrated time and resources on them to build their prestige and lure members away from the fighting groups. He helped them organize a "hall dance" (a dance in a rented hall, rather than in a member's home, which bestowed great prestige on a group), find a clubhouse, and become one of the more respected factions of the Stompers even though they did not include the major Stomper leaders. Marshall noted that after meetings, gang members who were unaffiliated with the Angels would wait on the stoop to find out what had happened and that a number eventually applied for membership. While Marshall did not succeed in breaking up the core of individuals who wanted to fight, he drew off potential fighters by providing resources and enhancing the prestige of an alternative group for those who tired of fighting or who might have joined a fighting gang for social reasons.[11]

Marshall's difficulty in reaching the core of fighters in the Stompers illustrates the central problem faced by street workers. Marshall could offer very little to the young men who were committed to constructing masculine identities through public posturing and street fighting. The gang worker had a reasonable hope of persuading peripheral members to break off from the gang, which was the tactic Marshall chose. And, as seen in chapter 6, the street worker provided an indispensable avenue of escape for those gang members who realized the terrible price they would pay by continuing to define their masculinity through street life. Street workers were able to reconnect these individuals to the world of working-class labor, but they could do little for those determined to be badmen.

Street workers offered their most valuable assistance in the area of job services. Despite a history of failure and even resistance to the job market, most adolescents needed to earn money, and gang workers' field notes indicate that the youths discussed work constantly. They expressed their distaste for the low-skilled, low-wage jobs available to them, but, driven by poverty, they desperately hunted for work. Some experienced repeated rejection in their job searches, but whether this occurred because of discrimination, a poor work history, or lack of qualifications is not always clear. Gang workers advised members about applying for jobs and on appropriate attire and etiquette, encouraged them to be realistic about their aspirations, and referred youngsters to agencies that specialized in hard-to-place workers. Steve Klein, a detached worker on the Lower East Side, was introduced to other youths by members of his gang as someone who could help them find jobs, which provided him with instant status in the neighborhood. Klein's group, the Spanish Kings, had abandoned street fighting, had tried drug pushing but found it both risky and morally troubling (or so they told Klein), and had come to the realization that yoking was their only viable alternative. The Kings struggled with this conclusion, but with Klein's assistance, they found work and apparently became reconciled to their prospects.[12]

In retrospect it seems surprising that the street workers accomplished as much as they did. A street worker had precious little to offer the adolescent gang, except advice, and most of his successes were with individuals or younger groups. A lot of what a street worker did was diversionary: organizing camping trips; car rides to an amusement park or the beach; or establishing a basketball league while trying to get his gang through the summer without anyone getting shot or imprisoned. According to the agencies, gang workers became "substitute fathers" (although no gang member has described the relationship in those terms); certainly there is evidence that they established close ties to individuals in their gangs. Street workers' intervention saved lives, and they provided links between the gang and conventional society. They eased a difficult transition into the labor market or into school and helped former gang members resign themselves to their position in the social structure. Much of what they did was traditional social work. But a central question remains: Why did gang members allow themselves to be counseled when the (usually overt) aim of that counseling was to break up their gang and force them back into a working-class world from which they had fled?

Gang leaders cooperated with street workers for their own purposes. Although gangs were initially suspicious of street workers, eventually having a street worker became a source of prestige, since it meant that a gang was bad enough to force official recognition of its reputation. In the status-conscious gang world, gangs watched the assignments of street workers carefully, noting which gangs had received workers and which actions earned them the required notoriety. (" 'Having a worker makes you a real 'down' club,' " a gang member told Lewis Yablonsky. " 'All 'bad' clubs have a 'man' trying to change them.' ") Street workers also sponsored mediation sessions that brought rival gang leaders together to negotiate differences and sign treaties. Mediation offered a convenient— and status-preserving—escape from confrontation, while it supplied gang leaders with renewed prestige and recognition.[13] Gang programs, even if underfunded and few in number, still provided resources (such as access to recreation programs or field trips) that members otherwise would not have had. Youth workers were useful in providing information about jobs (essential for those on parole) and for appearing in court as character witnesses when gang members were arrested. However, street workers could not really stop gang members from fighting or committing a crime. Although street workers could usually tell if something was up—the streets emptied, no one was hanging around the local candy store, gang members looked furtive when encountered—only if a member informed them about a specific plan were they in a position to interfere.

Street work sometimes had unanticipated results. Street work was supposed to destabilize gangs and get members to adjust to life beyond the gang. But, as criminologists Malcolm Klein and Walter Miller have argued, because new resources became available, street work could have the opposite effect of making gangs more cohesive and better organized. Peripheral members found additional reasons to participate in the gang and sometimes increased their interaction with it, while recruits eagerly anticipated the new benefits of joining. Gang leaders welcomed street workers because they believed they could use them when needed and otherwise ignore them.[14]

Gang leaders also encouraged particularly troubled members to engage in relationships with gang workers. Whether this was done altruistically, because these members had so many difficulties, or cynically, because gang leaders knew that the worker's attention would be focused elsewhere, is not clear. But the effect of what researchers Hans Mattick and Nathan Caplan call "stake animals" was to absorb the worker's attention. They satisfied the street worker's desire to be helpful, provided the sponsoring agency with evidence of successful counseling, and mired him in a time-consuming, energy-draining relationship.[15]

The relationship between gang member and gang worker resulted in a wily game of wits, but gang workers' notes, gang members' memoirs, and interviews with former gang members as well as retired Youth Board workers make it clear that it also went beyond that. Gang workers risked injury and death to prevent their gangs from fighting, and youths responded to their efforts. Several street workers exhibited battle scars where they had wrested knives or other weapons away from youths, and one Youth Board worker was shot in the face and another was beaten to death by factions of the gangs with which they were working.[16] No one endured the risk of injury, the endless hours on the street corner, the low pay, family or vacation time interrupted by frantic phone calls, and the tragedy of seeing young people maimed or killed without being completely dedicated to the welfare of youngsters. Vincent Riccio mourned the death by a heroin overdose of one of his boys decades after the event; Dan Murrow was invited to a reunion of the Fordham Baldies more than ten years after he left the Youth Board, and JT credited him with turning his life around; and Nestor Llamas was recalled fondly by former gang members in interviews. These workers established warm and personal relations with members of their gangs who, often lacking contact with understanding adults, embraced the acceptance a gang worker offered. The painfully difficult departures (" 'Hey, Steve, come around again— don't leave us,' " pleaded the Spanish Kings) when gang workers decided that their mission had been accomplished are evidence enough of the genuine relationships established by both sides. If some gangs used street workers for their own ends, and if gang workers were unable to turn most core members into socially productive adults, they still established close ties with a few and helped them make a break with the gang. Gang workers succeeded but the nature of that success was individual.[17]

The importance of this point cannot be overemphasized. Street work, with its concern for curbing gang fighting, tended to be crisis oriented, with the Youth Board shifting workers and resources to troubled neighborhoods as needed. The nature of the work meant that there was no provision to remain in a neighborhood or with a gang once fighting stopped. The philosophy was to flood an area and work with all the gangs to forestall further fighting. Once the crisis passed, workers and resources moved on to another part of the city. At the same time, workers with individual gangs ended their association with the gang when it was no longer deemed threatening—that is, when members were working or attending school, and hostilities had ceased. Youths were then left to their own devices and the community that had produced them was left unchanged. That aspect of the CAP program was ignored by the Youth Board and the private gang intervention projects, which were not rooted in the communities in which they worked. (To be fair, they also lacked the funding for long-term work.) Unfortunately, many individuals depended on the gang for a sense of security and well-being. Gangs, for all of their problems, were adolescent-created entities that were relatively autonomous and provided gang members with a place from which to view the adult world and the dominant society. Once the gang was broken up, those most committed to defining masculinity through street life and most resistant to yoking still had the opportunity to enter criminal careers, while those individuals most dependent on the gang structure drifted into drug use, as will be argued further in the next chapter. The price of the street worker's few individual successes was the many individual failures.

## INSTITUTIONAL INTERVENTION

The second form of intervention took place at the institutional level. Local churches, settlement houses, and recreation centers were rooted in the neighborhood and were natural hosts of gang intervention projects. Their goals included establishing links between the gang and the local institution and preventing gang fighting, but not necessarily organizing community residents to solve their own problems or inviting delinquents to participate in running the project. Institution-based gang projects delivered to gangs the social services that social workers or ministers thought most appropriate and overlooked the more democratic and empowering aspect of CAP's philosophy. The institutional approach had both theoretical and practical limitations, the most common of which was the difficulty in establishing a site as neutral turf controlled by the staff.

This problem of ownership is illustrated by the battles over the Manhattanville Neighborhood Center. Gang intervention in Manhattanville began after the Lions smashed tables and chairs and gouged walls and the ceiling in the center's dining room. Sociologist Harry Shulman, called in to consult with the center about starting a gang intervention project, pointed out that the institution could not simply exclude troublesome youngsters and hope that they would destroy property elsewhere, allow them to continue to vandalize property, or wait for the police to break up the gangs. Following his lead, the center hired four street workers to make contact with the neighborhood's warring Euro-American, Puerto Rican, and African-American gangs. (Manhattanville, or West Harlem, was the area west of Amsterdam Avenue and south of Washington Heights, discussed in chapter 2, and called "Mousetown" by Bradford Chambers.) Street workers did not intend to break up the gangs but wanted to establish contact with them and assist the center in creating a recreation program for them.

Shulman evaluated the project as it progressed and found that the street workers were quite successful in establishing rapport with their groups. At the end of six months, all had reported that their gangs invited them to participate in gang activities (including illegal ones), seemed genuinely moved by adult interest in their affairs, and were eager to enroll in center-sponsored athletic competition.[18] Although gang conflict eased, field notes recorded tension between Euro-American staff at the center and Puerto Rican gang members. ("She [a staff member] said something to the effect of his [a gang member] picking up his deceitfulness and his tendency toward lying from the rest of his tribe, the Puerto Ricans.") The center was caught up in the bitter ethnic succession battle in the neighborhood, and in the minds of most gang members (and at least some staff), it represented the declining Euro-American population. For a time, the center was a target for gangs of all ethnicities because none could establish ownership incontestably. However, over time it became the property of the Puerto Ricans, and staff members noted, with apparently little understanding, that few African Americans or Euro-Americans attended any longer. While the gangs were brought in and established their peace both with center staff and non-gang youth, it was because in the contest for control among the gangs, the Puerto Ricans had won.[19]

Establishing contacts between gangs and social and recreational institutions meant walking a fine line between luring gangs in and letting them control a site. The problem faced by the Manhattanville Neighborhood Center was by no means unique. Any site that brought different gangs together had the potential of being a flashpoint. The situation in Manhattanville was exacerbated by ethnic tension, but tense standoffs also occurred in neighborhoods where ethnic differences were not at issue.

Gangs saw recreational sites as valuable resources whose control added to their prestige. Failure to understand the gang's perspective doomed any attempt to use a recreational site to "reform" gang members. Instead of "taming" the gang, the recreation center became an additional source of gang pride and an incentive for adolescents to become gang members.

As both gang workers and institutions discovered, getting gang members working, involved in truce talks, or participating in recreational activities did not necessarily prevent them from fighting. Gang members may have accepted assistance when it was offered—and they may have been genuinely grateful for it—but that did not mean that they accepted adult direction. This should not have surprised social workers, although it made for embarrassing newspaper headlines. Gang members existed in both gang and non-gang worlds, and reinforcing ties to their community and to public or private institutions did not necessarily mean severing ties to the gang. For the gang member there was no contradiction between working toward what society called "social" and "anti-social" goals at the same time. A gang intervention project mediated between the institution and the gang, but it did not prevent the gang from pursuing its own goals. It brought the gang within an institutional setting, but once there, the gang incorporated the institution into its own cosmology.

There was an alternative to adult-dominated gang intervention that promised better results. The CAP philosophy of community empowerment suggested that control over a project be deliberately negotiated with its clients. It is interesting to note that some of the more successful intervention projects in New York were those that ceded significant control to the youths themselves and involved them in their own reform. Sometimes agencies did not come to this realization philosophically but discovered it pragmatically. In East Harlem, the Board of Education opened the Robert F. Wagner Sr. Youth and Adult Center on 120th Street in 1959, which sparked a contest for control among gangs. Anxious to keep gangs from battling over the site, the director summoned leaders of the eleven gangs in the area and warned them that conflict would result in closing the center, and he challenged them to establish a council that would meet weekly to resolve differences. The center became neutral turf, and the truce that existed there eventually was extended to the streets outside as well.[20]

Peer-based groups, usually run by older, former gang members and sponsored by local institutions, were the most successful in enlisting gang participation. Former gang members could speak to adolescents about gangs with greater credibility than could most social workers. Such projects rested on the recognition that while community leaders might not have formal training, they brought to a project respect earned by years of living and working in the community. Peer-based groups created their own tensions; they demanded a democratic operation, in which the sponsoring agency housed, but did not necessarily control, a gang intervention project. The East Harlem Youth Council, convened by JT after he was released from four years in reform school, is an example of such a project. JT formed the youth council after a bystander was killed during a confrontation between his former gang, the Viceroys, and a rival group. The youth council enrolled the leaders of East Harlem's Puerto Rican and Italian street clubs and met under the auspices of Dan Murrow at the Friends Neighborhood Group House, a project of the American Friends Service Committee. The Friends Group House proved to be a particularly congenial forum for such an endeavor because of the Quakers' emphasis on social activism and social justice. The council mediated conflicts that arose among gangs, staged theatrical events, and hosted dances and recreational activities. The East Harlem Youth Council incorporated gang leaders, however uneasily, into a structure that demanded their responsibility and participation. The council, while successful in mediating conflict, did not fit well into the Friends Neighborhood Group House. JT was insistent on doing things his way and eventually parted company with the Friends over issues of control and direction of the project.[21] (JT still runs a program for adolescents out of a storefront on 111th Street, just down the block from the former site of the Friends House.)

Projects that invited gang members to help shape them were all too rare. Granting respect to a gang member, inviting his participation in the governance of an institution, and acknowledging his social equality all gave at least minimal recognition to his masculinity, but few agencies and social workers were able to do that. Most institutional programs incorporated gangs into existing activities and then laid down the rules that gang members were supposed to obey. A gang member's experience with a settlement or recreation center was then fairly similar to what he encountered in school, where demands for orderly behavior were issued by alien authority. Since settlements and boys' clubs frequently had been created for earlier populations and had been left stranded by ethnic succession, adolescents stared across a class and ethnic divide at staff members unwilling to share power with newcomers, especially ones whose attire and demeanor crowed defiance. Gang members saw these institutions (as in the Manhattanville Neighborhood Center example) as alien impositions to be defied, vandalized, taken over, or simply ignored.[22] Institutional programs offered more in possibility than in reality.

## Community Intervention

Community-wide projects were the third form of gang intervention. The Lower East Side in Manhattan came closest to implementing the CAP model. Settlement houses and churches on the Lower East Side linked their gang intervention work, shared resources and information, involved parents in preventing violence, and established a fairly successful gang intervention program. The institutions, however, did not adopt a community empowerment model and remained firmly in control over the project. By the early 1960s they were growing out of touch with the changing population of the Lower East Side and faced demands that they become more representative of Puerto Rican and African-American residents. In the process of doing this, they created Mobilization for Youth as a mechanism for organizing the community, and in the end, it proved more radical than anything originally envisioned in the CAP model or by the Lower East Side agencies.

The Lower Eastside Neighborhood Association (LENA) sponsored gang intervention in the community. LENA, a collection of settlement houses, churches, and civic groups, formed in 1954 to combat increasing ethnic tensions in New York's traditional port-of-entry neighborhood. While there had been gangs in the area for a number of years, a series of interethnic clashes alerted the Henry Street Settlement to a new gang problem in the early 1950s. The Mayrose, a gang of Italian, Jewish, and a smattering of Irish youngsters on Henry Street, had been assaulting Puerto Rican adolescents on their way home from school. The Puerto Ricans had organized a chapter of East Harlem's Dragons and initiated raids into the Mayrose's territory. In addition, the Sportsmen formed

among the African-American youths living in the public housing projects and fought both the Mayrose and the Dragons. These were the main contenders, but a total of forty-five gangs were active on the Lower East Side by the mid-1950s. To prevent conflict, LENA began a series of intervention programs. They hired detached workers, established parent groups, formed a "rumbles committee" that toured the neighborhood in times of tension, created a project to intercept recruitment into the gangs, brokered gang disputes, organized recreational activities, found jobs for youths in the area, and headed off a number of gang conflicts. LENA's program achieved modest success in managing the gang problem.[23]

LENA's initial accomplishment was negotiating a gang truce in 1956 after two boys in the neighborhood were shot. Ethnic tension ran high as a Puerto Rican member of the Dragons shot an African-American youth in the foot and, in the same incident, badly wounded a Jewish boy. Three of the area's four major ethnic groups were involved in the incident, and the gangs began to choose up sides. Both victims were reported to be members of the Enchanters, and rumors flew that the Mayrose, the Enchanters, and the Sportsmen might unite to fight the Dragons, who in turn were expected to call on the East Harlem Dragons—their brother club—for assistance. LENA met separately with each of the gangs, as well as with several other gangs who, it was feared, might become jealous at the headlines and attention enjoyed by the main factions and try to initiate an incident themselves. Street workers organized daily bus trips into the country in order to occupy the gangs until a negotiating session could be arranged. The Youth Board assigned extra workers to the area and police added patrols. Meanwhile, the boy accused of the shooting, John Rodriguez, surrendered to his parish priest, who brought him to a LENA meeting where police took him into custody. Finally, five days after the shooting, representatives of the Dragons, Sportsmen, and Enchanters met under the auspices of Peter Brown, a partner in a prominent New York law firm and a former U.S. attorney, who negotiated a deal. The Mayrose eventually added their assent as well.[24]

The truce made headlines and not all of them were favorable. The treaty was standard fare, and as LENA pointed out, the negotiations it brokered among the rival gangs were similar to other mediation sessions

*Opposite page:* 7.1. Lower East Side.

held in the past that had attracted no media attention. The truce guaranteed individual gang members safe passage through each other's turf, limited the size of groups that might enter a neighborhood, agreed that all the gangs would work toward the establishment of a community center or "teen canteen," and planned for a one-day outing that the gangs would attend. The gangs agreed to report any truce violations to the clergymen who had arranged the negotiating session instead of handling matters themselves. LENA representatives mimeographed the agreement and distributed it throughout the Lower East Side along with a call for a community meeting. While residents at the community meeting were largely positive about the negotiations, the police commissioner immediately blasted the policy of negotiating with gangs. He charged LENA and the Youth Board with coddling criminals, and he ordered the police not to recognize gangs as "sovereign powers" and to step up their war against delinquency. Several of New York's newspapers took up the cry for old-fashioned "nightstick justice."[25]

Citizens and public officials had legitimate concerns about gang mediation. Negotiating with the help of a prominent attorney in front of television cameras and with swarms of newspaper reporters covering the story certainly increased the status of the gangs. Such publicity made the task of recruiting new members easier, gave gangs the recognition they desired, and meant that gang leaders could parade through the neighborhood with a newfound celebrity. The assistance of the Youth Board gave the treaty the stamp of municipal approval and seemed to recognize the city's division into spheres of influence controlled by adolescent gangs. Moreover, such truces required constant nurturing and rarely lasted very long, and one could ask if such a limited result was worth the benefits mediation conferred upon the gangs.

Yet there were few viable alternatives. "Nightstick justice"—allowing the cop on the beat to mete out punishment with his nightstick without bothering about charges or proving guilt or innocence—substantiated the belief among youths that they were the special targets of police brutality. Police relations with adolescents were largely adversarial: they ordered collections of youths loitering on the street corner to move on; frisked those who appeared to act suspiciously; and generally harassed youths encountered on patrol. Even gang workers complained of their treatment by police, who regarded them with barely concealed contempt. Gang members, well aware of police corruption, refused to grant them even a modicum of respect. In addition, police abused prisoners in order to extract confessions, and in these days before suspects had to be warned about self-incrimination and the right to an attorney, civil liberties were widely ignored. African-American and Puerto Rican gang members charged that a Euro-American police force overlooked the actions of Euro-American gangs and focused only on them. Instead of enforcing the peace, nightstick justice reinforced resentment and ethnic hostility.[26]

The second alternative, relying on the formal processes of the criminal justice system, was also problematical. Court action for those too old for juvenile court had repercussions that went beyond the punishment of a guilty party. The creation of a public record meant that families of gang members could be expelled from public housing projects because of the actions of their children. Although gang members proudly proclaimed their street names, they usually avoided having their family names identified for just this reason. More important, the courts were equipped to handle the aftermath of violence, not its prevention. The whole purpose of creating an agreement signed by the gangs was to forestall any additional violence and make a resort to the criminal justice system unnecessary.

Mediation, on the other hand, offered several advantages. The sessions were designed to handle problems informally and anonymously before trouble occurred. (The August 1956 mediation session was unusual in the publicity it attracted; most sessions involved only the disputants and Youth Board or agency representatives.) Intervention by community groups, with the support of social service agencies and the Youth Board, allowed gangs to save face and back away from a fight gracefully while establishing ties between gangs and concerned adults. And although treaties may have recognized the Balkanization of New York, that process had already occurred in the streets; treaties did not initiate it. Perhaps the most important part of mediation was that it granted the participants the respect they craved. It treated gang members as men, as equals able to resolve differences, and although this might have empowered them, as mediation opponents charged, it also enlisted them in the process of peacekeeping. Mediation was an agreement reached by the gang members themselves, with limited and concrete objectives, avenues of appeal, and a specific time frame for accomplishing its goals. For a mediation session to reach the agreement stage, all the parties had to believe that they had some "ownership" over the agreement. Even when mediation agreements broke down and had to be renegotiated, at the very least, they prevented retaliatory gang strikes and saved adolescents' lives.[27]

Still, managing the gang problem was not the same thing as solving it. While the reporters disappeared once overt tension declined, the situation in the Lower East Side remained precarious, and the same painstaking negotiations that produced the treaty were required to maintain it. LENA gang worker Milton Yale met with the Dragons for the first time in September 1956, just weeks after the truce agreement had been signed. Already the Dragons' leader was complaining that the Mayrose were violating the agreement, and he proposed a fair fight with fifteen members on a side to settle the territorial disputes. (A "fair one" in the gang world meant a one-on-one challenge, not the free-for-all implied by the Dragons' proposal, which probably would have led to a full-scale rumble.) Yale and Father Kilmer Myers of St. Augustine's Church, where the Dragons met, persuaded the leaders to observe the truce for a few days more until the entire gang could have a membership meeting. In the meantime, they went to work speaking with different gang members and lobbying for keeping the peace. At the gang meeting, several leaders who had been contacted by Myers and Yale argued for peace, and the split in the leadership allowed the members to vote to maintain the treaty.[28]

At the same time that Yale and Myers tried to manage the Dragons, members of the Henry Street Settlement House worked with the Mayrose. The Mayrose leader, Frankie F, had earlier confessed to hiding rifles in case of a "spic war" and had been persuaded to throw them into the East River. Frankie now agreed to participate in a meeting with the Dragons, but within days he threatened a Dragon member with a gun. The Dragon "escaped into his grandmother's house—F & his 4 friends banged on the door" trying to get him. Later that day a Mayrose member was stabbed, and around noon the following day the two groups met in the streets and began firing zip guns at one another. No one was hurt, but police arrested eleven youths and later picked up five more on illegal assembly and on Sullivan Law (carrying a concealed weapon) charges. About a week later, a "meeting [was] held at St. Augustine's church between 5 Mayrose & 5 P. R. [Puerto Rican] boys," and a truce agreement was reached. In the meeting, "both sides said they needed to know each other better." Two weeks later the truce still held and the gangs had gotten to know each other—perhaps too well, since the Dragons now proposed to the Mayrose that they launch a joint attack against their common enemy, the Sportsmen. All of these incidents occurred during a time when the gangs of the Lower East Side were thought to be at peace. No one except those intimately involved with the gangs knew of any tension.[29]

The series of meetings and behind-the-scenes efforts at persuading gang leaders to respect the peace extended past the early months of the truce. Field workers' notes show that skirmishes—fistfights, provocative, large-scale forays into each other's territory, shoving incidents at the dances sponsored by the church, and even shootings—occurred continuously, and slights or imagined slights threatened to send one group or another into battle. The famous truce of August 1956 happened to attract the media—there was little news in the languid end of summer and there had been a double shooting—who treated it as if it were a novelty. In fact, the negotiations that produced the treaty and later maintained it were typical of efforts to stop gang fighting by community organizations—such as LENA—with the help of the New York City Youth Board.[30] When these efforts broke down, or when new gangs attempted to establish a reputation by shooting someone, youth workers scrambled to repair the situation under the glare of public and political attention over the "revival" of gang hostilities and the "failure" of gang mediation.

The Lower East Side exploded into the news again on August 24, 1959, three years after the initial truce agreements. The night before, members of the Forsyth Street Boys tossed a Molotov cocktail and fired a .22-caliber rifle from a passing car at a group of Sportsmen sitting on benches outside the Lillian Wald Projects. One of the bullets struck fifteen-year-old Theresa Gee, a girlfriend of one of the Sportsmen, in the head, killing her instantly. Two other youths were wounded. The raid by the Forsyth Street Boys came in retaliation for a Sportsmen attack an hour or so earlier, in which one boy was shot in the nose and two others were stabbed. (One stabbing victim, Julio Rosario, fourteen, eventually died.) Later that evening the Sportsmen struck back and shot one Forsyth Street Boy and assaulted another.[31]

The murder of a young girl, a bystander to the Lower East Side turf wars, and the killing and wounding of seven other individuals, all in one twenty-four-hour period, created headlines about the resurgence of gang warfare. Yet LENA had been warning for months about the emergence of a new group—the Forsyth Street Boys—eager for status and reputation, and willing to challenge the established gangs to get it. Initially, the Sportsmen and the Forsyth Street Boys had been united against the Dragons, but then the Forsyth Street Boys switched sides. Skirmishes occurred throughout the spring and summer of 1959, first between the Sportsmen and the Dragons, and later between the Sportsmen and the Forsyth Street Boys. In the face of mounting tension, LENA had asked the Youth Board for extra street workers to head off a confrontation, but the Youth Board pleaded a manpower shortage. There were too many other gangs in too many other areas demanding attention, and the Youth Board left the Forsyth Street Boys uncovered.[32] Not even on the Lower East Side, where a community-wide network of institutions cooperated in gang intervention, where potentially troublesome gangs were identified to public authorities, and where gang members participated in the development of truces and agreements, could tragedy be averted. Even in this highly organized neighborhood, richly endowed with social institutions and sharing in an activist heritage, gang fighting was only managed.

Despite the emotion at the funerals of Theresa Gee and Julio Rosario, where families wailed, ministers begged for peace on the streets, and gang members swore vengeance, there was no further attempt at retaliation. LENA organized parents and local institutions to defuse the crisis. Angry Sportsmen threatened to organize a raid after Theresa Gee's funeral, but LENA found adults to take individual gang members home in cabs to prevent them from gathering. One gang leader asked LENA to get him out of the area so that he would not have to lead a reprisal attack. "He could not refuse to lead the attack without losing face, yet he knew his gang would not move without him. The youngster spent the night sleeping on the kitchen floor of the worker's apartment. The next day he was spirited away to an agency camp." By the time he returned, the crisis had passed and the police had patrols throughout the neighborhood—"there were two cops on every corner for a year," according to one informant. Father Kilmer Myers led a memorial procession of 250 candle-carrying marchers through the streets of the Lower East Side to commemorate the dead and pray for peace. Afterward, buses took fifty Sportsmen and their friends to a summer camp in upstate New York to avert further trouble. While street workers and community organizations had not broken up the gangs or prevented outbreaks of gang fighting, they succeeded in containing violence once it occurred.[33]

While LENA struggled to manage the relationships among the adolescent gangs in the neighborhood, it also sponsored a predelinquent gang project that intercepted younger children on their way to membership. The project, started by the Henry Street Settlement, worked with the younger members of the Mayrose and gradually added other gangs. The Mayrose, like many established gangs, were organized vertically into age-graded divisions that fed members into the Mayrose seniors as they progressed in age and daring. The three younger divisions, the Aces, the Junior Aces, and the Eagles, ranged in age from sixteen (Aces) down to seven (Eagles). The Henry Street Settlement established a basketball program for the Eagles, encouraged club meetings on its premises, included the boys in woodworking and drama programs, and visited and involved parents in their children's activities. The method with the younger children was the same as with the older cohorts—a group worker tried to undermine the influence of the leaders and substitute his own. The Eagles group worker found that initially the two leaders had more influence over behavior than he did, but "constant work with these two boys and their parents" meant that "Leonard and Mike are much more respectful of my authority and [with] the increased amount of control I have over them ... the behavior of the entire club has calmed down considerably."[34] This was the youngest division of the Mayrose, but LENA's program worked with the Aces and Junior Aces as well.

The Aces were the most troublesome of the younger groups and came to the agency's attention in 1955. "Their cohesiveness and aggressiveness was reminiscent of the patterns followed by well-established teen-age gangs in their younger years," and observers were sure that this was the rising generation of Mayrose members. The Aces exhibited little interest in the traditional settlement program except for basketball, and, as the group worker commented, "we gave them as much of this as possible." It took the worker six months to establish a relationship with the group, and it was a year and many tests before he believed they trusted him. The boys tried to con him into buying things for them, displayed goods stolen from stores and defied his demands that they return them, and acted aggressively toward other groups near the settlement. Gradually group members accepted his role and he was able to help a couple find part-time jobs and encouraged others to remain in school. At one point, the group worker suggested that the Aces take a trip together. The response of the boys was illuminating. " 'What Aces?' " they replied. " 'There ain't no more club.' " The success of the gang worker's effort can be measured in the wistful answer—although it took three years of work. LENA's program diverted younger children from gangs and involvement in illegal activities: of the sixty-three youngsters in the program, only five had appearances before Children's Court between March 1958 and March 1959, and none was from the Mayrose groups.[35]

In evaluating LENA's approach to the gangs, one must balance the deaths of Theresa Gee and Julio Rosario against the disruption of gang recruitment and the prevention of additional violence. On the whole, LENA's program was the most successful of the projects discussed so far. Although gang conflict did not disappear, gang workers from the settlements and parents cooperated to disrupt the cycle of attack and retaliation and negotiated agreements among the gangs, which allowed youths to pass unmolested through the neighborhood. LENA helped maintain a precarious balance of power, usually by getting the gangs to agree to convert to defensive fighting (that is, to protect themselves from attack but not to initiate raids). Parents, organized into a rumbles committee, took an active stance in preventing the spread of rumors and helping to get gang members out of the neighborhood when trouble was brewing. Community churches, settlement houses, and public authorities cooperated to supply recreational activities and to divert younger youths from becoming involved in gangs. These achievements of social work, while modest, were also real. Not all violence was prevented nor were the gangs broken up, but one wonders if "nightstick justice" would have accomplished as much.[36]

The Lower East Side did not fully incorporate CAP's philosophy, however. While community residents were organized to prevent violence, direction remained largely in the hands of the settlement houses. And even though gangs participated in the drafting and execution of agreements, they did so more as the clients than as the equals to the LENA agencies. Finally, most of the individuals who worked through LENA were Euro-Americans in a neighborhood that was becoming increasingly Puerto Rican and African American. As LENA searched for additional funding to expand its services, it encountered a demand that it do a better job of organizing the Lower East Side's indigenous communities. As it did so, LENA became swept up in confrontational politics with local landlords, public service agencies, and municipal authorities, as well as in a political backlash against community organizing.

## Mobilization for Youth

LENA turned to the federal government and the Ford Foundation to fund an expansion of its program. Planning for what became Mobilization for Youth (MFY)—a proposal not just to curb gang fighting, but to embed gang intervention into community organization and development—began in 1957. Planners visited Chicago to investigate the achievements of Clifford Shaw's Chicago Area Project, and they drew on the CAP model in formulating MFY. In 1962, MFY received funding from the Ford Foundation, the National Institute for Mental Health, the President's Committee on Juvenile Delinquency and Youth Crime, and the City of New York.[37]

LENA's timing had been fortuitous. The Ford Foundation was searching for ways to revitalize decaying urban communities, while President Kennedy's newly elected administration was committed to tackling the social problems that had festered during the Eisenhower years. Together the President's Committee on Juvenile Delinquency and the Ford Foundation transformed LENA's original proposal to extend its offerings of social services into a plan to empower the community and expand the availability of opportunity. Gangs would be prevented from forming by the combination of social services—such as job training—and the opening of channels of opportunity—job placement as well as subsidized employment. (MFY's larger historical significance was that it served as a prototype for Lyndon Johnson's War on Poverty.)[38]

MFY's social services were similar to what the Lower East Side settlements had been doing for years. MFY included educational and job training, several predelinquent youth projects, an expanded detached worker program, and a series of coffeehouses to provide youths with places of supervised recreation.[39] Five settlement houses cooperated in supporting detached workers, who had contact with an estimated fifteen to twenty gangs in the neighborhood over the program's four years of operation. Clearly detached workers and training did not represent a new departure in gang intervention.[40]

The coffeehouses were more innovative, but they repeated the history of other recreation programs that brought members of different gangs together. Teen canteens had been used in the past to provide gangs with places where members could dance, listen to music, or play pool; the coffeehouses were a more updated version. The turf issue, however, remained insolvable. Members of rival gangs shared the coffeehouses, at least initially, but their coexistence was barely peaceful and the policy of excluding non-members from the coffeehouses led to nearly nightly incidents. Members of the Sportsmen took over one of the coffeehouses, and the others gained reputations as hangouts for addicts and therefore were shunned by the gangs. The coffeehouses closed for periods of time as adult staff struggled to regain control of the premises, but MFY recognized that the program was a failure and closed the coffeehouses permanently in the spring of 1965. MFY proved no better able than the Manhattanville Neighborhood Center at dealing with the issue of control over a recreational site. MFY supplied new funding, but not necessarily new direction, to gang intervention programs.[41]

Even as the gang project fizzled out, MFY organizers focused on the other part of the program—organizing the community to confront the neighborhood's poor housing, unequal schools, and an indifferent city bureaucracy. In its community organizing, MFY proved to be much more innovative and more radical than in its gang intervention program, and it went beyond CAP's more cooperative style into a politics of confrontation. As a result, MFY succeeded in alienating local political and economic powers within the first few months of its operation. Staff members formed a housing clinic to assist residents in using legal channels to force landlords to bring their buildings up to code. When landlords did not cooperate, MFY–inspired tenant associations picketed those who failed to repair their buildings and began the Lower East Side rent strike of January 1964.

The process of working with community institutions followed a similar path. A parent education plan, designed to familiarize Puerto Rican families with the school system, led to confrontation with the New York City Board of Education. Mobilization of Mothers pressured principals to meet with them and redress grievances about the shortage of textbooks, institutional condescension toward Spanish-speaking parents and their children, and the general inadequacies of the local schools. After getting little response, parents organized a school boycott and picketed local schools, also early in 1964. At the same time, the Young Adult Action Group, designed to politicize delinquents, participated in the March on Washington, demonstrated for jobs, and, perhaps most provocatively, agitated for the creation of a civilian review board to investigate charges of police brutality. Everywhere the Lower East Side was astir, and MFY was roiling the waters.[42]

MFY's community organizing was much more confrontational than anything that CAP had done. It drew its inspiration from radicals, such as veteran organizer Saul Alinsky, who had participated in Clifford Shaw's CAP before parting company with him and who argued that Shaw's model was too limited. Alinsky believed that community organizing required forming neighborhood residents into power blocks able to negotiate on an equal footing with political and economic foes. MFY used this approach in organizing the Lower East Side. For MFY there was little doubt that gang members, like other residents of poor communities, could be converted into activists, but they discovered that doing this with public money invited a firestorm of political backlash.[43]

The reaction came quickly. The New York *Daily News* aired charges in August 1964 that the MFY staff was riddled with communists, that MFY had fomented rioting in Harlem in the summer of 1964, and that large sums of money had been misspent. Paul Screvane, president of the New York City Council and director of the city's antipoverty program, picked up on the charges and organized public hearings. (Screvane was interested in running for mayor and the investigation of MFY allowed him to make headlines in the local news.) State and federal officials began their own reviews of MFY's affairs, which included using paid informers and placing wiretaps on office telephones. Because of its confrontational politics and financial independence from the city, MFY had alienated Mayor Robert F. Wagner's administration and few mainline Democrats cared to defend it. In addition, a number of MFY board members representing the institutional interests of the Lower East Side—including some of the original LENA sponsors of MFY—had resigned as the organization became radicalized and moved into political confrontation. Welfare mothers with picket signs, poor people with lawyers, and delinquents calling for review of police actions went well beyond the traditional liberalism of the Lower East Side and the expectations of the original LENA supporters of MFY.

MFY had become isolated politically from its initial Lower East Side institutional supporters, from the local Democratic party, and from sources of power in the community. Although the charges against MFY proved groundless (no funds were misspent and, although leftist sympathies abounded, no communist infiltrators were found), the battered organization was forced to modify its course. Instead of organizing local residents, including gang members, to challenge schools that did not educate, to confront landlords who did not meet housing codes, or to defeat politicians who did not represent their constituents, MFY became absorbed with defending itself and preserving its future. In cold war New York, MFY's challenge to the economic and political establishment was turned aside through red-baiting. The executive director resigned—a sacrificial offering to political respectability—and MFY became more attuned to the political interests it had originally set out to attack.[44]

With its radical potential squelched, MFY settled back into a service provider role. It helped individuals earn high school equivalency degrees and find jobs, it counseled families, and it provided recreational resources. MFY still organized welfare mothers and continued to support community action programs, but any potential threat to the structures of power on the Lower East Side had been eliminated. In the future, antipoverty money would be coordinated through the mayor's office, thus limiting challenges to city hall.

The shift to social service also occurred in the gang prevention program. Concluding that gangs were no longer an important problem on the Lower East Side, MFY ended its detached worker program in 1966 and created "Adolescent Service Centers" that provided traditional social work—job and educational counseling—to adolescents.[45] LENA and MFY together helped to destabilize the Lower East Side's gangs and end gang fighting, but the result was not what anyone had anticipated. A new problem arrived with the decline of the gang. As Helen Hall, director of the Henry Street Settlement, commented, "While gang violence became less, a menacing new element crept into our neighborhoods: the teenage use of narcotics."[46]

MFY in its original conception may have offered the best opportunity to "reform" gangs. Linking adolescents to the economic and political transformation of their neighborhood promised to supply a larger purpose that could substitute for gang membership. Masculinity could be defined through resisting foes far more powerful than another neighborhood gang of adolescents. Alienation from the marketplace could have been approached collectively rather than handled individually through quitting or getting fired from jobs. Organizing might not have linked gang members to institutions in society, but it certainly would have connected them to their own communities. In the end, however, MFY's attempt to transform the community and to involve gang members in the process was defeated by political reaction, and its potential for transforming gangs remained unfulfilled.

Gang intervention took three forms in postwar New York and each had both successes and failures. Detached workers sometimes formed close personal relations with individual gang members and helped them make the transition out of the gang. But as the gang broke up, and individuals fell out of its orbit, they were left with nothing to replace the gang and still faced the same problems that had led them to gang membership originally. Institutionally based programs often were able to involve the gang in a recreational or equivalent program, but were less successful at dictating the terms of that involvement. The truces they arranged often were temporary and incomplete, and gangs were quite successful at using institutions for their own purposes. Broader community-based intervention projects, such as LENA, that reflected a more complete version of the CAP philosophy, were fewer in number, but enjoyed the greatest success in sustaining agreements among gangs, keeping the peace, and diverting younger youths from gangs. Their educational and social programs did not promise anything extraordinary, however, and they did not transform the choices poor adolescents faced. Mobilization for Youth attempted to go in a more radical direction, leading youth and the impoverished to confront landlords, schools, police, and city bureaucracies. Of course, becoming caught up in the turmoil of community action meant losing funds and creating powerful enemies who forced the program back into a more moderate path. Its potential for reforming gangs was never really tested.

Gang intervention in all of its forms attempted to disrupt the operations of the gang, especially gang fighting, and press youths into making conventional adjustments to working-class life. Because these programs defined the gang as the problem, rather than as a symptom of other problems, they were unprepared to confront the fundamental issues that had led adolescents to form gangs in the first place. These were the limits of liberal social reform. The result was that gang intervention, where it successfully disrupted gangs, inadvertently substituted individual deviance in the form of drug use for the collective resistance of the gang. By the mid-1960s, authorities decided that gangs were no longer the problem. They had been displaced by the rapid spread of heroin among New York's adolescents.

# Drugs, Politics, and Gangs, 1960–1975

$V$IC, a street-corner evangelist, held up his Bible to the crowd, warning them that it was the one thing they could rely on. " 'You can't count on the gang any more. . . . The gang is falling apart—the needle saw to that.' "[1] In the mid-1960s, street workers, gang members, journalists, and policy analysts agreed that New York's gangs had nearly disappeared, although they were less sure than Vic that heroin was the cause. Less than a decade later, however, gangs would reemerge, more active and more violent than before.

In this chapter I analyze the causes of both gang decline and resurgence. Despite Vic's hopes, gangs did not disappear during the 1960s, but they did fall below the threshold at which gang fighting was continuous. Public policy initiatives, such as police and Youth Board pressure and the gang intervention programs discussed in the previous chapter, finally began to bear fruit in the early 1960s. Later they were supplemented by the neighborhood-based political and social programs of Mayor John V. Lindsay's administration (1966–1973). During this same period, political radicals and civil rights organizers tried to engage gangs in larger political struggles, and finally, the war in Vietnam and a wartime boom economy drew older youths away from the streets. The combination of events depressed gang activity below the threshold level or the "tipping point."

The spread of heroin followed the decline of the gang. Gangs were a flimsy bulwark against heroin, insulating their members for a time and serving as a counterweight to the adolescent drug users in the neighborhood. After public policy initiatives and gang intervention projects successfully disrupted the gangs, heroin swept unimpeded through inner-city youth. While some gang members found that politics, the military, and employment substituted for the gang, for many adolescents, these were not viable alternatives. With the decline of the gang, heroin use remained as a way of rejecting the adult working-class world, and youths substituted a drug-using subculture for the gang subculture as a means of organizing life. Thus, even while gang fighting ebbed, addiction spread, and the juvenile delinquency rate and the overall crime rate soared in the 1960s as addicts searched for the means to pay for their habits.

Gangs reemerged fairly quickly in the 1970s. The same external factors that had limited gang fighting either were removed or, in a new context, operated differently. Returning veterans from Vietnam supplied the leadership that the draft and enlistments had removed from the neighborhood. A sudden decline in the city's economy after 1969 left adolescents again struggling to find work, while a retreat in the War on Poverty cut off avenues out of the streets. Neighborhood competition over the remaining antipoverty resources stimulated gang formation, while other gangs organized in response to the heroin plague and reconstituted themselves as a barrier to hard drug use. In different neighborhoods in the city the number of gangs once again passed the tipping point as adolescents hastened to organize.

## THE TIPPING POINT

The concept of a tipping point, introduced in chapter 1, is useful for understanding what happened to New York's gangs in the 1960s. The apparent "disappearance" of gangs was instead a significant decline. The decrease in the number of active gangs was sufficient to lessen the possibility of random contact and to lower the need for aggressive behavior on the part of the remaining gangs. Gangs did not disappear, but reports from several sources concurred that the number of active gangs was declining in the 1960s.

In the years after the violence-filled summer of 1959, which culminated with the murder of Theresa Gee on the Lower East Side and the Capeman and the Vampires' raid on a midtown Manhattan playground, public officials gladly announced a decline in gang activity. The Youth Board argued that the most significant change was the falling number of gang-related homicides in the summer months, when gangs traditionally were most active. After five gang-related homicides in July and August 1959, the Youth Board counted none for the same two months in 1960, one in 1961, two in 1962, and one in 1963. Although dire warnings appeared each spring that a new summer of gang violence was approaching (perhaps as a way of coaxing more money out of city hall), each fall the Youth Board reported fewer gang incidents. At the same time, the youth division of the police department reported a steady decline in active gangs, from 248 in 1961, to 184 in 1962, to 130 in 1965.[2]

According to the Youth Board's street workers, the gangs that remained were largely nonaggressive. Street workers maintained that only 15 percent of the gangs were "fighting gangs," with the rest listed either as defensive gangs or simply as street-corner groups. The declining number of fighting gangs in the early 1960s lessened the need to defend turf aggressively. Essentially, as the number of gangs fell below the tipping point, remaining gangs turned their attention from fighting to drinking, gambling, stealing, and narcotics use.[3]

A change in the forms of gang fighting preceded these reports of the decline of the fighting gang. In the late 1940s and early 1950s, large-scale rumbles had drawn hundreds of boppers to Brooklyn's Prospect Park or Coney Island or the Bronx's Orchard Beach over the Memorial Day weekend. Already by the mid-1950s, such ritualized conflicts had largely disappeared and even smaller prearranged rumbles became rare.[4] Instead gangs adopted new tactics featuring hit-and-run attacks by "suicide squads" that were harder for police to detect and prevent. These took the form of "knock knock," in which a gang member would go to a rival's residence, knock on the apartment door, and shoot whomever answered. (This was a serious escalation of violence since family members could easily be injured and non-boppers were by tradition off-limits in gang warfare.) More commonly, raiders would steal a car, drive into enemy turf, and spray a corner or meeting spot with shotgun blasts or rifle fire. Thus, violence became more deadly and was perpetrated by smaller cliques that seemed less concerned about hitting random targets. Fortunately, in the early 1960s, violence occurred less frequently as gangs retreated into more defensive postures.[5]

INTERVENTION

The decrease in gang activity was not an artifact of new reporting standards or of shifting media attention. Too many different sources produced for different purposes agree on the same point for this to be the case. Street workers, community agencies, police—in other words, those most knowledgeable about gang activities and those whose funding depended on a continuing gang problem—all reported that something was happening on the streets. For example, private agencies, such as Harlem Youth Opportunities Unlimited (Haryou) and Mobilization for Youth (MFY) on the Lower East Side, agreed with the Youth Board and the police that gang activity had diminished. Both of these programs originated with gang intervention and operated in Manhattan neighborhoods with traditions of very active gangs. Haryou claimed that forty fighting gangs had existed in central Harlem in the late 1940s during the height of gang activity in the area. By contrast, "the last gang eruption, according to police records, was in early 1963," and the number of fighting gangs had fallen to fourteen. According to MFY, the gang crisis peaked in 1959, and by the mid-1960s, the neighborhood gangs had either reached an accommodation or had broken up. (As noted in the previous chapter, MFY ended its gang outreach programs in 1966, concluding that gangs were no longer a problem.) Gangs did not disappear, but after years of effort, they had fallen below the threshold level.[6]

One reason for both the changing tactics of gang fighting and the subsequent decline in the fighting gang is the success of social control agencies in penetrating and disrupting the gang world. The gang world was not independent but a sphere of resistance hemmed in by working-class and middle-class authority. Adolescent gang members remained subject to the influence of parents and local adults, as well as probation officers, truant officers, and police. Since the 1950s, mediation by public and private agencies increased dramatically, particularly on the part of the Youth Board. The near quadrupling of the number of Youth Board workers from 40 to 150 between 1955 and 1965 meant that streetwise gang workers blanketed areas where trouble was brewing. Street workers identified and covered the potentially troublesome gangs in a neighborhood, prevented the spread of rumors, and worked with the gangs until the crisis had passed. They also encouraged reluctant warriors to warn them anonymously ("drop a dime") about impending conflicts so the police could be notified and fights prevented.[7]

The Youth Board also began to work more closely with the police department. Street workers had always tried to prevent rumbling and encouraged gang members to surrender their weapons, but they did not always inform police about gang activities or reveal who possessed weapons. In response to criticism from police and politicians, the Youth Board changed its policy in 1956. The Board told workers that they had to inform police about potential gang fights and the possession of weapons, even if it jeopardized their standing with the gang.[8] Although the police remained suspicious of street workers, who were still regarded as too sympathetic to gang members, the new policy improved communication and cooperation between the two city agencies. Instead of arriving after a fight had started and (sometimes) waiting until the violence died down before moving in, the police tried to prevent hostile forces from gathering.[9] They aggressively patrolled troubled neighborhoods and stopped suspicious-looking groups of teenagers for searches, confiscating anything that could be used as a weapon. The decline of the mass rumble throughout the city suggests that gangs adopted new tactics in the face of more effective Youth Board–police department cooperation.[10]

Private agencies were equally zealous in attempting to disrupt the gangs, as seen in the previous chapter. In Harlem, the Lower East Side, and East Harlem, agencies cooperated in their detached-worker and recreational programs, funded from private, municipal, and federal sources. Public social control agencies, settlement houses, and community organizations had set out to disrupt the gangs and curb gang fighting. By the early 1960s, after several years of cooperative and ever-increasing effort, they succeeded.

## Radical Politics

While social control agencies, settlements, and community organizations attempted to disrupt the gangs, other groups were at work trying to politicize them. Nationalist political parties—the Black Panthers (1967) and the Young Lords (1968)—organized in New York's neighborhoods,

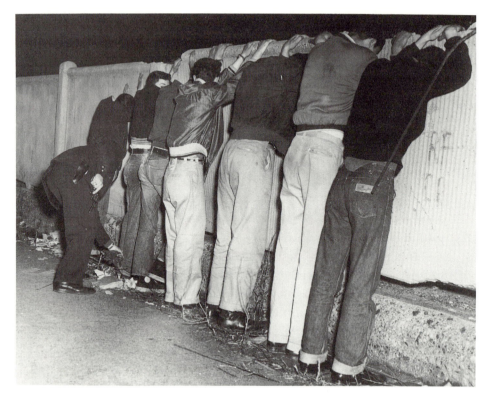

8.1. Boys' line-up at Pacific Street, Brooklyn, April 19, 1956.

the civil rights movement moved north and began to address de facto segregation and urban poverty, while ghetto riots exploded the myths of progress and equal opportunity.

Observers thought that the political restiveness of the inner city led to a reluctance on the part of street gangs to attack adolescents of similar ethnic background. As Black Panther Alfred Cain, Jr., recalled, even as a gang-fighting adolescent, "I could see that brothers killing brothers didn't make any sense." By spreading black and Puerto Rican nationalist consciousness, the Black Panthers and the Young Lords may have helped to depress gang violence.[11]

Some gang members chose to become revolutionaries. Gangbangers were natural recruits for revolutionary activity since they were accustomed to defying police and other authorities, and political organizing offered an appropriately masculine alternative to the self-defeating violence of gang conflict. The Panthers and the Lords wanted to assert control over their own communities, which gangs had been doing for years, and to resist the imperatives of the capitalist state. Theories of Black Liberation and Puerto Rican independence from U.S. colonialism gave form to the nonideological resistance expressed by gang members. Both the Black Panthers and the Young Lords, which combined appeals to socialism with ethnic nationalism, included a number of former boppers among their members.[12]

While the Panthers and the Lords lured individuals into political activity, they did not politicize the gangs themselves. The parties organized nationally, and gang activity in other cities was peaking even as New York's was declining. Therefore, the Black Panthers and the Young Lords did not prevent street gangs from organizing.[13] They were a route out of the gang, and they may have attracted youths who otherwise might have joined gangs. At best, they dampened the level of gang activity.

The civil rights movement operated in a similar fashion. Saul Bernstein, in a survey of gang intervention efforts in the mid-1960s, found little evidence of civil rights consciousness among northern gangbangers. While Gerald Suttles discovered that gang members in the Addams area did become involved in Chicago's civil rights struggles, it is equally notable that African-American gangs from a nearby neighborhood moved in to fill the vacuum left by the Addams gangs. In New York, efforts by MFY to organize delinquent youths into protest organizations foundered on the tensions between middle-class and street-oriented youth. The record of involvement in civil rights therefore is mixed. While willing to participate in the March on Washington or in local school boycotts, northern African-American and Puerto Rican gang members saw little relevance in the philosophy of nonviolence and in the approaches of an essentially southern civil rights movement. Abstract political goals held little appeal to gang members, and the civil rights movement involved few core gang members. But by organizing communities to pursue larger goals, the civil rights movement created a consciousness that probably discouraged gang fighting at least among African-American gangs.[14]

Ghetto rebellion also succeeded, at least for a time, in creating a larger racial consciousness that deterred intra-ethnic gang violence. In riots in Harlem and Bedford-Stuyvesant in 1964, in interracial disturbances in East New York in 1966, and in riots in East Harlem in 1967, African-

American and Puerto Rican youths vented their hostility toward a political and economic system that excluded them. There is no evidence of organized gang involvement in these riots; they were spontaneous explosions in which gang and non–gang members alike participated and united against a common foe, much as had occurred in the Harlem riot of 1943. But this was a short-term and largely instrumental unity. The gangs that remained were too identified with neighborhoods and too rooted in the defense of place, which offered them status and a sense of control, to be able to transcend their differences easily and unite.[15] Radical politics, civil rights organizing, and collective violence did not transform gangs from apolitical defenders of turf into a vanguard for community change. But by involving a critical number of youths, particularly potential leaders, they helped keep gang violence at bay.

### TERRITORIAL POLITICS

In the mid-1960s, as cities across the country went up in flames, it was not at all apparent to policymakers in New York that gang members there would ignore the call for revolution or be too narcotized to hear it. As political scientist Ira Katznelson has shown, city officials developed public policy initiatives that encouraged neighborhood rootedness as a way of preventing citywide protest.[16]

To prevent in New York the massive race riots experienced by other American cities, the administration of Mayor John V. Lindsay wanted to connect neighborhoods to city hall like the political machines had done in earlier decades. In a brilliant demonstration of the importance of place, Lindsay's Urban Action Task Force (UATF) delivered resources and city services to African-American and Puerto Rican neighborhoods that had been badly neglected, gathered street-level intelligence that could be used to prevent outbreaks of rioting, heard neighborhood grievances, and organized adolescents into community-based recreational and job programs. Through the task force, remaining gangs, or at least their leaders, were drawn into the political process where it mattered most to them—in the neighborhoods.

The UATF at its top (or umbrella) level coordinated city departments that otherwise bickered with each other and forced them to communicate. As Barry Gottehrer, special assistant to the mayor, recalled, often the first news of a potential riot or racial disturbance came in a phone call from the police department that squad cars had been dispatched to a neighborhood. To be more proactive, Gottehrer formed the task force, which included representatives of the police, sanitation, and fire departments, the borough presidents, the board of education, the city's antipoverty agencies, and the Youth Board, among others. City agencies shared information and coordinated the delivery of services, sometimes for the first time.

The most important work of the task force occurred at the neighborhood level. Neighborhood task forces were formed in each of eighteen high-risk communities, and each was chaired by a member of the umbrella group, who served as the "mayor's man" for the community. The neighborhood task forces brought together "community people, from the churches and from the streets, [who] participated in a weekly confrontation and dialogue with the municipal administration for their area." Neighborhoods made demands for city services, knowing they had a channel to top administrators at city hall, while the city officials used their contact with neighborhood groups to feel the pulse of the community. In addition, members of the neighborhood task force walked the streets to calm tensions and dispel rumors during times of crisis. Unlike MFY, which challenged established powers and protested at city hall, the neighborhood task forces channeled resources into neighborhoods and kept community groups focused on the neighborhood level.[17]

There were adolescent versions of the neighborhood task forces, too. The city set up youth councils in storefronts in each of the same eighteen key neighborhoods and hired "youth leaders" under the supervision of the Youth Board to organize local adolescents into summer recreation and employment programs. It is interesting to note that Barry Gottehrer did not refer to gangs either in his memos to the mayor and to other members of the Lindsay administration, or in his published memoirs, except to say that gangs were no longer a problem when Lindsay took office. Gottehrer recalled, "We were talent scouts for troublemakers with leadership ability . . . and the worse the kid, the happier we were to find him." Undoubtedly some of those kids were gang members who were most likely to satisfy both the leadership and the troublemaking requirements. The goal was to enlist youth in a process of community betterment, which was similar to the philosophy of the Chicago Area Project, discussed in chapter 7. The youth councils ran neighborhood cleanup campaigns, organized sports competitions, took youths on outings, and sponsored remedial educational programs. Using the federal money available through the War on Poverty, city officials staffed recreational programs and youth centers with the city's "worst kids." For these individuals, the youth council provided legitimacy, money, and an avenue out of the streets. According to one unsympathetic observer, Puerto Rican activist Alfredo Lopez, "Because of the low level of political consciousness, the poverty agencies were able to co-opt the gang's militancy by offering its members jobs."[18]

The argument that gangs were co-opted contains two fallacies. It ignores the decline in street gangs that was already apparent before Lindsay took office, and it romanticizes street gangs' political potential. Gang members' resistance to the world their parents inhabited was not "militant," but inchoate, not politicized as much as felt. Only a handful of gang members became politically involved. For the majority, their alienation coexisted with their need to live in the world and to supply their very material wants. As the history of intervention projects shows, gangs cooperated with programs offering them concrete advantages. Gang members were obsessed with finding work, especially work that might lead out of the dead-end service sector employment held by their parents and friends. But they were realistic enough to know that they had to start somewhere, and any program that seemed capable of supplying jobs, even bad jobs, gained support. Intervention programs may have gained more acceptance than Black Panthers or civil rights organizers because they offered something very tangible to extremely poor adolescents. Those gangs that remained in the late 1960s were not bought off as much as they were enlisted in programs that promised both individual and community improvement.

Barry Gottehrer vehemently denied the charge that the Lindsay youth programs were designed to buy off youth leaders. Gottehrer argued that street youths were smart enough to see through such cynical manipulation and that it would have failed miserably had it been tried. What the Lindsay administration offered was not a simple payoff for keeping the peace. Rather, adolescents received an opportunity to become involved in their communities, to prove that they could hold jobs and show up for work, and to define their masculinity in conventional ways—in sum, to act like "normal" adolescents. Like the Chicago Area Project, the youth councils linked adults and adolescents in defining and solving community problems in a democratic fashion. The main beneficiaries, however, were the leaders recruited by the program, who used their experience as a means of upward mobility. The Lindsay program allowed some youths an opening to enter the civil service bureaucracy, just like the Youth Board always had. In return for meaningful work, adolescents, including gang leaders, gave up the dead-end world of the streets, while the city gained a respite from gangs.[19]

The task forces and the youth councils proved their usefulness in Bedford-Stuyvesant and in East Harlem in the summer of 1967, when disturbances occurred but without massive destruction and loss of life. In Bedford-Stuyvesant, crowds stormed into the streets after police shot an African-American teenager. Task force members patrolled the neighborhood, dispelling rumors about the case, encouraging people to disperse, and preventing the outbreak of violence. In East Harlem, off-duty police officers intervening in a street brawl killed an armed assailant, which set off a week of disturbances. Although youth council and task force members did not prevent rioting, they helped limit its extent. The East Harlem Youth Council, which included a number of former gang members under the leadership of Arnold Segarra, helped disperse crowds and diffuse anger. In the aftermath of the rioting, the Youth Council won resources for the neighborhood—tangible evidence that with sufficient organization and pressure the political system might be made to work for the poor as well as the advantaged. Job and recreational programs were funneled through the Youth Council, which also lobbied successfully for the assignment of a case worker from the welfare department to assist community residents who came to the council for help. The Youth Council distributed jobs and welfare locally, like the political machine had, and cemented the ties between city hall and the neighborhoods. Not coincidentally, it also helped Segarra launch a career in politics.[20]

The Lindsay program could have contributed to the formation of more cohesive and powerful gangs. Like the gang intervention programs of the 1950s, it enhanced the prestige of the gang leaders who participated and provided resources for the neighborhood. But by the time these programs started, the number of gangs had already declined, and, with help from the Lindsay administration, youths with leadership abilities became absorbed in old-fashioned, community-based politics. The Lindsay policies contributed to maintaining the peace, prevented New York from exploding like other cities had done, and absorbed the energies of gang members that might otherwise have gone to street fighting.

## VIETNAM

The war in Vietnam, escalating at the same time that public and private social policies were disrupting gangs and engaging youths in their communities, had a dramatic impact on poor urban neighborhoods. At first, the war effort, with its voracious appetite for young men, helped reduce the pool of older gang members while spurring the domestic economy. Later, as will be discussed below, returning Vietnam veterans supplied leadership, tactics, and weapons to the gangs that began reorganizing in the 1970s.

The military had always served as a manly way out of the gang, but in the mid-1960s, enlistment was supplemented by the draft. Vietnam was, in historian Christian Appy's terms, a "working-class war" in which the disadvantaged bore the brunt of military service and combat, while the middle-class escaped more lightly. Historian George Flynn analyzed the pool of 1-A (draft eligible) males and found that participation in the military varied inversely with education, which serves as a proxy for class: where only 50 percent of college graduates in the 1-A pool participated in the military, 85 percent of high school dropouts did so. The less educated were also more likely to wind up in combat infantry units. One survey concluded that men from disadvantaged backgrounds were twice as likely as middle-class men to serve in the military and to see combat in Vietnam. Dramatic increases in draft call-ups began in 1966, and at the same time, standards for draftees dropped precipitously, which resulted in more poor and working-class men entering the service. Between enlistments and the draft, the pool of eligible gang members shrank after 1966.[21]

The number of youths available for gang membership was also reduced because the war economy spurred job growth in New York. Over 200,000 new jobs were created between 1965 and 1970, and the unemployment rate in New York City fell to 3.1 percent in 1968, which was a half point lower than the national average, while the unemployment rate for African Americans in the city was only 4 percent. One analyst concluded that New York in the mid- to late 1960s had the "strongest big city economy in the country."[22] Employment was a real possibility for those seniors tired of hanging around on the street corner.

As gangs splintered and their number fell below that needed to sustain conflict, members sometimes drifted, searching for alternatives to the gang. Summer recreation and jobs programs may have helped some, but they were not a permanent solution to the problems that led adolescents into the gang. Older youths faced the draft or took jobs, but for the younger adolescents in prime gang-formation age, those were not viable options. Youths on the Lower East Side, in the South Bronx, and in the city's other troubled neighborhoods looked for different ways to avoid the working-class world. Increasingly they turned to a form of deviance less immediately threatening than gang fighting, but one that in the end destroyed more lives. The effectiveness of the Youth Board, the police, and the social welfare agencies in disrupting the gangs inadvertently opened the door to heroin.

## THE SPREADING PLAGUE

Heroin was not new to city streets in the 1960s. In fact, it existed in the same neighborhoods in which gangs had proliferated. The timing of the heroin epidemic is crucial to understanding its effect on the city's gangs. The spread of heroin coincided with the rise of the gangs in the late 1940s, its use increased during the height of gang activity in the 1950s, and it existed independently of the gangs throughout this period. As seen in chapter 6, gang members weary of street fighting sometimes turned to heroin as a way of escaping the gang. But gangs generally did not have much tolerance for heroin users and heroin only nibbled at the edges of the gang. Studies showed repeatedly that heroin users and gang members, while living in the same areas, belonged to different social sets.[23] An adolescent was either a gangbanger or a junkie. As the gangs declined, however, heroin use became the default option for those adolescents wishing to avoid entering the adult working-class world.

New York was the nation's heroin capital, the center of national importation and distribution circles, as well as home to the majority of the nation's addicts. As supplies of heroin increased in the postwar period, the city not only drew addicts from throughout the nation, but it also witnessed an expanding local market. Increasingly heroin spread to the city's own, principally poor, youth. What author Claude Brown has called "the plague" swept over Harlem in the late 1940s and infected East Harlem, the Lower East Side, Bedford-Stuyvesant in Brooklyn, and the neighborhoods of the South Bronx in the early 1950s.[24] In 1951 members of the East Harlem Protestant Parish reported that "signs of increasing narcotics activity among teen-agers began to show late last summer here in our area. By late fall the staff and Parish members recognized that addiction was taking its toll among our youth." The spread of narcotics led the parish to form a Narcotics Anonymous group and to prepare educational materials for youngsters as they geared up to fight a new scourge.[25] The spread of heroin on the Lower East Side also dated to the early 1950s, when Italian and Irish youths obtained the drug in Italian East Harlem, New York's drug trafficking center. Soon the block on Henry Street between Clinton and Montgomery became known as "Junkies' Paradise" or "Junky Alley" because of the drug users and pushers who congregated there.[26]

According to city officials, heroin use grew alarmingly in the late 1940s and continued apace thereafter, with the most dramatic increases among adolescents. Although official statistics on heroin use have to be treated at least as gingerly as those on crime, they suggest the direction in which adolescent heroin use was moving. In 1951, narcotics arrests among adolescents were twenty-three times higher than in the base years, 1934–1938, while for adults the increase was only four and a half times.[27] The number of arrests for those twenty years old and younger on narcotics-related felonies and misdemeanors grew from 33 in 1946 to 521 in 1950, a sixteen-fold increase, while those for individuals twenty-one and older "only" tripled from 679 in 1946 to 1,961 in 1950.[28] In Central Harlem, the reported addiction rate nearly doubled from 22.1 per 10,000 in 1955 to 40.1 in 1961. Officials were aware of the epidemiological nature of narcotics use and pinpointed the Manhattan neighborhoods inhabited by African Americans and Puerto Ricans as suffering from the worst outbreaks.[29]

Adolescent gang members might have been expected to use heroin. The same African-American musical culture of bebop that gave gang members their name ("boppers") was characterized by heroin use. The hippest musicians, starting with Charlie Parker, the father of bebop, used heroin as part of their self-identity and it became almost synonymous with their cool style. " '[Heroin] was our badge,' " said musician Red Rodney. " 'It was the thing that made us different from the rest of the world.' " Heroin was an integral part of the scene for people who were really down with bop.[30] Since gang members borrowed language, style, clothing, and a way of walking from the bop musicians, it should have followed naturally that they borrowed their use of heroin as well. But they did not, and it was the gang that kept them clean.

At first, street gangs were eyed as likely purveyors and users of illegal narcotics, but a city-sponsored research project showed this was not the case. In their sample of heroin users, the research team found that adolescents learned about drugs in their neighborhoods, where the use of narcotics was common. Drug use began with peers, not pushers, and from observing family members, relatives, and friends who were narcotics users. Most important, narcotics users existed in a separate subculture from the neighborhood toughs, whose profile matched that of the gang member. Heroin addicts, instead of being masculine and aggressive defenders of reputation, were more "feminine" and concerned with appearance and clothing, the authors argued. They were the product of female-dominated households, and heroin use stemmed from their inability to assume a masculine role in society. Adolescent addicts, they concluded, were not tough gang members but "pretty boys" who would not look out of place in a "musical comedy chorus."[31]

While this report is marred by its homophobic stereotyping and its tendency to blame mothers for their sons' deviance, there is no reason to doubt its identification of a unique narcotics-user subculture. Narcotics users and gang members overlapped to a degree, but these were largely different groups of individuals. The researchers had distinguished what Richard Cloward and Lloyd Ohlin called a "retreatist" subculture, one that was analytically and empirically different from the "conflict" subculture that street gang members inhabited.[32]

A separate analysis of gangs by the same research team indicated that gangs were inimical to heavy narcotics use. Instead of pushing heroin, gangs pressured users to cut back on their heroin use or to stop it completely. Though some gangs tolerated pushers among their peripheral members (generally low-level dealers who sold heroin to support their own habits), these individuals did not peddle to fellow gang members. Only about a third of the over three hundred gang members surveyed had ever used heroin, and about a fifth of those who tried it had stopped by the time of the survey.

The research team formulated a two-stage hypothesis to explain gang development and heroin use. They argued that in the early stage, when most members were under eighteen, gangs were more cohesive and prone to gang fighting, and they participated in vandalism and competitive sports. As the gang aged, it moved into the second stage where it became less interested in conflict and rejected group activities as "kid stuff." Members became more concerned with employment, regular sources of income, and steady relationships with girlfriends, and they began to pull away from their adolescent peer group. It was in this stage that some members, unable to make this transition to manhood and fearful of forming heterosexual relationships, turned toward the habitual use of heroin as a way of remaining in the male-dominated world of the streets.[33]

This analysis of the progression of a gang member's career captures the sequential movement from fighting to drug use as some gang members separated from the gang. But it focuses too much on the alleged psychological problems of gang members. Gang members did not become drug users because they were effeminate, failed to establish relationships with girls, or because of a desire for an all-engulfing mother love. Their heroin use must be understood instead in terms of their relationship to the marketplace and the difficult choices they faced as they matured. They were ambivalent about entering the labor market while they were also wary of the increasing risks of remaining in the gang. Faced with difficult choices, young men resolved their dilemma through heroin use. It supplied them with a new group and a new subculture while allowing them to leave fighting and avoid the labor market. Their use of heroin and their entry into the world of hustling was not the expression of psychological dysfunction or of latent homosexuality, as the study implied. It was a refusal to accept the terms society offered working-class adolescents, and it substituted individual use of drugs for the collective resistance of gang membership.

Despite flaws in the heroin-user study, the most important point made—that heroin use and gang fighting did not mix—is corroborated by other evidence. A reporter, investigating the disappearance of the Assassins on Manhattan's Upper West Side in the mid-1960s, found the same pattern that the research team found a decade earlier. There were two principal and separate categories of adolescents in the neighborhood—gangbangers and junkies. "Although they are on pot, the Eagles, like most gangs, will not tolerate heroin addicts," Gertrude Samuels wrote. "The Eagles know that the only true allegiance of the addicts is to the source of their next fix."[34] As Manny Torres explained about his gang-banging days, "We didn't steal, didn't use dope. Most of us didn't even drink."[35] The heroin epidemic spread in the same neighborhoods where gangs prevailed, and at any point in time several gang members or former members could be found dabbling in heroin, but they generally were on their way out of the gang. Gangs served as a barrier—to be sure, only a flimsy one—to the spread of heroin. But as gangs broke up, their members were left awash in a sea of drugs.

## BARRIER BREACHED

The relationship between the collapse of a gang and heroin use became apparent almost immediately in gang intervention programs. When the Central Harlem gang project, organized by the Welfare Council in 1947, ended in 1950, the directors concluded that although their gangs had not participated in any fights, the project had not succeeded in preventing members from turning to drugs. The mandate had been to end acts of aggression, and little attention had been paid to the more deep-rooted problems facing adolescents, of which aggression was only a symptom.[36] Hugh Johnson, a street worker in Central Harlem who later rose to prominence in the Youth Board, also noted ruefully in an interview that "once the boys [in the Central Harlem project] had lost their precious reason for existence, bopping, many of them tended to withdraw from life altogether by becoming addicted to narcotics."[37] Former gang worker Nestor Llamas, analyzing the collapse of his South Bronx gang under police pressure after a homicide, found that members began using heroin. The police presence kept the gang on the defensive and forestalled any gang fighting. Stanley, formerly a low-status and peripheral member of the gang because of his drug use, now assumed a more central role. He started to hang around with the leaders, who had formerly shunned him but now turned to him as a supplier of heroin after the gang had fragmented.[38] Alfredo Lopez, commenting on Puerto Rican gangs in the city, wrote that "dope became popular when police repression made gang membership impossible." And from their observation of gangs on the Lower East Side, the organizers for Mobilization for Youth realized that a number of former boppers had become heroin users, and they warned that any new program would have to supply alternatives to the gang in order to contain the spread of heroin. "Often drug use tends to emerge," they cautioned, "when opportunities for conflict are no longer available," a finding that was echoed by the Youth Board as well. As the number of gangs fell below the threshold that sustained fighting, former boppers substituted the needle and the thrill of a heroin rush for the switchblade and the thrill of a rumble.[39]

Neighborhoods that had been gang bastions became overrun by heroin users as the gangs disappeared. As early as 1960, an investigation of New York's "toughest block"—East Harlem's 100th Street between First and Second Avenues—revealed that gangs no longer had a foothold there, but heroin users were everywhere. 100th Street had been Enchanter turf, but after most of the Enchanters had gone social and became the "Conservatives," the block had become a "business street" where drug pushing and using predominated. Youth Board workers reported that as former leaders got into drugs, so did their followers. While gang incidents declined in New York City, arrests for narcotics-related offenses soared, with a 10 percent increase between 1962 and 1963 alone. The citywide juvenile delinquency rate doubled between 1953 and 1963, from 23.6 per 1,000 five- to twenty-year-olds in 1953, to 50.6 per 1,000 seven- to twenty-year-olds a decade later. At the same time, violent crime, as signified by the adolescent homicide rate (fig. 2.2) and the number of adolescents charged with murder or manslaughter (fig. 2.3), continued to climb. Estimates of the number of heroin addicts in New York City varied widely between 25,000 and 60,000, with the majority of them under twenty-five years of age. While no one knew how many heroin users there actually were, the number of adolescent users had burgeoned since the early 1950s.[40]

Some contemporary commentators argued that heroin caused the collapse of the gangs. The evangelist David Wilkerson thought that heroin had destroyed the gangs, while Dion DiMucci, reflecting on his experience in the Fordham Baldies, maintained: "In one way you could say that junk broke up the gangs. When you were really high, the last thing you wanted to do was look for trouble." A number of my interviewees also claimed that heroin use led to the collapse of their gangs.[41]

Though the experience of these individuals is not "wrong," I do not find the argument that heroin killed the gangs persuasive. Gang members active in the '40s, '50s, and '60s all claimed that heroin use led to the end of the gangs, an observation that could not possibly be accurate since there were gangs (in fact, younger cohorts of their own gangs) present in their neighborhoods throughout this period. A more likely scenario is that individual members of their gang cohort began using heroin as a way out of the gang, an act that in memory is equated with the gang's demise as its strength began to be sapped. As other cohort members joined the workforce, went to jail, became involved in more organized criminal activity, or limited themselves to weekend membership, "their gang" disappeared and was replaced on the corner by a younger group. What changed in the 1960s was that the spread of the heroin epidemic interrupted this age-based process of gang succession.

With the decline in gang fighting, the gang lost much of its reason for existence. Although many gang members attributed feelings of intimacy, friendship, and belonging to their membership in a gang, it is undeniable that group cohesiveness had been reinforced by the ominous threats of surrounding gangs. As these threats disappeared, some members were free to resume more normal adolescent existences, while members whose identities had been especially bound up in conflict lost their basis for status in the adolescent world. As one interviewee put it, "Once you call a truce, what are you going to do?" These individuals still had to prove they had heart and they found a new challenge in heroin. For example, Youth Board worker Vincent Riccio found that as Brooklyn's Gowanus Boys became more interested in social events, "Polock," the war counselor, became even more aggressive and critical of Riccio's influence. With the gang turning social and new leaders being elected, "Polock" had lost his position with the group, and he eventually dropped out of the club and became an addict.[42] While some members were able to make adjustments to the demands of conventional society, others were unwilling to face the drudgery of the working world and found new meaning and new rituals in the drug subculture. With the decline in gang fighting, heroin became both a lure and a challenge.

The relationship between drug use and the decline of the gangs was synergistic: the collapse of the gangs furthered drug use and the rising tide of drug use eroded the remaining gangs' abilities to preserve their members and themselves. With the decline in gang organization and gang fighting, the gang became a less viable way for an adolescent to prove himself while heroin was an increasingly available alternative. The spread of heroin then disrupted the recruitment of new age cohorts to take the place of the retiring seniors. Public policy and gang intervention projects pushed the number of gangs below the threshold level in the early 1960s, but it was heroin that kept them there, as one epidemic gave way to another.

## THE RESURGENCE OF GANGS

Gangs had not entirely disappeared, however, and by 1970 or so, they seemed to be reorganizing. Since only eight to ten years had passed since gangs had been in their ascendancy, it is fair to question how real or extensive their decline had been.[43] If one reads accounts of declining gang activity closely, it soon becomes apparent that most reports came from Manhattan neighborhoods, rather than the Bronx or Brooklyn.[44] Other neighborhoods, especially in the outer boroughs, did not fare as well as the more famous Manhattan ones in the distribution of gang intervention programs and War on Poverty resources. In addition, heroin use radiated out of Harlem and the Lower East Side into Brooklyn and the Bronx, which also explains why gangs in Manhattan fell below threshold levels before gangs in other boroughs did. When journalists Fred Shapiro and James Sullivan analyzed the sources of the Bedford-Stuyvesant riot of 1964, they found twenty-two active gangs in the area.[45] Geoffrey Canada's account of growing up in the South Bronx in the mid-1960s reads no differently than those of Claude Brown, Piri Thomas, or Nicky Cruz, whose experiences in New York's street gangs occurred between one and two decades earlier.[46] Even as civil rights leaders such as Kenneth Clark proclaimed the dawning of a new age of racial harmony among African Americans, newspapers announced the murder of a member of the Pythons, an African-American gang from Bedford-Stuyvesant, by a member of the Chaplains, another African-American gang with roots going back to the 1940s.[47] Alfred Cain, Jr., a member of the Chaplains, recalled, "You had some young bloods out there still jitterbugging in '63 and '64."[48] Other boroughs followed the trend set in Manhattan, but they did so more slowly and unevenly. As in the past, neighborhood social ecology affected the levels of gang activity.

The decline in gang fighting had been relative, not absolute. It had been significant enough, however, that the Youth Board had concentrated its resources in neighborhood recreational centers and in contracting programs out to settlement houses. When gang fighting reemerged in the 1970s, the Youth Board was caught short and suddenly had to reinvent its street worker program and hire dozens of new workers.[49]

Gangs, as social phenomena, responded to the larger social and economic context in which they existed. As that context changed in the early 1970s, gangs passed the threshold level, first in one neighborhood, then in another. Neighborhood factors determined where gangs reorganized. Gangs in the South Bronx occupied a vacuum created by the absence of civil authority and reorganized in opposition to the devastating effects of the heroin plague. In Chinatown they emerged out of the fracturing of civil authority into hostile elements.

## CHINATOWN

Adolescent gangs appeared for the first time in New York's Chinatown in the mid-1960s, as gangs were declining elsewhere in Manhattan. Organized originally to protect Chinese-American students from attacks by African-American and Italian gangs on the Lower East Side, Chinese gangs exploded in size and number after the passage of the 1965 immigration reform act. (The immigration reform act removed the restrictive national quota on immigrants and allowed a flat quota of 20,000 annual immigrants for each nation. As a result, New York's Chinese population nearly doubled between 1960 and 1970, from less than 20,000 to slightly more than 37,000, with most of the increase coming in the second half of the decade.[50]) As they developed in this period, Chinese youth gangs were an expression of ethnic, political, and business rivalries that had existed for a long time in the Chinese community but which intensified after the liberalization of the immigration law. Gangs formed rather quickly based on place of origin (Toisanese, Cantonese, and Fujianese were the major Chinese groups, later supplemented by the Vietnamese) that was reflected in settlement patterns within an expanding, but still relatively contained, and eventually misnamed "Chinatown." The new, ethnic Asian gangs existed in close proximity to one another, developed intense rivalries, and fought each other rather than outsiders. In short, the neighborhood's social ecology pushed gangs in Chinatown above the threshold level while gangs elsewhere in New York were falling below it.

What made the gang situation in Chinatown unusual is that adults used gang rivalries and turned the gangs into economic as well as social entities. The takeoff of the Chinatown economy fueled feuds between two well-organized, traditional tongs, the Hip Sing and the On Leong, over gambling, racketeering, and political influence. Both sides employed adolescent street gangs as proxies in their struggle, and deadly rivalries broke out among the Flying Dragons (a youth gang affiliated with the Hip Sing), the Ghost Shadows, the Black Eagles, and the White Eagles, who were at various times affiliated with On Leong. Gang members worked as enforcers who collected debts, guarded gambling establishments, and protected the illegal enterprise of the tong for which they worked. Essentially the gang became a direct means of entry into adult organized crime. The Chinese gangs were defining turf in economic terms, something the gangs of the 1940s and 1950s had not done. And, as will be seen in the next chapter, this transformation in the meaning of turf and the role of the gang would eventually spread beyond Chinatown. Gangs were not only reorganizing, they were becoming something new.[51]

## THE SOUTH BRONX

Outside of Chinatown, the gang revival was centered in the South Bronx and gradually spread from there. By 1970, large swathes of the South Bronx had become a no-man's-land, with vacant and incinerated apartment buildings. Abandoned to arson and drugs, and without the political clout that yielded large amounts of antipoverty funding to Harlem and, to a lesser extent, to Bedford-Stuyvesant, the South Bronx existed in a social and political vacuum into which young people moved, creating their own social order.[52] The first reports of gangs appeared in 1970, and by the end of 1971, Lindsay administration officials estimated that between fifteen and twenty-five gangs had been established. These gangs developed affiliates in Harlem, Bedford-Stuyvesant, and the Lower East Side, while Euro-American gangs, especially in the north Bronx, organized to resist the migration of African Americans and Latinos into their neighborhoods and schools.[53]

As gangs made their reappearance in the South Bronx in the early 1970s, they announced their presence through attacks on addicts and heroin dealers, who were natural targets. Gangs claimed that they were defending their communities against drugs and drug users, a notion that police, in particular, scoffed at. The police feared romanticizing the gangs and turning them into community heroes. But given the traditional hostility gangs exhibited toward drug users, gang members' claims have some merit. Jill Jonnes, in her history of the South Bronx, commented that "these teenagers had seen their older brothers and sisters, even their parents, ravaged by 'smack.' They had come home to apartments burglarized by junkies and listened to tearful tales of muggings."[54] Carlos, a member of the Turbans, a South Bronx gang, reported that upon returning home from Vietnam, he " 'found junkies all over the streets, terrorizing people.' " The Turbans, Carlos said, beat up junkies and posted "Junkies Keep Out" signs with skull-and-crossbones emblems on Minford Place, the street where they headquartered. (This area had been an open-air market for drugs, with one resident recalling " 'on Charlotte and Minford they sold drugs like they were groceries.' ")[55] A number of gangs included former heroin users who had quit through the gang and probably found cathartic relief in their violence against heroin addicts. Burton Roberts, the Bronx district attorney, called the gangs vigilantes and asked, " 'Since when does a 15- or 16-year-old kid take it upon himself to be a judge and jury and inflict a penalty which the law doesn't inflict?' " Yet even Roberts was not entirely unsympathetic: " 'For the most part,' " he said, " 'these are good kids.' "[56] In sum, gang members had many reasons to despise junkies, and it is not at all illogical that adolescents with firsthand knowledge of the heroin scourge would organize to defend themselves against it. Attacks on junkies and dealers were extensions of the gangs' traditional defense of turf and became the basis for renewed gang organization.

Although gangs portrayed themselves as community defenders, they were not always the white knights they claimed to be. As the police rightly pointed out, gangs continued to engage in violence toward members of other gangs, and gang members still committed crimes. For example, gangs raised money through offering "protection" to area businesses that were thinly veiled extortion threats. Refusal to pay might result in a break-in, an act of vandalism, or even a firebombing.[57] Other actions had their roots in the traditional sources of gang conflict: claiming or defending turf, establishing or preserving reputation, and creating a masculine identity. One Bronx youth, a member of a graffiti writers group, recounted an invasion of a "hooky party" (a party held during school hours). The Black Pearls sponsored the party and had invited the graffiti artists, who were not gang members, but earned respect because they traveled unarmed and moved freely through the turfs of different gangs. Suddenly a heavily armed group of the Black Spades entered the abandoned building that served as a clubhouse. They turned on the lights, surveyed the scene, and selected a couple of youths to beat up. " 'Then they said, "All the graffiti artists, you, you, and you, split, because we don't want you guys to get involved. So you all just slip out." So we got out and when we got to the corner we heard bang, ting-a-ling, smash! But we just went upstairs, got on the train, made a tag [a wall writing], and went on about our business. But we didn't go back.' "[58] Gangs still observed certain rules—they selected their targets carefully and they let noncombatants go. However, the introduction of modern weapons also meant that a conflict between gangs could easily get out of hand. The Turbans, mentioned above for their antiheroin activities, maintained their rivalry with the nearby Javelins. A confrontation in the summer of 1972 between the two gangs sprayed gunfire all over the intersection of 173rd Street and Boston Road, leaving four innocent bystanders wounded.[59]

Even the attacks on the junkies were more violent than gang members admitted in a interview. The Immortals, another South Bronx gang, raided a "shooting gallery" (an apartment where heroin users could keep or rent "works" and shoot up) run by a young woman and raped and murdered her, while critically wounding her two male companions.[60]

The Youth Services Administration (the successor to the Youth Board) had gang intelligence reports that noted that the Savage Skulls and the Savage Nomads had attacked a group of junkies, killing two of them.[61] And in another incident, police found a drug pusher with six bullets in his body in the shape of a cross.[62] Gangs also had ulterior motives for their attacks on pushers. Dealers were rumored to use gangs to wipe out competitors, and at least one gang, the Turbans, had become involved in drug trafficking despite their claims of antiheroin vigilantism.[63] Gangs emerged in the 1970s in the South Bronx more heavily armed, more violent, and more independent of adult authority than before. The collapse of civil order in the South Bronx allowed youth gangs to create their own order on the streets.

## Gangs Rebound

A number of factors, including the war in Vietnam, led to the resurgence of street gangs. Returning veterans found that little had changed in their old neighborhoods other than the proliferation of drugs. (Undoubtedly some of these veterans returned with heroin habits; a survey of returning Vietnam veterans in 1971 found that over one-fifth used heroin or morphine while in Vietnam, and one-tenth used one or the other daily.)[64] Returning veterans helped reorganize gangs during the Vietnam era, just as veterans had after World War II. In both cases, war itself contributed to the normalization of violence.[65]

Veterans brought tactics, weapons, and heightened alienation back to their neighborhoods. The same reports about antidrug vigilantism note the presence of Vietnam veterans among the gangs. The Turbans were described as being made up nearly entirely of veterans, but generally the veterans were members, advisors, and suppliers of weapons in their gangs rather than the dominant force. The ages of gang members ranged from early adolescence to mid- to late twenties, and veterans fit the senior advisor role well. One Vietnam veteran put his skills to use as the war counselor for his gang, noting that " 'all I've ever been trained for is to kill people.' "[66] Gang workers reported seeing machine guns and other heavy armaments in gang arsenals, although the police discounted this. Even without machine guns, the gangs were better armed than their

1950s and 1960s predecessors. While Geoffrey Canada remembered guns as being a novelty in his South Bronx neighborhood as late as the mid-1960s, virtually all observers commented on the advanced firepower gangs packed in the early 1970s. The New York State Legislature's Subcommittee on the Family Court reported police seizures of automatic weapons and grenades, and Sergeant Craig Collins, the head of the New York City Police Department's Youth Gang Intelligence Squad in the Bronx, argued, "Today it's common for lots of gang members to have real guns. And it's my observation that these kids are much more ready to use weapons than gang members were in the '50s.'" "Home-mades" or zip guns were used only by very young boys and were held in contempt by most members, who fought with the real thing.[67]

The toll of violent confrontation mounted as weapons became more prevalent and more sophisticated. The total of fifty-seven gang-related homicides in 1972 was more than triple the number during any year in the 1950s. Although the number declined thereafter, gang-related homicides averaged forty-three per year in the mid-1970s. The distribution of victims was even more disturbing than their increasing number. Although bystanders had been hurt during gang wars in earlier decades (witness Theresa Gee), gangs generally avoided targeting adults or young children. When criminologist Walter Miller surveyed gangs in the 1970s, he found that whether by chance or by intention, nearly 40 percent of the victims of gang violence in New York were adults or children. Gangs reachieved threshold levels on New York City streets, but with the ready availability of weapons, they returned at an unparalleled level of mayhem. As one New York City policeman remarked, "'We should at least be thankful that these kids are such pitiful shots, otherwise there would be bodies all over the streets.'"[68]

Ethnic conflict sparked gang organization, again as it had in the 1940s. While most surveys commented that gang members were overwhelmingly African American and Hispanic in the 1970s, Euro-American gangs organized in the north Bronx, the farther reaches of Brooklyn, and in Queens to resist desegregation in the schools. (A survey of gang members by New York police in 1973 revealed that 55 percent were Hispanic, 36 percent African American, and 9 percent white.)[69] Italian areas in particular were flash points, and adults encouraged youths to defend the neighborhood against outsiders. The Arthur Avenue Boys, for example, inherited the turf of the Fordham Baldies and knew they could draw on the older men for support, with the "wiseguys" lurking in the background should things get out of hand. Incidents were usually isolated; African Americans and Hispanics traveled through these areas at their peril, with assaults on individuals and small groups fairly common, but with no reports of large-scale rumbling.[70]

Gangs exhibited a new level of political sophistication in the 1970s, and the same programs that helped end gang fighting in the 1960s now served as a catalyst for gangs' reorganization. Gangs, especially in the Bronx, eyed enviously the perks delivered by government programs to youths in other areas. Bronx gang members demanded their "fair share" of summer jobs and recreational activities, which in turn sparked demonstrations by East Harlem gang members who protested that their jobs had been allocated to the Bronx.[71] The message, as one community activist was quoted as saying, was " 'form gangs, be violent and you will receive your share of the gang money.' "[72]

Gangs realized that they could have more influence over policymakers if they organized. A group of five gangs, known as the Brotherhood, negotiated peace treaties with other gangs and met with the Bronx borough president's office to acquire a site for a clubhouse. They proposed to run a high school equivalency program and required that gangs affiliating with them work for the improvement of their communities. A successor to the Brotherhood was "the Family," a coalition of sixty-eight gangs organized under the auspices of the Ghetto Brothers after one of their members, twenty-five-year-old Cornell "Black Benjie" Benjamin, was killed trying to stop a gang fight. In Brooklyn, gangs also organized into an association called the Family and included gangs with the same names as those in the Bronx (Black Spades, Savage Nomads, and the Ghetto Brothers), which made the parallel obvious. These associations wanted to present a united front to the city in negotiating for summer jobs, recreational programs, and federal antipoverty projects. While the Bronx version of the Family soon broke up amid renewed rivalry, officials credited the publicity given the Ghetto Brothers for organizing the Family with helping to revive gangs around the city. Benjamin Ward, then deputy police commissioner for community affairs, argued that " 'these youths have lived through the anti-poverty and civil rights crusades. They've learned how to deal with the establishment. They know what you want to hear.' " Gangs were no longer just a matter of warlords and presidents, but of publicists and politicians as well. But by the time these gangs were organizing, the well of antipoverty funds was running dry.[73]

Assessing the gangs of the early 1970s is tricky because they were both more sophisticated than earlier gang generations in their understanding of the urban political economy and more violent in their reaction to it. " 'The kids in the gangs,' " according to Manuel Dominguez, a teacher in the South Bronx and an advisor to the Ghetto Brothers, " 'are the most romantic figures in the neighborhood.' " Bronx Borough President Robert Abrams saw things differently, arguing that gangs were responsible for a "reign of terror" in the Bronx. " 'I have seen youngsters who have been beaten. I have seen their scars. I have talked to their parents.' "[74] There is evidence for both of these positions. The well-publicized neighborhood cleanup campaigns, the rhetoric about community, the creation of educational programs, the peace negotiations, and efforts to drive out drugs and drug dealing were real enough and capture one side of the gangs. Gangs had learned how to use the press, how to echo the slogans of liberation movements, and how to negotiate with politicians and bureaucrats for recognition and jobs. But gang members continued to inhabit a world where expressive violence established one's reputation and manhood, where neighboring gangs rubbed up against each other and battled over turf, and where economic options outside of the illegal economy were becoming more limited. Advanced weapons made their conflicts more deadly and assured that more bystanders would become victims. There was romance, perhaps, in their rhetoric, but their reality was more harsh.

By the mid-1970s New York's street gangs had once again passed the tipping point and resurrected themselves as bulwarks against heroin use and as defenders of neighborhood turf. But, inevitably, gangs had changed. They had become more violent, the means of escaping the gang had become more limited, the neighborhood turfs they were defending had become more desperate, and gangs were more cut off than ever before from conventional society. New York's economy, which had percolated in the mid-1960s, soured after 1969, and the city lost an additional 340,000 jobs over the next five years, which culminated in a state of near bankruptcy. The city and federal funding that had supplied the gangs with jobs and recreational programs disappeared in the fiscal crisis that followed. The Youth Services Administration ended its street worker program, also a casualty of the fiscal crisis, thus eliminating another link between gangs and the adult world.

With fewer jobs, a smaller military, a shrinking civil service bureaucracy, vanishing antipoverty programs, and suppressed radicalism, the few constructive paths out of the gang world disappeared. What remained was the underground economy. As will be seen in the next chapter, the appearance of crack cocaine in the 1980s completed the cycle of change, as gangs became posses or crews, and turf developed an economic rather than a social meaning. Once again, gangs transformed themselves in response to their social and economic context.

## Comparing Gangs:

## Contemporary Gangs in Historical Perspective

O NE MORNING in East Harlem, waiting for an interviewee to arrive, I watched a group of young men standing on a nearby street corner. Sometimes one member of the group would walk over to the pay phone and answer it; at other times, another would stroll along the street for a short distance with a passerby. I noticed that several of them carried large wads of cash; they appeared to take no obvious notice of me. Across the street was one of those murals so common in inner-city neighborhoods, with names, artwork, slogans, and "RIP." After a while I averted my gaze, not wishing to offend or to appear more conspicuous than I already was, a tweedy, middle-aged white man loitering in a Hispanic and African-American community. My informant arrived, wading through the group at the corner, and we went inside his tire repair shop (which also served as a drop for the local numbers racket). My informant, a barrel-chested former boxer, started to talk about gangs in the 1950s and pulled up his shirt to show me the exit wound left by a bullet. Suddenly, a carload of the street-corner youths appeared outside his shop. The young men gathered slowly on the sidewalk in front of the store. First, one of his assistants went out to speak with them, and then, excusing himself, my informant stepped outside. Satisfied with what he told them, the young men piled back into the car and left. They wanted to borrow a wrench, he said. I realized that I had been cleared with the local dealers.

My informant, like several others I met in East Harlem, lived a life parallel to those led by the youths on the corner. They were aware of each other's existence and interacted when necessary, but my informants in the privacy of our conversations freely expressed their contempt for drug dealers. Their comments were unsolicited (although they may have been induced by a desire to affirm respectability with a middle-class researcher) and were made in the context of explaining the gangs of the 1950s and 1960s: whereas they had fought for honor, had codes of behavior, had defended the neighborhood, and had respected adults, these youths, motivated solely by profit, polluted their communities by peddling crack. Where they had been warriors, these young men were criminals. Clearly something—at least in the minds of my informants—had changed.

As I did more research into the gangs of the postwar period and had the chance to read more about contemporary gangs and observe some New York neighborhoods, it became clearer to me that the nature of the gang has indeed changed over the past two decades. In New York today it is rare to find named gangs and rarer still to see the open display of colors.[1] Gangs do not proclaim their alliances with brother gangs in other parts of the city, divide neighborhoods into fiefdoms, and demand allegiance from the adolescents residing there. Gang leaders no longer negotiate truces before reporters, teenagers do not fight with switchblades and zip guns, and there are no prearranged battles in parks. Girls are not necessarily organized as auxiliaries to male gangs, and they do not name themselves using the female diminutives of male gang names. The model that defined New York's gangs from the 1940s through the 1970s no longer applies. Yet it is clear from observing the knots of young men gathered day after day on the same street corners that gangs still exist even as their form and function are different.

In this conclusion, I would like to examine some of those differences. The most significant issue is the involvement of gang members in the drug trade and the effect that has on the meaning of turf. Drug dealing should be understood in the context of economic restructuring and the pervasiveness of the underground economy in inner-city neighborhoods. Gangs have also organized in new ways. While males still define their gender identities through the gang and in the same fashion as in the past, the relationship between male and female gangs has changed. The ethnic composition of gangs has also changed, as fewer Euro-Americans and more Asian Americans have become involved in gangs. Gang members stay active longer than in the past, which is a reflection of the continued deterioration of the urban economy. Violence, as suggested in the previous chapter, has become deadlier and gangs have become more isolated from conventional adult society as street worker projects have folded and recreational programs ("midnight basketball") have come under attack. The one thing that ties gang members to the larger society is the market, which has converted them from rebels into entrepreneurs, albeit of illegal goods and services.

Let me start by admitting that no one knows how many gangs or gang members there are in New York City, at least in part because there are no longer any agencies that work directly with gangs. After the Youth Services Administration was reorganized in 1976, a casualty of the city's fiscal crisis, the city lost the only source of information that was reasonably close to the gangs.[2] But even when the Youth Board published its studies of gangs, it was better at providing insight into why adolescents joined gangs, how they were organized, and what the bases for rivalries were than at counting the number of gangs or gang members. The alternative source, police department data, is unreliable: police intelligence reports are based on hearsay rather than any real contact with gangs, are infrequently updated, and do not reflect the fluidity of gangs, as many adolescents become peripheral members and then withdraw.[3] Much of the discussion that follows is based on analyses of the inner city's economic and social structure and on the ethnographic research of other scholars, which provides a rich but necessarily limited portrait of gangs and youth crime. Still, these studies make clear that gangs in their modern form remain an important part of the structure of urban neighborhoods.

As I reflected on my observations of drug dealing, I became increasingly convinced—despite the disclaimers of my informants—that the young men on the corner were the descendants of postwar gangs. They met reasonable sociological criteria that defined gangs: they congregated recurrently, exhibited territoriality, defended their turf, demonstrated cohesiveness, and were recognized by others as a group. They called themselves a posse or a crew rather than a gang, but then gangs in earlier decades had called themselves social and athletic clubs or cliques. Their weaponry was more advanced, and violent confrontations were more likely to end in serious injury or death, but those confrontations still involved issues of manhood, respect, and a personal reputation for toughness.[4] The major difference was that for many gangs, a fight over a park or a corner was no longer a battle to control a recreational space or to defend the integrity of the neighborhood but a struggle over a worksite. Already in the 1980s, the meaning of turf had changed, at least for those gangs involved in drug trafficking. For them, territory had less of a social meaning, one invested with concepts of ethnic pride and honor, and had acquired more of an economic one, in which gangs defended their market share. In the 1990s, this remains the same.[5]

## DRUG DEALING AND THE UNDERGROUND ECONOMY

The key question to be asked here is how extensive the involvement of street gangs is in the distribution and sale of illegal drugs. Looking at the problem of drug sales from a national perspective, there is no evidence that street gangs organize the drug trade or import drugs. That requires access to capital, abilities to corrupt law enforcement, and the creation of interurban transportation networks and levels of organization beyond the capacity of the average street gang. There are studies of several different cities showing no link whatsoever between organized drug dealing and street gangs. Occasional media reports that representatives of Los Angeles or Chicago gangs have been sighted in the American heartland organizing local youth into drug-selling franchises are fictions of hyperactive imaginations. Gangs emerge, as I have argued in chapter 8, because of local—even neighborhood-level—factors, although the broadcasting of gang culture through national media outlets means that a certain amount of copycatting exists. Gang members participate in crime as generalists rather than specialists; that is, they do not exhibit the characteristics of organized or professional crime. They are not focused on drug sales but peddle drugs along with hustling, stealing, burglarizing, and committing other illegal acts. They are not the organizers of national drug-selling networks.[6]

On the street level there is a different story to be told. Gangs do not organize the drug trade nationally, but it is clear that gang members—if not gangs as corporate entities—are involved in drug trafficking locally. In his study of gangs in three cities, criminologist Jeffrey Fagan found that nearly two-thirds of the gangs were involved in drug sales in some form, with slightly more than a quarter of them on a consistent basis.[7] Adolescents to perform the low-level and risky tasks of steering buyers, guarding stashes, packaging "product," fetching supplies, watching for police, and peddling on street corners or park benches. Gangs supply trustworthy individuals, who, as they ascend to more responsible positions or franchise their own operations, draw on their gang ties to form their own drug-selling networks.[8] Some gangs (what one researcher has called "corporate gangs") are heavily involved in drug selling, but in most gangs only individual members or small cliques graduate into the illegal economy, just as some gang members in previous decades did.[9] The underground economy, and drug dealing in particular, are so pervasive in the inner city that they provide an almost inescapable economic opportunity for work-starved adolescents.[10] Not all individuals are bold enough to try their hand in the underground economy, but gangs are one place to find those who are.

Drug dealing emerged only recently as a major occupation for adolescents. In New York, the process began with the passage of legislation that took effect in 1973 (the so-called Rockefeller drug laws) that mandated long prison terms for adult drug dealers. To avoid draconian legal penalties, dealers limited their exposure to arrest by using adolescent pushers, steerers, and carriers, who were subject to the milder treatment of the juvenile court. Two other factors—shifts in the importation of illegal drugs and in their marketing—were also involved. The traditional Mafia, with its centralized control over the importation and distribution of heroin, was displaced first by Cuban-American heroin dealers and later by rival South American cartels of cocaine exporters, who had trouble limiting entry into the illegal marketplace. A cocaine glut in the early 1980s led to a drop in price and the development of a new product—crack—that largely replaced powdered cocaine on inner-city streets. Crack refashioned the market for cocaine since it was sold in small, inexpensive quantities to less-affluent consumers.[11] Suddenly young men could prove their entrepreneurial abilities, earn a wage, obtain material goods that had been hitherto out of reach, and gain the admiration of the opposite sex and of their younger peers.[12] Together, changes in the law, new producers and new products, an expanding market, and a youthful population eager for work and opportunity converged to create an inner-city "enterprise zone" based on illegal drugs.

The incorporation of gang members into the underground economy has altered the meaning of gang membership. The gang has become another means of getting paid, and that is the most significant difference between modern gangs and those of the postwar period. Unlike adolescents in earlier periods, who joined gangs as a refuge from the low-skilled, exploitative work world, these youths enter the underground economy through their gang affiliation, and for them the gang has become an economic entity. Instead of creating a network based on mutual support or experiencing the gang as a buffer between adolescence and adult life, drug-selling gang members assume adult responsibilities and soon discover that they are expendable. They are, in novelist Richard Price's words, "clockers," the underground equivalent of McDonald's workers, better paid perhaps, but still exploited and subject to tremendous risks.[13]

Even those gangs not incorporated into drug-selling networks now act in a more utilitarian fashion. Recent studies of gangs have emphasized their interest in moneymaking: gangs provide "protection services" (extortion), steal and strip cars, or operate burglary rings. Gang members in the past had regular jobs, even if on an irregular basis, talked incessantly about finding work, and used the job referrals provided by their street workers. In other words, they had on-going encounters with the labor market, which provided a frame of reference for them. When they engaged in crime, it was for expressive purposes—joyriding, vandalism, and drunken brawls—at least as much as for utilitarian ones. Contemporary gang members are more cut off from the labor market and engage in crime in a more calculated fashion. Gang members still party and fight, but criminal activity is more purposeful.[14]

## ECONOMIC RESTRUCTURING

Economic restructuring provides the context for the new salience of drug dealing in the inner-city economy. Illegal activity has become not only the most tempting, but often one of the only viable economic options for adolescents acclimated to street culture and lacking middle-class social capital. Although New York's labor force in the legitimate economy has grown to 3.5 million workers, between 1969 and 1989 the manufacturing sector lost 460,000 jobs, with another 120,000 jobs lost in transportation and wholesale trade. These were replaced by white-collar, service positions in finance, insurance, real estate, and public social services.[15] Many of the new jobs require basic literacy and numeracy, and they are not available to adolescents without education, job skills, and a history of employment. Moreover, service sector jobs frequently demand knowledge of a proper office demeanor that is alien to masculine shop floor culture and the diametric opposite of the requirements of street culture. That is, service sector positions are "feminized," with large numbers of female employees and supervisors, and they require male workers to exhibit a subservience and docility that would be disastrous if shown on the streets. These positions have replaced the masculinized shop floor and dock worker jobs that working-class males traditionally used to support families and to maintain their gender identities. The construction trades remain an appropriately masculine and vital source of jobs, but entry still depends on family ties and ethnic background. The evolution of the economy has left few legitimate alternatives for working-class adolescents seeking to prove their masculinity.[16]

Economic restructuring has not affected all groups equally. Historical and ethnic factors have determined access to work in the legitimate economy and continue to do so. Historically, the labor force has been segmented, with industrial jobs relegated to Euro-Americans. As a result, African Americans, at least in New York, were relatively unaffected by the decline in manufacturing since they lacked access to these jobs to begin with. While African Americans have lost ground outside of manufacturing, they have been cushioned economically because of their hold over government bureaucracies.[17] Latinos, on the other hand, have had little success in the service economy, but they have been able to hold their own in the manufacturing sector as they replaced an aging white labor force. In other words, the number of whites in manufacturing declined more rapidly than the number of jobs, thus opening positions for Latinos in industries such as garment making, where they already had a foothold.[18] African-American and Latino youth, then, face difficult prospects in the legal marketplace, but for different reasons: African Americans find the public service sector friendliest to them, but it is an unlikely source of growth, requires a large educational investment, and demands social skills at odds with street culture, while Latinos remain vulnerable to job loss because as a group they are so heavily concentrated in the declining industrial sector. This combination of economic restructuring, unequal access to legitimate jobs, and discrimination in the job market propel inner-city youth into drug dealing and other forms of illicit economic activity.

Economic restructuring has also generated unregulated jobs on its margins—the licit sector of the underground economy. Garment manufacturing, for example, has declined greatly as a regulated industry, but sweatshops that pay well below the legal minimum wage and ignore legislation regarding hours of work and safety have proliferated. Gypsy cabs and vans ply inner-city streets where medallioned taxis refuse to go. Housecleaning, small contracting jobs, and other personal services are frequently unregulated, and employers ignore laws governing minimum wages, old-age and unemployment insurance, and worker's compensation. These goods and services support the well-being of the middle class at the cost of ill health and poverty for the workers who provide them.[19] Such sweated labor, frequently the province of illegal immigrants who are fearful of obtaining any legal redress, is part of the economic matrix that shapes the decision making of young Americans. If such exploitation is the wage of honest labor, adolescents reason, who needs it?

It is remarkable to see how well adolescents have identified strategies appropriate to the marketplaces they face, even if they are impeded from exercising them. Anthropologist Mercer Sullivan, in a 1989 comparative study of African-American, Latino, and Euro-American youths poised between criminal careers and the labor market, found that each group differed in access to both legal and illegal opportunity. African-American youths took schooling more seriously than the other two groups and hoped to enter the service sector as adults. Despite this accurate identification of employment trends, African-American adolescents were hampered by limited job experience and a lack of access to job networks as well as to more skilled forms of illegal activity. As a result, they engaged in fairly risky street crime to acquire income. Latino youths quit school the earliest to take manual labor jobs, which were available to them in nearby factories and warehouses and which provided traditional sources of employment for Latino males. They supplemented their income through burglary and were integrated into a widely tolerated underground economy that fenced stolen goods within the community. The Euro-American youths did not take education seriously and found blue-collar jobs through family connections that also shielded them from the criminal justice system. They had the opportunity to steal from employers and therefore rarely engaged in street crime or in illegal activities in their neighborhoods that would expose them to a likelihood of arrest. Class and ethnicity made the experience of each group slightly different.[20]

Faced with harsher criminal penalties as they aged, members of all three groups chose to enter the low-wage labor market, just as gang members leaving the streets in the 1950s and 1960s did. But given the restructuring of New York's economy, it is not clear how many would be able to earn a living there. Only a small number of African-American youths had obtained their GED degrees and had prepared themselves for the white-collar service sector; Latino, Euro-American, and other African-American adolescents were positioned only for the most vulnerable sectors of the economy. Sullivan thought it likely that in the future the youths would continue to supplement periods of low-wage work with periods of criminal activity.[21]

When anthropologist Philippe Bourgois studied Puerto Rican crack dealers in East Harlem, he found that his informants fit the same pattern. Bourgois's principal informants had all dropped out of high school to take manufacturing jobs. In each case, manufacturers moved or jobs ended, and workers had to scramble to find work or enter the underground economy. Several of Bourgois's informants attempted periodically to gain readmission into the mainstream economy even after long periods of drug selling. Bourgois describes in poignant detail the struggles of Primo, his chief informant, to handle the educational and behavioral requirements of work in a service sector job. Primo interpreted comments about his literacy, his Spanish accent, and his attempts to show initiative as racial and gender discrimination by his white, middle-class, female supervisors, who eventually fired him. Primo's abilities and his masculinity—which had never been challenged on the street—were severely tested in a setting that most middle-class people would have found routine.[22]

Adolescents still want to avoid the exploitation that their parents' generation faced, but as the personal costs of participating in the illegal economy escalate, they sometimes reconsider. In the past, many gang members resigned themselves to entering the low-wage marketplace once their gangbanging days were over, and they were able to find work. Primo's generation has found that it has lost even the opportunity to be exploited, as work in the legitimate economy, if it is to be found at all, is frequently temporary or has educational and behavioral requirements that are difficult to meet. In terms of the mainstream economy, the labor of inner-city youth has become superfluous.[23]

## WOMEN AND GENDER

There are many ways in which the experience of women in the gang world has remained the same. Male gang members still describe occasions of gang rape, refer to women in the most derogatory terms, and adhere to traditional patriarchal privileges, much as they did in the postwar era. Female gangs are usually affiliated with male ones, and males continue to outnumber females in the gang world by a ratio of about ten to one.[24] Female gang members form their primary social and sexual relationships with the males in their related gang, and membership in a gang or crew marks a transitional stage that ends with finding male partners or because of the demands of motherhood, just as occurred in the past. In some ways, one might argue that young women's position on the street has worsened with the spread of crack cocaine. Males exploit "crack whores" by trading sex for hits on the pipe under the most brutal and degrading circumstances.[25]

However, in contrast to the female victims of the drug economy, young women who are gang members have found more opportunity. Ethnographies of female gang members suggest that male prerogatives are being challenged, even if some aspects of female participation in street life remain unchanged. Female gangs are more independent than they were in the past. They control entry and discipline over their membership and resist male interference in gang affairs. There are also examples of female gangs that are independent of male ones, as well as examples of women who are integrated into male gangs, even in positions of leadership.[26]

Women accustomed to negotiating on the street can become active participants in the underground economy as adults. One of Philippe

Bourgois's female informants dealt cocaine and sold the rights to a corner after her husband was incarcerated, while one of sociologist Terry Williams's "cocaine kids" organized and ran a cocaine delivery business in partnership with a limousine and escort service. These young women understood that the underground economy offered an alternative to single motherhood and welfare, low-skilled service sector work, or dependency on frequently unreliable male partners. For them, associations on the street turned into channels for economic opportunity that did not exist twenty years earlier.[27]

## ETHNIC COMPOSITION

The appearance of Asian street gangs since the mid-1960s signifies an important change in the ethnic composition of the gang world. Chinese gangs first emerged in New York's Chinatown to defend Chinese youths against raids from other gangs, as discussed in chapter 8. However, Chinese youths are no longer threatened by outside groups, and Asian gangs have become involved more heavily in illegal enterprises. Asian gangs were among the first to be organized essentially for commercial purposes, including engaging in extortion, raiding homes to steal cash and valuables, and participating in protection rackets. Recently, Vietnamese and other Asian gangs have begun to contest Chinese gangs' position on the Lower East Side, in Queens, and in other areas of Asian settlement.[28]

The rise of Asian gangs has been matched by a decline of Euro-American ones. Although no census of gang members from the early decades exists, accounts by the New York City Youth Board and other sources make it clear that white and African-American gangs predominated in the 1940s, with Puerto Rican gangs added to the mix in the 1950s. White gangs have dwindled with ethnic succession in New York neighborhoods, although they still exist and defend the boundaries of white enclaves in such neighborhoods as Bensonhurst and Howard Beach in Brooklyn.[29] More recent estimates of gang membership nationally indicate that African Americans and Hispanics make up about 85 percent of gang members, with the remainder split about evenly between whites and Asians.[30] (I am excluding skinhead, biker, white supremacist, and neo-

Nazi groups, each of which poses its own set of social problems, because they are not particularly urban and do not meet my definition for gangs.) As the face of poverty has changed over time, so has the ethnic composition of urban gangs.

## GANG CAREERS

Gang members today are remaining active until later ages than before. While gangs in the past have included men in their twenties and even older, they were seniors or advisors, and gang researchers identified youths aged sixteen to eighteen as the most active members. Reports of young men "aging out" of the gang en masse after adolescence were exaggerated but still contained a kernel of truth as many young men married, found work, and accepted adult responsibilities and moved off the street corner. Recent studies of gangs indicate an increasingly "adult" profile. For example, the average age of gang offenders in homicide cases is nearly twenty years of age, with a range of up to forty. This again suggests that the changing economy has made it more difficult for adolescent males to assume the roles of manhood in the legitimate sector.[31]

The increasing age of gang members is important because of the example it provides to adolescents entering the gang. While gang members in earlier decades knew adults who engaged in street life, hustling, and criminal careers, they also knew young men who left the gang to enter working-class jobs, to return to school, or to use their gang experience to become street workers and rise through the social service bureaucracy. Adolescents, particularly in areas of concentrated poverty, now see large numbers of adults continuing to hang on the corner, joining the underground economy, or engaging in criminal activity. As sociologist William Julius Wilson has noted, "In such neighborhoods the chances are overwhelming that children will seldom interact on a sustained basis with people who are employed or with families that have a steady breadwinner."[32] Gangbangers and drug sellers are too often the most readily observable examples of successful manhood. The incentives for leaving the gang for a constructive adulthood are fewer than in the past, and thus the gang assumes a new importance in urban neighborhoods.

## VIOLENCE

The increase in violence is perhaps the most obvious change that has occurred over time. Advancing technology bears some responsibility for this. A shift from switchblades and zip guns to rifles and revolvers occurred unevenly in the past, but more recently, the widespread availability of automatic weapons has caused the death toll to rise. Though different cities use different definitions of what constitutes a gang-related offense, the trend in gang-related homicides and assaults is upward, regardless of definition, as is the overall adolescent homicide rate. In 1991, nearly half of the nation's homicide victims were young men between fifteen and thirty-four years of age.[33] Nationally, the rate of fourteen- to seventeen-year-olds arrested for committing homicide doubled between 1984 and 1991, after declining from 1980 to 1983. This paralleled the trend for eighteen- to twenty-four-year-olds, but the rate for the younger group was consistently double that of the older.[34] The rate at which young people are victimized by homicide also increased in the decade of the 1980s, most dramatically for African-American males.[35] Readers should not take too much hope from the recent downturn in homicide and other violent crime. The rates for both perpetrators and victims of homicide are cyclical rather than uniform, but unfortunately, as two veteran gang researchers have concluded, each cycle ends at a higher point than the previous one and then recedes to a higher plateau. Homicide has become endemic among adolescents, with gangs accounting for anywhere between 10 and 25 percent of the total, depending on location, and there is little evidence to suggest that this will change.[36]

In this Hobbesian world, the gang is both a source of stability and destruction. Adolescents refer to the necessity of having "back-up," and the gang provides a sense of security even as it makes its members obvious targets for rival gangs. The gang supplies goods to the community at a fraction of their original cost through fencing stolen items, weapons, or parts stripped from stolen cars, but its criminal endeavors add to the overall insecurity of inner-city life. Drug sales supply jobs and capital that fuel economic activity, but drug sales turn corners, buildings, and even whole blocks into a wasteland of hawkers, users, guards, and resident-hostages. The community survives, but only by cannibalizing itself. As one study of poverty in New York concluded, "For far too many people, the city has been transformed from a place of opportunity and hope to one of want and hopelessness."[37]

## ISOLATION

Gangs have also become more isolated from conventional society than they were in the past. The settlement house programs, the teen canteens, the church-sponsored mediation sessions, and the gang outreach of the Youth Board have largely disappeared. Gang members' reports of their activities suggest ever more intensive interaction with their peers once they join a gang and correspondingly fewer ties to other institutions, except for those in the criminal justice system. This means fewer restraints on adolescent behavior as well as the loss of opportunities to interact with adults who might model constructive social behavior, mediate conflict, and suggest alternatives to violence.[38]

I cannot claim that these programs, which were generally designed to make gangs conform to middle-class expectations, have been notably successful. Outreach or street work programs, while intended to disrupt the gang, sometimes contributed to its cohesion and longevity, especially when they existed in isolation from larger efforts to organize a community. Recreational programs that attempted to tame gang members through basketball or other sports ran the risk of being taken over by the gang, or they simply occupied the time of gang members without noticeably affecting their behavior. Community organizing put resources in the hands of gang members with unpredictable outcomes ranging from radical organizing that affronted institutional sponsors to criminal activity that appeared to be funded with public or foundation money. Even when gangs were managed successfully, as happened in certain Manhattan neighborhoods in the 1960s, new symptoms—heroin addiction—emerged that were at least as destructive to individual and communal well-being. Liberal social programming has not held the solution to the "gang problem," because it has focused largely on symptoms and helping individuals. Gangs have also proven to be remarkably resilient and able to turn these programs on their heads.

The most widely employed policy alternative, past and present, is police suppression. In our own time, police randomly search groups of (usually minority) adolescents, engage in mass sweeps of inner-city blocks, blockade neighborhoods, create databases of gang members and associates, and target gang leaders for arrest and incarceration. So far these tactics have not proven particularly effective in controlling gangs. Instead, they increase alienation among adolescents, violate civil rights, and, if anything, tend to promote identification with gangs and assist their internal cohesion. Moreover, they belie the promise of more sensitive "community policing" and, because of their lack of discrimination between gang members and non–gang members, they further the feeling of inner-city residents that they are under siege with as much to fear from the police as from gang members.

The lessons of Manhattan in the 1960s might suggest that only community mobilization can turn gangs into constructive forces. But radical organizing encountered the pragmatism of gang members, and only a small minority ever participated in political organizing. More important, mobilizers of the poor now confront a different political economy both at the local and at the national level. Instead of a municipality eager to build ties to its minority communities and a federal government committed to funding antipoverty programs, they find that the poor are on no one's agenda, and there is little support for creating political or economic opportunities for the poor.

Ironically, it is the marketplace that seems to have triumphed where liberal social programmers, conservatives, and radical organizers have failed. Where gangs once stood outside the market economy and offered an implicit critique of it, they now have become incorporated into the market, and gang members have moved from being potential rebels to becoming entrepreneurs. The economic marginalization of inner-city neighborhoods has forced gangs into becoming economic, rather than social, entities. Instead of seeing their gangs as a way of resisting the demands of American society, gang members view the gang as a way of achieving the dream of success and advancement. They still vow not to duplicate the fates of their parents in the low-wage economy, and to that extent they continue to defy the logic of the marketplace. Instead of taking their place at the bottom of the job queue, working hard, and waiting in vain for some reward for their labor, they choose to participate in illegal activities, which promise to shorten the process of gaining material goods. But it would be a mistake to interpret gang members' participation in the underground economy as a sign of rebellion against American society.

Crime, in Daniel Bell's terms, is an American way of life, and criminals are entrepreneurs unbound by society's conventions.[39] Their purpose is to climb the ladder of success, not upend it, and they choose illegal means because they are the most readily available. To the degree that legitimate economic opportunities do not exist, adolescents will use their gangs to create opportunities for themselves.

In the past, adolescents, alienated from the institutions of their society, responded to economic and social marginalization by forming street gangs. Gangs not only allowed them to postpone the demands of a dreary working-class adulthood, but they also created alternative standards by which to measure worth and define masculinity. Adolescent gangs fought for personal honor, in defense of place, and according to their own codes of conduct, but they also enforced ideals of ethnic separatism, engaged in sickening violence against each other, exploited adolescent girls, and offered a brutal rite of passage into manhood. This book, which opens with an account of a horrific murder, cannot be read nostalgically as a paean to a golden postwar age, when community reigned and masculine identity was secure.[40] Nonetheless, as this chapter shows, conditions in inner-city neighborhoods have worsened over the last twenty years, and it is not surprising to discover that gangs have adapted to them, so much so that even the gang members of the past have difficulty recognizing their descendants.

In 1968, the President's National Advisory Commission on Civil Disorders warned that we were dividing into "two societies, one black, one white—separate and unequal."[41] Our second society, which was never entirely black, now contains increasing numbers of Latinos and Asian Americans. This second society is geographically, socially, and economically isolated, and bridging the gap between our two societies remains our most pressing social problem. Until we can do that, adolescents in poor urban neighborhoods will continue to find employment through the underground economy and to establish their reputations through their gangs, and young men will continue to find violence essential to their creation of masculinity.

Let me give the final word in this book to Salvador Agron, with whom we began. In 1979, when asked to reflect on his impending freedom, Agron told a reporter from the *New York Times*:

> When they say, "Salvador, you're free," I smile because I know that to be free you need an environment, you have to have economic security, have a job and food, clothing and shelter. And when they say you're free and I go out there and I see those ghettos and I see this poverty, why, I say it's relative. Freedom is relative to the conditions. It seems to be very subtle, like something you chase.[42]

# NOTES

INTRODUCTION. THE CAPEMAN AND THE VAMPIRES

1. *New York Times*, August 31, 1959; *Daily News*, August 31, 1959; *New York Journal American*, August 31, 1959; *New York Post*, September 1, 1959; Wayne Phillips, "Walk in the Dark—On West 46th Street," *New York Times Magazine*, September 13, 1959, pp. 25ff.; and T. J. English, *The Westies: Inside the Hell's Kitchen Irish Mob* (New York: Putnam, 1990), pp. 47, 55.

2. "The People vs. Salvatore Agron, et al.," Stenographer's Minutes, vol. 1, pp. 208–22; Statement of Ewald Reimer, September 9, 1959; Statement of Hector Bouillerce, September 3, 1959—all in the New York County District Attorney's Office (hereafter cited as NYCDA); and *Daily News*, August 31, 1959.

3. *New York Times*, September 1, 1959.

4. For the juxtaposition of narrative accounts in an historical ethnography, see Greg Dening, *Mr. Bligh's Bad Language: Passion, Power and Theatre on the Bounty* (Cambridge: Cambridge University Press, 1992).

5. It is apparent in my interviews and in casual conversations with a variety of New Yorkers that the Capeman case made a lasting impression on a generation of city residents.

6. *Daily News*, August 31–September 5, 1959; *New York Herald Tribune*, August 31–September 6, 1959; *New York Journal American*, August 31–September 3, 1959; *New York Post*, September 1, 1959; *New York Times*, August 31–September 3, 1959; and *New York Mirror*, September 1, 1959, September 3, 1959.

7. "Petition for a Sanity Hearing," Supreme Court of the State of New York, Indictment #3604–59; *Daily News*, September 3–4, 1959; *New York Herald Tribune*, September 2, 1959, September 6, 1959; *New York Journal American*, September 2–3, 1959; *New York Mirror*, September 3, 1959; and *New York Post*, September 2, 1959.

8. *New York Herald Tribune*, September 4, 1959; *New York Post*, September 3, 1959; *Daily News*, September 6, 1959; and *New York Mirror*, September 20, 1959. On the distinction between "queers" and those who engaged in homosexual activity casually and who played male roles, see George Chauncey, Jr., "Christian

Brotherhood or Sexual Perversion? Homosexual Identities and the Construction of Sexual Boundaries in the World War One Era," *Journal of Social History* 19 (Winter 1985): 189–211. For a distinction between *activo* and *pasivo*, see Stephen O. Murray, "Machismo, Male Homosexuality, and Latino Culture," in *Latin American Male Homosexualities*, ed. Stephen O. Murray (Albuquerque: University of New Mexico Press, 1995), pp. 49–70.

9. Arthur Laurents, *West Side Story: A Musical* (New York: Random House, 1956), p. 10; Craig Zadan, *Sondheim & Co.* (New York: Macmillan, 1974), pp. 15, 19; *New York Journal American*, September 1, 1959; and *New York Post*, September 1, 1959.

10. Ronald H. Bayor, *Neighbors in Conflict: The Irish, Germans, Jews, and Italians of New York City, 1929–1941* 2d ed. (Urbana: University of Illinois Press, 1988); John T. McGreevy, *Parish Boundaries: The Catholic Encounter with Race in the Twentieth-Century Urban North* (Chicago: University of Chicago Press, 1996), pp. 9–13; Michael Omi and Howard Winant, *Racial Formation in the United States: From the 1960s to the 1990s*, 2d ed. (New York: Routledge, 1994), pp. 54–61; and David Roediger, *Towards the Abolition of Whiteness: Essays on Race, Politics, and Working Class History* (London: Verso, 1994).

11. Gerald Markowitz and David Rosner, *Children, Race, and Power: Kenneth and Mamie Clark's Northside Center* (Charlottesville: University of Virginia Press, 1996), pp. 98–109; Arnold R. Hirsch, "Massive Resistance in the Urban North: Trumbull Park, Chicago, 1953–1966," *Journal of American History* 82 (September 1995): 522–50; and Thomas J. Sugrue, "Crabgrass-Roots Politics: Race, Rights, and the Reaction against Liberalism in the Urban North, 1940–1960," *Journal of American History* 82 (September 1995): 551–78.

12. *New York Herald Tribune*, August 31, 1959, September 3, 1959; *Daily News*, September 1, 1959; *New York Journal American*, August 31, 1959; *New York Post*, September 3, 1959; "The People v. Salvatore Agron," Supreme Court of New York County, Indictment #3604–59, Stenographer's Minutes, September 12, 1966, pp. 108–9, 206; and "The 'Capeman' Reflects as Prison Release Nears," *New York Times*, October 3, 1979.

13. Memorandum from Edith Baikie to Dr. William J. Ronan, October 27, 1959; Letters from R. V. Henoy, September 2, 1959, Dr. John Manas, September 3, 1959, Fred Eidenbenz, September 3, 1959, and Sam Frohlich, n.d., Office Records, Governor Nelson Rockefeller, Subject Files, Youth, 1959–1962, reels 144–46. See newspaper dates already cited.

14. Winifred Raushenbush, "New York and the Puerto Ricans," *Harper's* 206 (May 1953): 78–83.

15. Jess Stearn, *The Wasted Years* (Garden City, N.Y.: Doubleday, 1959), pp. 83–95; and Interview with Seymour Ostrow, March 10, 1993.

16. *Daily News* August 31, 1959; *New York Journal American*, September 1, 1959; and *New York Times*, August 31, 1959.

17. *New York Journal American*, September 2, 1959, September 4, 1959; *Daily News*, September 1, 1959; *New York Times*, September 25, 1959; *New York Herald Tribune*, September 4, 1959; and Stanley Cohen, *Folk Devils and Moral Panics: The Creation of the Mods and Rockers* (New York: St. Martin's Press, 1980).

18. *New York Times*, September 8, 1959; Interview with Dan Murrow, February 28, 1993; and *Amsterdam News*, September 12, 1959, September 19, 1959, October 3, 1959. The only extant copies of *El Diario* that I have been able to find are in the possession of the Commonwealth of Puerto Rico's New York office, and they are too fragile to use.

19. Lewis Yablonsky, "The Violent Gang," *Commentary* 30 (August 1960): 125–30; idem, *The Violent Gang*, rev. ed. (New York: Penguin Books, 1970); Sam Kolman [pseud.], *The Royal Vultures* (New York: Permabooks, 1958); Stearn, *Wasted Years*; Harrison E. Salisbury, *The Shook-Up Generation* (New York: Harper and Brothers, 1958); and Vincent Riccio and Bill Slocum, *All the Way Down: The Violent Underworld of Street Gangs* (New York: Simon and Schuster, 1962), p. 33. See also Edith G. Neisser and Nina Ridenour, *Your Children and Their Gangs*, U.S. Children's Bureau Pub. No. 384 (Washington, D.C.: U.S. Government Printing Office, 1960), pp. 18–19.

20. *New York Times*, September 1–2, 1959; "Remarks by Mayor Robert F. Wagner," September 7, 1959, Wagner Papers, File 112, Box 161, New York City Municipal Archives; and Charles R. Morris, *The Cost of Good Intentions: New York City and the Liberal Experiment, 1960–1975* (New York: Norton, 1980).

21. *New York Times*, September 28, 1959; *New York Post*, September 3, 1959; and *New York Journal American*, August 31–September 1, 1959.

22. Transcript of Growman's Notes on Salvatore Agron, Transcript of Growman's Notes on Francisco Cruz, both NYCDA; Testimony of Hugh K. Johnson, "Respondent's Brief," Court of Appeals, State of New York, June 1961, p. 45; and *New York Times*, September 2, 1959.

23. Transcript of Growman's Notes on Francisco Cruz, Transcript of Growman's Notes on Salvatore Agron, Transcript of Growman's Notes on Raphael Colon, all NYCDA.

24. *New York Post*, September 1, 1959; *New York Herald Tribune*, September 3, 1959; *New York Journal American*, September 1, 1959, September 3, 1959; *Daily News*, September 5, 1959; and *New York Times*, September 2, 1959, July 22, 1960.

25. Ira Henry Freeman, "The Making of a Boy Killer," *New York Times Magazine*, February 18, 1962, pp. 14ff.; "Youth House Social Worker's Report," August 20, 1953, NYCDA; and untitled evaluation, NYCDA.

26. *New York Times*, September 1, 1959.

27. "The People vs. Salvatore Agron, et al." Stenographer's Minutes, vol. 1, pp. 209–11, NYCDA.

28. "Youth House Social Worker's Report," NYCDA.

29. Statement of Rafael Colon, August 31, 1959; Transcript of Growman's Notes on Salvatore Agron, NYCDA; and "The People v. Salvatore Agron," Supreme Court of the State of New York, Indictment #3604–59, Stenographer's Minutes, September 12, 1966, pp. 183–84, 188, 192–93, 200–201.

30. Alan Holden, "Summary of Psychiatric Report on Salvador Agron, Submitted February 15, 1966," Supreme Court of the State of New York, Indictment #3604–59.

31. Patricia Cayo Sexton, *Spanish Harlem* (New York: Harper and Row, 1965), p. 16; and "Brief for Appellant Salvatore Agron," Court of Appeals, June 1961, pp. 56–57, Supreme Court of the State of New York, Indictment #3604–59.

32. *New York Times*, January 29, 1975.

33. *New York Times*, October 3, 1979.

34. See chapter 3.

35. David Dawley, *A Nation of Lords: The Autobiography of the Vice Lords* (Prospect Heights, Ill.: Waveland Press, 1992), p. 4; and Dan Wakefield, *Island in the City: Puerto Ricans in New York* (New York: Corinth Books, 1957), p. 181.

36. Interview with JC, March 10, 1993; Interview with RG, April 23, 1993; Riccio and Slocum, *All the Way Down*, pp. 58–59; and Dawley, *Nation of Lords*, p. 7.

37. Salisbury, *Shook-Up Generation*, pp. 28–31; Riccio and Slocum, *All the Way Down*, p. 33; and Interview with WA, December 30, 1992.

38. Irving Spergel, *Racketville, Slumtown, Haulberg: An Exploratory Study of Delinquent Subcultures* (Chicago: University of Chicago Press, 1964), p. 42; Wakefield, *Island in the City*, pp. 126–27; Riccio and Slocum, *All the Way Down*, p. 30; Interview with ES, October 20, 1992; Visit with CL, September 1, 1959, and with JS, September 2, 1959, Field Reports, Box 1, Kenneth Marshall Papers, Schomburg Center for Research in Black Culture, New York Public Library.

39. Ruth Horowitz, *Honor and the American Dream: Culture and Identity in a Chicano Community* (New Brunswick, N.J.: Rutgers University Press, 1983).

40. R. W. Connell, *Masculinities* (Berkeley: University of California Press, 1995); James W. Messerschmidt, *Masculinities and Crime: Critique and Reconceptualization of Theory* (Lanham, Md.: Rowman and Littlefield, 1993); and Jack Katz, *Seductions of Crime: Moral and Sensual Attractions in Doing Evil* (New York: Basic Books, 1988). Although Katz captures the desire for transcendence among poor adolescents, he ignores the material need that drives it.

41. David D. Gilmore, *Manhood in the Making: Cultural Concepts of Masculinity* (New Haven: Yale University Press, 1990).

42. Salisbury, *Shook-Up Generation*, pp. 24–25; and Fox Butterfield, *All God's Children: The Bosket Family and the American Tradition of Violence* (New York: Avon Books, 1995), p. 289.

43. Spergel, *Racketville*, pp. 42–43; and Salisbury, *Shook-Up Generation*, p. 21.

## CHAPTER ONE. REMAKING NEW YORK

1. Ronald H. Bayor, *Neighbors in Conflict: The Irish, Germans, Jews, and Italians of New York City, 1929–1941* 2nd ed. (Urbana: University of Illinois Press, 1988), pp. 8–13.

2. Kenneth T. Jackson, "The City Loses the Sword: The Decline of Major Military Activity in the New York Metropolitan Region," in *The Martial Metropolis: U.S. Cities in War and Peace*, ed. Roger Lotchin (New York: Praeger, 1984), p. 153; Geoffrey Rossano, "Suburbia Armed: Nassau County Development and the Rise of the Aerospace Industry, 1909–1960," in ibid., pp. 73–74; Richard R. Lingeman, *Don't You Know There's a War On?: The American Home Front, 1941–1945* (New York: Putnam, 1970), pp. 63–64; Thomas Kessner, *Fiorello H. La Guardia and the Making of Modern New York* (New York: McGraw-Hill, 1989), pp. 539–40; and Dominic J. Capeci, Jr., *The Harlem Riot of 1943* (Philadelphia: Temple University Press, 1977), p. 61.

3. Kessner, *Fiorello H. La Guardia*, p. 539; Geoffrey Parrett, *Days of Sadness, Years of Triumph: The American People, 1939–1945* (New York: Coward, McCann and Geoghegan, 1973), p. 259; Lingeman, *Don't You Know There's a War On?*, p. 161; William M. Tuttle, Jr., *"Daddy's Gone to War": The Second World War in the Lives of America's Children* (New York: Oxford University Press, 1993), p. 241; and Harlem Youth Opportunities Unlimited, *Youth in the Ghetto: A Study of the Consequences of Powerlessness and a Blueprint for Change* (New York: Harlem Youth Opportunities Unlimited, 1964), table 29, p. 162.

4. Irving Shulman, *The Amboy Dukes* (New York: Avon, 1949), p. 26.

5. Edgar M. Hoover and Raymond Vernon, *Anatomy of a Metropolis: The Changing Distribution of People and Jobs within the New York Metropolitan Region* (Garden City, N.Y.: Doubleday, 1962), pp. 26–29, 32–37, 41–45, 113–19; John D. Kasarda, "Urban Change and Minority Opportunities," in *The New Urban Reality*, ed. Paul E. Peterson (Washington, D.C.: Brookings Institution, 1985), pp. 39–40 (the figures for job losses are derived from table 1, p. 44); John H. Mollenkopf, "The Postwar Politics of Urban Development," in *Marxism and the Metropolis: New Perspectives in Urban Political Economy*, ed. William K. Tabb and Larry Sawers (New York: Oxford University Press, 1978), pp. 130–31; and Twentieth Century

Fund, Task Force on the Future of New York City, *New York, World City* (Cambridge: Oelgschlager, Gunn and Hain, 1980), pp. 55–57.

6. Rossano, "Suburbia Armed," pp. 76–78.

7. Jackson, "The City Loses the Sword," p. 154.

8. Kasarda, "Urban Change and Minority Opportunities," p. 44.

9. George Sternlieb and James W. Hughes, "Is the New York Region the Prototype?" in *Post-Industrial America: Metropolitan Decline and Inter-Regional Job Shifts*, ed. George Sternlieb and James W. Hughes (New Brunswick: The Center for Urban Policy Research, Rutgers–The State University of New Jersey, 1975), pp. 122–23.

10. Suzanne Modell, "The Ethnic Niche and the Structure of Opportunity: Immigrants and Minorities in New York City," in *The Underclass Debate: Views from History*, ed. Michael B. Katz (Princeton: Princeton University Press, 1993), pp. 161–93; Roger Waldinger, *Still the Promised City? African Americans and New Immigrants in Postindustrial New York* (Cambridge, Mass.: Harvard University Press, 1996); and Bayor, *Neighbors in Conflict*, p. 23. See also John Bodnar, Roger Simon, and Michael P. Weber, *Lives of Their Own: Blacks, Italians, and Poles in Pittsburgh, 1900–1960* (Urbana: University of Illinois Press, 1982), pp. 28–52; Joe William Trotter, Jr., *Black Milwaukee: The Making of an Industrial Proletariat, 1915–1945* (Urbana: University of Illinois Press, 1985), chapter 1; and Stanley Lieberson, *A Piece of the Pie: Blacks and White Immigrants since 1880* (Berkeley: University of California Press, 1980), pp. 334–58.

11. James R. Grossman, *Land of Hope: Chicago, Black Southerners, and the Great Migration* (Chicago: University of Chicago Press, 1989); Philip Kasinitz, *Caribbean New York: Black Immigrants and the Politics of Race* (Ithaca, N.Y.: Cornell University Press, 1992); and Trotter, *Black Milwaukee*, pp. 165–71.

12. Ira Rosenwaike, *Population History of New York City* (Syracuse, N.Y.: Syracuse University Press, 1972), pp. 121, 139, 188–90.

13. Department of City Planning, City of New York, "Puerto Rican Migration to New York City," *Bulletin* (February 1957): 1–2.

14. Rosenwaike, *Population History*, pp. 188–90. However, in 1960 white youths aged fifteen to nineteen still outnumbered Puerto Rican and African-American youths in the same age group by about 3 to 1. This is based on tables in Rosenwaike, *Population History*, pp. 190, 197, 199.

15. Malcolm Gladwell, "The Tipping Point," *New Yorker*, June 3 1996, 32–38; H. Range Hutson, Deirdre Anglin, Demetrios N. Kyriacou, Joel Hart, and Kelvin Spears, "The Epidemic of Gang-Related Homicides in Los Angeles County from 1979 through 1994," *Journal of the American Medical Association* 274 (October 4, 1995): 1031–36; and Mark L. Rosenberg and Mary Ann Fenley, eds., *Violence in America: A Public Health Approach* (New York: Oxford University Press, 1991).

16. Irving Louis Horowitz, *Daydreams and Nightmares: Reflections on a Harlem Childhood* (Jackson: University Press of Mississippi, 1990), p. 2; and Jack Lait and Lee Mortimer, *New York: Confidential!* (New York: Crown, 1951), p. 120.

17. Capeci, *Harlem Riot of 1943*, pp. 32, 38, 58–59, 136, 161; Cheryl Lynn Greenberg, *"Or Does It Explode?" Black Harlem in the Great Depression* (New York: Oxford University Press, 1991), p. 15; Walter Davenport, "Harlem: Dense and Dangerous," *Collier's*, September 23, 1944, 11–13, 92; and Thomas Vietorisz and Bennett Harrison, *The Economic Development of Harlem* (New York: Praeger, 1970), p. 11.

18. James C. Scott, *Domination and the Arts of Resistance: Hidden Transcripts* (New Haven: Yale University Press, 1990). For an application of Scott's thesis, see Robin D. G. Kelley, "The Black Poor and the Politics of Opposition in a New South City, 1929–1970," in *The Underclass Debate*, pp. 293–333.

19. Horowitz, *Daydreams and Nightmares*, p. 5; Capeci, *Harlem Riot of 1943*, p. 136; Kwando Kinshasa in *Look for Me in the Whirlwind: The Collective Autobiography of the New York 21* (New York: Random House, 1971), p. 102; and Harlem Youth Opportunities Unlimited, *Youth in the Ghetto*, p. 116.

20. Harlem Youth Opportunities Unlimited, *Youth in the Ghetto*, p. 285; Capeci, *Harlem Riot of 1943*, pp. 35–37; Greenberg, *"Or Does It Explode?"*, pp. 18–20, 65–92, 218–19; Nathan Glazer and Daniel P. Moynihan, *Beyond the Melting Pot*, 2nd ed. (Cambridge, Mass.: MIT Press, 1970), p. 27; and Lieberson, *A Piece of the Pie*, pp. 342–58.

21. The median annual income of Harlem families was about $3,500, when $6,000 was the subsistence budget for a New York City family in 1967. Glazer and Moynihan, *Beyond the Melting Pot*, pp. 29–30; Vietorisz and Harrison, *Economic Development of Harlem*, pp. 22–23; and Mark J. Stern, "Poverty and the Life Cycle, 1940–1960," *Journal of Social History* 24 (Spring 1991): 531–33, 536.

22. Thirty percent of sixteen- to nineteen-year-old males in Harlem were unemployed in 1966 (which meant they were actively seeking employment), as compared to 10 percent of the total sixteen- to nineteen-year-old male population. Vietorisz and Harrison, *Economic Development of Harlem*, pp. 21–22.

23. On dependence on child labor, see Mark J. Stern, "Poverty and Family Composition since 1940," in *The Underclass Debate*, p. 244; and Claude Brown, *Manchild in the Promised Land* (New York: Penguin Books, 1965), p. 184.

24. Brown, *Manchild*, p. viii.

25. Christopher Rand, *The Puerto Ricans* (New York: Oxford University Press, 1958), p. 38; Virginia E. Sanchez Korrol, *From Colonia to Community: The History of Puerto Ricans in New York City, 1917–1948* (Westport, Conn.: Greenwood Press, 1983), pp. 22–27; C. Wright Mills, Clarence Senior, and Rose Kohn Goldsen, *The Puerto Rican Journey: New York's Newest Migrants* (New York: Harper, 1950), pp.

16–17, 56; and Iris Morales, in *Palante: Young Lords Party*, ed. Michael Abramson (New York: McGraw-Hill, 1971), p. 24. For slum life in Puerto Rico, see Oscar Lewis, *La Vida: A Puerto Rican Family in the Culture of Poverty—San Juan and New York* (New York: Random House, 1966).

26. Rand, *Puerto Ricans*, pp. 52–53; Mills et al., *Puerto Rican Journey*, pp. 43–44; Elena Padilla, *Up from Puerto Rico* (New York: Columbia University Press, 1958), pp. 22–23; Glazer and Moynihan, *Beyond the Melting Pot*, pp. 93, 97; and Nicholas Lemann, "The Other Underclass," *Atlantic Monthly* 268 (December 1991): 96–110.

27. Mills et al., *Puerto Rican Journey*, pp. 28–34; 66; Korrol, *From Colonia to Community*, pp. 39–40; and Department of City Planning, "Puerto Rican Migration," p. 2.

28. "The Puerto Rican Community of New York: A Statistical Profile," in *The Puerto Rican Community and Its Children on the Mainland: A Sourcebook*, 2d ed. Francesco Cordasco and Eugene Bucchioni (Metuchen, N.J.: Scarecrow Press, 1972), pp. 129, 134–35; Terry J. Rosenberg, *Residence, Employment and Mobility of Puerto Ricans in New York City* (Chicago: University of Chicago, Department of Geography, 1974), pp. 43–44, 56; and Clara E. Rodriguez, "Economic Survival in New York City," in *The Puerto Rican Struggle: Essays on Survival in the U.S.*, ed. Clara E. Rodriguez, Virginia Sanchez Korrol, and Jose Oscar Alers (Maplewood, N.J.: Waterfront Press, 1984), pp. 31–46. Of the over 21,000 academic diplomas granted by New York City high schools in 1963, only 1.6 percent went to Puerto Ricans and 3.7 percent to African Americans.

29. Edwin Torres, *Carlito's Way* (New York: Saturday Review Press, 1975), p. 6; Dan Wakefield, *Island in the City: Puerto Ricans in New York* (New York: Corinth Books, 1957), pp. 16–17; Winifred Raushenbush, "New York and the Puerto Ricans," *Harper's* 206 (May 1953): 78–83; and Oscar Handlin, *The Newcomers: Negroes and Puerto Ricans in a Changing Metropolis* (Garden City, N.Y.: Doubleday and Company, 1962), pp. 94–95.

30. Morris Eagle, "The Puerto Ricans in New York City," in *Studies in Housing and Minority Groups*, ed. Nathan Glazer and Davis McEntire (Berkeley: University of California Press, 1960), p. 149; and Nathan Kantrowitz, *Negro and Puerto Rican Populations of New York City in the Twentieth Century* (New York: American Geographical Society, 1969).

31. Maria, in *Growing Up Puerto Rican*, ed. Paulette Cooper (New York: New American Library, 1972), p. 125; Mills et al., *Puerto Rican Journey*, pp. 133, 152; Welfare Council of New York City, Committee on Puerto Ricans in New York City, *Report of the Committee on Puerto Ricans in New York City* (New York: Welfare Council of New York City, 1948), p. 25; Rand, *Puerto Ricans*, pp. 127, 129; Joseph P. Fitzpatrick, *Puerto Rican Americans: The Meaning of Migration to the Main-*

land (Englewood Cliffs, N.J.: Prentice-Hall, 1971), p. 109; Padilla, *Up from Puerto Rico*, pp. 76–81; and Clara E. Rodriguez, "Puerto Ricans: Between Black and White," in *The Puerto Rican Struggle*, pp. 20–30.

32. Rosenberg, *Residence, Employment and Mobility*, pp. 204–5; Committee on Puerto Ricans in New York City, *Puerto Ricans in New York City*, pp. 20–21; and Felipe Luciano in *Palante*, p. 29.

33. Mario, in *Growing Up Puerto Rican*, p. 104; Interviews with ES, October 20, 1992, Norman Eddy, July 7, 1992, Manny Diaz, July 29, 1992, Seymour Ostrow, March 10, 1993; and Piri Thomas, *Down These Mean Streets* (New York: Vintage Books, 1967).

34. Piri Thomas, *Savior, Savior, Hold My Hand* (Garden City N.Y.: Doubleday, 1972), pp. 46–48; Cooper, *Growing Up Puerto Rican*, pp. 116–17, 184; and Abramson, *Palante*, pp. 25, 32.

35. Eagle, "Puerto Ricans in New York City," pp. 148–49, 158–60; Committee on Puerto Ricans in New York City, *Puerto Ricans in New York City*, pp. 10–11; and Handlin, *The Newcomers*, p. 82.

36. Mark I. Gelfand, *A Nation of Cities: The Federal Government and Urban America, 1933–1965* (New York: Oxford University Press, 1975), pp. 61–64; Joel Schwartz, *The New York Approach: Robert Moses, Urban Liberals, and Redevelopment of the Inner City* (Columbus: Ohio State University Press, 1993), pp. 45–46; and Anthony Jackson, *A Place Called Home: A History of Low-Cost Housing in Manhattan* (Cambridge, Mass.: MIT Press, 1976), p. 210.

37. Gelfand, *Nation of Cities*, pp. 153–55.

38. Jackson, *Place Called Home*, pp. 230–31, 246; and Gelfand, *Nation of Cities*, pp. 155, 169, 199.

39. Gelfand, *Nation of Cities*, p. 209; and Robert Caro, *The Power Broker: Robert Moses and the Fall of New York* (New York: Knopf, 1974).

40. Leonard Wallock, "New York City: Capital of the Twentieth Century," in *New York: Culture Capital of the World, 1945–1965*, ed. Leonard Wallock (New York: Rizzoli, 1988), pp. 35, 43.

41. Carol Herselle Krinsky, "Architecture in New York City," in ibid., pp. 97–100; 106.

42. Schwartz, *New York Approach*, pp. 210–28, 238–39, 243–45, 276–89.

43. Caro, *Power Broker*, pp. 839–43, 850, 896–97; and Marshall Berman, *All That Is Solid Melts into Air: The Expression of Modernity* (New York: Simon and Schuster, 1982), p. 293.

44. New York City Planning Commission, *Tenant Relocation Report* (New York: New York City Planning Commission, 1954), p. 4.

45. Caro, *Power Broker*, pp. 859–63, 879–82.

46. Jackson, *Place Called Home*, p. 247; and Caro, *Power Broker*, pp. 962–65, 969–76.

47. City Planning Commission, *Tenant Relocation Report*, p. 8; Caro, *Power Broker*, pp. 971–72; and Samuel Lubell, *The Future of American Politics*, 3d ed. (New York: Harper and Row, 1965), pp. 93–94.

48. Capeci, *Harlem Riot of 1943*, pp. 140–41; Schwartz, *New York Approach*, pp. 55–58, 84–107, 113–16, 290; Richard Plunz, *A History of Housing in New York City: Dwelling Type and Social Change in the American Metropolis* (New York: Columbia University Press, 1990), pp. 253–57; Jill Jonnes, *We're Still Here: The Rise, Fall, and Resurrection of the South Bronx* (Boston: Atlantic Monthly Press, 1986), pp. 118–19; Joel Schwartz, "Tenant Power in the Liberal City, 1943–1971," in *The Tenant Movement in New York City, 1904–1984*, ed. Ronald Lawson and Mark Naison (New Brunswick, N.J.: Rutgers University Press, 1986), pp. 150, 160; and Woody Klein, *Let In the Sun* (New York: Macmillan, 1964), pp. 114–15. For other cities, see Arnold R. Hirsch, *Making the Second Ghetto: Race and Housing in Chicago, 1940–1960* (Cambridge: Cambridge University Press, 1983); and John F. Bauman, *Public Housing, Race, and Renewal: Urban Planning in Philadelphia, 1920–1974* (Philadelphia: Temple University Press, 1987).

49. Rosalie Genevro, "Site Selection and the New York City Housing Authority, 1934–1939," *Journal of Urban History* 12 (August 1986): 334–52.

50. Plunz, *A History of Housing*, pp. 224, 240–45, 268–72; and Jackson, *Place Called Home*, pp. 297–304.

51. Anthony F. C. Wallace, *Housing and Social Structure: A Preliminary Survey with Particular Reference to Multi-Story, Low-Rent, Public Housing Projects* (Philadelphia: Philadelphia Housing Authority, 1952), pp. 76–78.

52. Rosenwaike, *Population History*, p. 136.

53. Kenneth T. Jackson, *Crabgrass Frontier: The Suburbanization of the United States* (New York: Oxford University Press, 1985), pp. 196–209; and Douglas S. Massey and Nancy A. Denton, *American Apartheid: Segregation and the Making of the Underclass* (Cambridge, Mass.: Harvard University Press, 1993).

54. Jackson, *Crabgrass Frontier*, pp. 248–50; Caro, *Power Broker*, pp. 921–22, 927–30; and Gelfand, *Nation of Cities*, pp. 227–29.

55. Wallock, "New York City," p. 31; Jonathan Rieder, *Canarsie: The Jews and Italians of Brooklyn Against Liberalism* (Cambridge, Mass.: Harvard University Press, 1985); Robert Anthony Orsi, *The Madonna of 115th Street: Faith and Community in Italian Harlem, 1880–1950* (New Haven: Yale University Press, 1985); and Gerald Sorin, *The Nurturing Neighborhood: The Brownsville Boys Club and Jewish Community in Urban America, 1940–1990* (New York: New York University Press, 1990), p. 91.

56. Jackson, *Crabgrass Frontier*, pp. 215–16; Elaine Tyler May, *Homeward Bound: American Families in the Cold War Era* (New York: Basic Books, 1988), pp. 162–66; Arthur M. Johnson, "American Business in the Postwar Era," in *Reshaping America: Society and Institutions, 1945–1960*, ed. Robert H. Bremner and Gary W. Reichard (Columbus: Ohio State University Press, 1982), pp. 101–13; Roland Marchand, "Visions of Classlessness, Quests for Dominion: American Popular Culture, 1945–1960," in ibid., pp. 163–90; and John Barnard, "American Workers, the Labor Movement, and the Cold War, 1945–1960," in ibid., pp. 115–45.

57. See the series of studies published by the New York City Youth Board, which were typical of this genre: Sylvan S. Furman, ed. *Reaching the Unreached; Fundamental Aspects of the Program of the New York City Youth Board* (New York: New York City Youth Board, 1952); and New York City Youth Board, *How They Were Reached: A Study of 310 Children and Their Families Known to Referral Units* (New York: New York City Youth Board, 1954), for many references to "multi-problem families." See also James T. Patterson, "Poverty and Welfare in America, 1945–1960," in *Reshaping America*, pp. 193–221; and idem, *America's Struggle against Poverty, 1900–1980* (Cambridge, Mass.: Harvard University Press, 1981), pp. 79–85. A major exception to this was Herbert J. Gans, *The Urban Villagers: Group and Class in the Life of Italian Americans* (New York: The Free Press, 1965).

58. James Gilbert, *A Cycle of Outrage: America's Reaction to the Juvenile Delinquent in the 1950s* (New York: Oxford University Press, 1986).

59. Walter B. Miller, "Lower Class Culture as a Generating Milieu of Gang Delinquency," *Journal of Social Issues* 14 (1958): 5–19; Lewis Yablonsky, *The Violent Gang*, rev. ed. (New York: Penguin Books, 1970); and Herbert A. Bloch and Arthur Niederhoffer, *The Gang: A Study in Adolescent Behavior* (New York: Philosophical Library, 1958).

60. Harrison E. Salisbury, *The Shook-Up Generation* (New York: Harper and Brothers, 1958).


CHAPTER TWO. DISCOVERING GANGS


1. Thelma Neston to Mayor Fiorella La Guardia, September 24, 1945, La Guardia Papers, Box 3384, File 8, New York City Municipal Archives (hereafter NYCMA).

2. Howard S. Becker, *Outsiders: Studies in the Sociology of Deviance* (New York: The Free Press, 1963).

3. Walter B. Miller, "Lower Class Culture as a Generating Milieu of Gang Delinquency," *Journal of Social Issues* 14 (1958): 5–19; and idem, "American Youth

Gangs: Past and Present," in *Current Perspectives on Criminal Behavior*, ed. Abraham S. Blumberg (New York: Knopf, 1974): 210–39.

4. Stanley Cohen, *Folk Devils and Moral Panics: The Creation of the Mods and Rockers* (New York: St. Martin's Press, 1980).

5. Samuel Chotzinoff, *A Lost Paradise: Early Reminiscences* (New York: Knopf, 1955), pp. 85–87; Jenna Weissman Joselit, *Our Gang: Jewish Crime and the New York Jewish Community, 1900–1940* (Bloomington: Indiana University Press, 1983), pp. 26–28, 44; and Michael Gold, *Jews without Money* (Garden City, N.Y.: The Sun Dial Press, 1946), pp. 42–43. Obviously gangs existed prior to the 1940s; however, these were not adolescent or youth gangs acting independently of adult authority. See Herbert Asbury, *The Gangs of New York* (Garden City, N.Y.: Garden City Publishing Co., 1927); and Bruce Laurie, "Fire Companies and Gangs in Southwark: The 1840s," in *The Peoples of Philadelphia: A History of Ethnic Groups and Lower Class Life, 1790–1940*, ed. Allen F. Davis and Mark H. Haller (Philadelphia: Temple University Press, 1973), pp. 71–87.

6. "We Hold These Truths," undated memoir, Leonard Covello Papers, Box 51, Folder 13, Balch Institute for Ethnic Studies (hereafter cited as the Covello Papers).

7. Robert Anthony Orsi, *The Madonna of 115th Street: Faith and Community in Italian Harlem, 1880–1950* (New Haven: Yale University Press, 1985), pp. 17, 33; and "Letter from Angel Guadalpe to Mr. Fishman," October 22, 1938, Covello Papers, Box 53, Folder 16.

8. William Byron Forbush, *The Boy Problem: A Study in Social Pedogogy* (Boston: Pilgrim Press, 1902); J. Adam Puffer, *The Boy and His Gang* (Boston: Houghton Mifflin, 1912); Franklin Chase Hoyt, *Quicksands of Youth* (New York: Charles Scribner's Sons, 1921); Paul Hanly Furfey, *The Gang Age: A Study of the Preadolescent Boy and His Recreational Needs* (New York: Macmillan, 1926); Emory S. Bogardus, *The City Boy and His Problems: A Survey of Boy Life in Los Angeles* (Los Angeles: House of Ralston, 1926); Peter Gabriel Filene, *Him, Her, Self: Sex Roles in Modern America* (New York: Harcourt, Brace, Jovanovich, 1974); and E. Anthony Rotundo, "Boy Culture: Middle-Class Boyhood in Nineteenth-Century America," in *Meanings for Manhood: Constructions of Masculinity in Victorian America*, ed. Mark C. Carnes and Clyde Griffen (Chicago: University of Chicago Press, 1990): 15–36. Quotation from Furfey, *Gang Age*, p. 133. On adolescence, see Joseph F. Kett, *Rites of Passage: Adolescence in America, 1790 to the Present* (New York: Basic Books, 1977), chapter 8.

9. Frederic Thrasher, *The Gang: A Study of 1,313 Gangs in Chicago*, rev. ed. (Chicago: University of Chicago Press, 1963), pp. 60–61, 117–19, and the introduction by James F. Short, p. xxii.

10. Asbury, *Gangs of New York*, passim.

11. William Foote Whyte, *Streetcorner Society* (Chicago: University of Chicago Press, 1943), pp. 5–6.

12. The point here is not that "boy gangs" did not cause trouble—Thrasher makes it clear that they did—only that they did not cause enough trouble to merit a separate classification.

13. Marilynn S. Johnson, *The Second Gold Rush: Oakland and the East Bay in World War II* (Berkeley: University of California Press, 1993); William M. Tuttle, Jr., *"Daddy's Gone to War": The Second World War in the Lives of America's Children* (New York: Oxford University Press, 1993); and Irving Shulman, *The Amboy Dukes* (New York: Avon, 1949).

14. See Eric C. Schneider, *In the Web of Class: Delinquents and Reformers in Boston, 1810s–1930s* (New York: New York University Press, 1992), chapter 5.

15. Eleanor Lake, "Trouble on the Street Corner," *Common Sense* 12 (May 1943): 147–49; *New York Times*, March 21, 1943; and Allan M. Brandt, *No Magic Bullet: A Social History of Venereal Disease in the United States since 1880* (New York: Oxford University Press, 1985), pp. 167–68.

16. Victor W. Turner, *The Ritual Process: Structure and Antistructure* (Chicago: Aldine, 1969).

17. Marian Wolf, Harriet Boskey, and Pearl Harelick, "Report on Truancy," June 17, 1943, Covello Papers, Box 117, Folder 1.

18. Richard R. Lingeman, *Don't You Know There's a War On?: The American Home Front, 1941–1945* (New York: Putnam, 1970), pp. 333–34; Maurico Mazon, *The Zoot-Suit Riots: The Psychology of Symbolic Annihilation* (Austin: University of Texas Press, 1984); Stuart Cosgrove, "The Zoot-Suit and Style Warfare," *History Workshop Journal* 18 (Autumn 1984): 77–91; Bruce M. Tyler, "Black Jive and White Repression," *Journal of Ethnic Studies* 16 (1988): 31–66; and Robin D. G. Kelley, "The Riddle of the Zoot: Malcolm Little and Black Cultural Politics during World War II," in *Malcolm X: In Our Own Image*, ed. Joe Wood (New York: St. Martin's Press, 1992): 155–82.

19. Shulman, *The Amboy Dukes*, p. 2.

20. Malcolm X, *The Autobiography of Malcolm X* (New York: Grove Press, 1966), pp. 105–7. These themes are explored in Fritz Redl, "Zoot Suits: An Interpretation," *Survey Midmonthly* 79 (October 1943): 259–62; Eric Lott, "Double V, Double-Time: Bebop's Politics of Style," *Callaloo* 11 (1988): 597–605; and Dick Hebdige, *Subculture: The Meaning of Style* (New York: Methuen, 1979).

21. *New York Times*, March 3, 1943, April 12, 1944; James Gilbert, *A Cycle of Outrage: America's Reaction to the Juvenile Delinquent in the 1950s* (New York: Oxford University Press, 1986), pp. 24–29; "Juvenile Delinquency: War's Insecurity Lifts Youthful Crime 100%," *Life* 20 (April 8, 1946): 83–92; and Dominic J. Capeci,

Jr., "Fiorello H. La Guardia and the Harlem 'Crime Wave' of 1941," *The New York Historical Society Quarterly* 64 (January 1980): 7–29.

22. Office of War Information, "OWI 2564," October 1, 1943, Record Group 208, Entry E-82, Box 241, National Archives.

23. Mazon, *Zoot-Suit Riots*, pp. 86–87, 113; and Gilbert, *Cycle of Outrage*, pp. 31–32.

24. *New York Times*, June 11–12, 1943; and Kelley, "Riddle of the Zoot," pp. 160–62.

25. *New York Times*, August 17, 1942, August 19–21, 1942, March 16, 1943, March 20, 1943.

26. Claude Brown, *Manchild in the Promised Land* (New York: Penguin Books, 1965), p. 13; Thomas Kessner, *Fiorello H. La Guardia and the Making of Modern New York* (New York: McGraw-Hill, 1989), pp. 529–33; and Dominic J. Capeci, Jr., *The Harlem Riot of 1943* (Philadelphia: Temple University Press, 1977).

27. "R" quoted in Kenneth B. Clark and James Barker, "The Zoot Effect in Personality: A Race Riot Participant," *Journal of Abnormal and Social Psychology* 40 (1945): 145.

28. Nat Brandt, *Harlem at War: The Black Experience in WWII* (Syracuse: Syracuse University Press, 1996), pp. 44–45, 133–38.

29. Clark and Barker, "Zoot Effect," p. 146.

30. "Presentment of the August 1943 Grand Jury of Kings County," La Guardia Papers, Box 3384, File 10, NYCMA.

31. Harold X. Connolly, *A Ghetto Grows in Brooklyn* (New York: New York University Press, 1977), pp. 59–70. Belford is quoted in Capeci, "Harlem 'Crime Wave,'" p. 9.

32. *New York Times*, November 22, 1943.

33. *New York Times*, November 16–19, 1943, November 21–30, 1943, December 3, 1943, December 7, 1943; and Nathan R. Sobel, "Charge to the December Grand Jury," La Guardia Papers, Box 3385, File 8, NYCMA.

34. "Report of the Police Commissioner to the Mayor," November 20, 1943, La Guardia Papers, Box 3384, File 13, NYCMA.

35. Louis Schachter to Mayor La Guardia, July 19, 1943, and Edwards Cleaveland to Mayor La Guardia, July 29, 1945, La Guardia Papers, Box 3384, Files 1 and 8, NYCMA, plus additional correspondence in other files.

36. "Report of the Police Commissioner to the Mayor," p. 58.

37. Police Department Memo, from Commanding Officer, 11th Division, to Commanding Officer, Brooklyn West and Richmond Headquarters, August 17, 1943; Police Department Memo, from Commanding Officer, 13th Division, to Deputy Chief Inspector, Brooklyn East, August 31, 1945; and Police Department Memo, from Office of the Juvenile Aid Bureau, to the Chief Inspector, December

18, 1945. All materials are in the La Guardia Papers, Box 3384, Files 1 and 8, NYCMA.

38. Denial of the existence of gang problems is not, of course, unique to officialdom in postwar New York. See Malcolm W. Klein, *The American Street Gang: Its Nature, Prevalence, and Control* (New York: Oxford University Press, 1995), pp. 87–90.

39. Bradford Chambers, "Boy Gangs of New York: 500 Fighting Units," *New York Times Magazine*, December 10, 1944, p. 16; and Malcolm Gladwell, "The Tipping Point," *New Yorker*, June 3 1996, 32–38.

40. On defended communities, see Gerald D. Suttles, *The Social Order of the Slum: Ethnicity and Territory in the Inner City* (Chicago: University of Chicago Press, 1968).

41. Bradford Chambers, "The Juvenile Gangs of New York," *American Mercury* 62 (April 1946): 480–86, quotation, p. 481; and idem, "The Boy Gangs of Mousetown," *Reader's Digest* 53 (August 1948): 144–58, quotation, p. 148.

42. Bradford Chambers, "An Approach to the Gang," *Survey Midmonthly* 80 (September 1944): 256–58; *New York Times*, March 15–16, 1943; and Chambers, "Boy Gangs of Mousetown," p. 149.

43. *Brooklyn Eagle*, April 4, 1949.

44. Brooklyn Council for Social Planning, Minutes of the Board of Directors, December 11, 1946, August 6, 1947, September 29, 1947, March 16, 1948, June 24, 1948, Brooklyn Council for Social Planning Papers, Brooklyn Public Library; and *Brooklyn Eagle*, December 14, 1945, April 28–29, 1948.

45. Banome is quoted in Jill Jonnes, *We're Still Here: The Rise, Fall, and Resurrection of the South Bronx* (Boston: Atlantic Monthly Press, 1986), p. 114. See Ronald H. Bayor, *Neighbors in Conflict: The Irish, Germans, Jews, and Italians of New York City, 1929–1941*, 2d ed. (Urbana: University of Illinois Press, 1988), pp. 157–61, for ethnic settlement and hostility in the area.

46. *New York Times*, March 7, 1945, March 9, 1945; and *Daily News*, March 7, 1945.

47. Steve De Salvo, "Ten to One Odds," Thomas Foudy, "Race Prejudices," and Gaetano Riccio, "White vs. Black," all in Covello Papers, Box 57, Folder 12.

48. *New York Times*, September 29, 1945; *Daily News*, September 29, 1945; and *New York Sun*, September 28, 1945.

49. Leonard Covello, "Notes on the Racial Incident at Franklin," n.d., n.p., Covello Papers, Box 54, Folder 4.

50. "Excerpts from Investigative Bureau Report," Covello Papers, Box 54, Folder 9.

51. Chambers, "Juvenile Gangs of New York," p. 483.

52. Dane Archer and Rosemary Gartner, *Violence and Crime in Cross-National Perspective* (New Haven: Yale University Press, 1984), chapter 4. Archer and Gartner maintain that the U.S. after World War II was an exception to this, but another analysis shows clearly that U.S. homicide rates increased after the war. See Magaret A. Zahn, "Homicide in the Twentieth Century: Trends, Types, and Causes," in *Violence in America, Volume 1: The History of Crime*, ed. Ted Robert Gurr (Newbury Park: Sage, 1989), pp. 216–34.

53. Archer and Gartner, *Violence and Crime*, pp. 87–94.

54. Chambers, "Juvenile Gangs of New York," pp. 481, 485; *New York Times*, November 22, 1945, April 29, 1947; Interviews with JC, March 9, 1993; MD, July 7, 1992; NL, March 9, 1993; *Brooklyn Eagle*, March 4, 1949, March 6, 1949; *New York Sun*, May 20, 1946, May 12, 1948, March 1, 1949; Lewis Yablonsky, "The Violent Gang," *Commentary* 30 (August 1960): 129–30; and David C. Courtwright, *Violent Land: Single Men and Social Disorder from the Frontier to the Inner City* (Cambridge, Mass.: Harvard University Press, 1996), p. 211.

55. Ira H. Freeman, "A Teen-Age Gang Leader's Brutal Tale: How His Street Club Shot Its Way to Power," *Life* 44 (April 14, 1958): 126–28ff.; and Carl Joyeaux [pseud.], *Out of the Burning: The Story of a Boy Gang Leader* (New York: Crown Publishers, 1960). Freeman was the ghostwriter for Joyeaux's autobiography, which was published after he finished college. See Ira H. Freeman, "A Gang Leader's Redemption," *Life* 44 (April 28, 1958): 69–70ff.

56. Chambers, "Boy Gangs of Mousetown," pp. 151–52.

57. Roger Lane, "On the Social Meaning of Homicide Trends in America," in *Violence in America*, 1:55–79; idem, "Crime and Criminal Statistics in Nineteenth-Century Massachusetts," *Journal of Social History* 2 (1968): 156–63; and idem, *Violent Death in the City: Suicide, Accident, and Murder in Nineteenth-Century Philadelphia* (Cambridge, Mass.: Harvard University Press, 1979). For the general decline in violence, see Ted Robert Gurr, "Historical Trends in Violent Crime: Europe and the United States," in *Violence in America*, 1:21–54.

58. Zahn, "Homicide in the Twentieth Century," p. 219; and Courtwright, *Violent Land*, chapter 3 and p. 209.

59. New York State, Department of Health, Office of Biostatistics, *Annual Report*, 1940, p. cv.

60. Eric H. Monkkonen, *Police in Urban America, 1860–1920* (Cambridge: Cambridge University Press, 1981) argues that crime waves were really arrest waves with the exception of changes in homicide rates. See Lane, *Violent Death in the City*, 82–90, on undercounting homicides. Archer and Gartner, *Violence and Crime*, pp. 30–45, make the case for accuracy of criminal statistics in measuring crime trends.

61. Ralph W. Whelan, "Philosophy and Development of the Youth Board Program," in *Reaching the Unreached: Fundamental Aspects of the Program of the New York City Youth Board*, ed. Sylvan S. Furman (New York: New York City Youth Board, 1952), pp. 1–11; and James E. McCarthy and Joseph S. Barbaro, "Redirecting Teen-age Gangs," in ibid., pp. 98–126.

CHAPTER THREE. DEFENDING PLACE

1. See Werner Sollers, "Introduction: The Invention of Ethnicity," in *The Invention of Ethnicity*, ed. Werner Sollers (New York: Oxford University Press, 1989), pp. ix–xx, and Benedict Anderson, *Imagined Communities: Reflections on the Origin and Spread of Nationalism* (London: Verso, 1991).

2. Frederic Thrasher, *The Gang: A Study of 1,313 Gangs in Chicago*, rev. ed. (Chicago: University of Chicago Press, 1963); and Lewis Yablonsky, *The Violent Gang*, rev. ed. (New York: Penguin, 1970).

3. Gerald D. Suttles, *The Social Construction of Communities* (Chicago: University of Chicago Press, 1972), pp. 21–43; idem, *The Social Order of the Slum: Ethnicity and Territory in the Inner City* (Chicago: University of Chicago Press, 1968); Sally Engle Merry, *Urban Danger: Life in a Neighborhood of Strangers* (Philadelphia: Temple University Press, 1981); and Elijah Anderson, *Street Wise: Race, Class, and Change in an Urban Community* (Chicago: University of Chicago Press, 1990).

4. See Thrasher, *The Gang*, for the first position, and Suttles, *Social Order of the Slum*, for a study that links gangs and ethnicity without incorporating change.

5. My choices were made based on the availability of primary source material on gangs as well as the availablity of scholarly studies on these neighborhoods that allowed me to contextualize the gangs.

6. Yablonsky, *The Violent Gang*, chapter 2, reviews the Farmer incident. The quotation is on p. 42. My account differs in a number of ways. The quotations from gang members in Yablonsky are less detailed than those in the radio broadcast by Edward R. Murrow, and I have relied on Murrow's account. See "Who Killed Michael Farmer?" April 21, 1958, CBS Radio Network, on file with the Edward R. Murrow Library, Fletcher School of Law and Diplomacy, Tufts University (hereafter cited as "Who Killed Michael Farmer").

7. Richard E. Brotman, "An Analysis of Psychodynamic Processes of Change in Small Group Behavior in a Teen-Age Gang" (Ph.D. diss., New York University, 1955), pp. 85–88; and Bradford Chambers, "The Juvenile Gangs of New York," *American Mercury* 62 (April 1946): 480–86.

8. Yablonsky, *The Violent Gang*, pp. 61–62; and *New York Times*, February 23, 1958.

9. "Who Killed Michael Farmer," p. 52.

10. Murray Kempton, "Walking on Water," *New York Post*, February 14, 1958. Kempton covered the trial for the *Post* and his columns provide the most perceptive analysis of the case both at the time and since.

11. "Who Killed Michael Farmer," pp. 9–14. Murrow did not quote Farmer's dying words, nor were they reported in the press or introduced at the trial. See Irwin D. Davidson and Richard Gehman, *The Jury Is Still Out* (New York: Harper, 1959), p. 26. Davidson was the presiding judge.

12. Lee A. Lendt, *A Social History of Washington Heights, New York City* (New York: Columbia–Washington Heights Community Mental Health Project, 1960), pp. 21, 64–65; and Ira Katznelson, *City Trenches: Urban Politics and the Patterning of Class in the United States* (Chicago: University of Chicago Press, 1981), p. 85. See also Jess Stearn, *The Wasted Years* (Garden City, N.Y.: Doubleday, 1959), pp. 20–23.

13. Katznelson, *City Trenches*, p. 86.

14. Ronald Bayor, *Neighbors in Conflict: The Irish, Germans, Jews, and Italians of New York City, 1929–1941*, 2d ed. (Urbana: University of Illinois Press, 1988), p. 152; and Brotman, "Analysis of Psychodynamic Processes of Change," pp. 85–87.

15. Robert W. Snyder, "The Neighborhood Changed: The Irish of Washington Heights and Inwood since 1945," in *The New York Irish*, ed. Ronald H. Bayor and Timothy Meagher (Baltimore: Johns Hopkins University Press, 1996), pp. 442–45, quotation, p. 445; Bayor, *Neighbors in Conflict*, pp. 153–54; and John T. McGreevy, *Parish Boundaries: The Catholic Encounter with Race in the Twentieth-century Urban North* (Chicago: University of Chicago Press, 1996).

16. Bayor, *Neighbors in Conflict*, pp. 152–53; and Katznelson, *City Trenches*, p. 79. On networks, see Barry Wellman and Barry Leighton, "Networks, Neighborhoods, and Communities: Approaches to the Study of the Community Question," *Urban Affairs Quarterly* 14 (March 1979): 363–90; Elizabeth Bott, *Family and Social Network: Roles, Norms, and External Relationships in Ordinary Urban Families* (London: Tavistock Publications, 1957); and Snyder, "The Neighborhood Changed." I am indebted to Rob Snyder for suggesting that I look at network theory.

17. Bayor, *Neighbors in Conflict*, pp. 155–57; and Lendt, *Social History of Washington Heights*, pp. 72–76. On policemen residing in the area, see the *New York Times*, August 7, 1957.

18. Lendt, *Social History of Washington Heights*, pp. 21–22, 102, 109–10.

19. Ibid., p. 96; and Katznelson, *City Trenches*, p. 86.

20. For an ethnographic study with similar findings, see Jay MacLeod, *Ain't No Makin' It: Leveled Aspirations in a Low-Income Neighborhood* (Boulder: Westview Press, 1987). See Washington Heights Project, Office of the Mayor, Subject Files: Juvenile Delinquency, 1955–1958, Box 155, Folder: Juvenile Delinquency 2, 1957, Robert Wagner Papers, New York City Municipal Archives (hereafter cited as Mental Health Board Study, Wagner Papers, NYCMA) for evidence of African-American members in the Jesters and for cordial relations between the Jesters and African Americans in the neighborhood. This also follows the "guest model" found in Suttles, *Social Order of the Slum*, pp. 49–51.

21. *New York Times*, August 1–2, 1957; and *New York Mirror*, August 1, 1957.

22. Yablonsky, *The Violent Gang*, pp. 230–35, notes the mixed racial composition of the gangs but interprets the gang members' comments about race as another example of their individual psychopathologies.

23. *Amsterdam News*, August 10, 1957; *New York Times*, August 1, 1957; and *New York Post*, August 1, 1957.

24. Jack Katz, *Seductions of Crime: Moral and Sensual Attractions in Doing Evil* (New York: Basic Books, 1988), chapter 4.

25. Murray Kempton, "The Evidence," *New York Post*, February 7, 1958; idem, "The Lonely Crowd," *New York Post*, February 16, 1958; idem, "The Lucky Boy," *New York Post*, February 19, 1958; idem, "Wanton Boys," *New York Post*, March 20, 1958; idem, "The Chickens," *New York Post*, March 21, 1958; idem, "Apple Blossom Time," *New York Post*, March 25, 1958; and *New York Times*, March 2, 1958, March 6, 1958, March 12–13, 1958, March 19, 1958, March 21–22, 1958, March 25, 1958, April 8–9, 1958, April 16, 1958. The jury imposed its own racial distinctions in the case; two of the three defendants acquitted were Hills and McCarthy.

26. Interview with Manny Diaz, July 29, 1992.

27. Ronald H. Bayor, "The Neighborhood Invasion Pattern," in *Neighborhoods in Urban America*, ed. Ronald H. Bayor (Port Washington, N.Y.: Kennikat Press, 1982), 92–95; Robert Anthony Orsi, *The Madonna of 115th Street: Faith and Community in Italian Harlem, 1880–1950* (New Haven: Yale University Press, 1985), p. 17; Francesco Cordasco and Rocco G. Galatioto, "Ethnic Displacement in the Interstitial Community: The East Harlem Experience," *Phylon* 31 (1970): 302–12; and Frederic M. Thrasher, "Final Report on the Jefferson Park Branch of the Boys' Club of New York," October 21, 1935, pp. 82–89, Bureau of Social Hygiene Papers, unnumbered folder, reel 7, Rockefeller Archives (hereafter cited as BSH).

28. Orsi, *Madonna of 115th Street*, p. 17; and Bayor, "Neighborhood Invasion Pattern," pp. 96–97.

29. Robert Orsi, "The Religious Boundaries of an Inbetween People: Street Feste and the Problem of the Dark-Skinned Other in Italian East Harlem, 1920–1990," *American Quarterly* 44 (September 1992): 313–47; and Helen Parkhurst, *Undertow: The Story of a Boy Called Tony* (New York: Farrar, Straus and Company, 1963), p. 50.

30. Suttles, *Social Order of the Slum*, pp. 31–32; and Merry, *Urban Danger*.

31. Irving Spergel, *Racketville, Slumtown, Haulburg: An Exploratory Study of Delinquent Subcultures* (Chicago: University of Chicago Press, 1964), p. 23.

32. Thrasher, "Final Report," pp. 217–18.

33. *New York Herald Tribune*, March 26, 1933, quoted in Thrasher, "Final Report," p. 149.

34. This was confirmed in four interviews; the interviewees wished to remain anonymous. See also Spergel, *Racketville*, pp. 64–65, 157.

35. Quoted in Orsi, *Madonna of 115th Street*, p. 33. See also Spergel, *Racketville*, p. 13; and Parkhurst, *Undertow*, pp. 55–57.

36. See Suttles, *Social Order of the Slum*, pp. 107–12.

37. City Planning Commission, Department of City Planning, "East Harlem, Planning Area #308," pp. 4–9, 11–13, Box 1, Union Settlement Records, Social Welfare History Archives, University of Minnesota (hereafter SWHA).

38. Welfare Council of New York City, Committee on Puerto Ricans in New York City, *Report of the Committee on Puerto Ricans in New York City* (New York: Welfare Council of New York City, 1948), p. 19.

39. Virginia E. Sanchez Korrol, *From Colonia to Community: The History of Puerto Ricans in New York City, 1917–1948* (Westport, Conn.: Greenwood Press, 1983), pp. 85–117; and Elena Padilla, *Up from Puerto Rico* (New York: Columbia University Press, 1958), pp. 128–32, 188, 220. Again a comparison can be made to Suttles, *Social Order of the Slum*.

40. Padilla, *Up from Puerto Rico*, pp. 226–36, quotation, p. 232; Spergel, *Racketville*, pp. 19–20, 24–25, 63; and Dan Wakefield, *Island in the City: Puerto Ricans in New York* (New York: Corinth Books, 1957), p. 129.

41. Spergel, *Racketville*, pp. 3–7. Residents in Italian-dominated tracts had fewer operatives (22 percent) and service sector employees (15 percent), and a higher percentage of craftsmen (21 percent) and laborers (15 percent), with the latter working largely in highly paid construction trades. The proportion of white-collar employees was the same (22 percent) in both areas. These figures are subject to an ecological fallacy (one cannot assume that figures about Puerto Rican dominated census tracts are about Puerto Ricans per se), but they provide a rough approximation that is supported by other sources. See Welfare Council, *Puerto Ricans in New York City*, p. 20.

42. Piri Thomas, *Savior, Savior, Hold My Hand* (Garden City, N.Y.: Doubleday, 1972), p. 55; and interview with Manny Diaz, July 29, 1992.

43. See Ruth Horowitz, *Honor and the American Dream: Culture and Identity in a Chicano Community* (New Brunswick, N.J.: Rutgers University Press, 1983); Wakefield, *Island in the City*, p. 118; and Spergel, *Racketville*, pp. 19–20, 42–43.

44. *The Home News*, October 17, 1938, Box 53, Folder 14, for quotation. Committee for Racial Cooperation, "Report," Box 52, Folder 20, and D. Di Pino, "Interview with Lieutenant Haas of the 104th Street Station, Re: Italo-Porto Rican Riots," Box 53, Folder 14, both in Leonard Covello Papers, Balch Institute for Ethnic Studies (hereafter Covello Papers); and Orsi, *Madonna of 115th Street*, p. 17.

45. "Youth and Recreation in East Harlem: A Study of the Recreational Facilities for Teen Age Youth in East Harlem," May 1944, pp. 1–2, 6, Box 38, Folder 14, Covello Papers.

46. "Community Center for 31 West 110th Street," pp. 6–7, Box 73, Folder 13, Covello Papers; *New York Daily News*, April 29, 1957; East Harlem Youth Project of the United Neighborhood Houses of New York, Inc., "Report of the Director," October 1, 1944–June 1, 1945, pp. 39–41, Box 82, Folder 11, Henry Street Settlement Records, SWHA; and Interview with JC, March 9, 1993.

47. Thrasher, "Final Report," p. 93.

48. Gerald Meyer, *Vito Marcantonio: Radical Politician, 1902–1954* (Albany: State University of New York Press, 1989), pp. 112–14, 144; and Orsi, *Madonna of 115th Street*, pp. 71–73.

49. Patricia Cayo Sexton, *Spanish Harlem* (New York: Harper and Row, 1965), pp. 35–39; Meyer, *Marcantonio*, pp. 114, 145, 175; Bayor, "Neighborhood Invasion Pattern," pp. 96–97; Benjamin Alicea, "Christian Urban Colonizers: A History of the East Harlem Protestant Parish in New York City, 1943–1968" (Ph.D. diss. Union Theological Seminary, 1988), pp. 37–38; and Interview with Pete Pascale, December 29, 1992.

50. *Daily News*, April 29, 1957; Wakefield, *Island in the City*, p. 126; Padilla, *Up from Puerto Rico*, p. 231; Dan Wakefield, "The Gang That Went Good," *Harper's Magazine* 216 (June 1958): 36–43, quotation, p. 38; Interview with ES, March 7, 1994; and New York City Youth Board, *Reaching the Fighting Gang* (New York: New York City Youth Board, 1960), p. 46. For a similar situation in the Bronx, See Robert Rice, "Six Nights with a Teenage Gang," *New York Post*, June 3, 1958.

51. Harrison E. Salisbury, *The Shook-Up Generation* (New York: Harper and Brothers, 1958), p. 12.

CHAPTER FOUR. BECOMING MEN

1. Claude Brown, *Manchild in the Promised Land* (New York: Penguin Books, 1965), p. 265.

2. Michael S. Kimmel and Michael A. Messner, "Introduction," in *Men's Lives*, ed. Michael S. Kimmel and Michael A. Messner (New York: Macmillan, 1992), pp. 9–10; R. W. Connell, *Masculinities* (Berkeley: University of California Press, 1995); and James W. Messerschmidt, *Masculinities and Crime: Critique and Reconceptualization of Theory* (Lanham, Md.: Rowman and Littlefield, 1993).

3. Paul E. Willis, *Learning to Labour: How Working Class Kids Get Working Class Jobs* (Aldershot, England: Gower Publishing Co., 1977).

4. Felipe Luciano in *Palante: Young Lords Party*, ed. Michael Abramson (New York: McGraw-Hill, 1971), p. 29; and Douglas G. Glasgow, *The Black Underclass: Poverty, Unemployment, and Entrapment of Ghetto Youth* (New York: Vintage Books, 1981), pp. 57–60.

5. Dan Wakefield, *Island in the City: Puerto Ricans in New York* (New York: Corinth Books, 1957), pp. 151–53, 169–74.

6. Jamal, in *Look for Me in the Whirlwind: The Collective Autobiography of the New York 21* (New York: Random House, 1971), p. 122.

7. Carl Joyeaux, Jr. [pseud.], *Out of the Burning: The Story of a Boy Gang Leader* (New York: Crown Publishers, 1960); Ira H. Freeman, "A Teen-Age Gang Leader's Brutal Tale: How His Street Club Shot Its Way to Power," *Life* 44 (April 14, 1958): 126ff.; and idem, "A Gang Leader's Redemption," *Life* 44 (April 28, 1958): 69ff.

8. Georgie in *Palante*, p. 35. See also "Harlem Gang Leader," *Life* 25 (November 1, 1948): 106.

9. Brown, *Manchild*, p. 22.

10. Felipe Luciano, in *Palante*, p. 31.

11. Kenneth E. Marshall, "The Fighting Gang in Transition: A Study of the Structure and Functions of the Urban Adolescent Fighting Gang and an Analysis of Functionally Equivalent Deviant Group Modes" (Ed.D., diss., New York University, 1968), pp. 108–9; and New York City Youth Board (NYCYB), *Reaching the Fighting Gang* (New York: New York City Youth Board, 1960), pp. 35–36.

12. Interview with JT, December 28, 1992; and Warren Miller, *The Cool World* (Boston: Little, Brown and Company, 1959), p. 72.

13. Kenneth Marshall Process Records, May 4, 1951, Box 1, Kenneth Marshall Papers, Schomburg Center for Research in Black Culture, The New York Public Library (hereafter Schomburg Center).

14. Brown, *Manchild*, p. 22.

15. Piri Thomas, *Down These Mean Streets* (New York: Vintage Books, 1967), p. 64.

16. Interview with JT, December 12, 1992.

17. Joseph A. Fernandez with John Underwood, *Tales Out of School: Joseph Fernandez's Crusade to Rescue American Education* (Boston: Little, Brown and Company, 1993), p. 27.

18. NYCYB, *Reaching the Fighting Gang*, p. 55.

19. Kwando Kinshasa, in *Look for Me in the Whirlwind*, p. 102.

20. For an ethnographic study of school violence and the use of hallways, stairwells, and bathrooms, see John Devine, *Maximum Security: The Culture of Violence in Inner-City Schools* (Chicago: University of Chicago Press, 1996).

21. Dharuba, in *Look for Me in the Whirlwind*, p. 144.

22. Interview with JC, March 9, 1993.

23. Daniel Belknap Process Records, January 4, 1952, Box 1, Kenneth Marshall Papers, Schomburg Center.

24. For contemporary studies, see Jay MacLeod, *Ain't No Makin' It: Leveled Aspirations in a Low-Income Neighborhood* (Boulder: Westview Press, 1987); and Mercer L. Sullivan, *"Getting Paid": Youth Crime and Work in the Inner City* (Ithaca, N.Y.: Cornell University Press, 1989), pp. 54–55.

25. Marshall, "Fighting Gang," p. 176.

26. Ibid., 175–76.

27. Ali Bey Hassan, in *Look for Me in the Whirlwind*, pp. 128–29.

28. Raymond Williams, "Base and Superstructure in Marxist Cultural Theory," *New Left Review* 82 (November–December 1973): 3–16.

29. Anita S. Vogel and Mary Koval, *Youth in New York City: Out-of-School and Out-of-Work* (New York: New York City Youth Board, 1962), appendix, table 3. The comparable figures for females were 51 percent, 43 percent, and 19 percent.

30. Paul Osterman, *Getting Started: The Youth Labor Market* (Cambridge, Mass.: MIT Press, 1980), table 4.4, p. 66.

31. Willis, *Learning to Labour*; and MacLeod, *Aint No Makin' It*.

32. Vogel and Koval, *Youth in New York City*, pp. 14, 17.

33. Vincent Riccio and Bill Slocum, *All the Way Down: The Violent Underworld of Street Gangs* (New York: Simon and Schuster, 1962), p. 84.

34. NYCYB, *Reaching the Fighting Gang*, p. 58.

35. Paul L. Crawford, Daniel I. Malamud, and James R. Dumpson, *Working with Teen-Age Gangs: A Report on the Central Harlem Street Clubs Project* (New York: Welfare Council of New York City, 1950), p. 19.

36. Steve Klein, "Record Material on the Spanish Kings—A Puerto Rican Youth Gang" (New York: Mobilization for Youth, 1963). p. 2; and Thomas, *Down These Mean Streets*, pp. 98–104.

37. Daniel Belknap Process Records, July 3, 1952, Box 1, Kenneth Marshall Papers, Schomburg Center.

38. Marshall, "Fighting Gang," p. 177.

39. Fernandez, *Tales Out of School*, p. 26.

40. David M. Gordon, Richard Edwards, and Michael Reich, *Segmented Work, Divided Workers: The Historical Transformation of Labor in the United States* (Cambridge: Cambridge University Press, 1982), pp. 185–92; 200–210.

41. Osterman, *Getting Started*, pp. 6–8; 147–48.

42. Quoted in Crawford et al., *Working with Teen-Age Gangs*, p. 19.

43. Quoted in Kenneth Marshall, "Coffee Shops, Inc.: An Action Proposal," p. 7, Mobilization for Youth folder, Box 3, Kenneth Marshall Papers, Schomburg Center.

44. Interview with WC, October 21, 1992.

45. Brown, *Manchild*, pp. 294–95; and Shaba Om, in *Look for Me in the Whirlwind*, p. 5.

46. Marshall, "Fighting Gang," p. 105.

47. Stuart Henry, *The Hidden Economy: The Context and Control of Borderline Crime* (London: Robertson, 1978).

48. NYCYB, *Reaching the Fighting Gang*, p. 177.

49. Klein, "Spanish Kings," p. 23.

50. Ibid., p. 138.

51. Richard P. Rettig, Manual J. Torres, and Gerald R. Garrett, *Manny: A Criminal Addict's Story* (Boston: Houghton Mifflin, 1977), p. 176.

52. See Robin D. G. Kelley, *Race Rebels: Culture, Politics, and the Black Working Class* (New York: The Free Press, 1994).

53. See the works by these authors cited above. Also Harrison E. Salisbury, *The Shook-Up Generation* (New York: Harper and Brothers, 1958), p. 13; Interview with JG, May 25, 1995; and David Wilkerson, *The Cross and the Switchblade* (New York: Bernard Geis Associates, 1963), p. 149.

54. Bruce Kenrick, *Come Out the Wilderness: The Story of East Harlem Protestant Parish* (New York: Harper and Brothers, 1962), p. 17.

55. Dion DiMucci with Davin Seay, *The Wanderer: Dion's Story* (New York: Beech Tree Books, 1988), p. 28.

56. Brown, *Manchild*, p. 103.

57. Ibid., pp. 70–71; Marshall, "Fighting Gang," p. 52; Miller, *Cool World*, p. 126; and NYCYB, *Reaching the Fighting Gang*, p. 20.

58. Nicholas Pileggi, *Wiseguy: Life in a Mafia Family* (New York: Simon and Schuster, 1985), pp. 19, 21.

59. Bobby, in *Palante*, p. 32.

60. Joyeaux, *Out of the Burning*, p. 71.

61. Interview with JT, December 28, 1992.

62. Interview with RG, April 23, 1993. See also, Irving Spergel, *Racketville, Slumtown, Haulburg: An Exploratory Study of Delinquent Subcultures* (Chicago: University of Chicago Press, 1964), p. 63.

63. Marshall, "Fighting Gang," p. 78.

64. Vincent Riccio, Oral History, Columbia University Oral History Collection, part 2, p. 111.

65. Felipe Luciano, in *Palante*, p. 29.

66. Mario, in *Growing Up Puerto Rican*, ed. Paulette Cooper (New York: New American Library, 1972), pp. 103–4.

67. Robert Rice, "Six Nights with a Teenage Gang," *New York Post*, June 8, 1958.

68. Riccio and Slocum, *All the Way Down*, p. 100; and Riccio, Oral History, p. 157.

69. Marshall, "Fighting Gang," pp. 91–92.

70. Kenneth Marshall Field Reports, "Interview with JS," July 8, 1959, Box 1, Kenneth Marshall Papers, Schomburg Center.

71. Walter Bernstein, "The Cherubs Are Rumbling," *New Yorker* 33 (September 21, 1957): 128; and Riccio and Slocum, *All the Way Down*, p. 95.

72. Robert Rice, "Six Nights with a Teenage Gang," *New York Post*, June 4, 1957.

73. Salisbury, *Shook-Up Generation*, p. 22.

74. Crawford et al., *Working with Teen-Age Gangs*, p. 20; "Peacemaking Priest in Gangland," *Life* 43 (August 26, 1957): 89–91; Joseph Margolis, "Juvenile Delinquents: The Latter-Day Knights," *The American Scholar* 29 (Spring 1960): 211–18; and Miller, *Cool World*, p. 193.

75. Felipe Luciano, in *Palante*, p. 31.

76. John Clarke, Stuart Hall, Tony Jefferson, and Brian Roberts, "Subcultures, Cultures, and Class," in *Resistance through Rituals: Youth Subcultures in Postwar Britain*, ed. Stuart Hall and Tony Jefferson (London: Hutchinson, 1976), pp. 9–74.

77. Maxine Baca Zinn, "Chicano Men and Masculinity," in *Men's Lives*, p. 74; Hans Toch, *Violent Men: An Inquiry into the Psychology of Violence* (Chicago: Aldine, 1969); Jack Katz, *Seductions of Crime: Moral and Sensual Attractions in Doing Evil* (New York: Basic Books, 1988), chapter 3; and Richard Majors and Janet Mancini Billson, *Cool Pose: The Dilemmas of Black Manhood in America* (New York: Lexington Books, 1992), pp. 28–34.

78. James Gilligan, *Violence: Our Deadly Epidemic and Its Causes* (New York: G. P. Putnam, 1996), pp. 110–13; Katz, *Seductions of Crime*, pp. 88–93, 128–29, 247; Lawrence W. Levine, *Black Culture and Black Consciousness: Afro-American Folk Thought from Slavery to Freedom* (New York: Oxford University Press, 1977),

pp. 407–20; and Fox Butterfield, *All God's Children: The Bosket Family and the American Tradition of Violence* (New York: Avon Books, 1996), pp. 61–64.

79. Brown, *Manchild*, pp. 270–71; and Katz, *Seductions of Crime*, chapter 4.

80. Bobby, in *Palante*, p. 33.

81. NYCYB, *Reaching the Fighting Gang*, pp. 18–19; Spergel, *Racketville*, pp. 43, 74; and Crawford et al., *Working with Teen-Age Gangs*, p. 114.

82. Bobby, in *Palante*, p. 32.

83. Toch, *Violent Men*, originated these distinctions. For their application to gangs, see Ruth Horowitz, *Honor and the American Dream: Culture and Identity in a Chicano Community* (New Brunswick, N.J.: Rutgers University Press, 1983), chapter 5.

84. Kenneth Marshall Process Records, various dates, Box 5, Kenneth Marshall Papers, Schomburg Center.

85. Lumumba Shakur, in *Look for Me in the Whirlwind*, p. 148; and Horowitz, *Honor and the American Dream*, pp. 195–96.

86. Interview with ES, October 20, 1992.

87. Marshall, "Fighting Gang," pp. 126, 286.

88. Rettig et al., *Manny*, p. 18.

89. Kenneth Marshall Process Records, October 19, 1951, Box 5, Kenneth Marshall Papers, Schomburg Center.

90. Kenneth Marshall Process Records, n.d., Box 5, Kenneth Marshall Papers, Schomburg Center; and Interview with JT, December 28, 1992.

91. Nicky Cruz, *Run, Baby, Run* (Plainfield, N.J.: Logos Books, 1969), p. 50.

92. Brown, *Manchild*, p. 126; and Geoffrey Canada, *Fist, Stick, Knife, Gun: A Personal History of Violence in America* (Boston: Beacon Press, 1995), pp. 21–22.

93. Thomas, *Down These Mean Streets*, p. 51.

94. Brown, *Manchild*, p. 17.

95. Bobby, in *Palante*, p. 33. On the instrumentality of violence, see Philippe Bourgois, *In Search of Respect: Selling Crack in El Barrio* (Cambridge: Cambridge University Press, 1995), pp. 24–25.

96. William Foote Whyte, "A Slum Sex Code," *The American Journal of Sociology* 49 (July 1943): 24–31; and Ira L. Reiss, "Sexual Codes in Teen-Age Culture," *The Annals of the American Academy of Political and Social Science* 338 (November 1961): 56–57.

97. Horowitz, *Honor and the American Dream*, pp. 116–20; Gerald Suttles, *The Social Order of the Slum: Ethnicity and Territory in the Inner City* (Chicago: University of Chicago Press, 1968); Robert Anthony Orsi, *The Madonna of 115th Street: Faith and Community in Italian Harlem, 1880–1950* (New Haven: Yale University Press, 1985), pp. 115–17, 134–41; Herbert J. Gans, *The Urban Villagers: Group and Class in the Life of Italian Americans* (New York: The Free Press, 1965); Elena

Padilla, *Up from Puerto Rico* (New York: Columbia University Press, 1958); Peggy Reeves Sanday, *Fraternity Gang Rape: Sex, Brotherhood, and Privilege on Campus* (New York: New York University Press, 1990); and Bourgois, *In Search of Respect*, pp. 265–72. One need only read accounts of fraternity rapes or the extreme forms of sexual harassment in the military to be convinced that gang behavior was not aberrant.

98. Marshall, "Fighting Gang," p. 133; Joyeaux, *Out of the Burning*, p. 119; Salisbury, *Shook-Up Generation*, pp. 33–34; and Bourgois, *In Search of Respect*, pp. 205–12.

99. Joyeaux, *Out of the Burning*, p. 119.

100. Riccio, Oral History, pp. 164–65.

101. Interview with RG, April 23, 1993; and Salisbury, *Shook-Up Generation*, p. 33.

102. Thomas, *Down These Mean Streets*, pp. 15–16; Bob Collier, in *Look for Me in the Whirlwind*, p. 146; and C. Kilmer Myers, *Light the Dark Streets* (Garden City, N.Y.: Doubleday, 1961), p. 53.

103. Salisbury, *Shook-Up Generation*, p. 34; and Crawford et al., *Working with Teen-Age Gangs*, p. 96.

104. Joyeaux, *Out of the Burning*, p. 120.

105. Kenneth Marshall Process Records, October 1, 1951, Box 5, Kenneth Marshall Papers, Schomburg Center.

106. Kenneth Marshall, "Interview with JP," September 11, 1959, Field Reports, Box 1, Kenneth Marshall Papers, Schomburg Center.

107. Crawford et al., *Working with Teen-Age Gangs*, p. 16.

108. Riccio, Oral History, pp. 165–66; Salisbury, *Shook-Up Generation*, p. 34; and Wenzell Brown, *Monkey on My Back* (New York: Greenberg, 1953), p. 107.

109. Jerry Della Famina and Charles Sopkin, *An Italian Grows in Brooklyn* (Boston: Little, Brown and Company, 1978), p. 113.

110. Daniel Belknap Process Records, November 7, 1952, Box 1, Kenneth Marshall Papers, Schomburg Center.

111. Bourgois, *In Search of Respect*, pp. 207–8.

112. Riccio, Oral History, pp. 167, 168; and Kitty Hanson, *Rebels in the Streets: The Story of New York's Girl Gangs* (Englewood Cliffs, N.J.: Prentice-Hall, 1964), pp. 91–92.

113. Susan Brownmiller, *Against Our Will: Men, Women, and Rape* (New York: Bantam Books, 1975), p. 212.

114. Riccio and Slocum, *All the Way Down*, p. 111.

115. Quoted in Lewis Yablonsky, *The Violent Gang*, rev. ed. (New York: Penguin Books, 1970), p. 241.

116. Riccio, Oral History, p. 192; and Thomas, *Down These Mean Streets*, pp. 55–62.

117. Elijah Anderson, *A Place on the Corner* (Chicago: University of Chicago Press, 1978), p. 86; Mark S. Fleisher, *Beggars and Thieves: Lives of Urban Street Criminals* (Madison: University of Wisconsin Press, 1995), p. 165; and Albert J. Reiss, "The Social Integration of Peers and Queers," *Social Problems* (Fall 1961): 102–20. This is apparent also in the literature about sexual activity in prison. For an earlier period, see George Chauncey, Jr., "Christian Brotherhood or Sexual Perversion? Homosexual Identities and the Construction of Sexual Boundaries in the World War One Era," *Journal of Social History* 19 (Winter 1985): 189–211; and idem, *Gay New York: Gender, Urban Culture, and the Making of the Gay Male World, 1890–1940* (New York: Basic Books, 1994). The fluid boundaries between gay and heterosexual identities that Chauncey found continued for at least another decade after World War II.

118. Bourgois, *In Search of Respect*, pp. 210–11.

119. On culture as a mediating space, see Paul Gilroy, *"There Ain't No Black in the Union Jack": The Cultural Politics of Race and Nation* (Chicago: University of Chicago Press, 1991), pp. 16–17. Andrew Diamond was kind enough to bring this to my attention.

CHAPTER FIVE. MAKING A GANG CULTURE

1. Richard P. Rettig, Manual J. Torres, and Gerald R. Garrett, *Manny: A Criminal Addict's Story* (Boston: Houghton Mifflin, 1977), p. 24.

2. Here I disagree with Gerald D. Suttles, *The Social Order of the Slum: Ethnicity and Territory in the Inner City* (Chicago: University of Chicago Press, 1968), chapter 4, who so emphasizes the ethnic distinctiveness of language, clothing, and style that he misses the formation of a bop culture that transcended ethnicity.

3. Here I am criticizing the work of Lewis Yablonsky, *The Violent Gang*, rev. ed. (New York: Penguin Books, 1970); Walter B. Miller, "Lower-Class Culture as a Generating Milieu of Gang Delinquency," *Journal of Social Issues* 14 (1958): 5–19; Jack Katz, *Seductions of Crime: Moral and Sensual Attractions in Doing Evil* (New York: Basic Books, 1988); and Mark S. Fleisher, *Beggars and Thieves: Lives of Urban Street Criminals* (Madison: University of Wisconsin Press, 1995).

4. Dick Hebdige, *Subculture: The Meaning of Style* (New York: Methuen, 1979); Stuart Hall and Tony Jefferson, eds., *Resistance through Rituals: Youth Subcultures in Postwar Britain* (London: Hutchinson, 1976); Mike Brake, *The Sociology of Youth Culture and Youth Subcultures: Sex and Drugs and Rock 'n Roll?* (London: Routledge and Kegan Paul, 1980); William Graebner, *Coming of Age in Buffalo: Youth and*

*Authority in the Postwar Era* (Philadelphia: Temple University Press, 1990); and Raymond Williams, "Base and Superstructure in Marxist Cultural Theory," *New Left Review* 82 (November–December 1973): 3–16.

5. Grace Palladino, *Teenagers: An American History* (New York: Basic Books, 1996), chapter 7.

6. LeRoi Jones (Imamu Amiri Baraka), *Blues People: The Negro Experience in White America and the Music That Developed from It* (New York: William Morrow and Company, 1963), pp. 181–91; quotation, p. 181; David H. Rosenthal, *Hard Bop: Jazz and Black Music, 1955–1965* (New York: Oxford University Press, 1992), pp. 10–12, 15–16, 21–22; Ira Gitler, *Swing to Bop: An Oral History of the Transition in Jazz in the 1940s* (New York: Oxford University Press, 1985), pp. 3–5; Katrina Hazzard-Gordon, *Jookin': The Rise of Social Dance Formations in African-American Culture* (Philadelphia: Temple University Press, 1990); Steve Chibnall, "Whistle and Zoot: The Changing Meaning of a Suit of Clothes," *History Workshop* 20 (Autumn 1985): 56–81; and Eric Lott, "Double V, Double-Time: Bebop's Politics of Style," *Callaloo* 11 (1988): 597–605.

7. New York City Youth Board, *Reaching the Fighting Gang* (New York: New York City Youth Board, 1960), pp. 295–96; Harrison E. Salisbury, *The Shook-Up Generation* (New York: Harper and Brothers, 1958), pp. ix–x, 29–30; *New York World Telegram*, April 13, 1949; and Geoffrey Canada, *Fist, Stick, Knife, Gun: A Personal History of Violence in America* (Boston: Beacon Press, 1995), p. 71.

8. Edith A. Folb, *Runnin' down some lines: The Language and Culture of Black Teenagers* (Cambridge, Mass.: Harvard University Press, 1980), p. 40.

9. Graebner, *Coming of Age*, pp. 26–43; Dion DiMucci with Davin Seay, *The Wanderer: Dion's Story* (New York: Beech Tree Books, 1988); Anthony J. Gribin and Matthew M. Schiff, *Doo-Wop: The Forgotten Third of Rock 'n Roll* (Iola, Wisc.: Krause Publications, 1992), pp. 16–25; 34–36; 84–88; and Philip Groia, *They All Sang on the Corner: A Second Look at New York City's Rhythm and Blues Vocal Groups* (West Hempstead, N.Y.: Phillis Dee Enterprises, 1983).

10. Charlie Gillett, *The Sound of the City: The Rise of Rock and Roll*, rev. ed. (New York: Pantheon Books, 1983), pp. ix, 17–21.

11. David Nassaw, *Going Out: The Rise and Fall of Public Amusements* (New York: Basic Books, 1993), especially pp. 248–55; and David R. Roediger, *The Wages of Whiteness: Race and the Making of the American Working Class* (London: Verso, 1991).

12. Here I differ with William Graebner in his otherwise superb *Coming of Age*, p. 125.

13. Gillett, *Sound of the City*; *Brooklyn Eagle*, April 10, 1949; Gribin and Schiff, *Doo-Wop*, pp. 48–50; 65–66; Graebner, *Coming of Age*, pp. 29–34; and John A. Jackson, *Big Beat Heat: Alan Freed and the Early Years of Rock and Roll* (New York:

Schirmer Books, 1991). See Claude Brown, *Manchild in the Promised Land* (New York: Penguin Books, 1965), p. 171, for the evocative discussion of the term "baby" and its adoption by street gang members. See the extensive glossary in Folb, *Runnin' down some lines*, pp. 227–60.

14. Piri Thomas, *Down These Mean Streets* (New York: Vintage Books, 1967), p. 30.

15. Jeremy Larner and Ralph Tefferteller, *The Addict in the Street* (New York: Grove Press, 1964), p. 143; Carmelita, in *Growing Up Puerto Rican*, ed. Paulette Cooper (New York: New American Library, 1972), p. 154; and Canada, *Fist, Stick, Knife, Gun*, p. 71. For a contemporary analysis of "street signs," see Elijah Anderson, *Street Wise: Race, Class, and Change in an Urban Community* (Chicago: University of Chicago Press, 1990), pp. 167–77; on walking and style, see Richard Majors and Janet Mancini Billson, *Cool Pose: The Dilemmas of Black Manhood in America* (New York: Lexington Books, 1992), pp. 71–73.

16. Darla Milne, *Second Chance: The Israel Narvaez Story* (Wheaton, Ill.: Living Books, 1979), p. 63.

17. James Gilbert, *A Cycle of Outrage: America's Reaction to the Juvenile Delinquent in the 1950s* (New York: Oxford University Press, 1986), pp. 182–83; Graebner, *Coming of Age*, p. 49; Norman Podhoretz, *Making It* (New York: Random House, 1967), p. 21; Nicky Cruz, *Run, Baby, Run* (Plainfield, N.J.: Logos Books, 1969), pp. 38–39; and David Wilkerson, *The Cross and the Switchblade* (New York: Bernard Geis Associates, 1963), p. 66.

18. Carl Joyeaux, Jr. [pseud.], *Out of the Burning: The Story of a Boy Gang Leader* (New York: Crown Publishers, 1960), p. 111; Jerry Della Famina and Charles Sopkin, *An Italian Grows in Brooklyn* (Boston: Little, Brown and Company, 1978), p. 46; Stacy V. Jones, "The Cougars: Life with a Brooklyn Gang," *Harper's* 209 (November 1954): 42; and Kenneth E. Marshall, "The Fighting Gang in Transition: A Study of the Structure and Functions of the Urban Adolescent Fighting Gang and an Analysis of Functionally Equivalent Deviant Group Modes" (Ed.D. diss., New York University, 1968), p. 142.

19. Brake, *Sociology of Youth Culture*, pp. 22–27.

20. Graebner, *Coming of Age*, p. 46; and Gilbert, *Cycle of Outrage*, pp. 189–95.

21. *Brooklyn Eagle*, April 28, 1948; Rettig et al., *Manny*, p. 24; Joyeaux, *Out of the Burning*, p. 71; *New York World Telegram*, April 13, 1949, April 15, 1949; and William Barnard, *Jailbait: The Story of Juvenile Delinquency* (Garden City, N.Y.: Garden City Books, 1949), pp. 98–99.

22. Sam Kolman [pseud.], *The Royal Vultures* (New York: Permabooks, 1958), p. 28; Vincent Riccio and Bill Slocum, *All the Way Down: The Violent Underworld of Street Gangs* (New York: Simon and Schuster, 1962), p. 157; Vincent Riccio,

Oral History, Columbia University Oral History Collection, part 2, p. 44 (hereafter cited as Riccio, Oral History); and Salisbury, *Shook-Up Generation*, pp. 28–29.

23. Hebdige, *Subculture*; Brake, *Sociology of Youth Culture*, pp. 13–14; Malcolm X, *The Autobiography of Malcolm X* (New York: Grove Press, 1966), p. 78; Jones, *Blues People*, pp. 181–82, 190–91; and Brown, *Manchild*, pp. 98, 290–92.

24. Brown, *Manchild*, pp. 70–71.

25. Hebdige, *Subculture*, pp. 100–106; Alison Lurie, *The Language of Clothes* (New York: Random House, 1981), chapter 1; Elizabeth Wilson, *Adorned in Dreams: Fashion and Modernity* (Berkeley: University of California Press, 1987), chapter 9; and Kathryn E. Wilson, "Costume," in *Folklore: An Encyclopedia of Belief, Customs, Music, Tales, and Art*, ed. Thomas A. Green, 2 vols. (Santa Barbara, Calif.: ABC-CLIO Inc., 1997), 1:147–52.

26. Jones, "Cougars," p. 42; *Brooklyn Eagle*, June 20, 1950; and *New York Times*, March 24, 1958.

27. Salisbury, *Shook-Up Generation*, p. 46; Kitty Hanson, *Rebels in the Streets: The Story of New York's Girl Gangs* (Englewood Cliffs, N.J.: Prentice-Hall, 1964), p. 2; and *New York Times*, March 24, 1958.

28. Rettig et al., *Manny*, p. 22; and Kenneth Marshall Process Records, May 18, 1953, Box 1, Kenneth Marshall Papers, Schomburg Center for Research in Black Culture, New York Public Library (hereafter Schomburg Center). See also ibid., April 26, 1951, Box 5.

29. Interview with Nicky Cruz, February 24, 1993; DiMucci, *The Wanderer*, p. 47; New York City Youth Board, *Reaching the Fighting Gang*, p. 43; Hanson, *Rebels in the Streets*, p. 15; and Yablonsky, *The Violent Gang*, pp. 75–76.

30. See Yablonsky, *The Violent Gang*.

31. Richard E. Brotman, "An Analysis of Psychodynamic Processes of Change in Small Group Behavior in a Teen-Age Gang" (Ph.D. diss., New York University, 1955), p. 140.

32. Interview with RG, April 23, 1993.

33. Salisbury, *Shook-Up Generation*, p. 21.

34. Dan Wakefield, "The Gang That Went Good," *Harper's* 216 (June 1958), p. 39.

35. Joyeaux, *Out of the Burning*, pp. 71–72, 103; Rettig et al., *Manny*, p. 18; Salisbury, *Shook-Up Generation*, p. 23; R. Lincoln Keiser, *The Vice Lords: Warriors of the Streets* (New York: Holt, Rinehart and Winston, 1969), p. 59; and *New York World Telegram*, April 12, 1949.

36. Riccio and Slocum, *All the Way Down*, p. 34.

37. Craig Castleman, *Getting Up: Subway Graffiti in New York* (Cambridge, Mass.: MIT Press, 1982), especially chapter 5; and Jeff Ferrell, "The World Politics

of Wall Painting," in *Cultural Criminology*, ed. Jeff Ferrell and Clinton R. Sanders (Boston: Northeastern University Press, 1995), p. 278.

38. Salisbury, *Shook-Up Generation*, p. 4.

39. Herbert Kohl, "Names, Graffiti, and Culture," in *Rappin' and Stylin' Out: Communication in Urban Black America*, ed. Thomas Kochman (Urbana: University of Illinois Press, 1972), pp. 109–33; and Folb, *Runnin' down some lines*, pp. 81–83.

40. David Ley, *The Black Inner City as Frontier Outpost: Images and Behavior of a Philadelphia Neighborhood* (Washington, D.C.: Association of American Geographers, 1974), pp. 217–19.

41. Here I differ from subculturalists such as Albert K. Cohen, *Delinquent Boys: The Culture of the Gang* (Glencoe, Ill.: The Free Press, 1955).

42. As noted in chapter 3, East Harlem had five hundred candy stores. See Frederic M. Thrasher, "Final Report on the Jefferson Park Branch of the Boys' Club of New York," October 21, 1935, pp. 217–18, Bureau of Social Hygiene Papers, unnumbered folder, reel 7, Rockefeller Archives.

43. Joyeaux, *Out of the Burning*, pp. 144–46; New York City Youth Board, *Reaching the Fighting Gang*, pp. 29–30; Marshall, "Fighting Gang," p. 71; Hanson, *Rebels in the Streets*, pp. 24–25; and *Brooklyn Eagle*, March 2, 1949. Pool halls played similar functions for older youths.

44. New York City Youth Board, *Reaching the Fighting Gang*, pp. 29–30; Interview with RG, April 23, 1993; and Rettig et al., *Manny*, p. 17.

45. *Brooklyn Eagle*, April 28–29, 1948, April 10, 1949. See Irving Shulman, *The Amboy Dukes* (New York: Avon, 1949); and Wenzell Brown, *Monkey on My Back* (New York: Greenberg, 1953) for fictionalized accounts. For a modern one, see William Gale, *The Compound* (New York: Rawson Associates Publishers, 1977).

46. Cheryl Lynn Greenberg, *"Or Does It Explode?" Black Harlem in the Great Depression* (New York: Oxford University Press, 1991), p. 30.

47. New York City Youth Board, *Reaching the Fighting Gang*, pp. 74–75; Marshall, "Fighting Gang," pp. 286–88; and Joyeaux, *Out of the Burning*, pp. 210–12.

48. *Brooklyn Eagle*, April 12–13, 1949; Wakefield, "Gang That Went Good," p. 40; *New York Times*, March 10, 1958; and Riccio and Slocum, *All the Way Down*, p. 69.

49. Interview with JT, December 28, 1992; and Kenneth E. Marshall, "Milton Clark: Chapters from the Official and Unofficial Biography of a Delinquent Boy," pp. 52–53, unpublished paper, Box 3, Kenneth Marshall Papers, Schomburg Center.

50. See, for example, Felix M. Padilla, *The Gang as an American Enterprise* (New Brunswick, N.J.: Rutgers University Press, 1992), pp. 55–56.

51. Helen Parkhurst, *Undertow: The Story of a Boy Called Tony* (New York: Farrar, Straus, and Company, 1963), p. 49.

52. Cruz, *Run, Baby, Run*, p. 41.

53. Interview with JT, December 28, 1992.

54. DiMucci, *The Wanderer*, pp. 46–47; Rettig et al., *Manny*, p. 19; and Thomas, *Down These Mean Streets*, p. 50. See Martin Sanchez Jankowski, *Islands in the Street: Gangs and American Urban Society* (Berkeley: University of California Press, 1991), p. 12, for his initiation into the gangs he studied.

55. Harlan Ellison, *Memos from Purgatory* (New York: Pyramid Books, 1961), p. 53.

56. Gale, *The Compound*, pp. 52–54.

57. DiMucci, *The Wanderer*, p. 50.

58. Salisbury, *Shook-Up Generation*, pp. 46, 171; Keiser, *Vice Lords*, pp. 52–55; *New York World Telegram*, April 11, 1949; and Joyeaux, *Out of the Burning*, p. 158.

59. Rettig et al., *Manny*, pp. 20–22; New York City Youth Board, *Reaching the Fighting Gang*, pp. 35–36; and Joyeaux, *Out of the Burning*, p. 103.

60. Clarence Norman, Sr., is quoted in Myrna Katz Frommer and Harvey Frommer, *It Happened in Brooklyn: An Oral History of Growing Up in the Borough in the 1940s, 1950s, and 1960s* (New York: Harcourt, Brace and Company, 1993), p. 215; Francis A. J. Ianni, *Black Mafia: Ethnic Succession in Organized Crime* (New York: Simon and Schuster, 1974), pp. 147–48; *Brooklyn Eagle*, June 3, 1950; and *New York Times*, June 4, 1950, May 11, 1961.

61. New York City Youth Board, *Reaching the Fighting Gang*, pp. 98–99; 102–5; Yablonsky, *The Violent Gang*, pp. 94–98; and Jess Stearn, *The Wasted Years* (Garden City, N.Y.: Doubleday, 1959), pp. 107–8.

62. DiMucci, *The Wanderer*, p. 47; Joyeaux, *Out of the Burning*, p. 243; New York City Youth Board, *Reaching the Fighting Gang*, pp. 35–36, 94–95; and Interview with ES, October 20, 1992.

63. Riccio, Oral History, pp. 48, 58–59. On different forms of gang organization, see Jankowski, *Islands in the Street*.

64. Interview with RG, April 23, 1993.

65. C. Kilmer Myers, *Light the Dark Streets* (Garden City, N.Y.: Doubleday, 1961), p. 108.

66. On differences between white and African-American groups, see William Labov, "Rules for ritual insults," in *Rappin' and Stylin' Out*, pp. 287–88; Riccio, Oral History, pp. 170–71; Roger D. Abrahams, "Playing the Dozens," *Journal of American Folklore* 75 (1962): 209–20; and Folb, *Runnin' down some lines*, pp. 92–93.

67. Marshall, "Fighting Gang," p. 90.

68. Riccio, Oral History, pp. 171–72.

69. Brown, *Manchild*, p. 56.

70. Marshall, "Fighting Gang," p. 88; Folb, *Runnin' down some lines*, p. 93; and Lawrence W. Levine, *Black Culture and Black Consciousness: Afro-American Folk*

*Thought from Slavery to Freedom* (New York: Oxford University Press, 1977), pp. 344–58.

71. Roger D. Abrahams, "Joking: the training of the man of words in talking broad," in *Rappin' and Stylin' Out*, pp. 216–22; and Majors and Billson, *Cool Pose*, pp. 91–102.

72. Thomas Kochman, "Toward an ethnography of black American speech behavior," in *Rappin' and Stylin' Out*, pp. 258–61; and Folb, *Runnin' down some lines*, pp. 92–99.

73. Roger D. Abrahams, *Deep Down in the Jungle . . . Negro Narrative Folklore from the Streets of Philadelphia* (Hatboro, Penn.: Folklore Associates, 1964), pp. 32–34, emphasizes the need of an adolescent male to break away from the matrifocal black family by means of the dozens.

CHAPTER SIX. LEAVING THE GANG

1. See Ruth Horowitz, *Honor and the American Dream: Culture and Identity in a Chicano Community* (New Brunswick, N.J.: Rutgers University Press, 1983), pp. 177–97; and Joan W. Moore, *Going down to the Barrio: Homeboys and Homegirls in Change* (Philadelphia: Temple University Press, 1991), pp. 123–30. Unlike Moore, I distinguish between street life and gang membership.

2. Kenneth E. Marshall, "The Fighting Gang in Transition: A Study of the Structure and Functions of the Urban Adolescent Fighting Gang and an Analysis of Functionally Equivalent Deviant Group Modes" (Ed.D. diss., New York University, 1968), pp. 79–81, 119–20, 158, 276; Carl Joyeaux, Jr. [pseud.], *Out of the Burning: The Story of a Boy Gang Leader* (New York: Crown Publishers, 1960), p. 246; and Gertrude Samuels, "Death of a Youth Worker," *Saturday Evening Post* 236 (April 6, 1963): 75.

3. Dan Wakefield, "The Gang That Went Good," *Harper's* 216 (June 1958): 36–43; Norman Laden, "This Was a Gang," *New York Herald Tribune* September 13, 1959; Bruce Kenrick, *Come Out the Wilderness: The Story of East Harlem Protestant Parish* (New York: Harper and Brothers, 1962), pp. 216–17; and Interviews with Ramon Diaz, March 8, 1993, Norman Eddy, October 20, 1992, and WC, October 21, 1992.

4. Nicky Cruz, *Run, Baby, Run* (Plainfield, N.J.: Logos Books, 1969).

5. Malcolm W. Klein, *Street Gangs and Street Workers* (Englewood Cliffs, N.J.: Prentice-Hall, 1971); New York City Youth Board, *Reaching the Fighting Gang* (New York: New York City Youth Board, 1960), pp. 27–28; and Saul Bernstein, *Youth on the Streets: Work with Alienated Youth Groups* (New York: Association Press, 1964). See Dion DiMucci with Davin Seay, *The Wanderer: Dion's Story*

(New York: Beech Tree Books, 1988), p. 47; and the interview with Anthony Gourdine in Bruce Pollock, *When Rock Was Young: A Nostalgic Review of the Top 40 Era* (New York: Holt, Rinehart and Winston, 1981), p. 174. Mark S. Fleisher, *Beggars and Thieves: Lives of Urban Street Criminals* (Madison: University of Wisconsin Press, 1995), p. 115, takes peripheral membership as evidence of even greater marginality.

6. Horowitz, *Honor and the American Dream*, pp. 179–80.

7. Klein, *Street Gangs and Street Workers*, pp. 70–76.

8. Horowitz, *Honor and the American Dream*, p. 99; and Felix M. Padilla, *The Gang as an American Enterprise* (New Brunswick, N.J.: Rutgers University Press, 1992), pp. 56–57.

9. Cruz, *Run, Baby, Run*, p. 34. This is apparent in contemporary gangs as well. See, for example, Sanyika Shakur, *Monster: The Autobiography of an L.A. Gang Member* (New York: Penguin Books, 1993).

10. On "turning points," see Robert J. Sampson and John H. Laub, *Crime in the Making: Pathways and Turning Points through Life* (Cambridge, Mass.: Harvard University Press, 1993).

11. Claude Brown, *Manchild in the Promised Land* (New York: Penguin Books, 1965), pp. 127, 179, 271; Marshall, "Fighting Gang," pp. 309–10; and Richard P. Rettig, Manual J. Torres, and Gerald R. Garrett, *Manny: A Criminal Addict's Story* (Boston: Houghton Mifflin, 1977), p. 29.

12. Interview with JT, December 28, 1992; Darla Milne, *Second Chance: The Israel Narvaez Story* (Wheaton, Ill.: Living Books, 1979), p. 211; and Sampson and Laub, *Crime in the Making*, pp. 223–24.

13. Cruz, *Run, Baby, Run*, pp. 81–85, quotation, pp. 84–85.

14. Joyeaux, *Out of the Burning*, pp. 240–43.

15. Georgie quoted in *Palante: Young Lords Party*, ed. Michael Abramson (New York: McGraw-Hill, 1971), p. 35.

16. David Wilkerson, *The Cross and the Switchblade* (New York: Bernard Geis Associates, 1963); and Milne, *Second Chance*.

17. Interview with John Nolan, March 7, 1994; Cruz, *Run, Baby, Run*; and Sonny Arguinzoni, *Sonny* (La Puente, Calif.: Victory Outreach Publications, 1987). For a history of the Youth Board and its descendant, the Youth Services Administration, see Kurt Sonnenfeld, "Changing Perspectives on Youth Services as Seen through the Historical Development of the New York City Youth Board" (Ed.D. diss., Teacher's College, Columbia University, 1995).

18. Sampson and Laub, *Crime in the Making*, chapter 7.

19. Joshua B. Freeman, "Hardhats: Construction Workers, Manliness, and the 1970 Pro-War Demonstrations," *Journal of Social History* 26 (Summer 1993): 725–44.

20. Piri Thomas, *Savior, Savior, Hold My Hand* (Garden City, N.Y.: Doubleday, 1972), pp. 46–48; and Interviews with RG, May 5, 1993, and TS, July 27, 1993. On the importance of ethnic niches, see Roger Waldinger, *Still the Promised City? African Americans and New Immigrants in Postindustrial New York* (Cambridge, Mass.: Harvard University Press, 1996).

21. Georgie, in *Palante*, p. 42; and interview with AC, December 30, 1992.

22. Interviews with TS, July 27, 1993, and RG, May 5, 1993.

23. Interview with JC, March 10, 1993.

24. Moore, *Going down to the Barrio*, p. 128, in her sample of male gang members found that 11 percent enlisted in the military. See also Horowitz, *Honor and the American Dream*, pp. 180–81; and Sampson and Laub, *Crime in the Making*, pp. 219, 222–23.

25. Dharuba, in *Look for Me in the Whirlwind: The Collective Autobiography of the New York 21* (New York: Random House, 1971), p. 191; *New York Journal American*, April 21, 1949; and Interview with Harrison Lightfoot, May 1, 1994.

26. Marshall, "Fighting Gang," pp. 64, 82, 352; Joyeaux, *Out of the Burning*, p. 249; and Interview with NL, March 9, 1993.

27. Interviews with MR, December 23, 1996 and SN, December 22, 1993. Horowitz found the same thing in Chicago. See *Honor and the American Dream*, pp. 180–81.

28. Interview with ES, October 20, 1992.

29. Craig M. Cameron, *American Samurai: Myth, Imagination, and the Conduct of Battle in the First Marine Division, 1941–1951* (Cambridge: Cambridge University Press, 1994), pp. 64–66; W. Wayne Eisenhart, "You Can't Hack It Little Girl: A Discussion of the Covert Psychological Agenda of Modern Combat Training," *Journal of Social Issues* 31 (1975): 13–23; Helen Michalowski, "The Army Will Make a 'Man' Out of You," in *Reweaving the Web of Life: Feminism and Nonviolence*, ed. Pam McAllister (Philadelphia: New Society Publishers, 1982), pp. 326–36; Robert Jay Lifton, *Home from the War* (New York: Simon and Schuster, 1972), pp. 241–43; and Christian G. Appy, *Working-Class War: American Combat Soldiers and Vietnam* (Chapel Hill: University of North Carolina Press, 1993). Military manliness is not just an artifact of contemporary life; see Donald J. Mrozek, "The Habit of Victory: The American Military and the Cult of Manliness," in *Manliness and Morality: Middle-Class Masculinity in Britain and America, 1800–1940*, ed. J. A. Mangan and James Walvin (New York: St. Martin's Press, 1987), pp. 220–39.

30. Kenneth Marshall, "Notes on a Conference Held with Mr. Linda and Mr. Nottage of the Home Services Bureau," August 3, 1959, Kenneth Marshall Papers, Box 1, Schomburg Center for Research in Black Culture, New York Public Library (hereafter Schomburg Center). On nineteenth-century reform schools and the military, see John Clark Wirkkala, "Juvenile Delinquency and Reform in Nineteenth-Century Massachusetts: The Formative Era in State Care, 1846–

1879," (Ph.D. diss., Clark University, 1973). On military manpower needs, See George Q. Flynn, *The Draft, 1940–1973* (Lawrence: University Press of Kansas, 1993), pp. 138–39.

31. Frederic M. Thrasher, *The Gang: A Study of 1,313 Gangs in Chicago*, rev. ed. (Chicago: University of Chicago Press, 1963).

32. Teddy, in David Courtwright, Herman Joseph, and Don Des Jarlais, *Addicts Who Survived: An Oral History of Narcotic Use in America, 1923–1965* (Knoxville: University of Tennessee Press, 1989), pp. 49–50.

33. Vincent Riccio, Oral History, Columbia University Oral History Collection, part 2, pp. 58–59; Francis A. J. Ianni, *Black Mafia: Ethnic Succession in Organized Crime* (New York: Simon and Schuster, 1974), pp. 123–57, 206–14; and New York City Youth Board, *Reaching the Fighting Gang*, pp. 17, 20, 26.

34. Daniel Bell, "Crime as an American Way of Life: A Queer Ladder of Social Mobility," in *The End of Ideology*, ed. Daniel Bell (Glencoe, Ill.: The Free Press, 1960), pp. 115–36; and Interview with WC, October 21, 1992.

35. Robert Anthony Orsi, *The Madonna of 115th Street: Faith and Community in Italian Harlem, 1880–1950* (New Haven: Yale University Press, 1985), pp. 103–4; Francis A. J. Ianni, *A Family Business: Kinship and Social Control in Organized Crime* (New York: Russell Sage Foundation, 1972); and Humbert S. Nelli, *The Business of Crime: Italians and Syndicate Crime in the United States* (New York: Oxford University Press, 1976). Ralph Salerno's interview is in Courtwright et al., *Addicts Who Survived*, pp. 195–206, quotation, p. 202.

36. Interviews with RG, April 23, 1993, JC, March 9, 1993, TS, July 27, 1993. Richard A. Cloward and Lloyd E. Ohlin, *Delinquency and Opportunity: A Theory of Delinquent Gangs* (Glencoe, Ill.: The Free Press, 1960) argue that such a neighborhood structure should produce "criminal" rather than "conflict" gangs, but this is not supported by the evidence.

37. Jerry Della Famina and Charles Sopkin, *An Italian Grows in Brooklyn* (Boston: Little, Brown and Company, 1978), p. 44; Irving Spergel, *Racketville, Slumtown, Haulburg* (Chicago: University of Chicago Press, 1964); New York City Youth Board, *Reaching the Fighting Gang*, p. 58; Helen Parkhurst, *Undertow: The Story of a Boy Called Tony* (New York: Farrar, Straus and Company, 1963); and Riccio, Oral History, pp. 3, 225.

38. Interviews with Norman Eddy, October 20, 1992; JC, March 9, 1993, NL, March 9, 1993; and Ianni, *Black Mafia*, pp. 210–14; quotation, p. 211. Partiality toward whites occurred in the juvenile court as well; see Riccio, Oral History, p. 60.

39. On African-American organized crime, see Irma Watkins-Owens, *Blood Relations: Caribbean Immigrants and the Harlem Community, 1900–1930* (Bloomington: Indiana University Press, 1996), chapter 9.

40. Ianni, *Black Mafia*, pp. 72–104, 123–57, and "Harold Robinson" quoted on p. 149.

41. Interview with DS, March 7, 1994.

42. Ianni, *Black Mafia*, p. 290; Brown, *Manchild*, passim; and Fleisher, *Beggars and Thieves*, chapter 4.

43. Fleisher, *Beggars and Thieves*, pp. 143–46; and Philippe Bourgois, *In Search of Respect: Selling Crack in El Barrio* (Cambridge: Cambridge University Press, 1995), pp. 28–29.

44. See, for example, the series of case studies in New York City Youth Board (hereafter NYCYB), "Annual Review, 1951–1952," Brooklyn Council for Social Planning Papers, Brooklyn Public Library (hereafter BCSP); Isidor Chein, Donald L. Gerard, Robert S. Lee, and Eva Rosenfeld, with Daniel M. Wilner, *The Road to H: Narcotics, Delinquency, and Social Policy* (New York: Basic Books, 1964), pp. 172–74, 177–88; and Moore, *Going down to the Barrio*, p. 52.

45. Nestor Llamas, "The Social Processes of a Street Gang," *Journal of the Hillside Hospital* 13 (July–October 1964): 209; Walter Bernstein, "The Cherubs Are Rumbling," *New Yorker* 33 (September 21, 1957): 128; Vincent Riccio and Bill Slocum, *All the Way Down: The Violent Underworld of Street Gangs* (New York: Simon and Schuster, 1962), p. 99; Eugene Kinkead, "Sixteen," *New Yorker* 27 (November 10, 1951): 46, 53; Ianni, *Black Mafia*, pp. 154, 169; New York City Youth Board, *Reaching the Teen-Age Addict: A Study of Street Work with a Group of Adolescent Users* (New York: New York City Youth Board, c. 1961), p. 9; Warren Miller, *The Cool World* (Boston: Little, Brown and Company, 1959), pp. 43–44; Wenzell Brown, *Monkey on My Back* (New York: Greenberg, 1953), p. 126; Chein et al., *Road to H*, pp. 180–81; and Edward Preble and John J. Casey, "Taking Care of Business—The Heroin User's Life on the Street," *The International Journal of the Addictions* 4 (March 1969): 1–24.

46. Joseph A. Fernandez with John Underwood, *Tales Out of School: Joseph Fernandez's Crusade to Rescue American Education* (Boston: Little, Brown and Company, 1993), p. 40; and Spergel, *Racketville*, Mannie quoted on p. 54. On addicts combining work with heroin use, see Courtwright et al., *Addicts Who Survived*, pp. 213–30.

47. Interviews with RG, April 23, 1993, and TS, July 27, 1993; Daniel Belknap Process Records, July 28, 1952, Kenneth Marshall Papers, Box 1, Schomburg Center; and Moore, *Going down to the Barrio*, p. 66.

48. Brown, *Manchild*, pp. 103–4, 107–8, quotation, p. 153; and Chein et al., *Road to H*, pp., 11–12.

49. Paul L. Crawford, Daniel I. Malamud, and James R. Dumpson, *Working with Teen-Age Gangs: A Report on the Central Harlem Street Clubs Project* (New York:

Welfare Council of New York City, 1950), p. 17; and DiMucci, *The Wanderer*, p. 51.

50. Rettig et al., *Manny*, p. 36; and Llamas, "Social Processes of a Street Gang," p. 206. Cloward and Ohlin saw "retreatist" groups as a third, competing form of deviant response (after conflict and criminal gangs) to the lack of opportunity; see Cloward and Ohlin, *Delinquency and Opportunity*. While there were distinct subcultures, individuals moved from one to the other.

51. This admittedly crude estimate comes from my interviews; several interviewees mentioned that one-third of their peers died, one-third went to jail or became addicts, and one-third "made it." Moore, in *Going down to the Barrio*, pp. 124–30, concluded that about 40 percent became "squares."

52. Felipe Luciano, in *Palante*, p. 32; Riccio, Oral History, pp. 222–24; Irving Louis Horowitz, *Daydreams and Nightmares: Reflections on a Harlem Childhood* (Jackson: University Press of Mississippi, 1990), p. 15; and Joyeaux, *Out of the Burning*, p. 254.

53. Interviews with RG, April 23, 1993, TS, July 27, 1993, JT, December 28, 1992, and JG, May 24, 1994.

54. My informants agreed to be interviewed after having been contacted through the auspices of someone they knew; three individuals declined to be interviewed. The Reverend Norman Eddy introduced me to gang members he had worked with in East Harlem; Kurt Sonnenfeld provided the names of former Youth Board workers, five of whom had been gang members; the Reverend David Wilkerson introduced me to Nicky Cruz and Sonny Arguinzoni; and Dan Murrow gave me the names of several of the Fordham Baldies with whom he had worked. The three college professors volunteered to be interviewed after learning of my project. All told I interviewed twenty former gang members, whose membership in gangs covered the period from the late 1930s to the late 1960s. Obviously this is not a sample that is "representative" in a social scientific sense, but I have compared my interviews to field notes of gang workers, autobiographies, publications of the Youth Board, contemporary studies of gangs, as well as other sources, and I have no reason to doubt their veracity.

55. Joyeaux, *Out of the Burning*, p. 240.

## Chapter Seven. Intervening in Gangs

1. Vincent Riccio and Bill Slocum, *All the Way Down: The Violent Underworld of Street Gangs* (New York: Simon and Schuster, 1962), p. 153.

2. Ernest Burgess, Joseph Lohman, and Clifford Shaw, "The Chicago Area Project," National Probation Association, *Yearbook* (1937): 8–28; Solomon Ko-

brin, "The Chicago Area Project—A 25-Year Assessment," *The Annals of the American Academy of Political and Social Science* (March 1959): 19–29; and Steven Schlossman and Michael Sedlak, *The Chicago Area Project Revisited* (Santa Monica: The Rand Corporation, 1983).

3. James Russell Dumpson, "A Community Approach to Juvenile Delinquency: The Central Harlem Street Clubs Project," paper presented at the National Conference of Social Work, Cleveland, Ohio, June 14, 1949, pp. 4–5, 11, 13–14; "Youth Needs Help: Interim Report of the Central Harlem Street Clubs Project," Brooklyn Council for Social Planning Papers, Brooklyn Public Library (hereafter BCSP) pp. 4–6, 9; Paul L. Crawford, Daniel I. Malamud, and James R. Dumpson, *Working with Teen-Age Gangs: A Report on the Central Harlem Street Clubs Project* (New York: Welfare Council of New York City, 1950), pp. 39–49. 55, 58, 77–80, 123–26; and Robert Rice, "Profile: Hugh K. Johnson," *New Yorker*, December 23, 1961, p. 37.

4. Ralph W. Whelan, "Philosophy and Development of the Youth Board Program," in *Reaching the Unreached: Fundamental Aspects of the Program of the New York City Youth Board*, ed. Sylvan S. Furman (New York: New York City Youth Board, 1952), p. 2; James E. McCarthy and Joseph S. Barbaro, "Re-directing Teen-Age Gangs," in *Reaching the Unreached*, pp. 100–03; New York City Youth Board (NYCYB), "Annual Review, 1951–1952," pp. 5–7, BCSP; and Thomas M. Gannon, S.J., "Dimensions of Current Gang Delinquency," *Journal of Research in Crime and Delinquency* 4 (January 1967): 119–31.

5. Whelan, "Philosophy and Development of the Youth Board Program," pp. 5–6; Alice Overton, "Aggressive Casework," in *Reaching the Unreached*, pp. 51–61.

6. Riccio and Slocum, *All the Way Down*, p. 34; and Sam Kolman [pseud.], *The Royal Vultures* (New York: Permabooks, 1958), p. 28.

7. Dumpson, "Community Approach," pp. 8–9.

8. Richard E. Brotman, "An Analysis of Psychodynamic Processes of Change in Small Group Behavior in a Teen-Age Gang" (Ph.D. diss., New York University, 1955), pp. 112–25.

9. NYCYB, "Annual Review, 1951–1952," pp. 13–15, 46, 70, 80, 83–85, 97–98, 105, quotation, p. 46; and Brotman, "Psychodynamic Processes of Change," pp. 126–28.

10. Brotman, "Psychodynamic Processes of Change," pp. 128–40, 152–54.

11. McCarthy and Barbaro, "Re-directing Teen-Age Gangs," pp. 114–16.

12. Steve Klein, "Record Material on the Spanish Kings—A Puerto Rican Youth Gang" (New York: Mobilization for Youth, 1963), pp. 3, 8, 23, 41.

13. Lewis Yablonsky, *The Violent Gang*, rev. ed. (New York: Penguin Books, 1970), quotation p. 77. For an account of mediation, see ibid., pp. 93–98.

14. Kitty Hanson, *Rebels in the Streets: The Story of New York's Girl Gangs* (Englewood Cliffs, N.J.: Prentice-Hall, 1964), p. 12; Malcolm W. Klein, *Street Gangs and Street Workers* (Englewood Cliffs, N.J.: Prentice-Hall, 1971), pp. 136–39; and Walter B. Miller, "The Impact of a 'Total Community' Delinquency Control Project," *Social Problems* 10 (Fall 1962): 168–91.

15. Crawford et al., *Working with Teen-Age Gangs*, pp. 30, 34; Hans W. Mattick and Nathan J. Caplan, "Stake Animals, Loud-Talking, and Leadership in Do-Nothing and Do-Something Situations," in *Juvenile Gangs in Context: Theory, Research, and Action*, ed. Malcolm W. Klein and Barbara G. Meyerhoff (Englewood Cliffs, N.J.: Prentice-Hall, 1967), 106–19.

16. Interview with John Nolan, March 7, 1994; and Gertrude Samuels, "Death of a Youth Worker," *Saturday Evening Post* 236 (April 6, 1963): 74–76.

17. Marshall, "Fighting Gang," p. 105; and Klein, "Spanish Kings," p. 149.

18. "Report of the Street Club Project," Box 9, Folder: Manhattanville Community Center's Minutes, etc., 1948–1962, Harry Shulman Memorabilia, City College of New York (hereafter Shulman Papers, CCNY).

19. Quotation from "Report of the Street Club Project," p. 8, and "Report of the Teen-Age Division for Program Year 1953–1954," p. 3, Box 9, Folder: Manhattanville Center's Minutes, etc., 1948–1962, both in Shulman Papers, CCNY.

20. *New York Times*, August 8, 1960, October 9, 1960.

21. Interview with Dan Murrow, February 28, 1993; *New York Times*, December 24, 1959; Interview with JT, December 28, 1992; "Interest of Friend's Neighborhood Group in East Harlem Youth Council," Memo from Dan and Hope Murrow to Robert Gilmore et al., January 25, 1960, Folder: Administration, Regional Offices—Middle Atlantic—NY American Section Files, 1960, American Friends Service Committee (AFSC) Archives; and Richard Cloward, "The Friends Neighborhood Group: A Description and Informal Evaluation," Folder: Youth Services Division, Administration, Projects, East Harlem, 1967, AFSC Archives.

22. The Brownsville Boys Club was an exception, but as Gerald Sorin has shown, the club remained remarkably independent of adult control. See Gerald Sorin, *The Nurturing Neighborhood: The Brownsville Boys Club and Jewish Community in Urban America, 1940–1990* (New York: New York University Press, 1990).

23. Special LENA Gang Leadership Project, "Final Draft," Box 76, Folder 9, Henry Street Settlement Records, Social Welfare History Archives, University of Minnesota (hereafter SWHA); Mary Conway Kohler, "A Community Mobilizes to Combat Delinquency," Box 77, Folder 7, Henry Street Settlement Records, SWHA; Naomi Barko, "LENA and the 45 Gangs," *The Reporter* 23 (September

29, 1960): 26–28; C. Kilmer Myers, *Light the Dark Streets* (Garden City, N.Y.: Doubleday, 1961), pp. 29, 79–80, 110; and Helen Hall, *Unfinished Business in Neighborhood and Nation* (New York: Macmillan, 1971), pp. 222–27.

24. Rose Albert Porter, "Neighbors, Neighborhoods, and LENA," pp. 107–19, Box 77, Folder 5, Henry Street Settlement Records, SWHA; and *New York Times*, August 10–15, 1956.

25. Porter, "Neighbors, Neighborhoods, and LENA," pp. 130–42; and *New York Times*, August 16, 1956.

26. Vincent Riccio, Oral History, Columbia University Oral History Collection, Part II, pp. 60, 145, 150; Richard P. Rettig, Manual J. Torres, and Gerald R. Garrett, *Manny: A Criminal Addict's Story* (Boston: Houghton Mifflin, 1977), p. 22; and Interview with ES, October 10, 1992.

27. Porter, "Neighbors, Neighborhoods, and LENA," pp. 143–46. Yablonsky, *The Violent Gang* and Klein, *Street Gangs and Street Workers* are generally critical of gang intervention and mediation projects. As a trained mediator, I am obviously sympathetic to mediation's goals and methods.

28. "Interim Report on Special Gang Case Work Project," November 15, 1956, Box 76, Folder 9, Henry Street Settlement Records, SWHA.

29. Notes, Box 8, Folder "Henry Street Gangs," Ralph Tefferteller Papers, SWHA; and *Daily News*, October 13, 1956. See in particular "The Gangs at Peace," *New York Post*, August 11, 1957.

30. See, for example, "The War That Did Not Take Place," *Youth Board News* 7 (September 1955): 3–5.

31. *Daily News*, August 24, 1959; *New York Mirror*, August 24–25, 1959, August 28, 1959, September 10, 1959; *New York Post*, August 24, 1959; *New York Journal American*, August 24, 1959, August 28, 1959, November 8–11, 1959; and *New York Herald Tribune*, August 24–25, 1959.

32. "Notes on Sportsmen Dragon Conflict," January 1, 1959, "Report," May 27, 1959, and "Summer Report, 1959," all in Box 8, Folder "Henry Street Gangs," Ralph Tefferteller Papers, SWHA.

33. Kohler, "A Community Mobilizes to Combat Delinquency," p. 33; *New York Journal American*, August 28, 1959; Interview with SN, December 22, 1993; *Daily News*, August 29, 1959; and *New York Times*, August 29, 1959.

34. Henry Street Settlement Studies, "Pre-Delinquent Gang Project Annual Report," March 1959, pp. 43–60, quote p. 55, Henry Street Settlement Records, Box 66, Folder 8, SWHA.

35. Henry Street Settlement Studies, "Pre-Delinquent Gang Project Annual Report," March 1959, pp. 3, 63–72, quotations, pp. 64, 66, 71; and Hall, *Unfinished Business*, pp. 227–28.

36. For an evaluation of CAP and its successes, see Steven Schlossman, Gail Zellman, and Richard Shavelson, with Michael Sedlak and Jane Cobb, *Delinquency Prevention in South Chicago* (Santa Monica: Rand Corporation, 1984).

37. Daniel P. Moynihan, *Maximum Feasible Misunderstanding: Community Action in the War on Poverty* (New York: The Free Press, 1969); Herbert Krosney, *Beyond Welfare: Poverty in the Supercity* (New York: Holt, Rinehart and Winston, 1966); Donald Knapp and Kenneth Polk, *Scouting the War on Poverty: Social Reform Politics in the Kennedy Administration* (Lexington, Mass.: Lexington Books, 1971); Joseph H. Helfgot, *Professional Reforming: Mobilization for Youth and the Failure of Social Science* (Lexington, Mass.: Lexington Books, 1981), especially chapter 2; and Allen J. Matusow, *The Unraveling of America: A History of Liberalism in the 1960s* (New York: Harper and Row, 1984). See the announcement in the *New York Times*, June 1, 1962, p. 1.

38. Mobilization for Youth (hereafter MFY), *A Proposal for the Prevention and Control of Delinquency by Expanding Opportunities* (New York: Mobilization for Youth, 1961); Francis Fox Piven, "Politics and Planning: Mobilization as a Model," in *Justice and the Law in the Mobilization for Youth Experience*, ed. Harold H. Weissman (New York: Association Press, 1969), pp. 167–91; idem, "The Demonstration Project: A Federal Strategy for Local Change," in *Community Action against Poverty: Readings from the Mobilization Experience*, ed. George A. Brager and Francis P. Purcell (New Haven: College and University Press, 1967), pp. 83–103; Helfgot, *Professional Reforming*, pp. 24–28; Alice O'Connor, "Community Action, Urban Reform, and the Fight against Poverty: The Ford Foundation's Gray Areas Program," *Journal of Urban History* 22 (July 1996): 586–625.

39. Beverly Luther, "Overview of Group Services," in *Individual and Group Services in the Mobilization for Youth Experience*, ed. Harold H. Weissman (New York: Association Press, 1969), pp. 109–14; and MFY, *Proposal*, pp. 392–420.

40. Beverly Luther, "Group Service Programs and their Effect on Delinquents," in *Individual and Group Services*, pp. 117–19; Harold H. Weissman, "Overview of Employment Opportunities," in *Employment and Educational Services in the Mobilization for Youth Experience*, ed. Harold H. Weissman (New York: Association Press, 1969), pp. 25–34.

41. Luther, "Overview of Group Services," pp. 112–13; idem, "Group Service Programs," pp. 128–32; and idem, "Programs for the Adolescent Addict," in *Individual and Group Services*, p. 138.

42. Krosney, *Beyond Welfare*, pp. 22–25; Helfgot, *Professional Reforming*, pp. 72–81; and Beverly Luther, "Negro Youth and Social Action," in *Individual and Group Services*, pp. 151–61. On tension between community organizing and local agencies, see Schlossman and Sedlak, *Chicago Area Project Revisited*, pp. 104–9.

43. Schlossman and Sedlak, *Chicago Area Project Revisited*, pp. 101–2; Knapp and Polk, *Scouting the War on Poverty*, pp. 157–67; and Sanford D. Horwitt, *Let Them Call Me Rebel: Saul Alinsky—His Life and Legacy* (New York: Knopf, 1989).

44. Helfgot, *Professional Reforming*, pp. 143–44; Knapp and Polk, *Scouting the War on Poverty*, pp. 32–42, 157–67; Krosney, *Beyond Welfare*, pp. 22–32; Moynihan, *Maximum Feasible Misunderstanding*, pp. 122–24; and Alfred Fried, "The Attack on Mobilization," in *Community Development in the Mobilization for Youth Experience*, ed. Harold H. Weissman (New York: Association Press, 1969), pp. 137–62.

45. Luther, "Overview of Group Services," pp. 112–13; idem, "Group Service Programs," pp. 128–32; and idem, "Programs for the Adolescent Addict," p. 138.

46. Hall is quoted in Jeremy Larner and Ralph Tefferteller, *The Addict in the Street* (New York: Grove Press, 1964), p. 26. See also Hall, *Unfinished Business*, p. 245.


CHAPTER EIGHT. DRUGS, POLITICS, AND GANGS

1. David Wilkerson, *Twelve Angels from Hell* (Westwood, N.J.: Fleming H. Revell, 1965), p. 105.

2. *New York Times*, September 1, 1959, September 22, 1960, June 29, 1961, January 19, 1962, June 18, 1962, October 7, 1963, July 31, 1964, October 9, 1965, June 26, 1966; Gertrude Samuels, "They No Longer 'Bop,' They 'Jap,' " *New York Times Magazine*, March 7, 1965, pp. 40ff; Press Release, October 9, 1965, Subject Files: Juvenile Delinquency, 1961–1964, Box 157, Folder: Juvenile Delinquency 1965, Mayor Robert F. Wagner Papers, New York City Municipal Archives (hereafter NYCMA).

3. Thomas M. Gannon, S.J., "Emergence of the 'Defensive' Gang," *Federal Probation* 30 (December 1966): 44–48; and idem, "Dimensions of Current Gang Delinquency," *Journal of Research in Crime and Delinquency* 4 (January 1967): 119–31.

4. See, for example, Harlan Ellison, *Memos from Purgatory* (New York: Pyramid Books, 1961), pp. 106–12; Nicky Cruz, *Run, Baby, Run* (Plainfield, N.J.: Logos Books, 1969), pp. 49–50; Francis A. J. Ianni, *Black Mafia: Ethnic Succession in Organized Crime* (New York: Simon and Schuster, 1974), pp. 147–48; *New York World Telegram*, April 13, 1949; *Brooklyn Eagle*, May 14, 1950, May 16, 1950, June 3, 1950, June 11, 1953; and *New York Times*, May 11, 1961.

5. *New York Times*, June 20, 1960, January 20, 1962, June 18, 1962, June 9, 1964; Samuels, "They No Longer 'Bop' "; and Darla Milne, *Second Chance: The Israel Narvaez Story* (Wheaton, Ill.: Living Books, 1979), pp. 58–59.

6. Harlem Youth Opportunities Unlimited, *Youth in the Ghetto: A Study of the Consequences of Powerlessness and a Blueprint for Change* (New York: Harlem Youth Opportunities Unlimited, 1964), p. 141; Beverly Luther, "Group Service Programs and Their Effect on Delinquents," in *Individual and Group Services in the Mobilization for Youth Experience*, ed. Harold H. Weissman (New York: Association Press, 1969), pp. 115–35; and Kenneth E. Marshall, "The Fighting Gang in Transition: A Study of the Structure and Functions of the Urban Adolescent Fighting Gang and an Analysis of Functionally Equivalent Deviant Group Modes" (Ed.D. diss., New York University, 1968), p. 345.

7. Gannon, "Dimensions of Current Gang Delinquency," p. 46; *New York Times*, May 16, 1960; *New York Post*, July 20, 1961; and Helen Hall, *Unfinished Business in Neighborhood and Nation* (New York: Macmillan, 1971), p. 245.

8. Memorandum from James E. McCarthy, Deputy Executive Director, to Staff, Council of Social and Athletic Clubs, June 20, 1956, Box 119, Folder 6, Henry Street Settlement Records, Social Welfare History Archives, University of Minnesota. On the hostility between the Youth Board workers and the police, see Vincent Riccio, Oral History, Columbia University Oral History Collection, part 2, pp. 145, 150.

9. Gang members commented contemptuously about the police waiting until the violence had ended before intervening in a gang fight. See Katora and Lumamba Shakur, in *Look for Me in the Whirlwind: The Collective Autobiography of the New York 21* (New York: Random House, 1971), pp. 143, 149; and Richard P. Rettig, Manual J. Torres, and Gerald R. Garrett, *Manny: A Criminal Addict's Story* (Boston: Houghton Mifflin, 1977), p. 22.

10. Kenneth B. Clark, *Dark Ghetto: Dilemmas of Social Power* (New York: Harper and Row, 1965), p. 89.

11. See, for example, comments by Kenneth Clark, *New York Times*, July 31, 1964. Alfred Cain, Jr., is quoted in Paul Chevigny, *Cops and Rebels: A Study in Provocation* (New York: Pantheon, 1972), p. 7. Perhaps the most imaginative account of the possibilities for organizing gangs into revolutionary cells is Sam Greenlee, *The Spook Who Sat by the Door* (New York: Bantam Books, 1970). Robin Kelley brought this to my attention.

12. *Palante: Young Lords Party*, ed. Michael Abramson (New York: McGraw-Hill, 1971); and *Look for Me in the Whirlwind*, passim.

13. See, for example, Carl Husemoller Nightingale, *On the Edge: A History of Poor Black Children and Their American Dream* (New York: Basic Books, 1993), p. 21; Pennsylvania Economy League, *The Gang Problem in Philadelphia: Proposals for Improving the Programs of Gang-Control Agencies* (Philadelphia: Pennsylvania Economy League, 1974); and Walter B. Miller, "American Youth Gangs: Past and

Present," in *Current Perspectives on Criminal Behavior*, ed. Abraham S. Blumberg (New York: Knopf, 1974), pp. 225–26.

14. Saul Bernstein, *Alternatives to Violence: Alienated Youth and Riots, Race, and Poverty* (New York: Association Press, 1967), pp. 51–54; Gerald D. Suttles, *The Social Order of the Slum: Ethnicity and Territory in the Inner City* (Chicago: University of Chicago Press, 1968), pp. 133–34; Beverly Luther, "Negro Youth and Social Action," in *Individual and Group Services in the Mobilization for Youth Experience*, ed. Harold H. Weissman (New York: Association Press, 1969), pp. 151–61; Irving A. Spergel, "Youth Gangs and Urban Riots," in *Riots and Rebellion: Civil Violence in the Urban Community*, ed. Louis H. Masotti and Don R. Bowen (Beverly Hills: Sage Publications, 1968), pp. 143–56. For evidence from Philadelphia, see Barry Alan Krisberg, *The Gang and the Community* (San Francisco: R and E Research Associates, 1975), p. 55; and Miller, "American Youth Gangs," p. 227. On Chicago, see Amanda I. Seligman, " 'Their country is a Nation on no map': The Blackstone Rangers and Participation in the War on Poverty, 1967–1968" (Department of History, Northwestern University, photocopy), pp. 19–21.

15. Fred C. Shapiro and James W. Sullivan, *Race Riots: New York 1964* (New York: Crowell, 1964), pp. 175–76; Press Release, October 3, 1964, Subject Files: Juvenile Delinquency, 1961–1965, Box 157, Folder: Juvenile Delinquency (1) 1964, Wagner Papers, NYCMA; and Barry Gottehrer, *The Mayor's Man* (Garden City, N.Y.: Doubleday, 1975), pp. 4–7, 10–25, 37–38.

16. Ira Katznelson, *City Trenches: Urban Politics and the Patterning of Class in the United States* (Chicago: University of Chicago Press, 1981), pp. 135–89.

17. See Barry Gottehrer, "Report to Mayor John V. Lindsay," in Assistant to the Mayor Barry Gottehrer, Box: Summer Programs, 1968–1973, Folder: Summer Programs—Preparation materials, John Lindsay Papers, NYCMA, quotation, p. 8.

18. Gottehrer, *Mayor's Man*, p. 41; idem, "Report to Mayor Lindsay," pp. 20–21; "Report of the Citizens Summer Committee," October 2, 1967, in "Summer in Our City: New York City, 1967 and 1968," p. 13, in Assistant to the Mayor Barry Gottehrer, Box: Summer Programs, 1968–1973, Folder: Summer Programs—Preparation materials, John Lindsay Papers, NYCMA; and Alfredo Lopez, *The Puerto Rican Papers: Notes on the Re-emergence of a Nation* (Indianapolis: Bobbs-Merrill, 1973), p. 170.

19. Gottehrer, *Mayor's Man*, pp. 45–47, 67–68; and Charles R. Morris, *The Cost of Good Intentions: New York City and the Liberal Experiment, 1960–1975* (New York: McGraw-Hill, 1980), p. 66.

20. Gottehrer, *Mayor's Man*, pp. 70–75; idem, "Report to Mayor Lindsay," pp. 14–15, 20; and "Report of the Citizens Summer Committee," p. 13.

21. George Q. Flynn, *The Draft, 1940–1973* (Lawrence: University Press of Kansas, 1993), pp. 171, 233–34; Christian G. Appy, *Working-Class War: American Combat Soldiers and Vietnam* (Chapel Hill: University of North Carolina Press, 1993), pp. 23–24, 30–32; Lawrence M. Baskir and William A. Strauss, *Chance and Circumstance: The Draft, the War, and the Vietnam Generation* (New York: Vintage Books, 1978), pp. 8–9; and *New York Times*, May 18, 1964, December 5, 1966.

22. Morris, *Cost of Good Intentions*, p. 139.

23. See, for example, New York City Youth Board, *Reaching the Teen-age Addict: A Study of Street Club Work with a Group of Adolescent Users* (New York: New York City Youth Board, c. 1961), p. 9; and Lopez, *Puerto Rican Papers*, p. 173.

24. Claude Brown, *Manchild in the Promised Land* (New York: Penguin, 1965); and Jill Jonnes, *Hep-Cats, Narcs, and Pipe Dreams: A History of America's Romance with Illegal Drugs* (New York: Scribner, 1996).

25. Report to the Administrative Board, April 11, 1951, pp. 4–5, Box 3, East Harlem Protestant Parish Records, Union Theological Seminary; and *New York Times*, December 20, 1946.

26. Mobilization for Youth (MFY), *A Proposal for the Prevention and Control of Delinquency by Expanding Opportunities* (New York: Mobilization for Youth, 1961), pp. 9–10.

27. "The Department of Hospitals' Report on Teen-Age Narcotics Addiction," October 26, 1951, Subject Files: Narcotics, Box 88, Folder: Narcotics, 1950–1953, Mayor Vincent Impellitteri Papers, NYCMA; Memo from John J. Horwitz to Henry Epstein, January 26, 1955, "The Teen Age Narcotics Problem in Brief," Subject Files: Juvenile Delinquency, 1954–1955, Box 153, Folder: Juvenile Delinquency (2) 1955, Wagner Papers, NYCMA.

28. "Narcotics Arrests," Subject Files: Narcotics, Box 88, Folder: Narcotics, 1951–1953, Impellitteri Papers, NYCMA.

29. "Studies in the Epidemiology of Drug Use: Progress Report on the Second Study," October 1954, Subject Files: Juvenile Delinquency, 1954–1955, Box 153, Folder: Juvenile Delinquency (4) 1954, Wagner Papers, NYCMA; and Isidor Chein, Donald L. Gerard, Robert S. Lee, Eve Rosenfeld, with Daniel M. Wilner, *The Road to H: Narcotics, Delinquency, and Social Policy* (New York: Basic Books, 1964), pp. 32, 39–40. For Harlem addiction rates, see Jonnes, *Hep-Cats, Narcs, and Pipe Dreams*, p. 160.

30. Jonnes, *Hep-Cats, Narcs, and Pipe Dreams*, pp. 119–20, 130–37. Rodney is quoted on p. 119.

31. Chein et al., *The Road to H*, pp. 144–46, 216–18, 224–25.

32. Richard A. Cloward and Lloyd E. Ohlin, *Delinquency and Opportunity: A Theory of Delinquent Gangs* (Glencoe, Ill.: The Free Press, 1960).

33. Chein et al., *The Road to H*, pp. 11–12, 172–73, 180–83, 186–88, appendix K.

34. Samuels, "They No Longer 'Bop.' "

35. Rettig, et al., *Manny*, p. 18.

36. Paul L. Crawford, Daniel I. Malamud, and James R. Dumpson, *Working with Teen-Age Gangs: A Report on the Central Harlem Street Clubs Project* (New York: Welfare Council of New York City, 1950), pp. 78–82.

37. Robert Rice, "Profile: Hugh K. Johnson," *New Yorker*, December 23, 1961, p. 37.

38. Nestor Llamas, "The Social Processes of a Street Gang," *Journal of the Hillside Hospital* 13 (July–October 1964): 196–210. Nestor Llamas kindly provided me with a copy of his article. See also Frederick Johnson, *The Tumbleweeds: Somersaulting Up and Out of the City Streets* (New York: Harper and Row, 1977).

39. Lopez, *Puerto Rican Papers*, p. 173; MFY, *Proposal*, p. 85; and New York City Youth Board, *The Changing Role of the Street Worker in the Council of Social and Athletic Clubs* (New York: New York City Youth Board, 1965), pp. 6–7.

40. *New York Times*, July 25, 1960, June 18, 1962, July 8, 1962, April 16, 1964, June 9, 1964, June 26, 1966; "Speech—10/18/62," Subject Files: Narcotics, 1962–1965, Box 213, Folder: Narcotics 1962 (1), Wagner Papers, NYCMA; and "White Paper on Narcotics Addiction," October 24, 1965, Subject Files: Narcotics, Folder: Narcotics General, John Lindsay Papers, NYCMA. Delinquency rates can be found in *Juvenile Delinquency Rates: 1953 and Socio-Economic Characteristics for New York City* (New York: New York City Youth Board, 1954), p. 10; and *Juvenile Delinquency: 1963 and Selected Factors Related to Poverty* (New York: New York City Youth Board, 1964), p. 4.

41. Wilkerson, *Twelve Angels from Hell*, p. 105; Dion DiMucci with Davin Seay, *The Wanderer: Dion's Story* (New York: Beech Tree Books, 1988), p. 51; Warren Miller, *The Cool World* (Boston: Little, Brown and Company, 1959), p. 181; Brown, *Manchild*, p. 103; and Interviews with Nicky Cruz, February 24, 1993, RG, April 23, 1993, JG, March 8, 1993, and JC, March 10, 1993.

42. Interview with RG, March 8, 1993; and Riccio, Oral History, p. 236.

43. One scholar who questions this scenario is Walter B. Miller. See his "Youth Gangs in the Urban Crisis Era," in *Delinquency, Crime and Society*, ed. James F. Short, Jr. (Chicago: University of Chicago Press, 1976), pp. 91–128.

44. Edmund Newton, "New York Street Gangs: The Mini-Empires," *New York Post*, June 29, 1972. See Geoffrey Canada, *Fist, Stick, Knife, Gun: A Personal History of Violence in America* (Boston: Beacon Press, 1995), pp. 18–19, on gangs in the Bronx in the mid-1960s.

45. Shapiro and Sullivan, *Race Riots*, pp. 175–77.

46. See Canada, *Fist, Stick, Knife, Gun*.

47. See *New York Times*, July 31, 1964 for Kenneth Clark's comments. See Marshall, "The Fighting Gang," pp. 348–51, and *New York Times*, June 24, 1965, for the murder of Gregory Cunningham.

48. Quoted in Chevigny, *Cops and Rebels*, p. 7.

49. Commissioner Ted Gross, "Rationale and Proposal for an Approach to the Gang Problem," March–July 1972, Box: Mayor's Educational Task Force, 1972, Gangs J–Z, Folder: Gangs/YSA Workers and Assignments, John Lindsay Papers, NYCMA; and Edmund Newton, "New York's Street Gangs: Keeping It Cool," *New York Post*, June 30, 1972.

50. Carol Groneman and David M. Reimers, "Immigration," in *The Encyclopedia of New York City*, ed. Kenneth T. Jackson (New Haven: Yale University Press, 1995), pp. 584–85.

51. Memorandum, "Internecine Struggle between Chinatown Tongs," November 9, 1973, Box: Mayor's Educational Task Force, 1972, Youth Gangs A–I, Folder: Chinatown Youth Gangs, John Lindsay Papers, NYCMA; Peter Kwong, *The New Chinatown* (New York, 1987), pp. 110–12; Ko-lin Chin, *Chinatown Gangs: Extortion, Enterprise, and Ethnicity* (New York: Oxford University Press, 1996); and Betty Lee Sung, *Gangs in New York's Chinatown* (Washington, D.C.: Office of Child Development, Department of Health, Education and Welfare, 1977), pp. 24–29, 81.

52. Jill Jonnes, *We're Still Here: The Rise, Fall, and Resurrection of the South Bronx* (Boston: Atlantic Monthly Press, 1986), pp. 231–67; Dennis Smith, *Report from Engine Co. 82* (New York: Pocket Books, 1973); Robert Jensen, *Devastation/Resurrection: The South Bronx* (Bronx: Bronx Museum of the Arts, 1979), pp. 37–44; and Edmund Newton, "New York's Street Gangs," *New York Post*, July 1, 1972.

53. Memorandum, Gordon Davis to John Lindsay, December 6, 1971, Box: Mayor's Educational Task Force, 1972, Youth Gangs A–I, Folder: Gangs/Incidents/Police; Memo on Fighting Gangs from John Nolan to Deputy Commissioner Aguayo, Youth Services Agency, November 15, 1971, Box: Mayor's Educational Task Force, 1972, Youth Gangs A–I, Folder: Gangs/Profiles/Demands, John Lindsay Papers, NYCMA; and *New York Times*, April 18–19, 1972, January 16, 1973, July 2, 1973.

54. Jonnes, *We're Still Here*, p. 236.

55. Carlos is quoted in Edmund Newton, "New York's Street Gangs: They Call Themselves Cliques," *New York Post*, June 26, 1972. On conditions on Charlotte Street, see Jonnes, *We're Still Here*, p. 225.

56. Roberts is quoted in the *New York Times*, January 16, 1973.

57. *New York Times*, February 25, 1974.

58. Bama, quoted in Craig Castleman, *Getting Up: Subway Graffiti in New York* (Cambridge, Mass.: MIT Press, 1982), p. 93.

59. Edmund Newton, "New York's Street Gangs: What Kind of Summer?" *New York Post*, June 27, 1972.

60. Leonard Levitt, "The Rebirth of the Gangs," *Daily News*, August 20, 1972; and William Gale, *The Compound* (New York: Rawson Associates Publishers, 1977), pp. 31–34.

61. "Field Status/Incident Report—PM," June 1, 1972, Box: Mayor's Educational Task Force, 1972, Youth Gangs A–I, Folder: Gangs/Incidents/YSA, June 1972, John Lindsay Papers, NYCMA. See also Gale, *The Compound*, pp. 137–39.

62. *New York Times*, January 16, 1973.

63. Untitled draft, Box: Mayor's Educational Task Force, 1972, Youth Gangs A–I, Folder: Gangs/Profiles/Demands, John Lindsay Papers, NYCMA; and Gary Hoenig, *Reaper: The Story of a Gang Leader* (Indianapolis: Bobbs-Merrill, 1975), pp. 42–43, 48–49.

64. New York State Legislature, Subcommittee on the Family Court, *The Resurgence of Youth Gangs in New York City* (Albany, 1974), p. 2; H. Craig Collins, *Street Gangs: Profiles for Police* (New York: City of New York, Police Department, 1979), p. 9; and Baskir and Strauss, *Chance and Circumstance*, p. 134.

65. Dane Archer and Rosemary Gartner, *Violence and Crime in Cross-National Perspective* (New Haven: Yale University Press, 1984); Gale, *The Compound*, p. 104; and New York State Legislature, Subcommittee on the Family Court, *Armies of the Streets: A Report on the Structure, Membership and Activities of Youth Gangs in the City of New York* (Albany, 1974), p. 6.

66. Walter B. Miller, *Violence by Youth Gangs and Youth Groups as a Major Crime Problem in Major American Cities*, National Institute for Juvenile Justice and Delinquency Prevention, Office of Juvenile Delinquency Prevention, Law Enforcement Assistance Administration, U.S. Department of Justice (Washington, D.C.: U.S. Government Printing Office, 1975), p. 21; Memo on Fighting Gangs from John Nolan to Deputy Commissioner Aguayo, Youth Services Agency, November 15, 1971, Box: Mayor's Educational Task Force, 1972, Youth Gangs A–I, Folder: Gangs/Profiles/Demands, John Lindsay Papers, NYCMA; quotation in Newton, "New York's Street Gangs," *New York Post*, June 26, 1972; and Hoenig, *Reaper*, pp. 40–41.

67. Canada, *Fist, Stick, Knife, Gun*, p. 46; Gale, *The Compound*, p. 104; Collins, *Street Gangs*, pp. 82–83; Miller, *Violence by Youth Gangs*, pp. 41–42; and New York, Subcommittee, *Resurgence of Youth Gangs in New York City*, p. 7. Collins is quoted in *Daily News*, March 20, 1974.

68. Miller, *Violence by Youth Gangs*, pp. 30, 39; and New York, Subcommittee, *Resurgence of Youth Gangs in New York City*, quotation, p. 7.

69. Collins, *Street Gangs*, p. 42; and New York, Subcommittee, *Resurgence of Youth Gangs in New York City*, p. 3.

70. See, for example, memorandum from John Nolan to Deputy Commissioner Joe Aguayo, "Outlook for Weekend," March 16, 1972, Box: Mayor's Educational Task Force, 1972, Youth Gangs A–I, Folder: Gangs/Incidents/YSA March 1972; untitled draft, Box: Mayor's Educational Task Force, 1972, Youth Gangs A–I, Folder: Gangs/Profiles/Demands; "Night Incident Reports," August 14, 1974 and September 15, 1974, Box: Mayor's Educational Task Force, 1972, Youth Gangs A–I, Folder: Gang Reports 1974/75, John Lindsay Papers, NYCMA; and Newton, "New York's Street Gangs," *New York Post*, June 28, 1972.

71. *New York Times*, July 16, 1972.

72. Memorandum from Robert House to Lew Feldstein, John Sanderson, and Carl Irish, "Tension Observed in the North East Bronx," n.d., Box: Mayor's Educational Task Force, 1972, Youth Gangs A–I, Folder: Gang Correspondence, John Lindsay Papers, NYCMA.

73. Untitled notes and untitled draft, Box: Mayor's Educational Task Force, 1972, Youth Gangs A–I, Folder: Gangs/Profiles/Demands; Memorandum, Gordon Davis to John Lindsay, December 6, 1971, Box: Mayor's Educational Task Force, 1972, Youth Gangs A–I, Folder: Gangs/Incidents/Police; and Letter from Benjamin Ward to Carlton Irish, June 16, 1972, Box: Mayor's Educational Task Force, 1972, Youth Gangs A–I, Folder: Gangs/Profiles/Demands, John Lindsay Papers, NYCMA; *New York Times*, February 21, 1972. Ward is quoted in Newton, "New York's Street Gangs," *New York Post*, June 29, 1972.

74. Dominguez and Abrams are quoted in *New York Times*, April 19, 1972 and April 21, 1972, respectively.


CONCLUSION. COMPARING GANGS

1. There are exceptions, such as the Latin Kings, which is a citywide Latino gang. See Ed Morales, "King of New York," *The Village Voice*, December 10, 1996.

2. Kurt Sonnenfeld, "Changing Perspectives on Youth Services as Seen through the Historical Development of the New York City Youth Board" (Ed.D. diss., Teacher's College, Columbia University, 1995), pp. 302–4.

3. The problem with police data is suggested by the implausible conclusion that nearly half (47 percent) of the African-American male population between the ages of twenty-one and twenty-four is listed in the Los Angeles Police Department's gang database, as opposed to one-half of 1 percent of white males, 6 percent of Asian males, and 9 percent of Hispanic males. See California District Attorney (Los Angeles County), *Gangs, Crime, and Violence in Los Angeles: Findings and Proposals from the District Attorney's Office* (Los Angeles: Office of the District Attorney, 1992), pp. xxxii–xxxiii.

4. Joan W. Moore, *Going down to the Barrio: Homeboys and Homegirls in Change* (Philadelphia: Temple University Press, 1991), pp. 59–65; and Irving A. Spergel, "Youth Gangs: Continuity and Change," in *Crime and Justice: A Review of Research*, vol. 12, ed. Michael Tonry and Norval Morris (Chicago: University of Chicago Press, 1990), p. 189.

5. This statement is not true of the Los Angeles Hispanic gangs, where membership continues to be generational, the barrio has more than utilitarian meaning, and drug dealing and drug use have a long and different history than on the East Coast and in the Midwest. See James Diego Vigil, *Barrio Gangs: Street Life and Identity in Southern California* (Austin: University of Texas Press, 1988).

6. This point is made forcefully in Malcolm W. Klein, *The American Street Gang: Its Nature, Prevalence, and Control* (New York: Oxford University Press, 1995); John Hagedorn, *People and Folks: Gangs, Crime, and the Underclass in a Rustbelt City* (Chicago: Lake View Press, 1988), pp. 57–79; and Scott H. Decker and Barrik Van Winkle, *Life in the Gang: Family, Friends, and Violence* (Cambridge: Cambridge University Press, 1996), pp. 85–89. See also James A. Inciardi, "The Crack Violence Connection within a Population of Hard-Core Adolescent Offenders," in *Drugs and Violence: Causes, Correlates, and Consequences*, ed. Mario De La Rosa, Elizabeth Y. Lambert, and Bernard Gropper (Rockville, Md.: U.S. Department of Health and Human Services, 1990), 92–111; and Joan Moore, "Gangs, Drugs, and Violence," in *Drugs and Violence*, pp. 160–76.

7. Martin Sanchez Jankowski, *Islands in the Street: Gangs and American Urban Society* (Berkeley: University of California Press, 1991), pp. 120–21; Hagedorn, *People and Folks*; Decker and Van Winkle, *Life in the Gang*, pp. 62–63, 152–55; Stephen Koester and Judith Schwartz, "Crack, Gangs, Sex, and Powerlessness: A View from Denver," in *Crack Pipe as Pimp: An Eight-City Ethnographic Study of the Sex-for-Crack Phenomenon*, ed. Mitchell Ratner (New York: Lexington Books, 1993), 189–90; and Jeffrey Fagan, "The Social Organization of Drug Use and Drug Dealing among Urban Gangs," *Criminology* 27 (1989): 633–67. Fagan has also compared gang and non-gang youth samples drawn from similar populations, and found about one-third of male gang members were involved in drug sales, versus less than 10 percent of the non-gang male youths. See Jeffrey Fagan, "Social Processes of Delinquency and Drug Use among Urban Gangs," in *Gangs in America*, ed. C. Ron Huff (Newbury Park: Sage Publications, 1990), table 9.1, pp. 196–97.

8. Terry Williams, *The Cocaine Kids: The Inside Story of a Teenage Drug Ring* (Reading, Mass.: Addison-Wesley, 1989); and Moore, "Gangs, Drugs, and Violence," p. 169.

9. Philippe Bourgois, *In Search of Respect: Selling Crack in El Barrio* (Cambridge: Cambridge University Press, 1995); Felix M. Padilla, *The Gang as an American*

*Enterprise* (New Brunswick,N.J.: Rutgers University Press, 1992); and Carl S. Taylor, *Dangerous Society* (East Lansing: Michigan State University Press, 1990). Taylor has coined the term "corporate gang."

10. One study of self-reported drug dealers has found that dealing was a supplement to regular employment, again suggesting the extent of dealing in the inner city and the difficulty of subsisting on wages paid in the legal economy. See Robert MacCoun and Peter Reuter, "Are the Wages of Sin $30 an Hour? Economic Aspects of Street-Level Drug Dealing," *Crime and Delinquency* 38 (1992): 477–91.

11. David Durk with Arlene Durk and Ira Silverman, *The Pleasant Avenue Connection* (New York: Harper and Row, 1976); Williams, *Cocaine Kids*, pp. 5–8; Bourgois, *In Search of Respect*, pp. 73–75; Jeffrey Fagan, "Drug Selling and Licit Income in Distressed Neighborhoods: The Economic Lives of Street-level Drug Users and Dealers," in *Drugs, Crime, and Social Isolation: Barriers to Urban Opportunity,* ed. Adele V. Harrell and George E. Peterson (Washington, D.C.: Urban Institute Press, 1992), 102–3; Padilla, *The Gang as an American Enterprise*, pp. 14–15; Geoffrey Canada, *Fist, Stick, Knife, Gun: A Personal History of Violence in America* (Boston: Beacon Press, 1995), pp. 78–81; and California District Attorney, *Gangs, Crime, and Violence in Los Angeles*, p. 61.

12. See Taylor, *Dangerous Society,* pp. 59–60, for the importance of cash in establishing relations with the opposite sex.

13. Padilla, *The Gang as an American Enterprise*, pp. 6, 94–101; and Spergel, "Youth Gangs: Continuity and Change," p. 197. Taylor, *Dangerous Society,* offers the most extreme example of the effect of economic transformation on the gang. The best evocation of the world of street dealers is the novel by Richard Price, *Clockers* (Boston: Houghton Mifflin, 1992).

14. The rational, money-making aspect of contemporary gangs is stressed in Jankowski, *Islands in the Street*, which compared African-American, Hispanic, and white gangs, and in studies of Asian gangs, such as Ko-lin Chin, *Chinatown Gangs: Extortion, Enterprise, and Ethnicity* (New York: Oxford University Press, 1996).

15. Matthew Drennan, "The Decline and Rise of the New York Economy," in *Dual City: Restructuring New York*, ed. John Hull Mollenkopf and Manuel Castells (New York: Russell Sage Foundation, 1991), 25–41, especially table 1.5, p. 32; and Roger Waldinger, *Still the Promised City? African Americans and New Immigrants in Postindustrial New York* (Cambridge, Mass.: Harvard University Press, 1996), pp. 33–41.

16. Bourgois, *In Search of Respect*, chapter 4; Waldinger, *Still the Promised City?*, pp. 177–201; and Joshua B. Freeman, "Hardhats: Construction Workers, Manliness, and the 1970 Pro-War Demonstrations," *Journal of Social History* 26 (Summer 1993): 731–33. See Joan W. Moore, *Homeboys: Gangs, Drugs and Prison in the*

*Barrio of Los Angeles* (Philadelphia: Temple University Press, 1978), pp. 27–31, on the segmented economy.

17. Thomas Bailey and Roger Waldinger, "The Changing Ethnic/Racial Division of Labor," in *Dual City,* pp. 55–62; and Waldinger, *Still the Promised City?*, pp. 60–72.

18. Bailey and Waldinger, "Changing Ethnic/Racial Division of Labor," pp. 62–67; and Waldinger, *Still the Promised City?*, pp. 70–72.

19. Saskia Sassen, "The Informal Economy," in *Dual City,* pp. 79–101; and Moore, *Homeboys*, pp. 27–31.

20. Mercer L. Sullivan, *"Getting Paid": Youth Crime and Work in the Inner City* (Ithaca, N.Y.: Cornell University Press, 1989). On tolerance for the underground economy, see Stuart Henry, *The Hidden Economy: The Context and Control of Borderline Crime* (London: Martin Robertson, 1978).

21. Sullivan, *"Getting Paid,"* pp. 54–56, 117–18, 136–39, 179–84, 250. See MacCoun and Reuter, "Are the Wages of Sin $30 an Hour?" on supplementing low wages with drug selling. For a sense of the frustration and anger experienced by white adolescents, see Howard Pinderhughes, " 'Down with the Program': Racial Attitudes and Group Violence among Youth in Bensonhurst and Gravesend," in *Gangs: The Origins and Impact of Contemporary Youth Gangs in the United States,* ed. Scott Cummings and Daniel J. Monti (Albany: State University of New York Press, 1993), pp. 75–94.

22. Bourgois, *In Search of Respect*, pp. 137–52; and MacCoun and Reuter, "Are the Wages of Sin $30 an Hour?" pp. 484–85.

23. See Hagedorn, *People and Folks*; Vigil, *Barrio Gangs*, p. 9; Jankowski, *Islands in the Street*, pp. 45, 108; and Padilla, *The Gang as an American Enterprise*, p. 159. On labor redundancy, see Herbert J. Gans, *The War against the Poor: The Underclass and Antipoverty Policy* (New York: Basic Books, 1995).

24. Irving A. Spergel, *The Youth Gang Problem: A Community Approach* (New York: Oxford University Press, 1995), pp. 57–58. California District Attorney, *Gangs, Crime, and Violence in Los Angeles*, pp. 11–12, estimates female gang membership at no more than 6 percent of the total.

25. See Bourgois, *In Search of Respect*, pp. 205–10; Jankowski, *Islands in the Street*, p. 146; Fagan, "Drug Selling and Licit Income," pp. 135–36; and Philippe Bourgois and Eloise Dunlap, "Exorcising Sex-for-Crack Prostitution: An Ethnographic Perspective from Harlem," in *Crack Pipe as Pimp*, pp. 97–132.

26. Anne Campbell, "Female Participation in Gangs," in *Gangs in America*, pp. 163–82; Anne Campbell, *The Girls in the Gang: A Report from New York City* (Oxford: Basil Blackwell, 1984); Carl S. Taylor, *Girls, Gangs, Women and Drugs* (East Lansing: Michigan State University Press, 1993); Maria Hinojosa, *Crews: Gang Members Talk to Maria Hinojosa* (New York: Harcourt Brace, 1995), pp. 65–103;

Adrian Nicole LeBlanc, "Gang Girl: The Making of a Street Feminist," *New York Times Magazine*, August 14 1994, 26–33ff.; and Spergel, "Youth Gangs: Continuity and Change," pp. 219–20.

27. Bourgois, *In Search of Respect*, pp. 226–47; and Williams, *Cocaine Kids*, pp. 111–16.

28. Betty Lee Sung, *Gangs in New York's Chinatown* (Washington, D.C.: Office of Child Development, Department of Health, Education and Welfare, 1977); Chin, *Chinatown Gangs*; Ko-lin Chin, "Chinese Gangs and Extortion," in *Gangs in America*, pp. 129–45; James Diego Vigil and Steve Chong Yun, "Vietnamese Youth Gangs in Southern California," in ibid., pp. 146–62; and California District Attorney, *Gangs, Crime, and Violence in Los Angeles*, pp. 46–50.

29. On white gangs defending turf in Brooklyn, see Pinderhughes, " 'Down with the Program.' "

30. Spergel, *The Youth Gang Problem*, pp. 59–69; and Klein, *The American Street Gang*, pp. 105–10. Obviously the proportions differ somewhat depending on region.

31. Spergel, *The Youth Gang Problem*, pp. 55–56; Klein, *The American Street Gang*, pp. 104–5; Moore, *Going down to the Barrio*, p. 47; Hagedorn, *People and Folks*, pp. 38–41, 46; and California District Attorney, *Gangs, Crime, and Violence in Los Angeles*, p. 26.

32. Elijah Anderson, *Street Wise: Race, Class, and Change in an Urban Community* (Chicago: University of Chicago Press, 1990); and William Julius Wilson, *The Truly Disadvantaged: The Inner City, the Underclass, and Public Policy* (Chicago: University of Chicago Press, 1987), p. 57. There is a rejoinder of sorts in Mitchell Duneier, *Slim's Table: Race, Respectability, and Masculinity* (Chicago: University of Chicago Press, 1992), but Duneier's informants are of an older generation who expressed their own alienation from contemporary society.

33. Center for Disease Control, *Morbidity and Mortality Weekly Report* 43 (October 14 1994): 725–27; *New York Times*, January 1, 1994; Spergel, *The Youth Gang Problem*, pp. 33–40; and Malcolm W. Klein and Cheryl L. Maxson, "Street Gang Violence," in *Violent Crime, Violent Criminals*, ed. Neil Alan Weiner and Marvin E. Wolfgang (Newbury Park: Sage Publications, 1989), pp. 198–234.

34. *New York Times*, January 31, 1993.

35. *Philadelphia Inquirer*, October 30, 1994.

36. Klein and Maxson, "Street Gang Violence," p. 218; and Spergel, *The Youth Gang Problem*, p. 34.

37. See Jankowski, *Islands in the Street*, for the Hobbesian analogy. Emanuel Tobier, *The Changing Face of Poverty: Trends in New York City's Population in Poverty: 1960–1990* (New York: Community Service Society of New York, 1984), p. vi.

38. Decker and Van Winkle, *Life in the Gang*, pp. 187–90.

39. Jankowski, *Islands in the Street*, pp. 102–5, 119–26, 135; and Daniel Bell, "Crime as an American Way of Life: A Queer Ladder of Social Mobility," in *The End of Ideology: On the Exhaustion of Political Ideas in the Fifties*, ed. Daniel Bell (Glencoe, Ill.: The Free Press, 1960), pp. 115–36.

40. For a recent example, see Alan Ehrenhalt, *The Lost City: The Forgotten Virtues of Community in America* (New York: Basic Books, 1995).

41. *Report of the National Advisory Commission on Civil Disorders* (New York: Bantam Books, 1968), p. 1.

42. "The 'Capeman' Reflects as Prison Release Nears," *New York Times*, October 3, 1979.

# INDEX

Abrams, Robert, 244
"AC" (gang member), 174
Aces (Lower East Side gang), 209–10
adults: contemporary gangs isolated from, 248, 259–62; as discouragers of street fighting, 184, 190–97, 206, 208, 220; as enforcers, 238; gang support from, 53–54, 65, 68, 90–91, 93, 99–100, 121, 126, 150, 165, 242–43; as mentors for gang-leaving, 171–73, 176, 187, 188, 196; as organized crime recruiters, 180, 181; use of adolescents by, for drug dealing, 250. *See also* families; gang workers; organized crime
African Americans, 25; as criminals, 57, 60–62; employment discrimination against, xviii, 31, 36–37, 40, 115, 173, 180, 252, 253; in ethnically mixed gangs, 80, 86–91, 104; gangs among, 64–67, 73, 77, 81, 101, 181, 203, 237, 242–43, 256; gang style among, 57, 162–63; heroin use among, 230–31; on juvenile delinquency, 11–12; masculine models for, 124–25, 257, 259; migration of, to NYC, xix, 8, 27–28, 32, 50; nationalist sentiments among, 221–24; neighborhood expansion of, 9, 33, 35–37, 65–66, 83, 85–86, 210–11, 239; in NYC schools, 9, 67–70, 107–8, 113, 253, 270n.28; population statistics regarding, 32, 33, 36, 45–46, 102; riots involving, 59–60, 68–70, 222; as violence victims, 258. *See also* segregation
age succession (in gangs). *See* gangs: hierarchies in
Agron, Aurea (Salvador Agron's sister), 16–18

Agron, Gumersindo, 16–18
Agron, Salvador (the Capeman), xviii–xix, 3–8, 13–23, 26, 218, 262
alcohol, xviii, 121–22, 158, 161
Alinsky, Saul, 213
Alvarez, Louis, 89
*Amboy Dukes, The* (Shulman), 29–30, 56
American Friends Service Committee, 171, 200
American Labor Party, 62
Amsterdam Knights, 149, 191–92
*Amsterdam News*, 11–12, 88
Amsterdams (Washington Heights gang), 86
antipoverty funds, 211, 218, 226, 236, 239, 243–45
anti-Semitism, xviii, 86
Appy, Christian, 228
Archer, Dane, 71
Arguinzoni, Sonny, 173, 301n.54
armed services. *See* military
Arthur Avenue Boys (Bronx gang), 242–43
Asbury, Herbert, 54
Asians, 261; gangs among, 237–38, 247, 256
Assassins (gang), 132, 233
Avengers (gang), 122

"badman, the," 124–25
Bad Motherfuckers (gang), 120
Baldies. *See* Fordham Baldies
Balkans (gang), 149
Banome, Father, 66
Baraka, Imamu, 138
Barons (a Brooklyn gang), 144
Barons (another Brooklyn gang), 157
Bear Cats (Harlem gang), 73